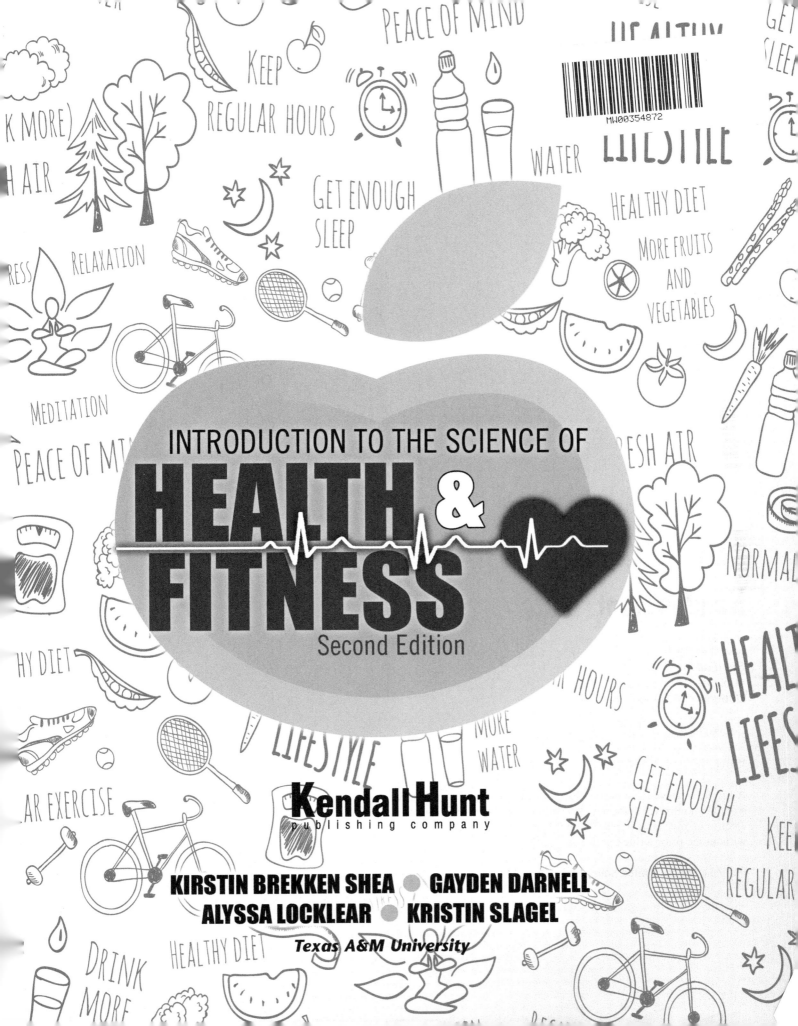

INTRODUCTION TO THE SCIENCE OF

HEALTH & FITNESS

Second Edition

Kendall Hunt
publishing company

KIRSTIN BREKKEN SHEA ● **GAYDEN DARNELL**
ALYSSA LOCKLEAR ● **KRISTIN SLAGEL**

Texas A&M University

Cover image © Shutterstock, Inc.

www.kendallhunt.com
Send all inquiries to:
4050 Westmark Drive
Dubuque, IA 52004-1840

Copyright © 2014, 2017 by Kendall Hunt Publishing Company

ISBN 978-1-5249-1664-0

Published in the United States of America

Brief Contents

Contents

Chapter 1
Wellness and Disease Prevention

OBJECTIVES

Students will be able to:

♦ Differentiate the definitions of health and wellness.
♦ Identify the seven elements of wellness.
♦ Explain the link between preventative behaviors and wellness.
♦ Discuss health behaviors that increase the quality and longevity of life.
♦ Identify the significance of *Healthy People 2020*.
♦ Differentiate between bacteria and viruses.
♦ Identify infection-prevention practices.

Adaptation of *Health and Fitness: A Guide to a Healthly Lifestyle*, 5th Edition, by Laura Bounds, Gayden Darnell, Kirstin Brekken Shea, and Dottiede Agnor. Copyright © 2012 by Kendall Hunt Publishing Company.

Emotional Wellness

Are you engaged in the process of Emotional Wellness?

Evaluate your own emotional wellness with this brief quiz.

- Am I able to maintain a balance of work, family, friends, and other obligations?
- Do I have ways to reduce stress in my life?
- Am I able to make decisions with a minimum of stress and worry?
- Am I able to set priorities?

If you answered "No" to any of the questions, it may indicate an area where you need to improve the state of your emotional wellness.

> *"Take care of your body with steadfast fidelity. The soul must see through these eyes alone, and if they are dim, the whole world is clouded."*
>
> **—Johann Wolfgang Von Goethe**

Health is a universal trait. The World Health Organization defines **health** as a "state of complete physical, mental, and social well-being and not merely the absence of disease or infirmity." Webster's Dictionary offers "the condition of being sound in body, mind, or spirit; especially: freedom from physical disease or pain . . . the general condition of the body" as a definition of health. However, health also has an individual quality; it is very personal, and unique.

Early on, definitions of health revolved around issues of sanitation and personal hygiene. Today, the definition of health has evolved from a basis of physical health or absence of disease, to a term that encompasses the emotional, mental, social, spiritual, and physical dimensions of an individual. This current, positive approach to health is referred to as wellness. **Wellness** is a process of making informed choices that will lead one, over a period of time, to a healthy lifestyle that should result in a sense of well-being.

Elements of Wellness

Wellness is a holistic approach to life that integrates mind, body, & spirit. Wellness emphasizes an individual's potential and responsibility for his or her own health. It is a process in which a person is constantly moving either away from or toward a most favorable level of health. Wellness results from the adoption of low-risk, health-enhancing behaviors. The adoption of a wellness lifestyle requires focusing on choices that will enhance the individual's potential to lead a productive, meaningful, and satisfying life.

It is the complex interaction of each of the seven elements of wellness that will lead an individual, over time, to a higher quality of life and better overall health and well-being. Constant, ongoing assessment of one's behaviors in the following dimensions is key to living a balanced life. In addition to the seven elements shown in Figure 1.1, there is discussion of other factors that influence wellness.

FIGURE 1.1

Seven Elements of Wellness

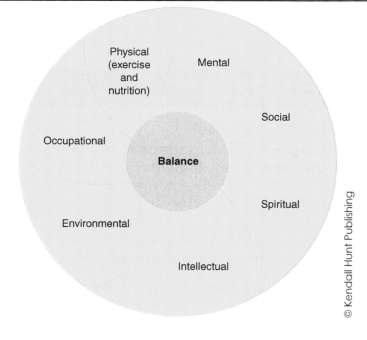

Emotional

Emotional wellness is being aware and accepting of not only your feelings and emotions but also the feelings and emotions of others. An individual who is emotionally healthy is able to enjoy life despite unexpected challenges and potential problems. Effectively coping with life's difficulties and unexpected events is essential to maintaining good health. Equally important to good personal wellness is the ability to understand your feelings and express those feelings or emotions outwardly in a positive and constructive manner. "Bottled-up" negative emotions can affect the immune system and result in chronic stress, which in turn can lead to serious illnesses such as high blood pressure and can potentially lead to a premature death.

The result of being emotionally well adjusted and being able to express emotions appropriately are healthy, mutually rewarding relationships with others and an overall enjoyment of life.

Intellectual

The mind can have substantial influence over the body. To be intellectually healthy, it is essential to continue to explore new avenues and interests and to regularly engage in new and ongoing learning opportunities and experiences. An individual must be open to new and different ideas & concepts. The more "unknowns" an individual faces or explores, the more opportunities he or she has to learn and grow intellectually.

Reading for pleasure, taking a dance class, learning a foreign language, traveling and learning about other cultures are all excellent ways to improve or maintain intellectual wellness. Truly well individuals are able to combine what they have learned through their formal education with what they experience outside of a traditional classroom.

Social

Social health is an individual's ability to relate to and interact with others. Socially healthy people are able to communicate and interact with the other people they come in contact with each day. They are respectful and caring of their family, friends, neighbors, and associates. A key component to being socially well is thinking about how one's actions impact, either positively or negatively, other people. For example, choosing to text while driving could impact the person texting by being killed in a car accident. Obviously their decision impacts them but, did they ever stop to think how their decision to text and drive would forever impact their family and friends or the police and paramedics who respond to the scene? Being socially well as an adult is more than being able to do well on a presentation, going out, or having friends. Although reaching out and communicating with others may be difficult or uncomfortable initially, it is extremely important to a person's social health and their overall sense of well-being.

Spiritual

Spiritual health helps a person achieve a sense of inner peace, satisfaction, and confidence it comes from within and can help give the sense that all is right with the world. A person's ethics, values, beliefs, and morals can contribute to their spiritual health. It can teach one to appreciate their own ethics, beliefs, morals and values and live a life true to them but at the same time it encourages a person to be tolerant of differences in other's ethics, values, morals and beliefs. Good spiritual health can help give life meaning and purpose.

Intellectual Wellness
Are you engaged in the process of Intellectual Wellness?

Evaluate your own intellectual wellness with this brief quiz.

- Am I open to new ideas?
- Do I seek personal growth by learning new skills?
- Do I search for lifelong learning opportunities and stimulating mental activities?
- Do I look for ways to use creativity?

If you answered "No" to any of the questions, it may indicate an area where you need to improve the state of your intellectual wellness.

© Yuri Arcus, 2012, Shutterstock, Inc.

The ability to relate and interact with others is important to a person's overall sense of well-being.

ELEMENTS OF WELLNESS

ELEMENT	SYMBOL	SYMBOL EXPLAINED	EXAMPLES
EMOTIONAL WELLNESS • The awareness and acceptance of feelings and emotions.		• The heart represents the general source of emotions (vs. the mind /brain as a symbol for rational thought).	• Fitness and exercise • Relationships with friends/family • Balancing work and family • Laughing and crying • Adequate sleeping patterns • Personal contact, ie. hugging
ENVIRONMENTAL WELLNESS • The recognition of interdependence with nature.		• The tree is a general, easy-to-identify representative of the natural realm.	• Reduce, reuse, recycle • Reusing materiels • Adopting Leave-No-Trace • Conserving water and fuels • Spend time in a state/national park • Finding value in surroundings • Positive workplace & attitude • Air quality
INTELLECTUAL WELLNESS • The openness to new concepts and ideas.		• A light bulb is a general representative for fresh thinking, innovation, and creativity.	• Reading & learning for fun • Participation in class, organization • Adopting a new hobby • Traveling • Adequate sleeping patterns • Self-help information
OCCUPATIONAL WELLNESS • The ability to enjoy a chosen career and/or contribute to society through volunteer activities.		• A gear with cogs or teeth represents a unit of labor or effort.	• Continuing education • Satisfying career/profession • Volunteering • Workplace safety • Exercise
PHYSICAL WELLNESS • The maintenance of a healthy body through good nutrition, regular exercise, and avoidance of harmful habits.		• An individual person represents the human body.	• Fitness and exercise; stretching • Personal hygiene • Walk/cycle to work • Know your numbers: cholesterol, blood sugar, blood pressure • Good nutrition • Adequate sleeping patterns • Regular medical/dental exams
SOCIAL WELLNESS • The ability to perform social roles effectively, comfortably, and without harming others.		• Three persons with connected hands represent harmony, networking, and friendship.	• Establish and maintain personal friendships • Community involvement • Attending social settings, ie. festivals, neighborhood events • Group fitness classes • Hobby/activity organizations
SPIRITUAL WELLNESS • The meaning and purpose of human existence.		• The sun represents the beginning and end of a day; a reflection of the source of growth and vitality in the universe. • Solar symbols can have meaning in astrology, religion, mythology, mysticism, and divination.	• Meditation; prayer • Religious affiliation • Explore and enjoy the flora & fauna of a wilderness area. • Watch a sunrise or sunset • Exercise • Freedom • Outdoor activities

Social Wellness

Evaluate your own social wellness with this brief quiz.

- Do I plan time to be with my family and friends?
- Do I enjoy the time I spend with others?
- Are my relationships with others positive and rewarding?
- Do I explore diversity by interacting with people of other cultures, backgrounds, and beliefs?

If you answered "No" to any of the questions, it may indicate an area where you need to improve the state of your social wellness.

Team or group fitness is an excellent way to enhance both physical and social wellness.

Physical

Physical wellness is maintaining a healthy body through regular exercise, good nutrition, and the avoidance of harmful habits. Ensuring good physical health begins with devoting attention and time to attaining healthy levels of cardiovascular fitness, muscular strength and endurance, flexibility, and body composition. When coupled with good nutritional practices such as consuming foods and beverages that are known to enhance good health rather than those that impair it, good sleep habits, and the avoidance of risky social behaviors such as drinking and driving or unprotected sexual intercourse, a physically healthy body results. This is the component that is most often associated, at first glance, with a person's health.

Occupational

An occupationally well individual is able to enjoy the career they have chosen and the way they contribute to society. They have chosen a path that is consistent with their own values, interests, and beliefs. Attaining occupational wellness begins with determining what roles, activities, and commitments take up a majority of an individual's time. These roles, activities, or commitments could include but are not limited to being a student, parenting, volunteering in an organization, or working at a part-time job while pursuing one's degree. It is when each of these areas are integrated and balanced in a personally and professionally fulfilling way that occupational wellness occurs.

Environmental

An individual's health and wellness can be substantially affected by the quality of their environment. An environmentally well individual recognizes that they are dependent on their natural environment just as the environment is dependent on them. They are aware that they have a responsibility toward the upkeep of environmental quality and have taken the time to identify ways in which they can be more environmentally "friendly." Access to clean air, nutritious food, sanitary water, and adequate clothing and shelter are essential components to being well. An individual's environment should, at the very least, be clean and safe.

Through wellness, an individual manages a wide range of lifestyle choices. How a person chooses to behave and the decisions he or she makes in each of the seven dimensions of wellness will determine their overall quality of life. Making an active effort to combining and constantly trying to balance each of the seven dimensions is key to a long and fulfilling life.

Ten Leading Causes of Death

You will see that lifestyle is only one component that works in tandem with other factors to make up good health and wellness.

Leading Causes of Death

Heart disease: 614,348 deaths per year
Cancer: 591,699 deaths per year
Chronic lower respiratory disease: 147,101 deaths per year
Stroke (cerebrovascular disease): 133,101 deaths per year

Spiritual Wellness

Are you engaged in the process of Spiritual Wellness? Evaluate your own spiritual wellness with this brief quiz.

- Do I make time for relaxation in my day?
- Do I make time for meditation and/or prayer?
- Do my values guide my decisions and actions?
- Am I accepting of the views of others?

If you answered "No" to any of the questions, it may indicate an area where you need to improve the state of your spiritual wellness.

Physical Wellness

Are you engaged in the process of Physical Wellness? Evaluate your own physical wellness with this brief quiz.

- Do I know important health numbers, like my cholesterol, weight, blood pressure, and blood sugar levels?
- Do I get annual physical exams?
- Do I avoid using tobacco products?
- Do I get sufficient amount of sleep?
- Do I have an established exercise routine?

If you answered "No" to any of the questions, it may indicate an area where you need to improve the state of your physical wellness.

Accidents (unintentional injuries): 136,053 deaths per year
Alzheimer's disease: 93,541 deaths per year
Diabetes: 76,488 deaths per year
Influenza and pneumonia: 55,227 deaths per year
Nephritis, nephritic syndrome, and nephrosis: 48,146 deaths per year
Intentional self-harm (suicide): 42,773 deaths per year

Addressing each dimension of wellness contributes to a well-rounded individual, as well as one's longevity. However, when reviewing the leading causes of death, we must acknowledge that unintentional injuries are high on the list. If we look specifically at people from 1 to 44 years of age, unintentional injury and violence account for over 50% of deaths each year, more than non-communicable and infectious diseases combined (National Center for Injury Prevention and Control, 2014). Therefore, in order to improve our chances to live a health and long life we must consider ways to reduce our risk of unintentional injuries.

Injury: The Leading Cause of Death among Persons 1–44

In 2010 in the United States, injuries, including all causes of unintentional and violence-related injuries combined, accounted for 50.6% of all deaths among persons ages 1–44 years of age—that is more deaths than non-communicable diseases and infectious diseases combined.

Injury Facts

- More than 180,000 deaths from injury each year—1 person every 3 minutes
- Leading cause of death for people ages 1–44 in the U.S.
- An estimated 2.8 million people hospitalized with injury each year

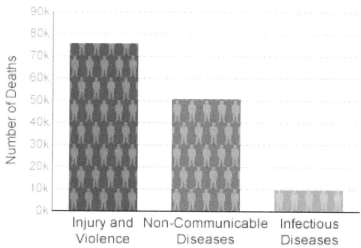

Injury Deaths Compared to Other Leading Causes of Death for Persons Ages 1–44, United States, 2010*

*Note: Injury includes unintentional injury, homicide, suicide, legal intervention, and those of undetermined intent. Non-communicable diseases include cancer, cardiovascular, kidney, respiratory, liver, diabetes, and other diseases. Infectious diseases include HIV, influenza, pneumonia, tuberculosis, and other infectious diseases. Data Source: National Vital Statistics System using CDC Wonder (http://wonder.cdc.gov).

10 Leading Causes of Death by Age Group, United States – 2014

Rank	<1	1-4	5-9	10-14	15-24	25-34	35-44	45-54	55-64	65+	Total
1	Congenital Anomalies 4,746	Unintentional Injury 1,216	Unintentional Injury 730	Unintentional Injury 750	Unintentional Injury 11,836	Unintentional Injury 17,357	Unintentional Injury 16,048	Malignant Neoplasms 44,834	Malignant Neoplasms 115,282	Heart Disease 489,722	Heart Disease 614,348
2	Short Gestation 4,173	Congenital Anomalies 399	Malignant Neoplasms 436	Suicide 425	Suicide 5,079	Suicide 6,569	Malignant Neoplasms 11,267	Heart Disease 34,791	Heart Disease 74,473	Malignant Neoplasms 413,885	Malignant Neoplasms 591,699
3	Maternal Pregnancy Comp. 1,574	Homicide 364	Congenital Anomalies 192	Malignant Neoplasms 416	Homicide 4,144	Homicide 4,159	Heart Disease 10,368	Unintentional Injury 20,610	Unintentional Injury 18,030	Chronic Low. Respiratory Disease 124,693	Chronic Low. Respiratory Disease 147,101
4	SIDS 1,545	Malignant Neoplasms 321	Homicide 123	Congenital Anomalies 156	Malignant Neoplasms 1,569	Malignant Neoplasms 3,624	Suicide 6,706	Suicide 8,767	Chronic Low. Respiratory Disease 16,492	Cerebro-vascular 113,308	Unintentional Injury 136,053
5	Unintentional Injury 1,161	Heart Disease 149	Heart Disease 69	Homicide 156	Heart Disease 953	Heart Disease 3,341	Homicide 2,588	Liver Disease 8,627	Diabetes Mellitus 13,342	Alzheimer's Disease 92,604	Cerebro-vascular 133,103
6	Placenta Cord. Membranes 965	Influenza & Pneumonia 109	Chronic Low. Respiratory Disease 68	Heart Disease 122	Congenital Anomalies 377	Liver Disease 725	Liver Disease 2,582	Diabetes Mellitus 6,062	Liver Disease 12,792	Diabetes Mellitus 54,161	Alzheimer's Disease 93,541
7	Bacterial Sepsis 544	Chronic Low. Respiratory Disease 53	Influenza & Pneumonia 57	Chronic Low Respiratory Disease 71	Influenza & Pneumonia 199	Diabetes Mellitus 709	Diabetes Mellitus 1,999	Cerebro-vascular 5,349	Cerebro-vascular 11,727	Influenza & Pneumonia 44,836	Diabetes Mellitus 76,488
8	Respiratory Distress 460	Septicemia 53	Cerebro-vascular 45	Cerebro-vascular 43	Diabetes Mellitus 181	HIV 583	HIV 1,174	Chronic Low. Respiratory Disease 4,402	Suicide 7,527	Unintentional Injury 48,295	Influenza & Pneumonia 55,227
9	Circulatory System Disease 444	Benign Neoplasms 38	Benign Neoplasms 36	Influenza & Pneumonia 41	Chronic Low Respiratory Disease 178	Cerebro-vascular 579	Cerebro-vascular 1,745	Influenza & Pneumonia 2,731	Septicemia 5,709	Nephritis 39,957	Nephritis 48,146
10	Neonatal Hemorrhage 441	Perinatal Period 38	Septicemia 33	Benign Neoplasms 38	Cerebro-vascular 177	Influenza & Pneumonia 549	Influenza & Pneumonia 1,125	Septicemia 2,514	Influenza & Pneumonia 5,390	Septicemia 29,124	Suicide 42,773

Centers for Disease Control and Prevention
National Center for Injury Prevention and Control

Data **Source:** National Vital Statistics System, National Center for Health Statistics, CDC.
Produced by: National Center for Injury Prevention and Control, CDC using WISQARS™.

- An estimated 31.7 million people treated in Emergency Department for injury each year
- Violence and injuries cost more than $406 billion in medical care and lost productivity each year

In general, there are a few common characteristics of an accident victim: young, male, prone to experimentation, more likely to take unnecessary risks and with poor impulse control (Thygerson, 1992). Please consider that all of these characteristics need not be met in order to be at risk of accidents and just because you are not in any of these groups does not mean you are not at risk. According to the research team of Frances E. Jensen and David K. Urion, of Children's Hospital Boston and Harvard Medical School, not only do adolescents have a slower to develop prefrontal cortex (responsible for controlling impulses and emotion and helping us understand cause and effect, right and wrong), but they are also often sleep deprived, have little exercise/activity on a regular basis and are constantly trying to multitask (Ruder, 2008). Does any of this sound familiar? Each of these has a negative effect on decision-making when it comes to accidents and violence. Consider a study conducted at the McLean Hospital Brain Imaging Center by Debroah Yurgelun-Todd and colleagues. They used functional magnetic resonance imaging to compare the activity of teen and adult brains. Because the prefrontal cortex is the last region of the brain to fully develop, they found that while adults could often use rational decision-making skills, teens lacked the ability to do the same. Similarly, Jay Giedd and colleagues at the National Institutes of Mental Health used brain imaging to measure the structure, as opposed to activity, of adolescent brains when compared to adults, finding that development of the frontal lobe continues well into one's early twenties (Talukder, 2013).

Motor Vehicle Safety

The leading cause of unintentional death is motor vehicle crashes. In 2009, over 35,900 individuals died in motor vehicle crashes in the United States. The 15–24 year-old age group had nearly 8,000 deaths for that year (NSC, 2011).

One of the leading factors in motor vehicle crashes is driver inattention. According to the National Highway Traffic Safety Administration (NHTSA), nearly 80 percent of crashes involve some form of driver inattention. This signifies the importance of the driving task and that the need for attention is critical (NHTSA, 2010).

Distracted Driving

Operating a motor vehicle is the single most dangerous activity that we do on a daily basis and yet we feel confident that we can drive and do others things at the same time.

We pride ourselves in our ability to multitask. We have been conditioned to think that we are more productive and successful if able to focus on more than one thing at a time. But can we truly multitask?

John Medina, author of *"Brain Rules"* says, "research shows that we can't multitask. We are biologically incapable of processing attention-rich inputs simultaneously." The brain focuses on ideas and concepts one after another instead of both at the same time. The brain must let go of one activity to go to another, taking several seconds. According to Professor Clifford Nass at Stanford University, the more that you multi-task, the less productive you become.

When we operate a motor vehicle, many things can be considered distractions. Any secondary activity like texting, talking on a cell phone, putting on make-up, eating and drinking, adjusting your music and even your GPS can all cause problems while driving. Taking your eyes off the road for as little as

---

Occupational Wellness

Are you engaged in the process of Occupational Wellness? Evaluate your own occupational wellness with this brief quiz.

- Do I enjoy going to work most days?
- Do I have a manageable workload at work?
- Do I feel that I can talk to my boss and co-workers with problems arise?

If you answered "No" to any of the questions, it may indicate an area where you need to improve the state of your occupational wellness.

Environmental Wellness

Are you engaged in the process of Environmental Wellness? Evaluate your own environmental wellness with this brief quiz.

- Do I recycle?
- If I see a safety hazard, do I take the steps to fix the problem?
- Do I volunteer time to worthy causes?
- Am I aware of my surroundings at all times?

If you answered "No" to any of the questions, it may indicate an area where you need to improve the state of your environmental wellness.

two seconds can be dangerous. We have added more distractions by using our smart phones for Facebook, Twitter and other social media.

There are 3 main types of distraction:

- Visual—taking your eyes off the road. For example, glancing down at your phone or changing songs on your CD player or iPod
- Manual—taking your hands off the wheel. Examples range from hand held cell phone use, texting, eating or changing clothes
- Cognitive—taking your mind off the task. Daydreaming or your current emotional state could play a role in your attention on the driving task.

All three types can be a serious, life-threatening practice.

Statistically, distracted driving has passed drunk driving as the number one safety concern for the driving public. Drivers on cell phones are more impaired than drivers with a .08 BAC, which is considered legally intoxicated in all states.

This is not to say that drinking and driving is not a serious problem, it brings to light, the impact of distracted driving. What about an intoxicated driver on a cell phone or texting? and the odds of being involved in an accident increases greatly.

According to NHTSA research, distraction-related fatalities represented 16 percent of overall traffic fatalities in 2009. Nearly 5,500 people were killed and 448,000 were injured in crashes involving a distracted or inattentive driver (NHTSA, 2009).

We know what distractions are out there, but what can we do to solve this problem? With nearly 5,500 fatalities in 2009 that number will only continue to grow unless we, as the driving public, make some positive changes. Legislation may work to some degree but changing our behavior is crucial in solving this problem.

U.S. Department of Transportation Secretary, Ray LaHood, cautions that researchers believe the epidemic of distracted driving is likely far greater than currently known. Police reports in many states still do not document routinely whether distraction was a factor in vehicle crashes, making it more difficult to know the full extent of the problem.

With that in mind, The Department of Transportation has hosted two Distracted Driving Summits in Washington, D.C., the most recent in September of 2010. Many states have considered passing laws prohibiting cell phone use and texting while driving. There are 30 states, and the District of Columbia that have banned text messaging for all drivers. Twelve of these laws were enacted in 2010 alone.

Changing your behavior and encouraging your friends to change may help bring an end to the senseless tragedy of distracted driving.

For more information on Distracted Driving visit there websites: enddd.org—the official U.S. Government Website for Distracted Driving distraction.gov—sponsored by the Department of Transportation (DOT) "Faces of Distracted Driving" caseyfeldman foundation.org.

Drowsy Driving

Fatigue on the road can be a killer. It happens frequently on long trips, especially long night drives. There is no test to determine sleepiness and no laws regarding drowsy driving; therefore, it is difficult to attribute crashes to sleepiness. According to the NHTSA, drowsy driving accounts for approximately 100,000 accidents each year, injuring 71,000 and producing 1,550 fatalities (NHTSA, 2011). In a 2006 poll conducted by the National Sleep Foundation (NSF, 2007) reported driving a vehicle while feeling drowsy during the prior year, with 37 percent reporting that they actually dozed off while driving. It is equally as dangerous if not more dangerous to drive when you are drowsy than intoxicated. Some drivers abstain from alcohol but no one can resist the need to sleep. People are less likely to admit that they are feeling fatigued and therefore continue to drive when drowsy, leaving it up to self-regulation. Results from a recent study by the Stanford Sleep Disorders Clinic, performed by Dr. Nelson Powell, concluded that the sleepy drivers performed the same as the drunk drivers on basically all skills tested.

The leading cause of accidental death is motor vehicle accidents.

The NSF has created the "Drive Alert . . . Arrive Alive" campaign to help people become aware of the dangers of drowsy driving. One very important detail pointed out by this campaign is that people fall asleep more often on high-speed, long, boring, and rural highways. The more monotonous the drive, the more likely the driver will suffer some fatigue. According to the NSF, drivers who pose a greater risk for drowsy driving are those who are sleep deprived, drive long distances without breaks, drive through the night, drive alone, or those drivers with undiagnosed sleep disorders. Shift workers also pose a greater threat because they typically have non-traditional work schedules. Young people are more prone to sleep-related crashes because they typically do not get enough sleep, stay up late, and drive at night. NSF has a few warning signs to indicate that a driver may be experiencing fatigue. These include not remembering the last few miles driven, drifting from their lane, hitting rumble strips, yawning repeatedly, having difficulty focusing, and having trouble keeping the head up. The NSF also offers these tips for staying awake while driving:

- Get a good night's sleep.
- Schedule regular stops.
- Drive with a companion.
- Avoid alcohol.
- Avoid medications that may cause drowsiness.

If anti-fatigue measures do not work, of course the best solution is sleep. If no motels are in sight and you are within one to two hours of your destination, pull off the road in a safe area and take a short twentyto thirty-minute nap.

Most drowsy driving crashes involve males between the ages of 16–25 (NSF, 2008). Because of this growing problem, many colleges and universities, are providing awareness programs to try to prevent this tragedy from occurring.

In any kind of motor vehicle crash, a seat belt may save your life! The lap/shoulder safety belts reduce the risk of fatalities to front seat passengers of cars by 45 percent and for trucks by 60 percent. They also reduce the severity of injuries by 50 percent for cars and 65 percent for trucks (NSC, 2008).

Air bags combined with safety belts offer the best protection. There has been an overall 14 percent reduction in fatalities since adding air bags to vehicles (NSC, 2008). Buckle up!

Traumatic Brain Injury (TBI) can be caused by a bump, blow, or jolt to the head that disrupts normal brain function. An estimated 1.7 million people sustain a TBI annually in the U.S., killing 52,000. The leading cause of TBI deaths is motor vehicle traffic injuries, with the highest death rate among adults 20–24 years old.

Crime Awareness and Campus Security Act of 1990   The Clery Act was named for Jeanne Clery, a 19-year-old freshman who was raped and murdered in her dorm room at Lehigh University in 1986. Her parents were later informed that there had been thirty-eight violent crimes on this campus and the students were unaware of this problem. As a result, her parents, Connie and Howard Clery, along with other campus crime victims, convinced Congress to enact the law known as the "Crime Awareness and Campus Security Act of

Fire Safety 101

A Factsheet for Colleges & Universities

Every year college and university students experience a growing number of fire-related emergencies. There are several causes for these fires; however most are due to a general lack of knowledge about fire safety and prevention.

The U.S. Fire Administration (USFA) offers these tips to help reduce and prevent the loss of life and property in dormitory and university housing fires.

The Facts

In cases where fire fatalities occurred on college campuses, alcohol was a factor. There is a strong link between alcohol and fire deaths. In more than 50% of adult fire fatalities, victims were under the influence at the time of the fire. Alcohol abuse often impairs judgment and hampers evacuation efforts. Cooking is the leading cause of fire injuries on college campuses, closely followed by careless smoking and arson.

The Cause

Many factors contribute to the problem of dormitory housing fires.

- Improper use of 911 notification systems delays emergency response.
- Student apathy is prevalent. Many are unaware that fire is a risk or threat in the environment.
- Evacuation efforts are hindered since fire alarms are often ignored.
- Building evacuations are delayed due to lack of preparation and preplanning.

- Vandalized and improperly maintained smoke alarms and fire alarm systems inhibit early detection of fires.
- Misuse of cooking appliances, overloaded electrical circuits, and extension cords increase the risk of fires.

Safety Precautions

- Provide students with a program for fire safety and prevention.
- Teach students how to properly notify the fire department using the 911 system.
- Install smoke alarms in every dormitory room and every level of housing facilities.
- Maintain and regularly test smoke alarms and fire alarm systems. Replace smoke alarm batteries every semester.
- Regularly inspect rooms and buildings for fire hazards. Ask your local fire department for assistance.
- Inspect exit doors and windows and make sure they are working properly.
- Create and update detailed floor plans of buildings, and make them available to emergency personnel, resident advisors, and students.
- Conduct fire drills and practice escape routes and evacuation plans. Urge students to take each alarm seriously.
- Do not overload electrical outlets and make sure extension cords are used properly.
- Learn to properly use and maintain heating and cooking appliances.

www.usfa.fema.gov

1990." The law was amended in 1992 and 1998 to include rights to victims of campus sexual assault and to expand the reporting requirements of the colleges and universities. In 1998, the law was officially named the "Clery Act."

The Clery Act requires all colleges and universities to accurately report the number of campus crimes per category to the campus community and prospective students. Follow up with your campus Police Department to find out how this report is dispersed to current & prospective students, staff, & faculty. College campuses have often been the site for criminal activity. These offenses include sex offenses, robbery, aggravated assault, burglary, arson, and motor vehicle theft. Hate crimes as well as hazing issues can be included in the reports as well as alcohol and weapons violations. Approximately 80 percent of the crimes that take place on college campuses are student-on-student, with nine out of ten felonies involving alcohol or other drugs.

As of 2002, the Clery Act also requires all states to register sex offenders, under Megan's Law, if they are students or employees of the college or university. This information is available to the campus police as well as students who request such information.

Under this law, colleges and universities can be fined for failure to report campus crimes. Omission of this information is not only illegal but it poses a threat to students' safety. The fines send a strong message for schools to take the obligation of reporting crimes and protecting students seriously.

Current Issues Impacting College Campuses:
High risk drinking
Illegal drug use
Prescription drug use
Sexual assault
Stalking
Relationship violence
Hazing
Hate crimes
Fire safety

Source: The Clery Center for Security on Campus http://clerycenter.org/national-campus-safety-awareness-month.

A Wellness Profile

Living well requires constant evaluation and effort on an individual's part. The following list includes important behaviors and habits to include in your daily life:

- Be responsible for your own health and wellness. Take an active role in your life and well-being.
- Learn how to recognize and manage stress effectively.
- Eat nutritious meals, exercise regularly, and maintain a healthy weight.
- Work towards healthy relationships with friends, family, and significant others.
- Avoid tobacco and other drugs; use alcohol responsibly, if at all.
- Know the facts about cardiovascular disease, cancer, infections, sexually transmitted infections, and injuries. Utilize this knowledge to protect yourself.
- Understand how the environment affects your health and take appropriate measures to improve it.
  (adapted from Insel & Roth, 2009)

FIGURE 1.2

Healthy vs. unhealthy years of life expectancy

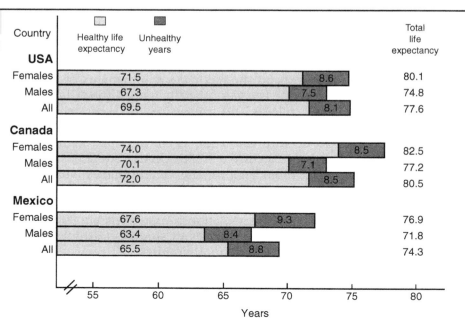

Sources: World Health Organization and National Center for Health Statistics

By regularly evaluating your lifestyle and making small changes, you can maintain a healthy lifestyle. There are significant benefits to choosing healthy behaviors early on. The earlier these healthy behaviors are achieved, the more graceful aging will be. In Figure 1.2 the life expectancy is differentiated between healthy life expectancy and unhealthy years. In the CDC graph "10 Leading Causes of Death by Age Group" on page 7, the number one cause of death is unintentional injury until the age of 44. After age 44, the leading causes of death are cancer and heart disease. These two figures demonstrate how critical it is that healthy behavior choices are made now rather than waiting until an injury or disease has occurred.

© hxdbzxy/Shutterstock.com

The best way to avoid injuries and disease is through prevention. There are three types of prevention: primary, secondary and tertiary. **Primary prevention** utilizes behaviors to avoid the development of disease. This can include getting immunizations, exercising regularly, eating healthy meals, limiting exposure to sunlight, using sunscreen, having safe drinking water, and guarding against accidents. The focus of this textbook will be primary prevention to help individuals choose behaviors that will prevent disease and premature death.

Secondary prevention is aimed at early detection of disease. This can include blood pressure screenings, mammograms, and annual pap tests to identify and detect disease in its earliest stages. This is before noticeable symptoms develop, when the disease is most likely to be treated successfully. With early detection and diagnosis, it may be possible to cure a disease, slow its progression, prevent or minimize complications, and limit disability. Another goal of secondary prevention is to prevent the spread of communicable diseases. In the community, early identification and treatment of people with communicable diseases, such as sexually transmitted infections, not only provides secondary prevention for those who are infected but also primary prevention for people who come in contact with infected individuals.

Tertiary prevention works to improve the quality of life for individuals with various diseases by limiting complications and disabilities, restoring function, and slowing or stopping the progression of a disease. Tertiary prevention plays a key role for individuals with arthritis, asthma, heart disease, and diabetes.

Researchers at the Human Population Laboratory of the California Department of Health published the following list of healthrelated behaviors that have been associated with good health and a long life. These behaviors include:

■ 1. Regular exercise
■ 2. Adequate sleep
■ 3. A good breakfast
■ 4. Regular meals

■ 5. Weight control
■ 6. Abstinence from smoking and drugs
■ 7. Moderate use of (or abstinence from) alcohol

It was shown that by following six of the seven listed behaviors, not only is an individual's quality of life greatly improved, but also, men could add eleven years to their lives and women could add seven years to their lives.

Disease Prevention

What happens if you *don't* follow these recommendations for a longer, healthier life? A shortened lifespan, perhaps, along with increased risk of illness and injury.

Illnesses, or infections, are most often caused by bacteria and viruses. These two microorganisms differ in many ways. The most significant difference is that antibiotics can treat bacterial infections, but they are generally ineffective against viral infections (Mayo Clinic, 2014).

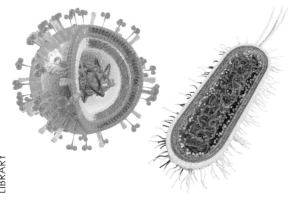

Bacteria

Bacteria are single-celled microorganisms that can replicate on their own (outside of a host) and thrive in almost any type of environment. Many bacteria are actually harmless and some even live inside the human body. For example, hundreds of species of bacteria called intestinal microflora exist in the digestive system. These organisms assist with fiber digestion, synthesize certain vitamins, and interfere with pathogens (Gorbach, 1996). Harmful bacteria make up less than 1% of the total number of bacteria species. When these infectious bacteria are introduced into the body, they reproduce quickly. Many give off toxins, which make you sick and cause symptoms. Illnesses caused by bacteria include strep throat (caused by streptococcus), staph infections (caused by staphylococcus) and E. coli infections.

Fortunately, modern medicine offers a powerful tool for fighting bacterial infections – antibiotics. These medications either kill bacteria or prevent them from reproducing. It is important that you follow antibiotic instructions carefully, as each time someone takes these medications, they might increase the chance that bacteria become resistant to the treatment. Finishing an entire course of antibiotics is an important step in preventing antibiotic resistance (Medline Plus, 2017).

Antibiotic Resistance

FIGURE 1.3

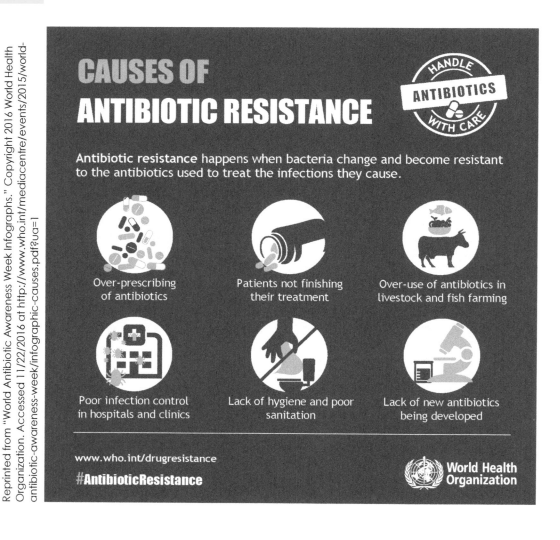

As seen in Figure 1.3, antibiotic resistance is not only caused by over-prescribing or not finishing antibiotics. Healthcare, sanitation, and agriculture industries all contribute to possible changes in bacteria that make them resistant to the antibiotics designed to treat the infections they cause. The World Health Organization (WHO) identifies antibiotic resistance as one of the biggest threats to food security, global health, and development today. According to WHO, infections such as pneumonia, gonorrhea, and tuberculosis are becoming increasingly more difficult to treat because they do not respond to traditionally-prescribed antibiotics. Without changes to the ways antibiotics are prescribed by physicians and veterinarians and handled by the general public, WHO warns that we may be headed toward a post-antibiotic era, where minor illnesses can kill once again. Infection-preventing practices, such as hand washing, hygienic food preparation, avoiding contact with people who are sick, safer sex, and up-to-date vaccinations can help prevent the need for excessive antibiotic prescriptions (WHO, 2016).

Viruses

Smaller than bacteria, viruses require a living host (such as a human, animal, or plant) to reproduce. When a virus enters a host, it invades the cells, re-programming them to reproduce the virus. This illness-causing, sometimes deadly, re-programming can affect the liver, blood, respiratory system, or any other area. Examples of viruses that cause illnesses include Norovirus (inflammation of the stomach or intestines), Influenza, Ebola, and Zika. While symptoms of bacterial and viral infections are often similar, the treatment protocols are very different.

Antibiotics are not effective against viruses at all. Anti-viral drugs can slow the progression of the illness and help reduce symptoms, but the body's immune system is often the only defense against the virus itself. Avoiding the prescription of antibiotics for an illness that is possibly caused by a virus is another stop in preventing antibiotic resistance. Some viruses, such as Human Papilloma Virus and Hepatitis B, can be prevented with vaccines.

Another unique characteristic of viruses is their ability to delay replication once inside a cell. These two processes are called the lytic cycle and the lysogenic cycle. When a virus uses the lytic cycle, it invades a cell and immediately starts making copies of its genetic material. The virus's proteins assemble to form a protein coat, and the components come together to form complete and functional viruses. Eventually, enough new viruses are formed that the cell to lyse, or break open, releasing all of the viruses out into the environment. These viruses then invade nearby cells, and the process continues. The alternative to this process is the lysogenic cycle. In this slow-moving cycle, a virus invades a cell and combines with the host's genetic information, but it does not replicate. These viruses have repressor genes that allow them to remain dormant or latent until a trigger (like exposure to a bacteria) weakens the repressor gene. When the host tries to repair itself, the virus becomes active, breaks open the cell, and begins to invade other ones (Khan Academy, accessed 2017).

Meningitis, the common cold, and influenza are diseases that college students may face. Knowing whether they are caused by a bacteria or virus can help students understand their severity, treatment and prevention.

Meningitis

One illness that can be caused by both bacteria and viruses is meningitis. This disease causes an inflammation of the tissue that covers the brain and spinal cord. The severity, symptoms, treatment, and prevention for the two types of meningitis differ, but college students are at risk for both due to their close contact with large numbers of people.

Viral Meningitis

The most common, but least severe, type of meningitis is viral. Non-polio enteroviruses are the most usual cause of viral meningitis in the United States. Not everyone infected with these viruses will develop meningitis; infection depends on the strength of the immune system. Babies under one month old and adults with weakened immune systems because of medications or recent organ or bone marrow transplantations are at highest risk. The virus is spread through close contact with an infected individual.

The symptoms of viral meningitis vary with the age of infected individuals. All ages can experience fever, sleepiness, lethargy, and loss of appetite. Adults can also experience headache, stiff neck, sensitivity to light, and vomiting. These symptoms are similar to those of bacterial meningitis, so an examination by a healthcare provider is essential in determining the type of meningitis and corresponding treatment.

Diagnosis is achieved through testing swabs from the nose, throat, or rectum, drawing blood, or drawing fluid from around the spinal cord (spinal tap). Most cases of viral meningitis get better on their own in 7–10 days with the infected individual practices standard self-care, such as adequate nutrition, hydration, and rest.

No vaccines are available to prevent meningitis caused by non-polio enteroviruses. People can lower their chance of contracting meningitis by following the infection-preventing practices shown in Figure 1.4.

FIGURE 1.4

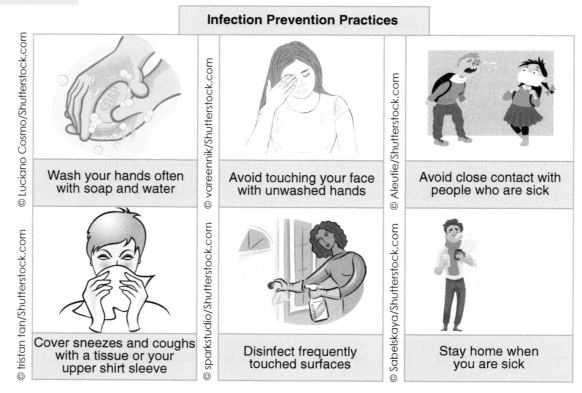

Infection Prevention Practices

Wash your hands often with soap and water

Avoid touching your face with unwashed hands

Avoid close contact with people who are sick

Cover sneezes and coughs with a tissue or your upper shirt sleeve

Disinfect frequently touched surfaces

Stay home when you are sick

© Luciano Cosmo/Shutterstock.com
© tristan tan/Shutterstock.com
© vareennik/Shutterstock.com
© sparkstudio/Shutterstock.com
© Aleutie/Shutterstock.com
© Sabelskaya/Shutterstock.com

Bacterial Meningitis

Less common than viral meningitis, bacterial is the more severe of the two types of infections. Infections can be very serious and even deadly, with death occurring within just a few hours in some cases. Even though most people with bacterial meningitis recover, long-term complications such as brain damage, hearing loss, and learning disabilities can follow.

The type of bacteria that causes meningitis varies depending on the age of the person infected. Adolescents and young adults are most at risk for *Neisseria meningitides* and *Streptococcus pneumoniae*. Outbreaks of *N. meningitides* have been reported on college campuses due to the community living setting making it easy for diseases to spread. Fortunately, the bacteria that cause meningitis are not as contagious as viruses that cause the cold or the flu. Transmission of bacterial meningitis occurs through the exchange of respiratory or throat secretions during close (kissing or hugging) or lengthy contact, especially when residing in the same household. Anyone who has contact with a person who has meningitis should be seen by a healthcare provider to determine their risk and need for preventive antibiotics.

© Rawpixel.com/Shutterstock.com

The initial, common symptoms of bacterial meningitis are: sudden onset of fever, headache, and stiff neck. Other symptoms may include: nausea, vomiting, sensitivity to light, and altered mental status (confusion). These symptoms typically present in 3–7 days after exposure. Seizures and coma are much later signs of meningitis. As soon as someone suspects they have meningitis, they should see a healthcare provider. A diagnosis is made by sampling blood or cerebrospinal fluid. Testing blood or fluids helps determine the specific bacteria that caused the meningitis, which guides the treatment with antibiotics and determination of the severity of infection. For maximum effectiveness, it is essential that antibiotic treatment (and preventive antibiotics for others, if necessary), begin as soon as possible.

Because college students spend a great deal of time with large groups of people, they are more at risk for contracting meningitis than other populations.

Vaccines for three types of bacteria that cause meningitis are available. The CDC identifies these vaccines as the most effective way to protect yourself against certain types of bacterial meningitis. The meningococcal, pneumococcal, and Hib vaccines are all part of the recommended vaccination schedule for children and adolescents (CDC, 2017).

Common Cold and the Flu

The common cold and influenza (the flu) are both respiratory illnesses, but are caused by different viruses. The symptoms are similar, but special testing within the first few days of illness can help determine if an individual has the flu. Symptoms of a cold tend to be more mild and short-lived, and do not lead to more serious health complications or hospitalizations. Table 1.1 differentiates between cold and flu symptoms (CDC, 2017).

Treatment for the cold involves rest, hydration, and over-the-counter or homeopathic treatments to help relieve symptoms. If the flu virus is identified within 2 days of illness, antiviral medications can be administered to decrease the severity and shorten the duration of the illness. Antiviral drugs can also help prevent flu-related complications. These medications are a treatment only and do not prevent future flu infections.

Table 1.1 Differentiates between Cold and Flu Symptoms

Symptom	Cold	Flu
Runny nose	✓	✓
Congestion	✓	✓
Sore throat or coughing	✓	✓
Fever		✓
Muscle or body aches		✓
Headache		✓
Fatigue		✓

Flu Vaccine

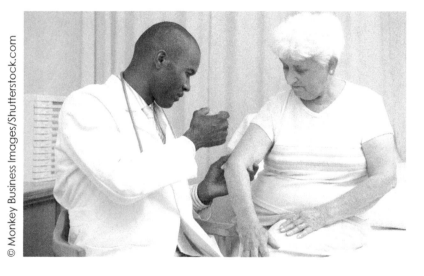

While there is no cure for the flu, certain strains of influenza can be prevented with a flu vaccine. This vaccine is unlike others because it is seasonal, meaning that people need to get a different vaccine each year in order to be protected. Researchers develop the seasonal flu vaccine by determining which strains of the flu virus are expected to be most prevalent during the upcoming flu season (which typically runs October through May in the United States). Current flu vaccines cause the recipient to develop antibodies against the flu approximately two weeks after the vaccine. These antibodies provide protection against the three (trivalent vaccines) or four (quadrivalent vaccines) flu strains included in the shot. The vaccines are made with either inactive flu viruses (meaning they cannot cause flu symptoms) or no flu viruses at all. This refutes the myth that people "get the flu" from the flu shot. Beginning in 2010, the CDC's Advisory Committee on Immunization Practices voted for universal flu vaccines in the United States. Since then, everyone who is six months of age and older has been recommended to receive a flu shot, with rare exceptions. Those who should not receive a flu shot include infants younger than six months and individuals with life-threatening reactions to the flu vaccine or vaccine ingredients. People with Guillian-Barre Syndrome and those with allergies to eggs should talk to a healthcare provider before receiving the vaccine. In the event of a vaccine shortage, people with the following conditions should receive priority:

- Children between 6 months and 4 years of age
- Adults ages 50 and older
- Household contacts and caregivers of anyone in the above-mentioned age groups
- Those with compromised immune systems
- Healthcare workers
- Nursing home and chronic-care facility residents
- Those with chronic cardiovascular, renal, hepatic, pulmonary, metabolic, and neurologic disorders
- Women who are or will be pregnant during flu season (CDC, 2016)

Flu vaccines can significantly reduce the spread and severity of the seasonal flu. An CDC study reported in the August 2016 Clinical Infections Diseases journal that flu-related hospitalizations were reduced by half in adults over age 65 who received the flu vaccine (CDC, 2016). Vaccines can also make the flu infection shorter or milder if someone does get the virus after vaccination. Researchers constantly strive to improve the effectiveness of the flu vaccine. In addition to the seasonal flu, scientists study avian, swine, and international flu strains to increase protection and prevention across the globe (Figure 1.5).

FIGURE 1.5

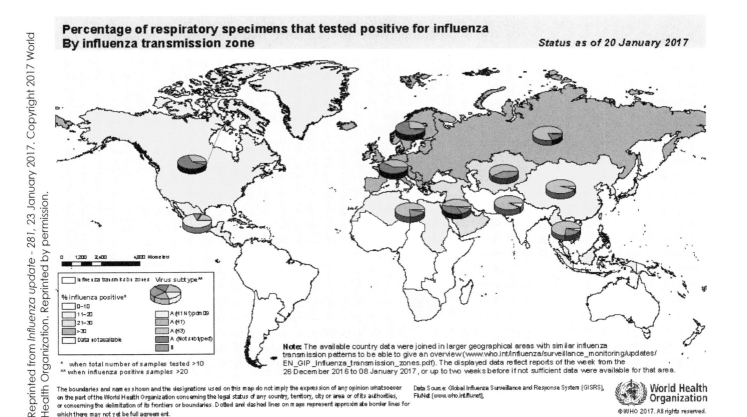

Percentage of respiratory specimens that tested positive for influenza By influenza transmission zone — *Status as of 20 January 2017*

Healthy People 2020: Improving the Health of Americans

There are twelve major public health areas, which include leading health indicators. They are:

- Access to health services
- Clinical preventive services
- Environmental quality
- Injury and violence
- Maternal, infant, and child health
- Mental health
- Nutrition, physical activity, and obesity
- Oral health
- Reproductive and sexual health
- Social determinants
- Substance abuse
- Tobacco

www.healthypeople.gov/2020/LHI.default.aspx

There are four major factors that influence personal health:

1. personal behavior
2. heredity
3. environment
4. access to professional health care personnel

The importance of prevention is made clear in *Healthy People 2020. Healthy People* was first developed in 1979 as a *Surgeon General's Report.* It has been reformulated since 1979 as *Healthy People 1990: Promoting Health/Preventing Disease, Healthy People 2000: National Health Promotion and Disease Prevention and Healthy People 2010; Objectives for Improving Health.* The original efforts of these programs were to establish national health objectives and to serve as a base of knowledge for the development of both state-level and community-level plans and programs to improve the nation's overall health. Much like the programs *Healthy People 2020* is based on, it was developed through broad consultation programs and the best and most current scientific knowledge in the public and private sectors. It is also designed in a way that will allow communities to measure the success rates, over time, of the programs they choose to implement.

Healthy People 2020 has four overarching goals. The first goal is to attain high quality, longer lives free of preventable disease, disability, injury, and premature death. The second goal is to achieve health equity, eliminate disparities, and improve the health of all groups. The third goal is to create social and physical environments that promote good health for all. One last goal is to promote quality of life, healthy development, and healthy behaviors across all life stages.

In conclusion, health is "a state of complete physical, mental, and social well-being and not merely the absence of disease or infirmity" according to the World Health Organization. By definition, health is a universal trait. Due to the fact that personal behaviors are one of the four major factors that influence a person's lifespan and quality of life, health also takes on a very individual and unique quality.

The idea of wellness is an individual-based approach to health. Wellness is grounded in behavior modification strategies that result in the adoption of low-risk, health-enhancing behaviors. By balancing the seven components of wellness—emotional, intellectual, social, spiritual, physical, occupational, and environmental—a person can, to some degree, prevent disease and premature death.

Each decade, since the 1979 *Surgeon General's Report,* the nation has refined its health agenda—first through *Healthy People* 1990 through *Healthy People 2000: National Health Promotion and Disease Prevention* through *Healthy People 2010: Objectives for Improving Health,* and currently through *Healthy People 2020.* When an attempt is made to understand the four goals of *Healthy People 2020* and connect the topic areas of this program with these goals, the overwhelming importance of prevention in promoting an individual's level of wellness is made clear.

References

Centers for Disease Control and Prevention: Bacterial Meningitis (25 January 2017). Retrieved from https://www.cdc.gov/meningitis/bacterial.html

Centers for Disease Control and Prevention, National Center for Injury Prevention and Control (2014). The leading cause of death for persons 1–44 in U.S.

Centers for Disease Control and Prevention, National Center for Injury Prevention and Control (2014). FASTSTATS: Leading causes of death.

Centers for Disease Control and Prevention: New CDC Study: Influenza Vaccination Reduces Risk of Hospitalization by More Than Half Among

Seniors (2 August 2016) Retrieved from https://www.cdc.gov/flu/news/study-vaccination-hospitalization.htm

Centers for Disease Control and Prevention: Preventing Seasonal Flu with Vaccination (10 November 2016). Retrieved from https://www.cdc.gov/flu/protect/vaccine/index.htm

Centers for Disease Control and Prevention: Viral Meningitis (15 June 2016). Retrieved from https://www.cdc.gov/meningitis/viral.html

Corbin, C. B., Welk, G. J., Corbin, W. R. and Welk, K. A. *Concepts of Physical Fitness* (16th ed). McBrown. 2010.

Finkelstein, E. A., Corso, P. S., and Miller, T. R., Associates. Incidence and Economic Burden of Injuries in the United States. New York, NY: Oxford University Press. 2006.

Floyd, P., Mims, S., and Yelding-Howard, C. *Personal Health: Perspectives and Lifestyles* (4th ed). Morton Publishing Co. 2007.

http://ahha.org http://wellness.ndsu.nodak.edu/education/dimensions.shtml

http://who.int/aboutwho/en/definition.html

http://www.cdc.gov/nchs/data/hp2k99.pdf

http://www.healthypeople.gov/2020/default.aspx

http://www.m-w.com/dictionary.htm

http://www.wellnesswise.com/dimensions.htm

Gorbach, S. (1996). *Medical microbiology*. Galveston, TX: University of Texas Medical Branch at Galveston.

Hyman, B., Oden, G., Bacharach, D., and Collins, R. *Fitness for Living* (3rd ed). Kendall-Hunt Publishing Co. 2006.

Insel, P. M. and Roth, W. T. *Core Concepts in Health* (12th ed). McGraw Hill Publishing. 2009.

Khan Academy: Viral Replication: Lytic and Lysogenic (accessed January 2017). Retrieved from https://www.khanacademy.org/test-prep/mcat/cells/viruses/v/viral-replicaiton-lytic-vs-lysogenic

Mayo Clinic: Bacterial vs Viral Infections: How Do They Differ? (24 October 2016) Retrieved from "http://www.mayoclinic.org/diseases-conditions/infectious-diseases/expert-answers/infectious-disease/faq-20058098" \h disease/faq-20058098

Medline Plus: Bacterial Infections (17 January 2017) Retrieved from https://medlineplus.gov/bacterialinfections.html

National Vital Statistics System, National Center for Health Statistics, CDC.

NCIPC: Web-based Injury Statistics Query and Reporting System (WISQARS) http://www.cdc.gov/injury/wisqars

Payne, W. A., Hahn, D. B., and Lucas, E. B. *Understanding Your Health* (10th ed). McGraw Hill Publishing. 2008.

Pruitt, B.E. and Stein, J. *Health Styles*. Allyn & Bacon. 1999.

Ruder, Debra Bradley. (2008). The teen brain: a work in progress. *Harvard Magazine*, 8–10.

The Clery Center for Security on Campus. http://clerycenter.org/national-campus-safety-awareness-month

Talukder, Gargi. (2013). Decision-making is still a work in progress for teenagers. http://brainconnection.brainhq.com/decision-making-is-still-a-work-in-progress-for-teenagers/

Thygerson, Alton L. (1992). Safety. Boston, MA: Jones and Bartlett Publishers.

World Health Organization: Antibiotic Resistance (October 2016). Retrieved from http://www.who.int/mediacentre/factsheets/antibiotic-resistance/en/

Wellness Initiative/University of Nebraska-Lincoln

Wellness The Total Package, 2nd Edition.

Chapter 2
Scientific Inquiry

© Billion Photos/Shutterstock.com

OBJECTIVES

The student will be able to:

♦ Recognize the steps and limitations of the scientific method.
♦ Explain the constructs of scientific inquiry.
♦ Identify the levels of scientific studies.
♦ Differentiate between reliability and validity.

"All truths are easy to understand once they are discovered; the point is to discover them"

– Gaileo Gailie

The word science might conjure up memories of high school chemistry experiments or images of researchers squinting into microscopes in a lab. These activities certainly comprise some aspects of science, but the field is not limited to bubbling test tubes and Petri dishes. Science is a process of questioning, investigating, and experimenting that leads to discoveries, breakthroughs, and often, even more questions. Children learning to wash their hands, doctors prescribing antibiotics, and public policies preventing cigarette smoking in public areas are all rooted in science.

Scientific exploration often begins with a process called the **Scientific Method**. This is practiced in classrooms, laboratories, and other research arenas as a methodical approach to answering questions and determining conclusions. Figure 2.1 provides a visual representation of this method.

- *Observation* – The research process begins with an individual making an observation about something that interests him. For example, an observation could be, "The US Olympic teams used chocolate milk as a post-exercise recovery aid in 2016".
- *Question* – An observation leads to a question, where the investigator wonders why something occurs or what the result of an intervention, or change, might be. A question posed after the above example could be, "Will drinking chocolate milk after a workout help college students (non-competitive athletes) recover faster?
- *Hypothesis* – A hypothesis is a prediction of the expected outcomes of an experiment, sometimes written as an "If… then" statement. Using the chocolate milk question, a testable hypothesis would be, "If students drink chocolate milk after their workouts, then their recovery time will be decreased".
- *Experiment* – The researcher then designs an experiment that tests the hypothesis. In an actual experiment, at least two groups or specimens are tested, using one as a control with no intervention or change, and the other with the condition(s) to be tested. Conducting a formal experiment is not always feasible due to lack of funds, time, or resources. Sometimes an "experiment" can be collecting data from existing sources, like peer-reviewed literature. The chocolate milk example falls in this category. College students would probably not conduct a formal experiment where they measured recovery time after drinking chocolate milk, but they can research previous studies of groups who drank chocolate milk after workouts.

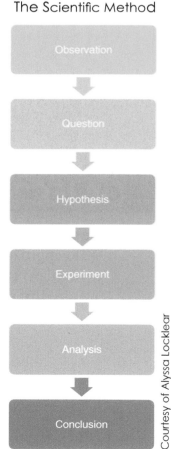

FIGURE 2.1

The Scientific Method

Observation

Question

Hypothesis

Experiment

Analysis

Conclusion

- *Analysis* – Results from the experiment or study are interpreted through graphs, charts, and written explanations.
- *Conclusion* – The researcher states if the hypothesis is proved or disproved and offers recommendations for future studies. Variables and other challenges encountered in the experiment are also discussed. A conclusion in the chocolate milk study might be that the student proves the hypothesis with findings from his research. The conclusion could also be that additional experiments or studies are needed, and the researcher is not able to prove or disprove the hypothesis yet.

Not all research follows this method exactly, and this process is not always accessible to the general public. Many people desire to conduct their own research on health issues, treatment options, prevention techniques, and healthcare alternatives. In reality, there is no one scientific method. The process of **Scientific Inquiry** opens the door to individuals, regardless of their research focus or educational background, to conduct their own investigations into the plethora of "expert" health information available. The National Academy of Sciences reports the National Research Council's explanation of the process as,

"Scientific Inquiry refers to the diverse ways in which scientists study the natural world and propose explanations based on the evidence derived from their work. Inquiry also refers to the activities of students in which they develop knowledge and understanding of scientific ideas, as well as an understanding of how scientists study the natural world."

(National Science Education Standards, 1996)

Possible sources of information in the scientific inquiry process may include:

- Books and other sources of background information
- Experimental evidence
- Trusted sources

The abundance of health information can be overwhelming. Guidance is available on how to effectively and efficiently identify credible sources of information. Cornell University offers an Evidence-Based Living blog, and one of their articles includes the following questions to help readers determine the usefulness of any type of information that is reported in the news:

1. *Access to the original source* – Evidence-Based Living recommends that readers go back to the original source of information before believing what is presented in the media. News reports or other articles that do not provide access to this resource leave readers wondering if the information is real or not.
2. *Reliance on a single study* – According to Evidence-Based Living, systematic reviews should be the first source that readers investigate when searching for the truth about a product or recommendation. These are comprehensive reviews of many pieces of literature on the same subject that can indicate if the same finding is generated repeatedly, or just in isolated cases. Relying on just one or two research reports to prove a point is not reliable.

3. *Quick or confusing generalizations* – Headlines like "Lose 20 pounds in a week!" or "Eating blueberries prevents cancer" are certainly attention-grabbing, but they do not describe the whole body of research. By isolating interesting bits of information and reporting them outside the context of the whole study, reporters create a sense of urgency in readers. This may lead them to making hasty or illogical decisions if they do not read the entire article and investigate the original source of the information.

(Cornell University, 2011)

By following these constructs, lay health researchers can more accurately verify the sources of information and see past sensational headlines. Terms often used in research reporting include **reliable** and **valid**. Although these are sometimes used interchangeably, they describe different attributes of research. **Reliability** of a test refers to the extent to which an experiment, test, or other measuring procedure yields the same results on repeated trials (Mirriam Webster). **Validity** indicates the extent to which a measuring device measures what it intends or purports to measure (The Free Dictionary).

Credible experiments are both reliable and valid.

As references are provided for the information contained in an article or news report, readers must also understand that not all research is equal. Different types of studies yield different levels of confidence in results due to how rigorous they are and the potential for error. The Evidence Pyramid (Figure 2.2) illustrates the levels of research; those higher on the pyramid are more rigorous and have less margin of error.

Types of Study Designs

A **Meta-analysis** takes a systematic review one step further by combining all the results using accepted statistical methodology.

Systematic Reviews usually focuses on a specific clinical question and conducts an extensive literature search to identify studies with sound methodology. The studies are reviewed, assessed, and the results summarized according to the predetermined criteria of the review question.

Randomized, controlled clinical trials. A prospective, analytical, experimental study using primary data generated in the clinical environment. Individuals similar at the beginning are randomly allocated to two or more groups (treatment and control) and the outcomes of the groups are compared after sufficient follow-up time.

A study that shows the efficacy of a diagnostic test is called a prospective, blind comparison to a gold standard study. This is a controlled trial that looks at patients with varying degrees of an illness and administers <u>both</u> diagnostic tests—the test under investigation and the "gold standard" test— to *all* of the patients in the study.

Cohort studies identify a large population who already has a specific exposure or treatment, follows them over time

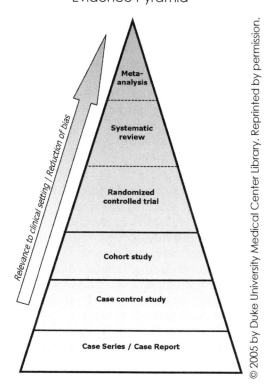

Figure 2.2
Evidence Pyramid

Relevance to clinical setting / Reduction of bias

Meta-analysis

Systematic review

Randomized controlled trial

Cohort study

Case control study

Case Series / Case Report

(prospective), and compares outcomes with another group that has not been affected by the exposure or treatment being studied. Cohort studies are observational and not as reliable as randomized controlled studies, since the two groups may differ in ways other than in the variable under study.

Case control studies are studies in which patients who already have a specific condition or outcome are compared with people who do not. Researchers look back in time (retrospective) to identify possible exposures. They often rely on medical records and patient recall for data collection. These types of studies are often less reliable than randomized controlled trials and cohort studies because showing a statistical relationship does not mean than one factor necessarily caused the other.

Case series and **Case reports** consist of collections of reports on the treatment of individual patients or a report on a single patient. Because they are reports of cases and use no control groups with which to compare outcomes, they have no statistical validity.

Healthy People 2020

The Office of Disease Prevention and Health Promotion, under the US Department of Health and Human Services (HHS), coordinates the Healthy People Initiative. As described in Chapter 1, this framework provides national quantitative health promotion and disease prevention goals for 10-year periods. The first three Healthy People initiatives set targets for reducing health disparities and burdens, but did not include recommendations for how to achieve these targets and did not consider the effectiveness or cost of these efforts. To initiate Healthy People 2020, the HHS asked a committee of public health experts to develop "evidence- based" recommendations for this document.

Evidence-Based Public Health

Origins of the Movement toward Evidence-Based Public Health Practice

Evidence-based public health (EBPH) has its roots in clinical epidemiology and evidence-based medicine (EBM). During the 1970's and 1980's, evidence accumulated that expert reviews and recommendations from expert panels frequently failed to include relevant studies and produced suboptimal conclusions. It was not clear what aspects of health care practices were associated with better health outcomes. EBM was developed in response to this experience, and as a means to explore which combination of specific services and medical conditions lead to improved health outcomes in actual practice, and for whom. EBM originated in the management of individual patients, where the best available evidence was combined with patient preferences and knowledge of local resources to improve decision making.

More recently, EBM has focused primarily on clarifying aspects of medical decision making that can be made on a scientific basis, recognizing that judgments about appropriate treatment often depend on individual factors (e.g., values or quality of life). Preventive services have been in the vanguard of this movement. In 1984, the U.S. Preventive Services Task Force (USPSTF) was established to build on the work of the Canadian Task Force on the Periodic Health Examination (established almost a decade earlier). The general medical community began focusing on EBM in the 1990's, employing scientific methods to assess which diagnostic or therapeutic strategies would produce the best medical outcomes.

What Is "Evidence-Based" Public Health Practice?

Evidence-based public health practice is the development, implementation, and evaluation of effective programs and policies in public health through application of principles of scientific reasoning, including systematic uses of data and information systems and appropriate use of behavioral science theory and program planning models. Just as EBM seeks to combine individual clinical expertise with the best available scientific evidence, evidence-based public health draws on principles of good practice, integrating sound professional judgments with a body of appropriate, systematic research. There has been strong recognition in public health of the need to identify the evidence of effectiveness for different policies and programs, translate that evidence into recommendations, and increase the extent to which that evidence is used in public health practice.

As with clinical interventions, planning to address population-based health problems typically takes place within a context of limited resources. Decision-makers should invest in proven, cost-effective solutions. Evidence for the effectiveness of interventions—such as programs, practices, or policies—can be used to provide a rationale for choosing a particular course of action, or to justify the allocation of funding and other resources.

There is demand for evidence at many levels: practitioners use it for program planning and internal policies, local managers use it to make decisions about which programs to support, and senior managers within government and health care organizations use it to set priorities and make policy and funding decisions. A recent important example is the Patient Protection and Affordable Care Act (PPACA) which instituted a policy to cover all services receiving an A or B recommendation from the USPSTF with no copayment in all new health care plans.

(Courtesy of the Department of Health & Human Services, Developing Healthy People 2020, 2010)

Impact of National Health Goals

National health goals, such as those in Healthy People 2020, may seem far-removed from everyday health decisions. However, we have been impacted by advancements in public health research for decades. Skepticism almost always accompanies this research; sometimes it is well-founded, and sometimes it is falsely swayed by public opinion or well-funded advertisements. For example, the link between cigarette smoking and lung cancer was first identified in multiple studies in several countries in the 1930s through early 1950s. Despite these published reports, only one-third of doctors surveyed in 1960 agreed with the notion that cigarettes should be considered a major cause of lung cancer. This same survey also revealed that 43% of doctors were regular smokers. Tobacco companies tried to distract users from the reports by heavily advertising in the media and promoting new, "safer" products. The 1964 Surgeon General Report recognized cigarette smoking as a cause of lung cancer

© turgaygundogdu/Shutterstock.com

in men, and is considered a turning point in the tobacco education and regulation. (Proctor, 2012). Today, the negative health consequences of tobacco use are widely accepted, but decades of scientific inquiry were required for this agreement.

The process of scientific inquiry is still a thriving practice in the research of foods and artificial products. For example, the debate surrounding the positive and negative impact of eggs is supported on both sides by randomized clinical trials showing benefits and drawbacks of egg consumption. Artificial sweeteners were originally advertised as a healthy, low-calorie sugar alternative, but new investigations reveal possible negative health outcomes when consumed in high doses.

Scientific inquiry is taught in classrooms to help students understand that science is more than just memorization of facts. In inquiry-based instruction, students recognize the role that their existing knowledge and beliefs hold in their understanding of the world around them. By experiencing scientific phenomena and processing the new information, students build on their body of knowledge and draw new conclusions. Teaching scientific inquiry in a social environment (like team-based learning), allows students the opportunity to learn from others' viewpoints and challenges them to revise or defend their own way of thinking. Science is not limited to a laboratory; any place where ideas are challenged, creativity is encouraged, and alternative explanations are revealed, discoveries are made.

So, before spending money on the latest fitness gadget, embarking on a cleansing diet, or switching from one treatment regimen to another, consider engaging in scientific inquiry. This fascinating process constantly adds to one's body of knowledge and enhances their interaction with the physical world.

References

Cornell University: Evidence Based Living. (5 February 2011). Retrieved from http://evidencebasedliving.human.cornell.edu/2011/02/05/weird-science-reporting-my-saturdays-with- usa-weekend/

Developing Healthy People 2020: Evidence-Based Clinical and Public Health: Generating and Applying the Evidence (26 July 2010). Retrieved from http://www.healthypeople.gov/2010/hp2020/advisory/pdfs/EvidenceBasedClinicalPH2010.pdf

Duke University Medical Center Library: Evidence Based Medicine Resources (2005). Retrieved from https://mclibrary.duke.edu/sites/mclibrary.duke.edu/files/public/guides/ebmresources.pdf

National Science Education Standards (National Academy of Sciences, 1996, p.23, 116–120).

Proctor, R. (2012). The history of the discovery of the cigarette-lung cancer link: evidentiary traditions, corporate denial, global toll. *Tobacco Control*. 21, 81–99. doi :10.1136

US National Library of Medicine: Medline Plus Guide to Healthy Web Surfing (20 April 2015). Retrieved from: https://medlineplus.gov/healthywebsurfing.html

Chapter 3
Body Systems

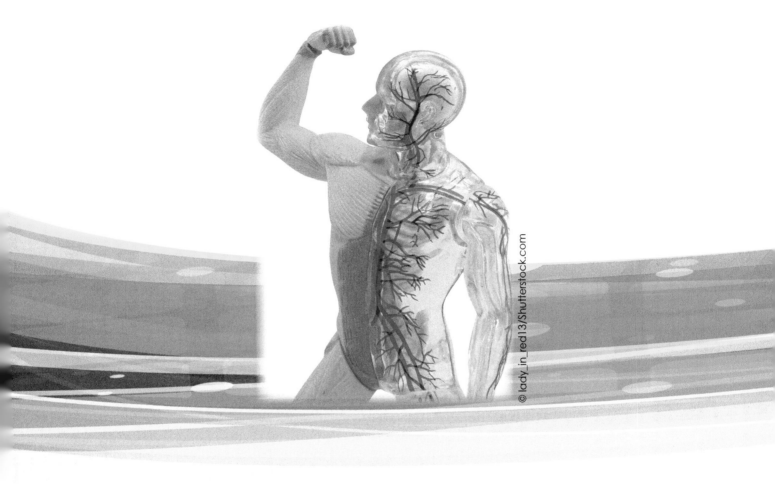

© lady_in_red13/Shutterstock.com

OBJECTIVES

Students will be able to:

- ◆ Compare and contrast anatomy and physiology.
- ◆ Describe the requirements for homeostasis.
- ◆ Use anatomical and directional terms to identify major body regions, sections, and cavities.
- ◆ Describe biometric measurements used to assess the function of body systems.

From *Introduction to Anatomy and Physiology* by John Erickson. Copyright © 2010 by Kendall Hunt Publishing Company. Reprinted by permission.

"Take care of your body. It's the only place you have to live in."

—Emanuel James "Jim" Rohn

In the world around us there are few things more awesome or complex than the human body. The adult human body has about 60 trillion cells. For example, the human brain contains roughly 100 billion nerve cells, about the same number of neurons as there are stars in the Milky Way. These nerve cells allow us mental abilities of complex reason, creativity, and thought far beyond those of other living organisms. Consider the cardiovascular system. If you take the entire network of blood vessels inside your body and place them end-to-end, they would measure 60,000 miles! In other words, you could wrap your blood vessels around the earth two and one-half times.

When we study anatomy and physiology, we make sense of the ways our body responds. We get insight into why a physician prescribes a specific treatment or therapy. We also understand how to keep our bodies fit and more able to defend against injury and disease. Better yet, we are able to realize how intricate and amazing the interactions of all of the systems that keep us in balance and functioning normally truly are.

Anatomy

Anatomy is the study of structure, including attachments, shape, size, location, and general appearance. The anatomist is intent on describing what a specific structure in the body looks like, and giving it a descriptive name, usually in Latin. For example, anatomists studying the upper arm found a muscle that is attached in two places on one end and only one on the other. They noted its placement and the direction the muscle runs. They studied the muscle under the microscope to determine its composition. They named the muscle *biceps* (two heads) *brachii* (arm) (Figure 3.1).

Divisions of Anatomy

The study of anatomy can be divided into two categories: gross anatomy and microscopic anatomy. It is essential to study both to achieve a more complete understanding of the structure of the human body.

Macroanatomy (Gross Anatomy)

The anatomist may study some region or organ in the body without the aid of magnification; this is known as *macroanatomy*, or *gross anatomy*. For example, the macroanatomist (gross anatomist) may study bones, muscles, or perhaps internal organs such as the heart, brain, or intestine. In the laboratory, this area of study often involves dissection.

Microanatomy

Some anatomists are interested in the cells and tissue that compose a particular organ. To study these, this anatomist would need some type of magnification, usually a microscope. The study of very small objects such as cells and tissue is referred to as *microscopic anatomy*. The quantity of structures seen in the microscope depends on the level of magnification. When using relatively low magnification, the anatomist views groups of cells or tissue. *Cytology* is the study of cells. Looking at individual cells within that tissue requires high magnification. The study of tissue is known as *histology*.

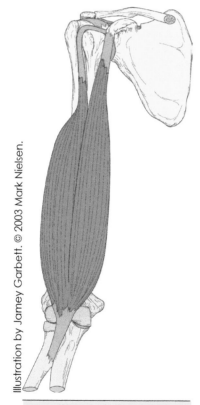

Illustration by Jamey Garbett. © 2003 Mark Nielsen.

FIGURE 3.1

Upper Limb—Biceps Brachii Muscles

Physiology

Physiology, the study of function, seeks to answer the question, "How does it work?" For example, while the anatomist may describe the location of a muscle, where it is attached, its diameter, and length, the physiologist explains how it is able to shorten to cause movement. Another example of how function and structure complement each other is that the anatomist describes the heart and blood vessels—defining internal structures, types of tissue composing the organs and location of each structure of the cardiovascular system—in order to provide a clear perspective of the overall system for transportation of substances throughout the body. The physiologist explains the processes that cause the heart to contract, the dynamics involved with forcing blood through vessels and how changes in vessel diameter affect the cardiovascular system and tissue surrounding its capillaries. Each system affects the function of other systems allowing us to maintain homeostasis of essential parameters for normal function, to allow us to survive and even thrive in our environment, and to reproduce our species. A physiologist is aware of the anatomy (structure), especially microscopic anatomy, when formulating a description of the processes an organ goes through in order to perform its function. Once a person has a general understanding of the physiology of the body, it becomes easier to understand how the body's systems interact to maintain constancy, growth, and development, while guarding against external threats.

Criteria for Life

Humans are affected by both living and nonliving things in the environment. It will be useful in our study to define the criteria that are required to determine if something is living or not.

> **Criteria for Life**
> - Organization
> - Response to stimuli
> - Growth
> - Reproduction
> - Movement
> - Metabolism and excretion

Living organisms have the ability to respond both to internal needs and to changes in the environment; this also includes the ability to produce offspring. Bear in mind, the organism or object in question must meet all of the criteria sometime during its existence to be considered living—this may not be as obvious as it appears to be on the surface.

Consider three objects to determine if they are living or nonliving: this textbook, a virus, and a rabbit. A virus is a piece of cellular instructions, DNA or RNA, surrounded by a protein coat or envelope.

Organization

Organization refers to the status of the organism or object's internal contents. Are internal structures present that have particular functions in specific areas or are the contents totally random? Are the internal structures of this book arranged in organized patterns or are they random? The intent is to be organized and the content is in distinct groups. The internal content of the virus is also highly organized. If we viewed the rabbit internally, we would rapidly determine that its organs were organized and in specific locations.

Response to Stimuli

The next factor to consider is responsiveness to stimuli. When a living organism is touched or manipulated in some way, it will respond of its own accord. We can touch or even shake this book, but it cannot make a response; the same is true of the virus. The rabbit, on the other hand, will be very quick to respond.

Growth

Another factor necessary for life is the ability to grow or mature. This book cannot grow of its own accord and it is as mature as it will ever be. The virus also remains unchanged throughout its existence. The rabbit, however, will grow rapidly and mature as long as it is maintained.

Reproduction

Reproduction is another important defining factor. Can the object or organism produce offspring just like itself? This book cannot reproduce. The virus can reproduce but not of its own accord—the virus injects its genetic material into a living cell, causing that cell to produce more viruses. The rabbit, on the other hand, is the big winner in this category. It is important to understand that within this category we include the ability to pass on genetic traits to offspring and the potential for changes, or mutations. Although the printing press can produce many books, each book cannot reproduce itself. Genetic changes can occur in viruses. In fact, it is often the rapid mutation of viruses that causes serious outbreaks of diseases around the world every year. While rabbits do change their genetics over time, those changes, without human intervention, would normally occur over hundreds or even thousands of years. Reproductive organs also produce hormones that influence growth, development, and tissue repair.

Movement

Living organisms also have the ability to move. Many can change position or location to accommodate their needs and all have some kind of movement internally. Rabbits move quickly in their environment, but their internal movement is also continually active throughout life. The transport of viruses is the result of some other cause such as air currents, water flow, or bodily fluid. If this book starts moving on its own, get rid of it—fast.

Metabolism and Excretion

All living things need energy to do whatever processes are essential for life. The energy needed to maintain life comes from the sun. Living organisms must find a way to either convert the energy from the sun into a form they can use or consume other organisms that have made that conversion. That process falls into a category of chemical reactions known as *metabolism*. The ingredients in food that are used by organisms to extract energy, form new body components, and assist body functions are called nutrients. Once an organism has obtained the energy it needs from nutrients, the by-products are removed by the process of *excretion*. This book does possess energy—if the pages are burned, the book will give off heat energy, but it did not, by its own chemical reactions, convert energy into the form it has. A virus is not involved in the conversion of energy either. The rabbit eats plants that have captured solar energy and stored it chemically as glucose (sugar). Glucose is a nutrient from which the rabbit extracts this chemical energy to be able to perform its own functions. By-products from the breakdown of glucose, such as carbon dioxide and water, as well as unusable plant material are excreted from the rabbit's body.

All six of these criteria must be present at some time during the organism or object's existence for it to be considered living. The book may have one of the criteria (organization), but it lacks the others. Viruses, even though they are active in the process of causing diseases, are not living because they do not possess all of the criteria for life. The rabbit possesses all six criteria, allowing us to consider it as a living organism. Humans meet all of these standards, although it is more obvious for some criteria than others.

Requirements to Sustain Life

There are some requirements that humans must have in order to maintain life.

Requirements to Sustain Human Life
- Oxygen
- Water
- Nutrients
- Heat
- Atmospheric Pressure

Oxygen

Humans need oxygen to extract the maximum amount of energy from the nutrients they take in. For example, some very active muscles consume large quantities of energy and have such a strong demand for oxygen that they possess special molecules called *myoglobin* to hold extra oxygen to meet the need. Deprive brain cells of oxygen for more than 6 minutes and they begin to die. There are some organisms that do not require oxygen for survival, but to humans it is essential.

Water

Water is found almost everywhere in our body. It is transported in our blood-stream. It bathes the outside of our cells. Approximately 60 to 80% of our body weight is due to water. Running short of liquid (dehydration) can cause our blood to thicken (increase viscosity) and draw some of the water out of cells making it more difficult for them to perform their functions. Severe loss of water can have serious results. Over-hydration is also possible if an individual drinks excessive quantities of water in a very short period of time. The resulting dilution of blood causes cells to swell and interferes with the rate of chemical reactions. The consequences can also be very serious.

Nutrients

Nutrients are not just the chemicals from which to extract energy. They are also used to form proteins essential for the construction of muscle and enzymes. Fats are needed to make cell membranes. Nucleic acids form DNA and RNA, which form cellular instructions and are essential components in the transfer of information. Other nutrients such as vitamins and minerals are essential for chemical reactions to occur.

Heat

A constant internal body temperature is maintained to allow all normal bodily functions to occur. If we become too hot or too cold, chemical reactions essential for life are unable to continue at rates necessary to sustain life.

Atmospheric Pressure

The air around us pushes on us much like stepping into the ocean causes the water to press on us from all sides. This is known as *atmospheric pressure*. It is the difference in pressures between the air outside of us and the air inside our lungs, created by changing chest volume that allows us to breathe and to exchange oxygen and carbon dioxide with the air.

Without supplying all of these requirements humans would not be able to survive.

Homeostasis

In the human body, or in any living organism for that matter, there is a need to maintain certain parameters such as temperature, water balance, hormone levels, blood pressure, and oxygen and carbon dioxide concentration within a constant range. If this is not accomplished, the individual becomes sick. The term for regulating various parameters inside a living body within a specific range is called **homeostasis**. More precisely, homeostasis is defined as the dynamic constancy of the internal environment of the body. In order to keep things constant, each parameter requires a *control center* to be able to cause changes when the level in the body is not where it should be.

This center receives input from sensors, or *receptors,* that determine the current level in the body and compares that reading to a standard, or *set point,* that indicates what it should be. If the control center determines that the current level in the body is out of range, it will activate a system known as an *effector* to produce the appropriate change to bring that parameter back within the homeostatic range.

For example, let's say the temperature set point of my body is 98.6°F. The control center for temperature is found in an area of my brain known as the *hypothalamus.* Temperature sensors inform the hypothalamus about my current temperature. If my actual temperature goes over the set point—for example, 99.5°F, my hypothalamus will activate the cooling process (effector) and I will sweat. If, on the other hand, my internal temperature becomes too cold, my hypothalamus will cause me to shiver—a process that generates heat and warms my body. By constantly comparing my actual body temperature with the set point, my hypothalamus maintains my internal body temperature at a constant level to regulate homeostasis (Figure 3.2).

FIGURE 3.2

Homeostasis of Body Temperature.
(a) Sweating to cool the body is the result of increased internal temperature.
(b) Shivering increases body heat when the individual is cold.

FIGURE 3.3

Negative Feedback. The controller compares the level of a specific parameter detected by a receptor with the set point, desired level. When the detected level is at the low end of the desired range, the controller stimulates the effector to increase its output of that parameter. The change is monitored by the receptor and sent to the controller. When the level reaches the high end of the appropriate range the controller decreases the output of the effector. In this way, stimulation of the effector results in a reversal of the need.

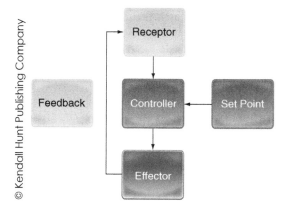

Negative Feedback

The process by which the body maintains parameters within a specific range is known as negative feedback (Figure 3.3). It is considered negative feedback because the response of the effector results in the controller reversing its direction of control. For example, if the level of thyroid hormones in the blood, detected by receptors in the hypothalamus, began to reach the lower levels of its normal range (set point), the controller, the hypothalamus, would stimulate the thyroid gland (effector) to increase its hormone production resulting in an increase in thyroid hormones in the blood. As the level of this hormone increases it reaches the upper limit of the desired level. The hypothalamus then decreases its stimulation of the thyroid gland causing thyroid hormone levels in the bloodstream to decrease, which will again cause a reversal of the controller as the levels reach the lower limit again. And so the process continues causing the levels to weave back and forth within the homeostatic range.

Positive Feedback

There are times that require exceptional changes in the body, such as childbirth. For this situation, positive feedback is used. *Positive feedback* is the special case in which the response actually increases the need. It enhances the initial stimulus (same direction). For instance, a woman is nine months pregnant, the gestation period is complete and it is time for labor to begin. Positive feedback is required. The hypothalamus (control center) causes the pituitary gland (effector) to release a small amount of the hormone oxytocin, which causes a slight uterine contraction. This contraction stimulates the release of more oxytocin causing an even stronger contraction. The cycle continues with each contraction stimulating more oxytocin until birth occurs. There are additional steps, but the general process is due to positive feedback.

Intrinsic and Extrinsic Regulation

When the control process occurs within the system it is regulating, we call this *intrinsic regulation (auto-regulation)*. When the control comes from a source outside the system it is designated as *extrinsic regulation*. For example, the digestive system produces hormones that tell its own digestive organs to perform tasks essential for the breakdown of food. That is intrinsic regulation because it comes from within the system. The brain can also alter our digestive system by speeding it up or slowing it down. Because the brain is outside the digestive system, its control of digestion is extrinsic regulation.

Organization of the Human Body

There are two perspectives when we consider the organization of the body. One organizes the body into systems; the other views the organization from simplest to most complex.

Levels of Organization

When studying the body, there are differing levels of complexity on which to focus (Figure 3.4):

- **Chemical level**—Atoms make up everything around us, including our bodies. Those atoms bond together to form molecules: atoms and molecules are the chemical makeup of all matter. The interaction of molecules within our cells allows performance of the functions necessary for life.

FIGURE 3.4

Hierarchy of Body Structure

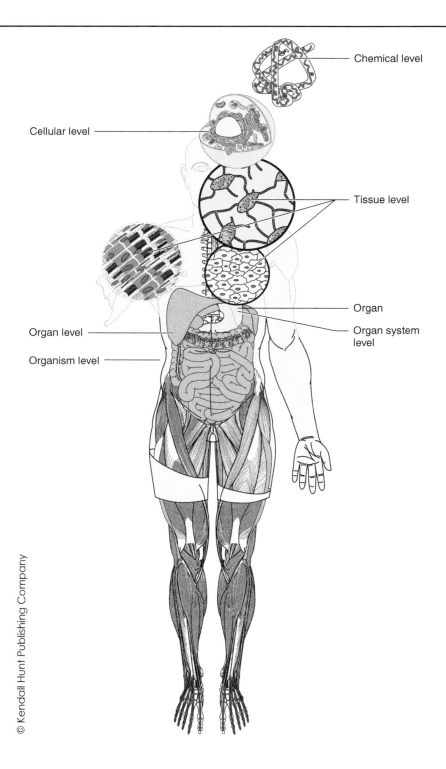

- **Cellular level—Cells** are the smallest unit of life. All living organisms are composed of cells. Within most cells are specialized structures known as *organelles* that act as miniature organs to allow the cell to accomplish its purpose. (Note: Organelle is to a cell as an organ is to the organism.) When you understand the function of one cell, you can better comprehend the activities of all cells.

- **Tissue level—Tissues** are groups of similar cells that work together with the same purpose. While the human body is made up of around 60 trillion cells, there are only four basic tissue types:
  a. Epithelium
  b. Connective tissue
  c. Muscle tissue
  d. Nervous tissue
- **Organ level—**Tissues, working together to achieve a common function, form **organs**. For example, the stomach is composed of tissue designed to secrete chemicals and mix those secretions with food while protecting the stomach lining from self-destruction. Stomach tissue is very different from brain tissue, which conducts impulses for communication, or heart muscle, which contracts rhythmically to pump blood throughout the body. An organ is made up of particular types of tissue designed to perform a specific set of functions. In many cases, an organ is the primary location in the body where its specific activity is accomplished.
- **Organ system level—**When various organs work together to perform a common function, they form an **organ system**. For example, the esophagus, stomach, and small and large intestines are all organs of the digestive system. Organ systems allow us to grow, develop, reproduce, and interact with the world around us.
- **Organism level—**All organ systems working together to support a living entity is called an **organism**, including humans.

Systems of Organization (refer to Figure 3.5)

- The *integumentary system*—the skin and underlying connective tissue—provides a barrier around the body, not only to keep hazardous substances from entering our body, but also to keep essential chemicals and fluids inside our body from being lost. It also possesses sensory receptors to keep us aware of the environment.
- The *skeletal system* is made up of our bones and joints. It provides a framework on which to attach other organs. It provides protection of internal contents and movement when muscles attached to our bones cause them to change position. Bones are also the site for storage of minerals and production of blood cells.
- The *muscular system* contains skeletal muscle attached to bones to cause movement. In the face, skeletal muscle attaches to skin to change facial expression. Skeletal muscle is a major source of body heat resulting from metabolism required to provide energy involved with contraction.
- The *nervous system* provides rapid communication throughout the body allowing us to assess, decide, and initiate action.
- The *endocrine system* allows glands to produce slow, sustained communication with other parts of the body.
- The *cardiovascular system* transports blood throughout the body, providing a method to carry substances wherever needed. It moves heat from deep inside the body to the skin for release into the environment. It also contains cells for defense and components for clotting.
- The *lymphatic system* collects excess tissue fluid, cleans it, and returns it to the bloodstream for recirculation. It is also a location for production and storage of many of our disease-fighting cells.

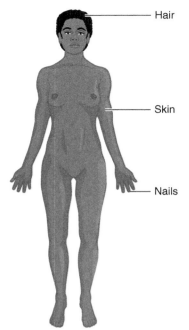

Integumentary System—
Isolates internal contents
of the body from external
access. It senses the
environment, releases
heat, and produces
vitamin D.

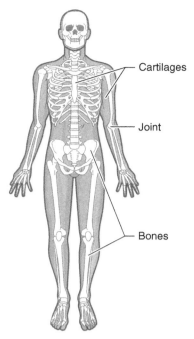

Skeletal System—Provides
support and protection. It
results in movement when
muscles attached to bone
contract. It is also the site
for blood cell production
and mineral storage.

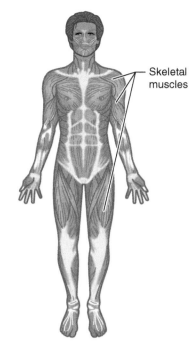

Muscular System—Due to its
attachments between bones or
bone and skin, the muscles
contract to cause movement.

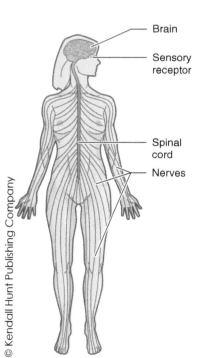

Nervous System—Provides
rapid communication, sensing
of the environment, analysis
and decision making, and
stimulation of muscle.

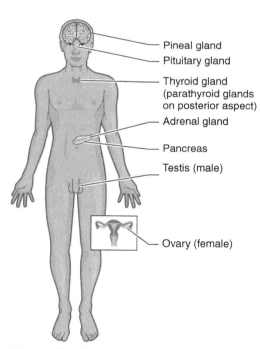

Endocrine System—Provides slow
sustained communication between
cells through chemical messages
(hormones) released into the
bloodstream.

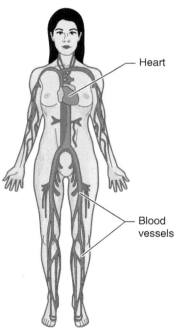

Cardiovascular System—
Consists of a pump (the
heart) and vessels through
which substances can be
transported in the blood
throughout the body. It also
provides defense and clotting
of blood.

FIGURE 3.5

11 Systems of the Body

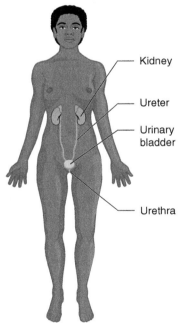

Lymphatic System—Collects and cleans excess tissue fluid and returns it to the bloodstream. It is responsible for immunity.

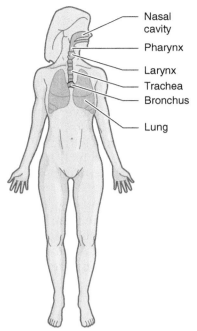

Respiratory System—The location where atmospheric gases can exchange with blood. It also assists with controlling blood pH.

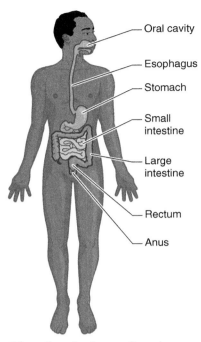

Digestive System—Breaks down nutrients to their simplest components then absorbs those nutrients into the bloodstream.

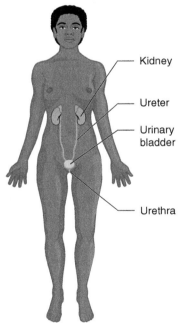

Urinary System—Removes excess or unwanted substances from the plasma and excretes them from the body. It stimulates red blood cell production and assists in the control of pH. It is also involved in the control of blood pressure.

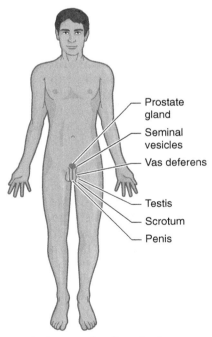

Male Reproductive System—Provides sperm containing half the male's genetic code and provides a mechanism for the sperm to be appropriately delivered. It also produces hormones responsible for male characteristics.

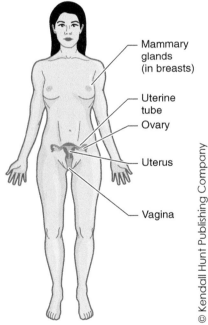

Female Reproductive System—Produces ova containing half the female's genetic code and provides a location for the fertilized ovum to develop until it is able to function outside the mother's body. It also produces hormones responsible for female characteristics.

FIGURE 3.5

11 Systems of the Body (*continued*)

- The *respiratory system* exchanges oxygen and carbon dioxide between the body and the air around us. It is also essential in the control of the amount of acid or base (pH) in our blood.
- The *digestive system* extracts nutrients from the food we eat and then breaks it down to its simplest components so it can be absorbed into the bloodstream and transported to the rest of the body. After the desired nutrients have been removed, the digestive system prepares the remaining material for excretion from the body.
- The *urinary system* extracts excess substances in the blood and excretes them from the body. It is also an active participant in the control of acid and base balance in our blood (pH) as well as in red blood cell production.
- The *reproductive system* produces cells that provide the essential information in the form of DNA (chromosomes) to produce another human being. Each gender provides half of the needed chromosomes. This system also produces hormones that affect metabolism, growth, and development of the individual.

Anatomical Terms

Anatomists devised a set of terms that describes the relationship of various structures in the body with nearby points. These clear, precise terms, understandable by everyone in the field, were necessary in order to adequately define structures. This system is also used in the medical field for communication.

Anatomical Position

When we discuss anatomical terms, it is important that we always consider the body to be in the **anatomical position**. This position is an erect individual with upper extremities extended at the sides, and palms and toes forward (Figure 3.6). It does not matter if the real person is actually lying down or even standing on his head—we refer to body parts as if the person was standing in front of us in the anatomical position.

Directional Terms

It is extremely helpful to have a set of common terms that all anatomists and professionals in the medical field can use to specifically locate body parts. Often individuals who have access to medical records are amazed how often these terms are employed. They are typically used in terms of relationships—that is, how one location relates to another. Following is a list of common directional terms and a brief definition followed by an example. The directional terms in the list are paired so the even-numbered terms give the opposite direction of the preceding odd-numbered term. For example, number two on the list, posterior, signifies direction toward the back and indicates the opposite of number 1, anterior, toward the front. Remember we always assume we are looking at our subject standing in the anatomical position. The terms in parentheses are equivalent terms used to indicate anatomical relationships.

1. *Anterior (ventral)* (Figure 3.7b)—Toward the front of the body (toward the front of the chest). My sternum (breastbone) is anterior to my heart.
2. *Posterior (dorsal)* (Figure 3.7a)—Toward the back of the body (toward the spine). My vertebral column is posterior to my heart.
3. *Superior (cranial)* (Figure 3.7b and c)—Above (toward the head). My chin is superior to my shoulders.

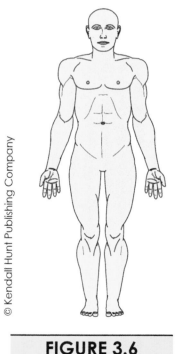

FIGURE 3.6

Anatomical Position

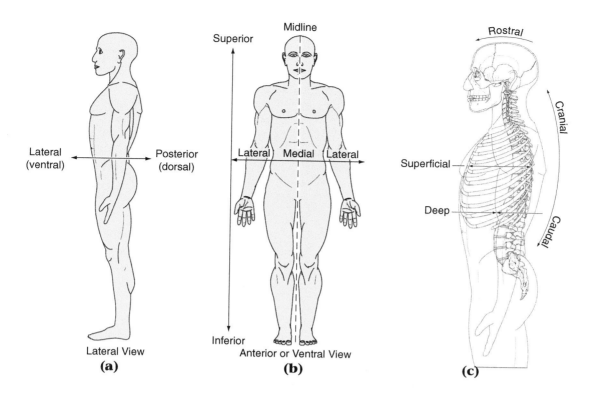

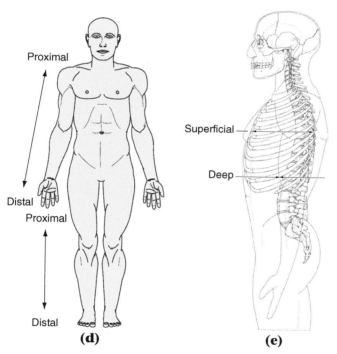

Illustration by Jamey Garbett. © 2003 Mark Nielsen.

FIGURE 3.7

Terms of Direction

An anatomist may describe a specific location in the following manner, "The occipital bone forms much of the *inferior posterior* cranium. The foramen magnum is a large hole on the *medial inferior* surface of the occipital bone where the spinal cord exits the skull." Replacing anatomical terms with their definition, we would read, "The occipital bone forms much of the cavity that is *below and behind* the rest of the bones surrounding the brain. The foramen magnum is a large hole that is located *closest to the midline on* the lower surface of the occipital bone where the spinal cord exits from the skull (Figure 3.8a).

A physician may write in his/her notes, "An 18-year-old female received a 2-centimeter *superficial* cut *superior and lateral* to the left eye." Substituting the definitions of the terms listed above, we would rewrite the physician's notes as, "An 18-year-old female received a 2-centimeter cut that is *close to the surface of the skin* found *above and toward the side of* the left eye *farthest away from the midline*" (Figure 3.8b).

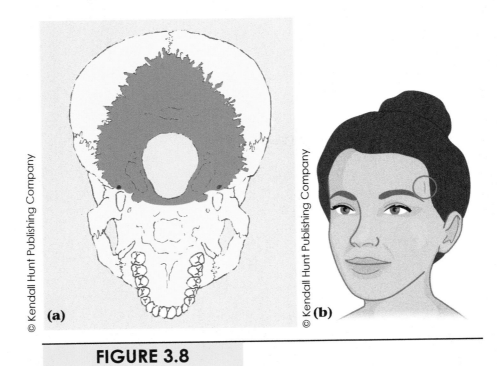

(a) © Kendall Hunt Publishing Company

(b) © Kendall Hunt Publishing Company

FIGURE 3.8

4. *Inferior (caudal)* (Figure 3.7b and c)—Below (toward the feet or tail). My lips are inferior to my nose.
5. *Medial* (Figure 3.7b)—Toward the midline. If a line is drawn through the body from the top of the head, down through the nose, through the middle of the trunk, and between the two lower extremities, the midline has been identified. Whatever is closest to the midline is medial. My eyes are medial to my ears.
6. *Lateral* (Figure 3.7a)—Toward the side or away from the midline. My shoulders are lateral to my clavicle (collarbone).
7. *Proximal* (Figure 3.7d)—Nearest to the trunk or attachment site of limb. This term can be used in other ways, but for our purposes we will use it on the extremities. The shoulder and hip are the most proximal structure of the extremities. My elbow is proximal to my wrist.
8. *Distal* (Figure 3.7d)—Farthest from the trunk. Going from the trunk down the extremities, if the area of interest is farther away from the reference point, it is distal. My heel is distal to my knee.

9. *Superficial* (Figure 3.7e)—Toward the surface. Note that toward the surface is not the same as toward the front. My spine is also superficial to my heart. Even though it is posterior to my heart, my spine is still closer to the surface.

10. *Deep* (Figure 3.7b)—Toward the center of the body. My intestine is deep to my navel.

When we use these anatomical terms, we often refer to two points. The first is the area of interest and the second is a reference point. When we understand anatomical direction, we can use these terms to give a precise, detailed explanation of the situation. For purposes of clarity, it is often useful to use more than one anatomical term to precisely locate a point of interest. These anatomical terms become a major component of the language used by anatomists and medical practitioners.

Anatomical Regions of the Body

The human body can be divided into general regions for identification of structures (Table 3.1; see also Figures 3.9 and 3.10 on pages 48 and 49). The head is referred to as the **cephalic region**. The neck is the **cervical region**. The **thoracic region** is commonly known as the chest. The area of the trunk inferior to the thoracic region and superior to the pelvic region is known as the **abdominal region**. The thoracic and abdominal regions and their contents are separated by the major muscle of breathing—the **diaphragm**. At the inferior end of the abdomen are the hip bones, or pelvis, designated as the **pelvic region**.

The upper and lower extremities form the appendages. Although commonly called the *arm,* anatomists prefer to call it the *upper extremity* because it is more than just the upper arm and forearm—it is also the wrist and hand.

TABLE 3.1 ♦ Anatomical Landmarks

Abdominal	Anterior trunk between ribs and pelvis
Axillary	Armpit
Brachial	Arm
Buccal	Area of the cheek
Carpal	Wrist
Cephalic	Head
Cervical	Region of the neck
Digital	Fingers and toes
Femoral	Thigh
Nasal	Area of the nose
Oral	Mouth
Orbital	Area of the eye
Pelvic	Area of the pelvis
Pubic	Area of the genitalia
Tarsal	Ankle
Thoracic	Chest
Umbilical	Navel
Vertebral	Area of the spine

FIGURE 3.9

Anatomical Landmarks of
the Body—Anterior View

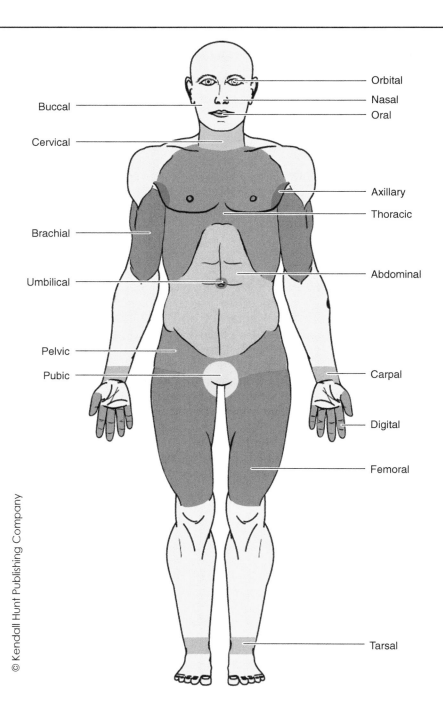

Orbital

Nasal

Oral

Buccal

Cervical

Axillary

Thoracic

Brachial

Abdominal

Umbilical

Pelvic

Pubic

Carpal

Digital

Femoral

Tarsal

Technically, the arm is between the shoulder and elbow. The lower extremity consists of the thigh, calf or leg, ankle, and foot. Commonly we often misrepresent the lower extremity by calling it *leg*, which is actually located between the knee and ankle.

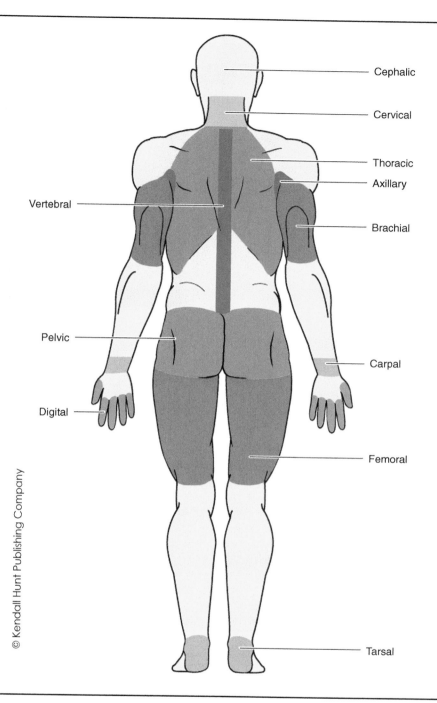

FIGURE 3.10

Anatomical Landmarks of the Body—Posterior View

- Cephalic
- Cervical
- Thoracic
- Axillary
- Vertebral
- Brachial
- Pelvic
- Carpal
- Digital
- Femoral
- Tarsal

Adapted from Anatomy I and Physiology Lecture Manual

FIGURE 3.11

Anatomical Planes

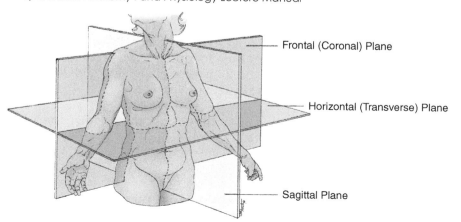

- Frontal (Coronal) Plane
- Horizontal (Transverse) Plane
- Sagittal Plane

Adapted from Anatomy I and Physiology Lab Manual

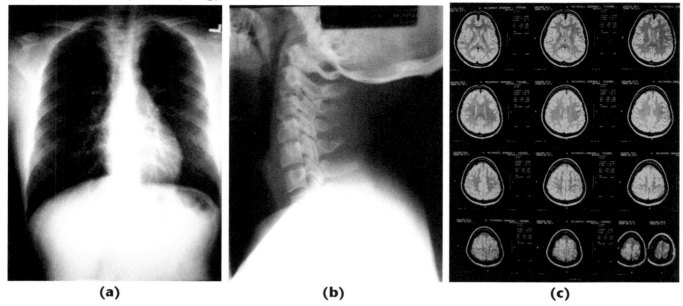

(a)   (b)   (c)

FIGURE 3.12

Views of the Body from Differing Planes. (a) X-ray of the thorax in the frontal plane. (b) X-ray in the sagittal plane. (c) CAT scan of the brain in the transverse plane.

Anatomical Planes

Today there are numerous, noninvasive methods for viewing the body: X-rays, CAT scans, MRIs, PET scans, bone scans, nuclear scans, and others. When an observer understands the view from which these pictures were taken, it makes an enormous difference in his or her understanding of the images. Just like there are the three dimensions of length, width, and depth, when we look at an object, the body can also be viewed or sectioned in three dimensions known as **anatomical planes** (Figure 3.11 on page 47).

- The **frontal plane,** or coronal plane, divides the body into anterior and posterior sections and appears to be taken from the front. It can also be taken back to front. One-inch slices, or *sections,* taken through a person's body, as can be done with MRI, would start at the toes and nose and work toward the back or vice versa.
- The **sagittal plane** divides the body into right and left sections and is a view from the side (lateral view). They can be taken from either side. If an MRI is made of the whole body in the sagittal plane, it would begin at one hand and make sections through the body to the other hand.
- The **transverse plane,** or **horizontal plane**, or cross section passes the body of an organ perpendicular to its long axis. It would divide slices of the body or organ, into superior and inferior sections. If a whole body MRI was taken in the transverse plane, it would begin at the top of the head and end at the feet or vice versa.

With a little practice it becomes a fairly simple task to recognize the appropriate plane in which a scan was taken (Figure 3.12).

Abdominal Quadrants

The abdomen can be divided into four **abdominal quadrants**, or sections. This is simply done by drawing imaginary lines through the navel (umbilicus);

one is vertical and the other horizontal (Figure 3.13). This can be very useful in determining potential problems with the abdominal contents. The right-upper quadrant contains mostly the liver. On the underside of the liver is the gallbladder. In the posterior right-upper quadrant is the right kidney. The left-upper quadrant contains the stomach, pancreas, and spleen with the left kidney in the posterior abdomen. The right-lower quadrant contains mostly the digestive system; best known in this area is the appendix. The left-lower quadrant is also primarily digestive system. The S-shaped sigmoid colon is the structure that commonly receives the most attention in the left-lower quadrant because of irritable bowel syndrome (IBS) or spastic colon.

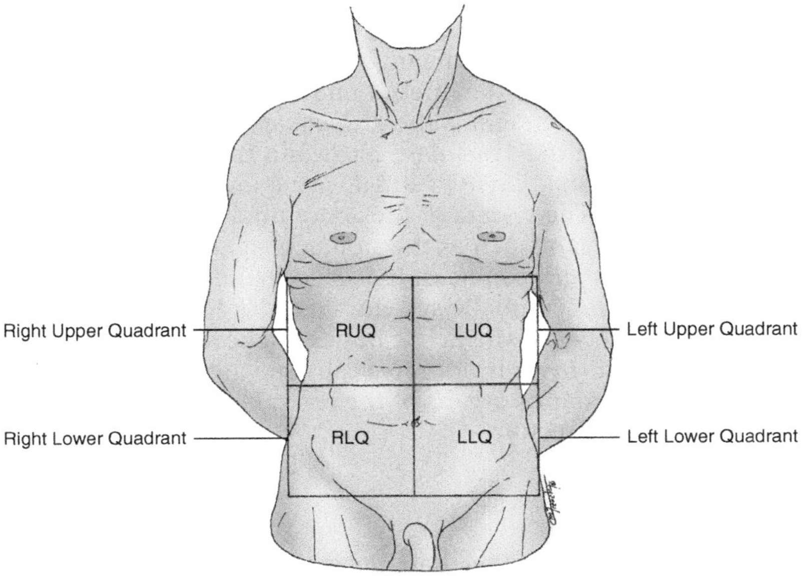

Adapted from Anatomy I and Physiology Lecture Manual

FIGURE 3.13

Abdominal Quadrants

Right Upper Quadrant — RUQ | LUQ — Left Upper Quadrant

Right Lower Quadrant — RLQ | LLQ — Left Lower Quadrant

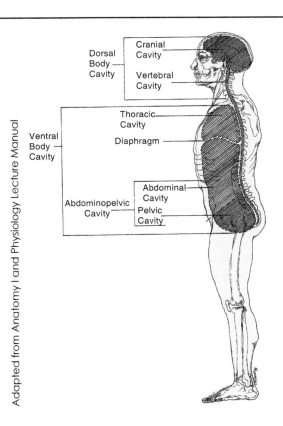

Adapted from Anatomy I and Physiology Lecture Manual

FIGURE 3.14

Body Cavities

Dorsal Body Cavity
Cranial Cavity
Vertebral Cavity

Ventral Body Cavity
Thoracic Cavity
Diaphragm

Abdominopelvic Cavity
Abdominal Cavity
Pelvic Cavity

Body Cavities

Human **body cavities,** or internal spaces within the body, can be divided into two general sections: the dorsal and ventral cavities (Figure 3.14).

1. The *dorsal cavity* is toward the back and has two divisions:
   - The cranial cavity contains the brain.
   - The vertebral cavity is a space in the vertebrae for the spinal cord.
2. The *ventral cavity* contains two divisions as well. The organs in the ventral cavity are referred to as **viscera.**
   - The *thoracic cavity* primarily contains the lungs and heart. The lungs are surrounded by a membrane known as *pleura.* Between the two lungs is an area known as the *mediastinum.* This section contains all other organs within the chest other than lungs. Included in the mediastinum is the heart, which is surrounded by a tissue sac known as the *pericardium.* The thoracic and abdominal cavities are separated by the diaphragm, which is the major muscle of breathing and is attached to the inferior end of the rib cage.
   - Below the diaphragm is the *abdominopelvic cavity.* It is composed of two sections: the *abdominal cavity* and the *pelvic cavity.* The entire abdominopelvic cavity is lined with a membrane known as the *peritoneum.* The viscera of the abdominal cavity include most of the digestive organs such as the stomach, small intestine, colon, liver, gallbladder, and pancreas. It also contains the spleen, which is an organ of the lymphatic system. Posterior to the peritoneum are the kidneys. Between the pelvic bones is a bowl-shaped space known as the *pelvic cavity.* It is not physically separated from the abdominal cavity. It contains organs of the reproductive system, urinary bladder, and rectum.

Biometrics

Throughout this chapter you have learned the requirements necessary to sustain life, how the body is organized using systems, and how to communicate more clearly about the body using appropriate terminology. Along with this knowledge, biometrics are used to measure the health of a body system as well as the body, in general. A **biometric measurement** is a measurement of a physical characteristic, such as height, weight or resting heart rate that is used to indicate current health and future risk of illness or disease. Once benchmarks are established, continuing to accurately measure, assess and track many biometrics over a lifetime can provide a better understanding of health. For example, the Centers for Disease Control and Prevention (CDC), suggests using biometric measurements, such as body mass index (BMI), blood pressure, and aerobic fitness tests, as part of a workplace health promotion program.

The following is a brief description of the biometrics used for this course. Throughout this course, you will have the opportunity to measure many biometrics, establish benchmarks for yourself, and compare your results with current norms. This information can be used by you and others on your healthcare team, to help predict risk of disease and identify effective prevention strategies to keep your organs, systems and overall body working well.

One quick and easy biometric often recorded regarding overall health is a person's body weight. While this measurement is easy to take, inexpensive and available to most, body weight is not the most descriptive metric to use when assessing general health and risk of disease. **Body Composition** is one of five health-related fitness components and considered one of the best overall health indicators. Body Composition measurements estimate the percentage of body fat compared to lean muscle mass, such as muscle, bone and water. Body weight may fluctuate throughout the day, can be affected by hydration (and even by what you wear on the scales), but body composition remains consistent.

There are several techniques to calculate body composition, ranging from simple field-based options, such as skinfold testing, to more elaborate options, like the BOD POD or DEXA, conducted in a laboratory or office setting. The ideal body fat range for college-aged males is 12–18% and for college-aged females is 18–23%. It is generally accepted that a range of 10–22 percent for men and 20–32 percent for women is considered satisfactory for good health (ACSM).

Another option, **Body Mass Index** (BMI, see Table 3.2), is a ratio between height and weight, used to determine if your body weight is within a healthy range.

$$BMI = \frac{weight\ in\ kilograms}{height\ in\ meters\ squared}$$

A BMI under 18 is considered underweight, while a BMI of over 25 is considered overweight and above 30 is considered obese. But keep in mind that BMI does not take into account the composition of the weight used in its calculations and that special populations may not be able to use BMI

TABLE 3.2

Body Mass Index Table

To use the table, find the appropriate height in the left-hand column labeled Height. Move across to a given weight (in pounds). The number at the top of the column is the BMI at that height and weight. Pounds have been rounded off.

BMI	19	20	21	22	23	24	25	26	27	28	29	30	31	32	33	34	35
Height (inches)								Body Weight (pounds)									
58	91	96	100	105	110	115	119	124	129	134	138	143	148	153	158	162	167
59	94	99	104	109	114	119	124	128	133	138	143	148	153	158	163	168	173
60	97	102	107	112	118	123	128	133	138	143	148	153	158	163	168	174	179
61	100	106	111	116	122	127	132	137	143	148	153	158	164	169	174	180	185
62	104	109	115	120	126	131	136	142	147	153	158	164	169	175	180	186	191
63	107	113	118	124	130	135	141	146	152	158	163	169	175	180	186	191	197
64	110	116	122	128	134	140	145	151	157	163	169	174	180	186	192	197	204
65	114	120	126	132	138	144	150	156	162	168	174	180	186	192	198	204	210
66	118	124	130	136	142	148	155	161	167	173	179	186	192	198	204	210	216
67	121	127	134	140	146	153	159	166	172	178	185	191	198	204	211	217	223
68	125	131	138	144	151	158	164	171	177	184	190	197	203	210	216	223	230
69	128	135	142	149	155	162	169	176	182	189	196	203	209	216	223	230	236
70	132	139	146	153	160	167	174	181	188	195	202	209	216	222	229	236	243
71	136	143	150	157	165	172	179	186	193	200	208	215	222	229	236	243	250
72	140	147	154	162	169	177	184	191	199	206	213	221	228	235	242	250	258
73	144	151	159	166	174	182	189	197	204	212	219	227	235	242	250	257	265
74	148	155	163	171	179	186	194	202	210	218	225	233	241	249	256	264	272
75	152	160	168	176	184	192	200	208	216	224	232	240	248	256	264	272	279
76	156	164	172	180	189	197	205	213	221	230	238	246	254	263	271	279	287

Source: www.nhlbi.gov

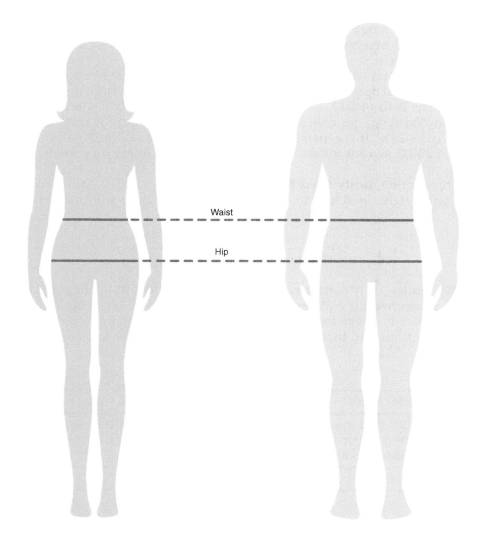

to accurately estimate the healthy range of weight for their body type. For example, young children, older sedentary adults, individuals with a large amount of muscle mass, and pregnant or lactating women should use another method to assess healthy weight.

Additional low cost, field-based measurements include **waist circumference and waist-to-hip ratio**. Both options focus on the amount of abdominal fat present, giving participants the appearance of an "apple-shaped" body. In a follow-up to the Nurses' Health Study, one of the largest and longest studies investigating risk factors for major chronic diseases in women, researchers found that even women with a "normal weight" and BMI less than 25 were at higher risk if they were carrying more weight around the waist. This represents a presence of more metabolically active, visceral fat (abdominal fat surrounding the liver and other abdominal organs) which releases fatty acids, inflammatory agents and hormones negatively affecting cholesterol, triglycerides, blood glucose and blood pressure.

Scientists agree that both waist-to-hip and waist circumference measurements seem to be equally effective in estimating risk of future illness and disease. So practically speaking, the single measurement required of the waist circumference makes it preferable to many.

The Harvard School of Public Health reports that the American Heart Association and the National Heart, Lung, and Blood Institute identify a waist circumference of greater than 35 inches for women and 40 inches for men as abdominal obesity, which increases risk of type 2 diabetes and cardiovascular disease (2017).

Oxygen Uptake

VO₂ Max is the nomenclature for maximum oxygen uptake, the measurement of the maximum amount of oxygen that an individual can utilize per minute of physical activity. VO₂ Max is expressed as milliliters of oxygen per kilogram of body weight per minute (ml/kg/min). As aerobic capacity increases, so does VO₂ Max. VO₂ Max is considered the best indicator of cardiovascular fitness. Unfortunately, measurement in a laboratory takes time, equipment, and technicians to administer the tests. Another, more practical, option used to measure cardiovascular fitness is timing the completion of a 1.5 mile run and using the data to complete the following calculation:

$$VO_2\, max\, (ml \bullet kg^{-1} \bullet min^{-1}) = 88.02 - (0.1656 \times BW) - (2.76 \times time) \times (3.16 \times gender*)$$

Where: BW = body weight in kilograms and time = 1.5 mile run time to the nearest 100th of a minute). For gender, substitute 1 for males and 0 for females.

(National Strength and Conditioning Association's Essentials of Personal Training, 2012)

Heart Rate

An individual's **heart rate** is expressed in beats per minute. Resting heart rate is someone's heart rate when he or she is at rest, or not exerting themselves. An average resting heart rate (RHR) for adults is 60–100 beats per minute. When examined along with other biometrics like blood pressure and cholesterol, resting heart rate can help indicate an individual's cardiac health and risk for future health problems (Harvard Health Publications, 2016). Heart rate increases with physical activity, and the level of increase can determine the intensity of the exercise and if the individual is receiving cardiorespiratory benefit. Several methods for determining a cardiovascular training zone exist, and one of the most common is the Karvonen formula. Developed by Dr. Martti Karvonen and originally published in 1957, this formula has proven accurate in measuring maximum heart rate and is positively correlated with maximal oxygen uptake (Camarda, et al. 2008).

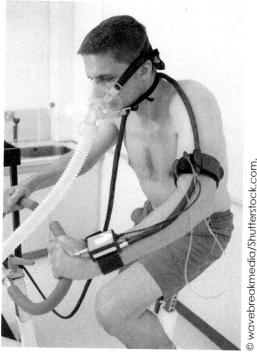

© wavebreakmedia/Shutterstock.com.

Karvonen Formula

Determining Target Heart Rate Zone (THRZ)

Take your resting heart rate early in the morning before you rise, counting for sixty seconds. Use your index and middle finger to palpate either your carotid

© Khakimullin Aleksandr/Shutterstock.com

(neck) or radial (wrist) artery. It is best to do this three different times and then average the three resting heart rates.

Finding your target heart rate zone is beneficial so that you can determine at any given time during a workout how hard your heart is working. This gives you feedback that helps you construct a proper workout that matches your goals. Working out with intensity high enough to bring the heart rate above the minimum threshold is important to attain cardiovascular benefits of exercise.

EXAMPLE:

AGE: 20 yr. old RESTING HEART RATE: 68 bpm

Formula for calculating Maximum Heart Rate (Max HR) 220 − age (in years) = Maximum Heart Rate	*Example* 220 − 20 = 200 beats per minute (bpm)
Formula for calculating Heart Rate Reserve Max HR − Resting HR = Heart Rate Reserve	*Example* 200 − 68 = 132 beats per minute
Formula for calculating Threshold of Training HR HR Reserve × 60% Plus Resting HR = Threshold of Training HR	*Example* 132 × .60 = 80 bpm 80 + 68 = 148 bpm
Formula for calculating the Upper Limit of the THRZ HR Reserve × 85% Plus Resting HR = Upper Limit for the THRZ	*Example* 132 × .85 = 112 112 + 68 = 180 bpm

The target zone for this 20-year-old with a resting HR of 68 bpm is 148 − 180 bpm.

Divide these numbers to get a 10-second working heart rate 24–30 bpm/10 sec

Your age: _____ Your Resting HR _____ bpm

Max HR = 220 − _____ = _____

Max HR − RHR = HR Reserve _____ − _____ = _____

HR Reserve × 60% + RHR = Minimum Threshold
_____ × .60 = _____ + _____ = _____

HR Reserve × 85% + RHR = Upper Limit
_____ × .85 = _____ + _____ = _____

Your target heart rate zone is _____ bpm (60%) to _____ bpm (85%)

Blood Pressure

Blood pressure is the force of the blood flowing through blood vessels. It is measured in millimeters of mercury, which is the element originally used in blood pressure gauges and remains the standard unit of measurement for pressure in medicine. Systolic blood pressure (top number) is the measurement of how much pressure the blood exerts against the artery walls when the heart beats. Diastolic blood pressure (bottom number) is the pressure on the artery walls when the heart is between beats, or at rest. The American

This chart reflects blood pressure categories defined by the American Heart Association.

Blood Pressure Category	Systolic mm Hg (upper #)		Diastolic mm Hg (lower #)
Normal	less than 120	and	less than 80
Prehypertension	120–139	or	80–89
High Blood Pressue (Hypertension) Stage 1	140–159	or	90–99
High Blood Pressue (Hypertension) Stage 2	160 or higher	or	100 or higher
Hypertensive Crisis (Emergency care needed)	Higher than 180	or	Higher than 110

* Your doctor should evaluate unusually low blood pressure readings.

FIGURE 3.15

This chart reflects blood pressure categories defined by the American Heart Association.
Source: American Heart Association

Heart Association offers a guide for categories of blood pressure readings and corresponding risk levels (Figure 3.15).

Cholesterol

Blood **cholesterol** levels indicate the amount of cholesterol and triglycerides in the blood. A blood test called a lipoprotein panel can describe the following levels:

- Total cholesterol. Total cholesterol is a measure of the total amount of cholesterol in your blood, including low-density lipoprotein (LDL) cholesterol and high-density lipoprotein (HDL) cholesterol.
- LDL cholesterol. LDL, or "bad," cholesterol is the main source of cholesterol buildup and blockages in the arteries.
- HDL cholesterol. HDL, or "good," cholesterol helps remove cholesterol from your arteries.
- Triglycerides (tri-GLIH-seh-rides). Triglycerides are a type of fat found in your blood. Some studies suggest that a high level of triglycerides in the blood may raise the risk of coronary heart disease, especially in women.

If it's not possible to have a lipoprotein panel, knowing your total cholesterol and HDL cholesterol can give you a general idea about your cholesterol levels.

Testing for total and HDL cholesterol does not require fasting. If your total cholesterol is 200 mg/dL or more, or if your HDL cholesterol is less than 40 mg/dL, your doctor will likely recommend that you have a lipoprotein panel. (Cholesterol is measured as milligrams (mg) of cholesterol per deciliter (dL) of blood.)

The tables below show total, LDL, and HDL cholesterol levels and their corresponding categories. See how your cholesterol numbers compare to the numbers in the tables below.

Total Cholesterol Level	Total Cholesterol Category
Less than 200 mg/dL	Desirable
200–239 mg/dL	Borderline high
240 mg/dL and higher	High

LDL Cholesterol Level	LDL Cholesterol Category
Less than 100 mg/dL	Optimal
100–129 mg/dL	Near optimal/above optimal
130–159 mg/dL	Borderline high
160–189 mg/dL	High
190 mg/dL and higher	Very high

HDL Cholesterol Level	HDL Cholesterol Category
Less than 40 mg/dL	A major risk factor for heart disease
40–59 mg/dL	The higher, the better
60 mg/dL and higher	Considered protective against heart disease

Triglycerides also can raise your risk for heart disease. If your triglyceride level is borderline high (150–199 mg/dL) or high (200 mg/dL or higher), you may need treatment. (National Heart Lung and Blood Institute, 2016)

Muscular Endurance: Push-up and Curl-up (Crunch) Testing

Standardized testing for muscular endurance measures the ability of a muscle group to perform repeated contractions against a load. As part of a complete fitness assessment, muscular endurance tests can help an individual develop a well-rounded training program and determine risk for cardiovascular disease and other conditions.

The American College of Sports Medicine authored testing procedures and fitness categories for **push-up and curl-up tests**. The push-up test is conducted in the standard position for males and in the modified "knee push up" position for females. For all participants, the maximal number of pushups performed in the correct position without forcible strain or rest is counted as the score. The curl up, or crunch, test is administered the same for males and females.

Participants lie in a supine position with knees bent at 90 degrees and arms extended at their sides. They slide their hands 12 cm forward or up their thighs just past the knee cap to create spinal flexion of 30 degrees. The curl ups are performed to a metronome beat of 40 beats per minute, and the test ends either when the subject reaches 75 curl ups or the cadence is broken. Participants receive a fitness category rating based on the number of successful push-ups and curl-ups permformed.

Future chapters will provide more details about these biometrics and others, and how students can establish baseline measurements to track health changes across a lifetime. Collecting data about your own body can help you take important steps toward preventing or delaying your risk of many health conditions.

References

American Heart Association: Understanding Blood Pressure Ratings. (12 January 2017). Retrieved from https://www.heart.org/HEARTORG/Conditions/HighBloodPressure/GettheFactsAboutHighBloo dPressure/Understanding-Blood-Pressure-Readings_UCM_301764_Article.jsp

Brekken Shea, K., Darnel, G., Agnor, D., & Netherland, B. (2014). *Introduction to the science of health and fitness.* Dubuque, IA: Kendall Hunt

Camarda, SR. et al. (2008). Comparison of maximal heart rate using the prediction equations proposed by Karvonen and Tanaka. *Arquivos Brasileiros de Cardiologia.* 91 (5). DOI 10.1590/S0066-782X2008001700005

Coburn, J.W. & Malek, M.H. (Eds). (2012). *National strength and conditioning association's essentials of personal training.* Champaign, IL: Human Kinetics.

Harvard Health Publications: Your Resting Heart Rate Can Reflect Your Current and Future Health. (17 June 2016). Retrieved from http://www.health.harvard.edu/blog/resting-heart- rate-can-reflect-current-future-health-201606179806

National Heart Lung and Blood Institute: How is High Blood Cholesterol Diagnosed? (8 April 2016). Retrieved from https://www.nhlbi.nih.gov/health/health-topics/topics/hbc/diagnosis

Pescatello, L.S., Arena, R., Riebe, D., & Thompson, P.T. (Eds.). (2014). *American college of sports medicine's guidelines for exercise testing and prescription.* (9th edition). Philadelphia, PA: Wolters Kluwer Health.

Waist Size Matters. https://www.hsph.harvard.edu/obesity-prevention-source/obesity- definition/abdominal-obesity/

Workplace Health Promotion: Workplace Health Glossary. Retrieved from: https://www.cdc.gov/workplacehealthpromotion/tools-resources/glossary/glossary.html#B

Chapter 4
Stress and Mental Health

© 2012, Shutterstock, Inc.

OBJECTIVES

Students will be able to:

- ♦ Define stress and describe ways in which stress can manifest itself.
- ♦ Introduce general tips to help individuals positively cope with stress.
- ♦ Describe the negative health complications that can result from unmanaged stress.
- ♦ Establish a link between preventative behaviors and stress.
- ♦ List characteristics of good stress managers.
- ♦ Establish a link between unmanaged stress and its detrimental effect on psychological health.

Adaptation of *Health and Fitness: A Guide to a Healthy Lifestyle*, 5th Edition, by Laura Bounds, Gayden Darnell, Kirstin Brekken Shea, and Dottiede Agnor. Copyright © 2012 by Kendall Hunt Publishing Company.

- Introduce the concept of self-talk and explain the effects positive and negative self-talk can have on an individual's stress level and its impact on the person's psychological health.
- Show the links between stress, depression and suicidal behaviors.
- Define eating disorders: who is at risk, what are the causes, what are the symptoms, how serious are they, and what can be done to help someone with an eating disorder.

"Those who suffer from mental illness are stronger than you think. We must fight to go to work, take care of our families, be there for our friends, and act 'normal' while battling unimaginable pain."

—HealthyPlace.com

Stress, both positive and negative forms, has always been a part of life. One cannot hope to live and thrive without facing stressful situations daily. Most Americans live a fast-paced, over-booked lifestyle each day in an attempt to make the most of their time and talents. Due to the fact that "working under the gun" has become the rule rather than the exception, stress has become one of the most common detriments to the overall health and well-being of Americans.

Wellness and Stress

Stress was defined by Hans Selye as the nonspecific response to demands placed on the body. "Nonspecific response" alludes to the production of the same physiological reaction by the body regardless of the type of stress placed on the body. Physiologically, when an individual is confronted with a stressor they will experience a surge of adrenaline that causes the discharge of cortisol and the release of endorphins. This, in turn, will increase the person's blood pressure and heart rate, preparing him or her to take immediate action.

While the physiological way in which all people react to stress is the same, the way a person physically, emotionally, or behaviorally reacts to a specific stressor can vary greatly. This is due in part to the fact that when facing the exact same event or circumstance it might be perceived as highly stressful and draining to one person but simply stimulating and exciting to someone else. The ways in which people outwardly react to stressful situations are a personal physical and emotional response to the stimuli. These responses can be either positive or negative.

Eustress is a positive stress that produces a sense of well-being. It is a healthy component of daily life. It can be harnessed to improve health and performance. Examples of activities or events that might initiate a positive stress response include competitive sports, graduation from school, dating, marriage, the birth of a baby, or a long awaited vacation. Eustress can help channel nervous energy into a top-notch performance.

Distress is negative stress. It is a physically and mentally damaging response to the demands placed upon the body. Distress is generally associated with changes that interrupt the natural flow of a person's life. Excessive schoolwork, loss of a job, breaking up with a significant other, or illness or death of a loved one are examples of activities or situations that may produce a negative stress response from an individual. When distress occurs, it is typical to see deterioration in the affected individual's health and performance.

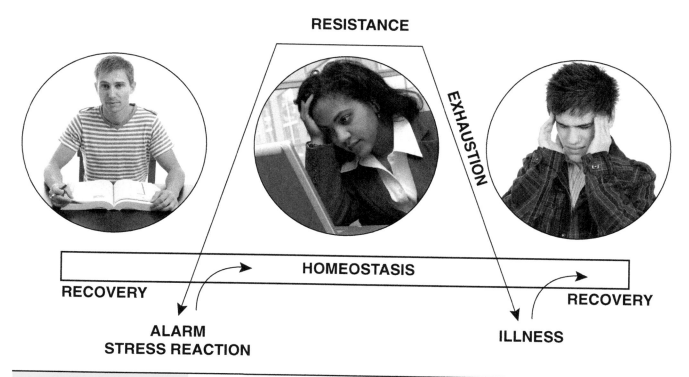

FIGURE 4.1

© Hugo Silveirinha Felix, 2009, Shutterstock, Inc.

© Rob Marmion, 2009, Shutterstock, Inc.

© Rui Vale de Sousa, 2009, Shutterstock, Inc.

The way each person chooses to manage the stressors that occur in life will, to a large degree, determine overall physical and emotional well-being. An individual's body naturally attempts to maintain a state of homeostasis, or balance, so that it can continue to function in an effective manner. When a stressful situation presents itself, an "alarm" is triggered. Then either the person deals with the situation and the body recovers and returns to a state of homeostasis, or the attempts to avoid or resist the stressor eventually result in exhaustion or illness (see Figure 4.1).

Stress is not the cause of illness, but when it goes on for long periods of time or is particularly irritating, it can become harmful by weakening an individual's immune system. This increases that person's risk of getting sick.

Uncontrolled or unmanaged stress can lead to a variety of negative health consequences such as coronary heart disease, high blood pressure, ulcers, irritable bowel syndrome, migraine headaches, and insomnia.

Certain forms of stress are not only normal but necessary in everyday life. However, the results of continual or inappropriately managed stress can cause disruptions that can be serious or severe to an individual's emotional, intellectual, social, spiritual, physical, occupational, and/or environmental health.

It is extremely important for an individual to determine how he or she handles or reacts to stressors, especially if the stress is ongoing. The way stress manifests or "shows itself" is going to vary depending on an individual's personality and past experiences.

There are typically four ways in which stress can manifest itself:

1. Emotionally
   * Do you always feel rushed, without enough time to get all that is needed done well or done at all?
   * Do you find it difficult to relax?

- Are you irritable and moody, or easily angered?
- Do you feel helpless or hopeless?
- Do you want to cry for no apparent reason?
- Is it difficult for you to listen or pay attention to your friends without being distracted?
- Is it hard for you to fall asleep even on days when you are exhausted?
- When you do fall asleep, is it difficult to stay asleep?

2. Mentally
   - Are you indecisive in many areas of your life?
   - Is it difficult for you to concentrate?
   - Do you regularly have bad dreams or nightmares?
   - Do you have negative thoughts, including suicidal thoughts?

3. Behaviorally
   - Has your appetite changed so that you have gained or lost significant amounts of weight?
   - Are you neglecting yourself/your appearance?
   - Have you curtailed social activities?
   - Have you taken to substance abuse, such as cigarette smoking, drug use, or excessive alcohol or coffee intakes?

4. Physically (see Figure 4.2)
   - Do you have an increased heart rate or blood pressure?
   - Can you feel your own heart beat?
   - Do you feel out of breath or have tightness in your chest?
   - Do you suffer from frequent headaches or muscle aches due to chronic tension?
   - Is it difficult for you to digest food—leading to nausea or diarrhea?
   - Do you suffer from frequent attacks of infections such as influenza or sore throats?

FIGURE 4.2

Stress Effects on Body

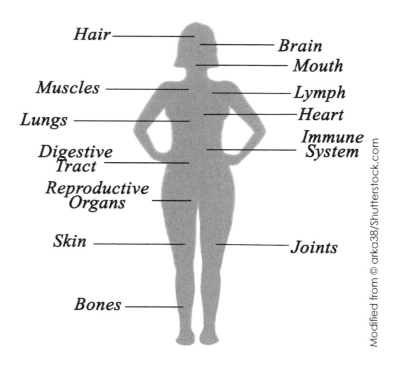

Hair — Brain — Mouth — Muscles — Lymph — Lungs — Heart — Digestive Tract — Immune System — Reproductive Organs — Skin — Joints — Bones

Modified from © arka38/Shutterstock.com

Physical Effects of Stress

The physical effects of stress are striking in these photographs taken at the beginning and near the end of President Abraham Lincoln's terms as President of the United States.

Lincoln before (1861) Lincoln after (1865)

Left photo: Brady's National Photographic Portrait Galleries, photographer. President Abraham Lincoln, three-quarter length portrait, seated, May 16, 1861, LC-USZ62-15179. Retrieved from the Library of Congress, https://www.loc.gov/item/2009630687/. (Accessed January 26, 2017.); right photo: Gardner, Alexander, photographer. Abraham Lincoln, three-quarter length portrait, seated and holding his spectacles and a pencil, Feb. 5, 1865, LC-DIG-ppmsca-19469. Retrieved from the Library of Congress, https://www.loc.gov/item/cwp2008000004/PP/. (Accessed January 26, 2017.)

Recognizing how stress affects their lives allows individuals to recognize stressful situations and to immediately deal with, or cope with, something that has the potential to compromise their overall well-being.

While uncontrolled or unmanaged stress can lead to negative health consequences, there are a number of ways to control stress. What works for one person will not necessarily be helpful to someone else. It is important to recognize the stressor (see Figure 4.3) and determine the most effective way(s) to relieve, reduce, or eliminate that particular stressor. Another key to successfully managing stressors is to use a strategy that produces positive results, rather than a strategy that creates additional stress. Also, to be successful with stress management, give a particular stressor only the amount of energy it warrants—do not give a "10 cent" stressor $10 worth of time or energy. The following are general tips that can help maintain a healthy lifestyle and can prepare an individual to cope with many of the stressors found in everyday life.

1. Deal with the cause:
   Finish the task, talk to the person, fix the tire, write the letter, make the call—do what needs to be done to deal with the situation. The longer a situation gets put off, the more stress it can create.

STRESSORS IN THE LIVES OF COLLEGE STUDENTS	
Drug use	Military obligations
Academic competition	Social alienation, anonymity
College red tape	Love/marriage decisions
Religious conflicts	Illness and injury
Choice of major/future job	Lack of privacy
Sexual pressures	Parental conflict
Family responsibilies	Time management
Loneliness Depression Anxiety	Alcohol use
Money troubles	

FIGURE 4.3

Stressors in the Lives of College Students

Source: Adapted from W. W. K. Hoeger, L. W. Turner, and B. Q. Hafen. Wellness Guidelines for a Healthy Lifestyle. Wadsworth/Thomson Learning, 2007.

2. Put the situation into perspective: How important is it really? How important will this be tomorrow, in six months? Most situations that tax physical/mental energies will soon be inconsequential and forgotten. Determine if anything can be done about the situation, or if it is a situation that calls for acceptance.

3. Pace yourself:
    No one can be in "high gear" all the time. Too often individuals stop to "smell the roses" only after the first accident or heart attack. Set short and intermediate goals—reward yourself upon reaching these goals.

4. Laugh at life and at yourself:
    Humor is a wonderful tool. Laughing is internal jogging! She or he who laughs . . . lasts! See the humor in people and the absurdity of situations. Read the "funny pages."

5. Develop quality relationships:
    Seek social and emotional support systems—individuals who care, love, and will listen to you. Express feelings constructively. Be there for others and allow others to be there for you in the good times and in the bad times.

6. Time management needs to be life management:
    Look at goals and responsibilities from a bigger perspective; this can help with decision making. Streamline activities by breaking big, imposing jobs into small components and list each activity in a daily planner. Seek assistance when it is needed; don't try to do everything yourself—delegate! Avoid common "time killers" (see Figure 4.4).

7. Look at situations and people in a different light—try an attitude adjustment: Is your perception of the situation, event, or person correct? Is there another way to handle things, or is there another possible way to answer the problem? Go easier on yourself and on others. It is unreasonable to expect perfection from yourself or from others. Perfection is a "moving target" and causes constant stress. Take care of the things you can; don't worry about the things that are beyond your control.

8. Balance fun and responsibility:
    Family, society, and community encourage and command constant work and responsibility. It is important to contribute and to meet responsibilities, but it is also important to find enjoyment and fun in life as well. Do something you find enjoyable on a regular basis and don't feel guilty!

FIGURE 4.4

Common Time Killers

COMMON TIME KILLERS	
• Watching television	• Talking on the telephone
• Listening to radio/music	• Worrying
• Sleeping	• Procrastinating
• Eating	• Drop-in visitors
• Daydreaming	• Confusion (unclear goals)
• Shopping	• Indecision (what to do next)
• Socializing/parties	• Interruptions
• Recreation	• Perfectionism (every detail must be done)

From Hoeger/Hoeger. *Principles and Labs for Fitness and Wellness (with Personal Daily Log and CengageNOW, InfoTrac® Printed Access Card)*, 9E. © 2008 Brooks/Cole, a part of Cengage Learning, Inc. Reproduced by permission. www.cengage.com/permissions.

9. Exercise and eat sensibly:
   Exercise is one of the best stress-busters. Schedule exercise into your life. Walk, bike, swim, stretch, and recreate. Good food in proper proportions is also essential to good health and is an excellent way to reduce the negative effects stress may have on your life.

When an individual is able to identify stress management techniques that work with her or his personality and lifestyle, it can be extremely beneficial to be proactive in recognizing potential sources of stress so that they can be dealt with before they become detrimental to the individual's overall well-being.

Stress and Sleep

Sleep is crucial to functioning day-to-day. It allows the brain and the body to rest and recharge. The tension from unmanaged or unresolved stress often causes physiological arousal during non-REM (rapid eye movement) sleep that results in insomnia. Insomnia prevents an individual from sleeping or causes them to awaken throughout the night or too early in the morning.

Balance fun and responsibility. Do something you enjoy on a regular basis and don't feel guilty.

Five Ways Stress Robs You of Sleep
1. Stress prevents you from getting enough sleep
2. Stress negatively impacts the quality of your sleep
3. Stress increases your risk of insomnia
4. Stress sends your brain into over-drive and keeps you from falling asleep
5. Stress can be a catalyst for a cycle of sleep deprived nights

Stress Measurement Scale

There are several scales or scientific instruments that have been designed in an attempt to measure an individual's level of stress. The Student Stress Scale that is shown in Figure 4.5 has been modified from the Holmes and Rahe's Life Events Scale (1967) to gauge the stress level and corresponding health consequences for collegeaged adults.

In the Student Stress Scale, each event, such as beginning or ending school, is given a score that represents the amount of readjustment a person has to make in life as a result of the change. To determine a stress score, add up the number of points corresponding to the events that have happened during the past six months or are likely to occur within the next six months.

People with scores of 300 points or higher have a high health risk. Individuals scoring between 150 and 300 points have about a fifty-fifty chance of developing a serious health condition within the next two years. People scoring below 150 points have a one-in-three chance of developing a serious health condition.

It is imperative that individuals recognize the potential stressors that occur in their lives. However, it is equally important that individuals also acknowledge an overall level of stress. By doing this, a proactive "deal with it" approach can be taken. This lessens the negative impact that stress can have on overall well-being and allows them to become good stress managers (see Figure 4.6).

FIGURE 4.5

Student Stress Scale

1.	Death of a close family member	❏	100	❏
2.	Death of a close friend	❏	73	❏
3.	Divorce between parents	❏	65	❏
4.	Jail term	❏	63	❏
5.	Major personal injury or illness	❏	63	❏
6.	Marriage	❏	58	❏
7.	Fired from job	❏	50	❏
8.	Failed important course	❏	47	❏
9.	Change in health of a family member	❏	45	❏
10.	Pregnancy	❏	45	❏
11.	Sexual problems	❏	44	❏
12.	Serious argument with close friend	❏	40	❏
13.	Change in financial status	❏	39	❏
14.	Change of major	❏	39	❏
15.	Trouble with parents	❏	39	❏
16.	New girl- or boyfriend	❏	38	❏
17.	Increased workload at school	❏	37	❏
18.	Outstanding personal achievement	❏	36	❏
19.	First quarter/semester in college	❏	35	❏
20.	Change in living conditions	❏	31	❏
21.	Serious argument with instructor	❏	30	❏
22.	Lower grades than expected	❏	29	❏
23.	Change in sleeping habits	❏	29	❏
24.	Change in social activities	❏	29	❏
25.	Change in eating habits	❏	26	❏
26.	Chronic car trouble	❏	26	❏
27.	Change in number of family get-togethers	❏	26	❏
28.	Too many missed classes	❏	25	❏
29.	Change of college	❏	24	❏
30.	Dropped more than one class	❏	23	❏
31.	Minor traffic violations	❏	20	❏

Source: Adapted from T. H. Holmes and R. H. Rahe, 1967, *Journal of Psychosomatic Research,* 11:213.

Self-Talk Your Way to Reduced Levels of Stress and an Improved Life

What Is Self-Talk?

Self-talk is the constant interpretation of the different situations that individuals find themselves in throughout each day. It is that "inner voice" that determines one's perception of a situation. Conscious thoughts, as well as subconscious thoughts, are part of a person's inner voice. Negative or positive self-talk begins early in most individuals' lives and can determine the impact stress has on each person's life.

Negative or Positive Self-Talk

Negative self-talk such as "I am going to fail my test" or "there is no way I can run that far or fast or perform that move" is self-defeating. Negative interpretation of a situation will often make that situation more stressful than it needs to be.

Replacing negative thoughts or self-talk with positive thoughts can decrease stress levels and improve a person's productivity and overall outlook. There is a line between thinking something and feeling it! People changing the way they think can allow them to change the way they feel.

Some tips for reducing stress and improving your quality of life through the use of positive self-talk are listed in the margin of page 33.

Thinking positively is a habit. Like any other habit, it will take time and practice to master—but health benefits such as decreased negative stress, reduced risk of coronary heart disease, and improved coping skills make it time well spent.

FIGURE 4.6

CHARACTERISTICS OF GOOD STRESS MANAGERS

Good stress managers
- are physically active, eat a healthy diet, and get adequate rest every day.
- believe they have control over events in their life (have an internal locus of control).
- understand their own feelings and accept their limitations.
- recognize, anticipate, monitor, and regulate stressors within their capabilities.
- control emotional and physical responses when distressed.
- use appropriate stress management techniques when confronted with stressors.
- recognize warning signs and symptoms of excessive stress.
- schedule daily time to unwind, relax, and evaluate the day's activities.
- control stress when called upon to perform.
- enjoy life despite occasional disappointments and frustrations.
- look success and failure squarely in the face and keep moving along a predetermined course.
- move ahead with optimism and energy and do not spend time and talent worrying about failure.
- learn from previous mistakes and use them as building blocks to prevent similar setbacks in the future.
- give of themselves freely to others.
- have a deep meaning in life.

From Hoeger/Hoeger. *Principles and Labs for Fitness and Wellness (with Personal Daily Log and CengageNOW, InfoTrac® Printed Access Card)*, 9E. © 2008 Brooks/Cole, a part of Cengage Learning, Inc. Reproduced by permission. www.cengage.com/permissions.

Stress and Its Impact on Mental Health

While stress in general, and specifically unmanaged stress, can have a negative impact on a person's physical health, the detrimental impact it can have on mental health can be equally devastating.

There are many types of mental health disorders. Schizophrenia, depression, general anxiety disorders, bipolar disorders, and panic disorders are just a few of the mental health disorders that can cause havoc in a person's life. These disorders typically include chronic or occasional dysfunctional feelings and/or a lost sense of self worth that may often limit the extent to which an individual participates in life's daily activities.

Who Gets Mental Health Disorders?

According to the 1996 Surgeon General's Report on Physical Activity and Health, one out of two Americans will suffer from some sort of mental health disorder at some point in their lifetime. The many different types of mental health disorders affect 90 million people. Mental health disorders are far-reaching. They affect not only the individual with the disorder but also the people who have intimate and social relationships with them. Mental health disorders have a far-reaching "ripple effect."

Depression and Stress

Depression is a mental health disorder that is prevalent among college populations. One of the reasons college students are particularly vulnerable to depression is that for many students, they face large amounts of unresolved stress. College is a time filled with challenging, new, different, and stressful situations (refer back to Figure 4.3).

It is important to realize that unmanaged stress and depression can quickly become a vicious cycle. The more depressed an individual is, the less day-to-

Jenny's Story

Jenny Smith was diagnosed with bipolar disorder, a condition characterized by severe mood swings from total elation to utter depression. Jenny was hospitalized off and on, and after trying all available drug therapy to no avail, Jenny was told to expect to be in and out of psychiatric hospitals for the rest of her life. Jenny decided to learn hatha yoga. Hatha yoga incorporates breathing, postures, and meditation that relax and strengthen the body. Smith noticed that her panic attacks subsided (a symptom of her bipolar disorder) with her daily yoga practice. Smith now feels better and successfully manages her disorder with the anti-depressant Paxil and daily yoga practice. She has taught her 11-year-old daughter relaxation through simple breathing techniques, and now her daughter's panic attacks have also subsided. Some mental health disorders are genetic in nature. Smith's grandmother committed suicide due to depression, and Smith is determined to spread the word that she believes yoga has literally saved her life.

(Weintraub, 2000)

day stress and the fewer activities can be coped with and the more depressed the person becomes.

While stress often plays a major roll in depression, another type of depression also has a biological basis—endogenous depression. In this instance, a person's family mental health history can help determine if a genetic predisposition toward depression exists. This knowledge allows them to take a proactive approach toward diagnosing and battling this mental health condition.

Everyone has occasional feelings of being down or sad at some point. However, when depression results in a person crying a great deal, feeling hopeless, or being unable to take pleasure in life, professional help should be sought so that a life-threatening situation does not occur.

Aside from or along with professional counseling, individual therapy or group therapy can be beneficial to an individual battling with depression. Prescription medications can be another important tool when coping with depression. They may or may not be necessary depending on each individual's situation.

Exercise has also been shown to be effective in treating mild to moderate cases of depression. Thirty-three percent of all inactive adults consider themselves depressed. "A recent review of more than 20 years of studies found that aerobic exercise and strength training are equally effective in treating depression, can reduce anxiety in patients with panic disorders and can be an important part of treatment for people with schizophrenia" (Payne, 2000).

Recently a charity conducted a survey that found that 83 percent of those with mental health problems looked to some form of exercise to help improve their mood or reduce the amount of stress they felt they were under (news.bbc.co.uk). While exercise plays a vital role in reducing the negative impact mental health disorders have on a person's life, it should not be considered a total replacement for other treatments, and patients should always work with and under the close care of a physician.

James Blumenthal, a psychologist at Duke University Medical Center, conducted a study comparing the effects of exercise and drugs on depression. The 156 participants were broken up into three different groups:

© Andresr, 2009, Shutterstock, Inc.

Exercise has been shown to help in the treatment of mild to moderate depression.

1.   exercise only,
2.   antidepressants only,
3.   exercise and antidepressants.

After sixteen weeks, the researchers found that all three groups showed the same amount of improvement on standard measures for depression. An interesting note concerning the participants using exercise as a method of dealing with their depression was that not only did the exercise have a positive impact on their level of depression, but it also improved their cognitive functioning ability (bbc.news.health).

It is critical to realize that for an individual dealing with any type of mental illness, therapy through counseling and/or the use of prescription medications is not a sign of weakness or personal failure. Accepting these means of help requires strength and courage to face the fact that there is a problem and to fight/prevail against a life-draining force. An individual with a mental illness receiving any type of therapy is much the same as a visually impaired person wearing glasses or contacts, or a hearing impaired individual using a hearing aid.

Suicidal Behavior and Stress

Another area in which stress can affect an individual's mental health is thoughts of or attempts at suicide. College students are particularly vulnerable to this problem. Nationwide each year, approximately one in 10,000 college students commits suicide; many more college students have suicidal thoughts.

Most people who contemplate or actually do commit suicide want something in their "world" to change. It may be one thing that will greatly impact their life if it changes or goes away, or it may be a lot of the "little things" that have added up. Often, a suicidal individual does not really want to die; it is just that the person has run out of ways or ideas on how to make that needed change occur.

Intense pressure or stress, along with feelings of depression, alcohol misuse, drug abuse, or a personal loss such as a breakup or lack of academic success, are common causative factors in suicides. Anyone expressing suicidal thoughts should be taken seriously. Friends, roommates, or whoever should seek out help for a suicidal individual immediately.

Typical signs that an individual is contemplating suicide could include:

- skipping classes,
- giving away personal possessions,
- withdrawing from friends,
- withdrawing from "normal" activities,
- engaging in risky behaviors not normal for that person.

An effective tool for helping someone get past suicidal thoughts or desires is counseling to help change the way he or she is thinking and coping. Medications can also be very effective in the prevention of suicidal behaviors. Hospitalization may be needed as well, in order to prevent suicide. The key to helping a suicidal or potentially suicidal individual is for those around them to be aware and actively involved in seeking out help for the person who is at risk.

Eating Disorders and Stress

Eating disorders are medically identifiable, potentially life-threatening mental health conditions related to obsessive eating patterns. Eating disorders are not new— descriptions of self-starvation have been found as far back as medieval times.

Even though more young men are succumbing to eating disorders each year, the mental health condition is typically thought of as a woman's disease. Unfortunately, even grade school girls can feel pressure to "fit in"

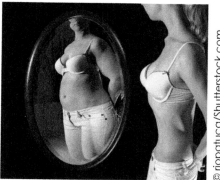

Anorexics and bulimics tend to suffer from low self-esteem and depression and typically have a distorted view of themselves.

FIGURE 4.7

Major Risk Factors for
Eating Disorders

Biological

Dieting
Obesity/overweight/pubertal weight gain

Psychological

Body image/dissatisfaction/distortions
Low self-esteem
Obsessive-compulsive symptoms
Childhood sexual abuse

Family

Parental attitudes and behaviors
Parental comments regarding appearance
Eating-disordered mothers
Misinformation about ideal weight

Sociocultural

Peer pressure regarding weight/eating
Media: TV, magazines
Distorted images: toys
Elite athletes as at-risk groups

Source: White, Jane. "The Prevention of Eating Disorders: A Review of the Research on Risk Factors with Implications for Practice." *Journal of Child and Adolescent Psychiatric Nursing*, Vol. 13, No. 2, April 2000.

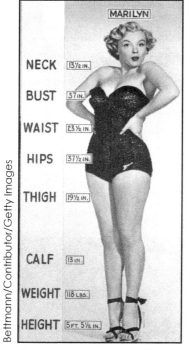

Body image is affected by a person's attitudes and beliefs, as well as outside influences such as family, social pressures, and the media.

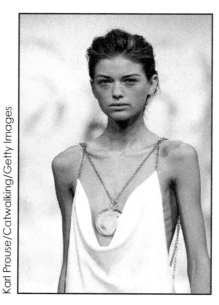

or look thin. This can be very troubling and disruptive to young girls struggling to build a positive body image.

Typically, a person with an eating disorder seeks perfection and control over their life. Both anorexics and bulimics tend to suffer from low self-esteem and depression. They often have a conflict between a desire for perfection and feelings of personal inadequacy. Such persons typically have a distorted view of themselves, in that when they look into a mirror, they see themselves differently than others see them. Narcissism, or excessive vanity, can be linked to both anorexia and bulimia. (see Figure 4.7)

Eating disorders are often accompanied by other psychiatric disorders, such as depression, substance abuse, or anxiety disorders. Eating disorders are very serious and may be life-threatening due to the fact that individuals suffering from these diseases can experience serious heart conditions and/or kidney failure—both of which can result in death. Therefore, it is critically important that eating disorders are recognized as real and treatable diseases.

Body Image

The media, advertising, and the fashion industry portray women, as well as men, as thin (or fit), beautiful, and youthful. This is an ideal that is difficult to attain and nearly impossible to maintain. It is important to note that glamorous magazine cover models' pictures are airbrushed with imperfections deleted, so that the final product is an almost perfect unachievable image. It wasn't too long ago that the ideal for a woman's body was "fat is where it's at" instead of the current preoccupation with "thin is in." Many of the great masters' paintings portray the female image as having desirable traits such as soft, round, and fleshy bodies. The 50's had curvy movie stars such as Marilyn Monroe. In the 60's, the Twiggy look was in. In the 70's, it was Farrah Fawcett Fit. In the 80's, it was the fit look with Cindy Crawford. In the 90's, Kate Moss exemplified the gaunt heroin look. As Americans grow in size, the current unobtainable look is very thin. The Body Mass Index of Playboy models and Miss America contestants lowered significantly from the 1970's to the 1990's. Even wealthy celebrities who can afford personal chefs, trainers, registered dieticians, and top consultants sometimes battle with their weight.

A person's body image is how a person sees him or herself in his or her mind. Body image is affected by a person's attitudes and beliefs, as well as by outside influences such as family, social pressures, and the media. It is important to have good perspective. If you are an "apple" and naturally carry excess fat in your abdominal area, when you gain weight you will become a larger "apple" or you may lose weight and become a smaller "apple." The same is true for "pear" shaped individuals who carry their excess fat in their hips and buttocks. You cannot become a different shape, nor can you diet down to a thin waif. Accept yourself for who you are; then work on behavior changes to become healthier. The fringe benefit to becoming healthier is that you will most likely fit better in your jeans. You will also feel better while you reduce your risk of heart disease and diabetes.

Anorexia Nervosa

Anorexia nervosa is a state of starvation and emaciation, usually resulting from severe dieting and excessive exercise. An anorexic will literally stop eating in an effort to control body size.

Most, if not all, anorexic individuals suffer from an extremely distorted body image. People with this disease look in a mirror and see themselves as overweight or fat even when they have become dangerously thin.

Major weight loss is the most visible and the most common symptom of anorexia. Anorexic individuals often develop unusual eating habits, such as

Ways to Love Your Body

- Become aware of what your body does each day, as the instrument of your life, not just an ornament for others.
- Think of your body as a tool. Create a list of all the things you can do with this body.
- Walk with your head held high, supported by pride and confidence in yourself as a person.
- Do something that will let you enjoy your body. Stretch, dance, walk, sing, take a bubble bath, get a massage.
- Wear comfortable styles that you really like and feel good in.
- Decide what you would rather do with the hours you waste every day criticizing your body.
- Describe ten positive things about yourself without mentioning your appearance.
- Say to yourself "Life is too short to waste my time hating my body this way."
- Don't let your weight or shape keep you from doing things you enjoy.
- Create a list of people who have contributed to your life, your community, the world. Was their appearance important to their success and accomplishment? If not, why should yours be?
- If you had only one year to live, how important would your body image and appearance be?

By Margo Maine, Ph.D. and Eating Disorders' Awareness and Prevention

avoiding food or meals, picking out a few "acceptable" foods and eating them in small quantities, or carefully weighing and portioning foods. Other common symptoms of this disease include absent menstruation, dry skin, excessive hair on the skin, and thinning of scalp hair. Gastrointestinal problems and orthopedic problems resulting from excessive exercise are also specific to this illness.

Anorexic individuals can lose between 15 and 60 percent of their normal body weight, putting their body and their health in severe jeopardy. The medical problems associated with anorexia are numerous and serious. Starvation damages bones, organs, muscles, the immune system, the digestive system, and the nervous system.

Between 5 and 20 percent of anorexics die due to suicide or other medical complications. Heart disease is the most common medical cause of death for people with severe anorexia.

Long-term irregular or absent menstruation can cause sterility or bone loss. Severe anorexics also suffer nerve damage and may experience seizures. Anemia and gastrointestinal problems are also common to individuals suffering from this illness.

The most severe complication and the most devastating result of anorexia is death.

Bulimia Nervosa

Bulimia nervosa is a process of bingeing and purging. This disorder is more common than anorexia nervosa. The purging is an attempt to control body weight, though bulimics seldom starve themselves as anorexics do. They have an intense fear of becoming overweight, and usually have episodes of secretive binge eating, followed by purging, frequent weight variations, and the inability to stop eating voluntarily. Bulimics often feel hunger, overeat, and then purge to rid themselves of the guilt of overeating.

Bulimic individuals are often secretive and discreet and are, therefore, often hard to identify. Typically, they have a preoccupation with food, fluctuating between fantasies of food and guilt due to overeating. Symptoms of bulimia can include cuts and calluses on the finger joints from a person sticking their fingers or hand down their throat to induce vomiting, broken blood vessels around the eyes from the strain of vomiting, and damage to tooth enamel from stomach acid.

Because purging through vomiting, the abuse of laxatives, or some other compensatory behavior typically follows a binge, bulimics usually weigh within the normal range for their weight and height. However, like individuals with anorexia, they often have a distorted body image and fear gaining weight, want to lose weight, and are intensely dissatisfied with their bodies.

While it is commonly thought that the medical problems resulting from bulimia are not as severe as those resulting from anorexia, the complications are numerous and serious. The medical problems associated with bulimia include tooth erosion, cavities, and gum problems due to the acid in vomit. Abdominal bloating is common in bulimic individuals. The purging process can leave a person dehydrated and with very low potassium levels, which can cause weakness and paralysis. Some of the more severe problems a bulimic can suffer are reproductive problems and heart damage, due to the lack of minerals in the body.

Binge-Eating Disorder

People with binge-eating disorder typically experience frequent (at least two days a week) episodes of out-of-control eating. Binge-eating episodes are associated with at least three of the following characteristics: eating much more rapidly than normal; eating until an individual is uncomfortably full; eating large quantities of food even when not hungry; eating alone to hide the quantity of food being ingested; feeling disgusted, depressed, or guilty after overeating. Not purging their bodies of the excessive calories they have consumed is the characteristic that separates individuals with binge-eating disorder from those with bulimia. Therefore, individuals suffering from this disease are typically overweight for their height and weight.

Fear of Obesity

Fear of obesity is an over-concern with thinness. It is less severe than anorexia, but can also have negative health consequences. This condition is often seen in achievement-oriented teenagers who seek to restrict their weight due to a fear of becoming obese. This condition can be a precursor to anorexia or bulimia if it is not detected and treated early.

Activity Nervosa

Activity nervosa is a condition in which the individual suffers from the ever-present compulsion to exercise, regardless of illness or injury. The desire to exercise excessively may result in poor performance in other areas of that individual's life due to the resulting fatigue, weakness, and unhealthy body weight.

Female Athlete Triad   In 1991, a team was formed by the American College of Sports Medicine to educate, initiate a change, and focus on the medical management of a triad of female disorders that included disordered eating, amenorrhea, and osteoporosis (ACSM, 1991). A triangle is used to depict these disorders because the three are interlinked. Disordered eating behaviors result in weight loss and subsequent loss of body fat that halts menstruation. When amenorrhea occurs, calcium is lost and a decline in bone mass occurs. This in turn causes osteoporosis and can easily result in stress fractures. Many times the inactivity necessary to allow stress fractures to heal causes depression that often leads an individual back into disordered eating behaviors, and the cycle continues (see Figure 4.8).

Who Is at Risk?

By far, more women than men succumb to eating disorders; however, the incidence of eating disorders in men is believed to be very underreported.

It is estimated that one in every hundred teenage girls is anorexic. Anorexia usually occurs in adolescent women (90 percent of all reported cases), although all age groups can be affected. It is estimated that one in every five college-bound females is bulimic.

Individuals living in economically developed nations, such as the United States, are much more likely to suffer from an eating disorder, due to the dual factors of an abundance of available food and external, societal pressure. College campuses have a higher incidence of people with eating disorders, and upper-middle-class women who are extremely self-critical are also more

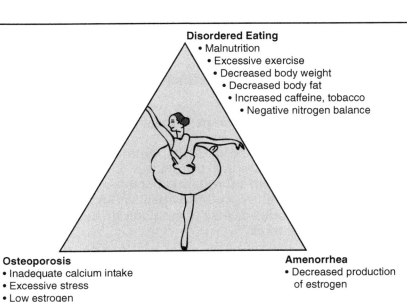

Disordered Eating
• Malnutrition
• Excessive exercise
• Decreased body weight
• Decreased body fat
• Increased caffeine, tobacco
• Negative nitrogen balance

Osteoporosis
• Inadequate calcium intake
• Excessive stress
• Low estrogen
• Decreased bone mineral content
• Injury
• Depression

Amenorrhea
• Decreased production of estrogen

FIGURE 4.8

The Female Athlete Triad

I Have Won

One Woman's Recovery from Binge-Eating Disorder

It was a constant nagging voice in my mind, whispering promises of protection, comfort and a life of numbness. I didn't realize it was my enemy, disguised as a savior. This is what my eating disorder was to me. I have been struggling with binge-eating disorder for eight years, and after a year of therapy I am learning how to tell that voice to go away and to love, trust and respect myself and my values.

I have countless memories of daytime binges when my roommates were in class, even digging through the trash to retrieve a half-eaten candy bar or piece of cake. I withdrew from my friends, missed out on beach parties, and felt lonely, scared and completely out of control every waking moment of the day. I became deeply depressed and couldn't face emotional issues that had been with me for a long time. That voice gave soothing promises of a way out, a way to forget, an excuse for any failures or disappointments, and a way to slowly. . . die.

My friends and family were aware there was a problem but I spent years denying the truth. I would tell them I just loved to eat and I just needed to start exercising more. All the while my weight kept slowly growing. I would think constantly about changing, going on a diet, but the diet day would come and I couldn't do it, so I would retreat to the voice and let it take charge. I finally accepted that I had a problem when I was in school completing a Master's Degree in Counseling. I had to constantly analyze myself and my life for projects and papers and could no longer deny the issues at hand.

I entered into therapy and honestly wasn't prepared for the difficulty that lay ahead. I had to confront my demons, that voice, examine every horrible issue that I had suppressed and once again learn how to live life. I learned that I can do other things when I find myself in front of the refrigerator and I am not physically hungry. I can take walks, call my husband, or put together a puzzle. I also had to relearn my body's signals for hunger and fullness and to trust that my body will tell me what I need and when I need it.

Although still in recovery, I can clearly see how far I've come, and I can see the light at the end of the tunnel. I now spend time speaking about eating disorders and volunteering at the Massachusetts Eating Disorder Association. I want people to know that there is hope and that recovery is possible. The voice no longer whispers to me; I now shout at it, "I don't need you anymore. I love myself. I have won!"

by Cathy King, M.S.

A special thanks to the Massachusetts Eating Disorder Association

Source: *Courtesy of the Massachusetts Eating Disorder Association*

likely to become anorexic. Being aware of the groups at risk can be a large step toward prevention.

Activities such as dance and dance team, gymnastics, figure skating, track, and cheerleading tend to have higher instances of eating disorders. An estimate of people suffering from anorexia and bulimia within these populations is 15–60 percent. Male wrestlers and body builders are also at risk due to the unsafe practice of attempting to shed pounds quickly in an attempt to "make weight" before a competition.

Causes of Eating Disorders

The causes of anorexia and bulimia are numerous and complex. Cultural factors, family pressure, psychological factors, emotional disorders, and chemical imbalances can all contribute to eating disorders.

Forty to 80 percent of anorexics suffer from depression.

Forty to 80 percent of anorexics suffer from depression, as reduced levels of chemical neurotransmitters in the brain have been found in victims suffering from both eating disorders and depression. Links between hunger and depression have been discovered through research, which contributes to the depression a person with an eating disorder may feel.

For some bulimics, seasonality can adversely affect them, causing the disorder to worsen during the dark, winter months. Another startling statistic is that the onset of anorexia appears to peak in May, which is also the peak month for suicides.

Family factors are also critical. One study showed that 40 percent of all 9- to 10-year-old girls were trying to lose weight, many at the encouragement of their mothers. Mothers of anorexics are often overinvolved in their child's life, while mothers of bulimics are many times critical and detached.

It is clear that many people who suffer from eating disorders do not have a healthy body image. From an early age, there is enormous pressure in our culture from society, family, friends, the media, and often from one's self to achieve the unachievable and unnecessary "perfect" body. A woman's self-worth is too often associated with other people's opinions, which in many cases put unrealistic emphasis on physical attractiveness.

Ways to Help

The best course of action for a person who suspects they know someone with an eating disorder is to be patient, supportive, and not judge the individual. Learn what you can about the problem by consulting an eating disorder clinic or counseling center (common on college campuses), and offer to help the ill person seek professional help.

Often, individuals suffering from an eating disorder do not realize or will not admit that they are ill. For this reason, seeking help or continuing/completing treatment for the disorder is often difficult.

Medical treatment is often necessary for eating disorders. However, it is extremely encouraging to note that eating disorders can be treated and a healthy weight and relationship with food can be restored. Because of the complexity of eating disorders, the best and most successful treatment is usually a combination of counseling, family therapy, cognitive behavior therapy, nutritional therapy, support groups, and drug therapy. Treatment, many times, includes a hospital stay and is usually resisted by the patient. Support for the anorexic or bulimic person by friends and family and the realization of the severity of the problem is critical to successful treatment of the illness.

References

Ballard, D. "A Dozen Ways to Stress-Proof Your Life." 2002.

Corbin, C.B. and Lindsey, R. *Concepts of Physical Fitness.* McBrown. 2008.

Donatelle, R. J. *Access to Health* (9th ed). Allyn & Bacon. Boston. 2006.

Floyd, P., Mims, S., and Yelding-Howard, C. *Personal Health: Perspectives and Lifstyles.* Morton Publishing Co. 2007.

Hahn, D. B. and Payne, W. A. *Understanding Your Health.* McGraw-Hill. 2008.

Hales, D. *An Invitation to Health* (8th ed). New York: Brooks/Cole Publishing Company. 1999.

Hales, D. *An Invitation to Health* (Brief 2nd ed). Belmont, CA: Wadsworth Thomson. 2002.

Hoeger, W. and Hoeger, S. A. *Principles and Labs for Fitness and Wellness* (9th ed). Brooks/ Cole Publishing Company. 2008.

Hoeger, W. W. K. and Hoeger, S. A. *Lifetime Physical Fitness and Wellness: A Personalized Program* (8th ed). Belmont, CA: Thomson Wadsworth. 2005.

Holmes, T. H. and Rahe, R. H. Student Stress Scale. *Journal of Psychosomatic Research, 11,* 213.

http://ahha.org

http://healthed.tamu.edu/stress.htm

http://indiana.edu/~health/stress.html

https://sleep.org/articles/sleep-and-stress/

http://stress.about.com/od/optimismspitituality/a/positiveselftalk.html

http://umm.edu/health/medical/reports/articles/stress

http://www.huffingtonpost.com/2014/09/17/stress-and-sleep_n_5824506.html

http://who.int/aboutwho/en/definition.html

http://www.healthdepot.com

http://www.med.nus.edu.sg/pcm/stress

http://www.m-w.com/dictionary.html

http://www.nimh.nih.gov/publicat/eatingdisorder.com

http://www.reachout.com.au/default.asp?ti=2249

http://www.selfcounseling.com/help/depression/suicide.html

http://www.acsm.org

http://www.cdc.gov/nccdphp/sgr/pdf/chap4.pdf

Hyman, B., Oden, G., Bacharach, D., and Collins, R. *Fitness for Living.* Kendall-Hunt Publishing Co. 2006.

Payne, W. A., Hahn, D. B. *Understanding Your Health* (6th ed). St. Louis, MO: Mosby. 2000.

Peterson, M. S. *Eat to Compete* (2nd ed). St. Louis, MO: Mosby. 63146

Powers, S. K., Todd, S. L., and Noland, U. J. *Total Fitness and Wellness* (2nd ed). Boston: Allyn & Bacon. 2005.

Prentice, W. E. *Fitness and Wellness for Life* (6th ed). New York: WCB McGraw-Hill. 1999.

Pruitt, B. E. and Stein, J. *Health Styles.* Boston: Allyn & Bacon. 1999.

Robbins, G., Powers, D., and Burgess, S. *A Wellness Way of Life* (4th ed). New York: WCB McGraw-Hill. 1999.

Rosato, F. *Fitness for Wellness* (3rd ed). Minneapolis: West. 1994.

Roth, G. *Why Weight? A Guide to Compulsive Eating.* New York. Penguin Group. 1989. Student Health Services, Texas A&M University. *Guidelines for Helping a Friend with an Eating Disorder,* 2002.

Webmaster@noah.cuny.edu

Weinttraub, Amy. Yoga: It's Not Just An Exercise. *Psychology Today,* Nov. 2000.

Chapter 5
Hypokinetic Conditions and Lifestyle Choices

Photo courtesy of Sarah Burns

OBJECTIVES

Students will be able to:

◆ Identify the major hypokinetic diseases and how activity impacts the disease.
◆ Identify cardiac risk factors and strategies to reduce controllable risk factors.
◆ Integrate various strategies to combat obesity.

Adaptation of *Health and Fitness: A Guide to a Healthly Lifestyle,* 5th Edition, by Laura Bounds, Gayden Darnell, Kirstin Brekken Shea, and Dottiede Agnor. Copyright © 2012 by Kendall Hunt Publishing Company.

"When health is absent, wisdom cannot reveal itself, art cannot become manifest, strength cannot be exerted, wealth is useless and reason is powerless"

—Herophilies, 300 B.C.

Why should we exercise? The simple answer is that our brains and our bodies work optimally when we undergo the stress of activity on a regular basis. The health of many Americans has declined in the last 30 years as we have eaten more, become more sedentary, and with the explosion in technology. It has been firmly established that physical activity should be a part of our daily lives. Exercise enhances weight management and overall wellness by burning calories, speeding up metabolism building muscle tissue, and balancing appetite with energy expenditure. More importantly, an active lifestyle decreases health risk and typically makes you feel good and feel good about yourself. The Centers for Disease Control (CDC) have reported that lifestyle is the single greatest factor affecting longevity of life. This chapter examines diseases that afflict people in developed countries like the United States.

These diseases are called **hypokinetic** because they are associated with too little activity: the prefix "hypo" means low and "kinetic" refers to movement. Kraus and Rabb first coined the term hypokinetic in 1961. Hypokinetic diseases include the leading causes of death, such as coronary heart disease and cancer, as well as debilitating conditions such as low back pain, osteoporosis, obesity, diabetes, and many mental health disorders. In 1992 the American Heart Association (AHA) identified inactivity as a major cardiac risk factor. In 2012 a new emphasis in human performance studies was added called inactivity physiology. The Greek physician Hippocrates, born in 460 BC, quipped "walking is man's best medicine."

The 1996 Surgeon General's Report is a landmark report that, after a comprehensive review of literature, traced the link between physical activity and good health (see Figure 5.1). According to the 1996 Surgeon General's Report, we are all encouraged to try and expend 150 calories extra each day, above and beyond a normal routine. It is clear that regular consistent activity can decrease the potential of having a hypokinetic disease.

FIGURE 5.1

Landmark Report: **1996 U.S. Surgeon General's Report: Physical Activity and Health**

1. Males and females of all ages benefit from regular physical activity.
2. Significant health benefits can be obtained by moderately increasing daily activity on most, if not all, days of the week.
3. Additional health benefits can be gained through greater amounts of physical activity.
4. Physical activity reduces the risk of premature mortality in general, and of coronary heart disease, hypertension, colon cancer, and diabetes mellitus in particular.

Prevention of Hypokinetic Conditions: Move Every Day

Simply changing our lifestyle to include more physical activity can reduce the incidence of many hypokinetic conditions. **Lifestyle activity** is movement that is intentionally expending extra energy rather than searching for opportunities to conserve energy with convenient devices like remote controls. An example of increasing lifestyle activity would be to take the stairs rather than the elevator when possible. Students who walk across big campuses between classes rather than take the bus expend more energy. One day might not have a significant impact; however, at the end of the semester the cumulative effects of walking can add up to enhanced health. Lifestyle activity is sometimes easier to incorporate into a hectic schedule. Try taking a ten-minute active study break to walk, jump rope, do some push-ups, practice a sun salutation or stretch.

Planned exercise is important for fitness benefits. It isn't important whether or not you take up jogging, swimming, CrossFit, or salsa dancing. What is critical is that you enjoy the activity so that you will stay committed, hopefully throughout your lifetime. Plan it! Don't leave your exercise to chance, because chances are, you won't have time. If you hate to run, don't take up marathon training. To be successful with your planned workout program, set realistic goals. Research indicates that specific goal setting greatly enhances your chance of success. Create behaviors that will support your goals. Enlist the help of friends and family. Try to establish a routine, such as meeting your roommate at the campus recreation center after class every Monday, Wednesday and Friday. Plan activity breaks throughout your day. Both lifestyle activity and planned exercise are significant to long-term good health.

Overall weekly caloric expenditure from extra activity in your life can decrease your overall health risk. For example, expending an extra 500-1,000 calories per week can decrease overall

Choosing to be more active daily, such as gardening, walking rather than driving, parking farther away from your destination and taking the stairs can make a surprising dent in your energy reserves.

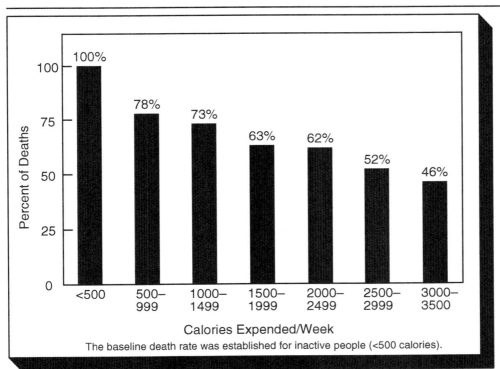

FIGURE 5.2

Deaths Decrease as Caloric Expenditure Increases

Calories Expended/Week
The baseline death rate was established for inactive people (<500 calories).

Source: Data from C. Bouchard et al. *Exercise Fitness and Health.* Champaign, IL: Human Kinetics Publishers, 1990.

health risk (see Figure 5.2). Expending an extra 1,000-2,000 calories per week can decrease overall health risk more and also moderately increase cardiovascular fitness. An expenditure of 2,000-3,500 calories per week can decrease overall health risk, as well as significantly increase cardiovascular fitness over time. Typically expending beyond 3,500 calories per week can increase risk of musculoskeletal injuries, burnout, or the possibility of an obsession with exercise. As in all areas of life, balance and common sense are important. The bottom line is that we all have to make the choice, daily, to move more. Our life depends on it.

Students who walk to class rather than ride are increasing their lifestyle activity.

Avoid "Sitting Disease"

Are you sitting right now? As a species we have evolved from active hunter-gatherers to primarily sedentary beings. Technology continues to change our lives in many positive ways-but a side effect is that we tend to sit for many of the activities that occupy our time-exclusive of planned physical activity. Long sitting times have been linked to increased risk of heart disease, colon cancer, foggy brain, strained neck, a weakened core, tight hip flexors and risk of osteoporosis. Even those people who have a regular routine of running 2 miles several mornings a week need to consider how much they are sitting the rest of the day. Standing desks have become popular alternatives to reduce sitting time at work and in schools. A less expensive solution is setting an alarm every hour while studying or at work for a 5 minute posture or walk break to break up the time you are seated. A study published in the American Journal of Preventive Medicine in 2016 concluded that excessive sitting for 11 or more hours a day increased of premature death by 12%. Excess sitting time was responsible for 3.8% of all-cause mortality in the 54 countries that were included in the analysis; this risk is independent of physical activity. So why not stand up and move a little?

If you must sit for long periods of time, take frequent breaks to stand and stretch.

© ATurner, 2012, Shutterstock, Inc.

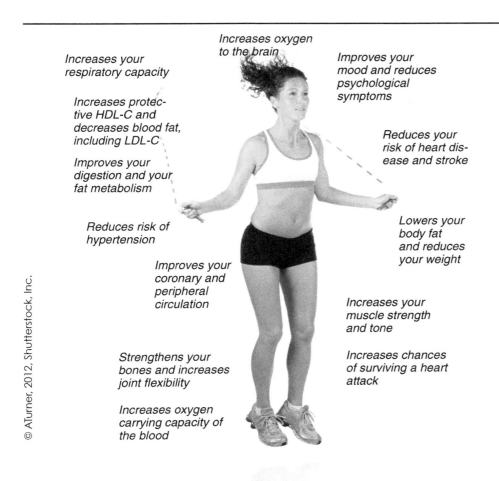

FIGURE 5.3

Benefits of Exercise: Consistent physical activity affects cardiovascular disease by one or more of these mechanisms.

Types of Hypokinetic Conditions

Cardiovascular Disease (CVD)

The cardiovascular system is responsible for delivering oxygen and other nutrients to the body. The major components of the cardiovascular system are the heart, blood, and the vessels that carry the blood. Cardiovascular disease (CVD) is a catch-all term that includes several disease processes including various diseases of the heart, stroke, high blood pressure, congestive heart failure, and atherosclerosis. The heart muscle may become damaged or lose its ability to contract effectively. The vessels that supply the heart with oxygen may become blocked or damaged and subsequently compromise the heart muscle. Finally, the peripheral vascular system (all of the vessels outside the heart) may become damaged and decrease the ability to provide oxygen to other parts of the body.

The good news is that between 2003–2013, deaths due to cardiovascular disease declined 38% (AHA, 2016). The bad news is that in 2014, for the first time since 1980, the life expectancy in the United States did not increase (CDC, 2017). CVD still claims one in three deaths in the United States. Many of the risk factors for CVD are lifestyle-related and therefore preventable, yet Americans, including women, are much more likely to die from CVD than anything else. The cost of CVD is very high, both in dollars and in productivity lost. Health Impact Goals 2020 and the Million Hearts Initiative are efforts to coordinate public, private, and governmental resources to focus on the positives, on prevention. As part of Health Impact Goals 2020, the AHA developed **7 Metrics of Cardiovascular Health**. MyLifeCheck.org is a part of a campaign to increase awareness of positive attributes of health. Check it out.

The good news is that being active can reduce heart disease by 30–40% and stroke by 25% when the exercise is moderate to vigorous. (AHA, 2016) So what are you waiting for?

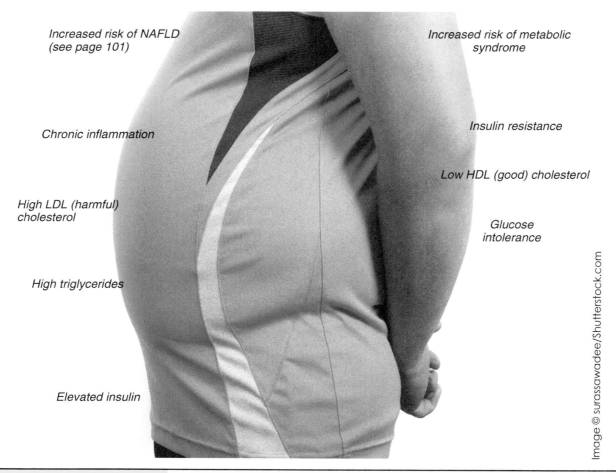

Increased risk of NAFLD
(see page 101)

Increased risk of metabolic
syndrome

Chronic inflammation

Insulin resistance

High LDL (harmful)
cholesterol

Low HDL (good) cholesterol

Glucose
intolerance

High triglycerides

Elevated insulin

Image © surassawadee/Shutterstock.com

FIGURE 5.4

Consequences of Visceral Obesity

The risk of cardiovascular disease and type 2 diabetes is increased by all of these factors. Note: sedentary, thin people can also have visceral fat.

Who Is at Risk for CVD?

The landmark Surgeon General's Report (Satcher, 1996) placed **physical inactivity** as a significant risk factor for cardiovascular diseases and other health disorders. Most sedentary Americans are at risk. "About 85.6 million Americans are living with some form of cardiovascular disease or the after-effects of stroke." (AHA, 2016 update) Many factors can predispose a person to be at risk for CVD. Sedentary living, habitual stress, smoking, poor diet, high blood pressure, diabetes, obesity, high cholesterol, and family history can all increase risk. Advancing age increases risk. Males typically have a higher risk than women until women are post-menopausal, then risk evens out. Misconceptions still exist that CVD is not a real problem for women. Because more women have heart attacks when they are older, the initial heart attack is more likely to be fatal. It is important for women to realize that CVD is an equal opportunity killer. Just like men, more women die from heart disease than anything else.

Certain populations have an inherently higher health risk such as African Americans and Hispanics. Genetic predisposition is a strong factor; familial tendencies toward elevated triglycerides, fat distribution (abdominal fat accumulation denotes a higher health risk than hip/thigh accumulation of fat), and high **low-density lipoprotein cholesterol (LDL-C)** levels increase risk. LDL-C is a blood lipid that indicates a higher cardiac risk. Saturated fat intake tends to increase LDL cholesterol. Dr. William Franklin of Georgetown University

Medical School in Washington claims that anyone who has a close relative who has had a heart attack should begin monitoring his heart with regular stress tests when he is 45. If your father died in his 40's of a heart attack, then you should be concerned a decade earlier in your 30's. Variables such as age, gender, race, and genetic makeup may place you at a higher or lower risk but cannot be changed. These can be termed unalterable risk factors.

CVD Prevention

Cardiovascular disease is the leading cause of death in the United States. "On average, approximately 2200 Americans die of CVD each day, and average of 1 death every 40 seconds." (AHA, 2016 update) Since you cannot change your age, your sex, and who your parents are, focus on what you *can* change. These risk factors include but are not limited to: diet, drug use, tobacco use, cholesterol levels, obesity, high blood pressure, and last but definitely not least, physical inactivity. This is a critical point, since activity level is a risk factor that can be easily modified and is often overlooked (Figure 5.6). Choosing to be more active can prevent many of the diseases discussed in this chapter. With this being the case, consider your own risk. How can you adjust your current lifestyle habits to decrease your risk? Refer back to the Benefits of Exercise (Figure 5.3) to determine how exercise helps CVD.

C-reactive protein: a protein produced by the liver that is normally present in trace amounts in the bold serum but is elevated during episodes of acute inflammation (as associated with chronic infection or coronary artery disease).

Plasma homocysteine: an amino acid produced in the body that is related to atherosclerosis and increased risk for other types of CVD.

Omega-3 fatty acids: fatty acids found in fish such as salmon and tuna, and also in the oils of some nuts and seeds. Omega-3 fatty acids are beneficial in reducing risk of CVD.

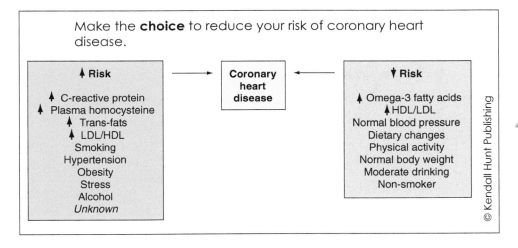

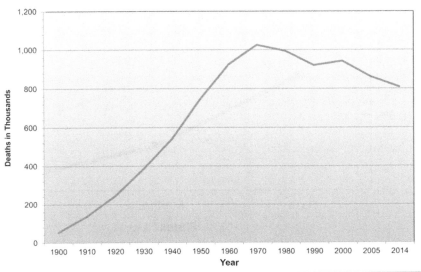

FIGURE 5.5

Deaths attributable to cardiovascular disease (United States: 1900-2014)

Source: National Center for Health Statistics

Claudette's Story

"I consider myself to be relatively healthy and I exercise for about ninety minutes every morning. I started having pain in my chest and face during my exercising, and finally went to the cardiologist. I never thought that the pain in my face could be related to my heart, so I was shocked when the tests showed that I had had a heart attack. I thought I was too young, but my father died of a heart attack when he was only 38, so I had family history as a risk factor. After my second heart attack, I knew that I needed to help get the message out. **Women need to know** that heart disease is their biggest health threat."

Source: National Heart, Lung and Blood Institute, National Health Institute.

FIGURE 5.6

Relationship between Different Levels of Fitness and Death Due to Cardiovascular Disease among Men and Women

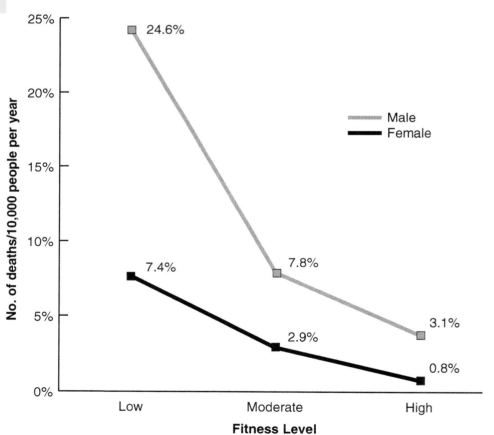

Source: Blair et al., Physical fitness and all-cause mortality: A prospective study of healthy men and women. *Journal of the American Medical Association* 262(17): 2395–2401, 1989. (Adapted from S. N. Blair, N. W. Kohl, III, R. S. Paffenbarger, Jr., D. G. Clark, K. H. Cooper, and L. W. Gibbons. Physical fitness and all-cause mortality: A prospective study of healthy men and women.)

The "ABCS" of heart disease and stroke prevention

Aspirin therapy
Blood pressure control
Cholesterol control
Smoking cessation

CVD and stroke are largely preventable for a significant part of the lifespan. High blood pressure, high cholesterol, and smoking continue to put people at risk of heart attack and stroke. To address these risk factors, the Centers for Disease Control and Prevention is focusing many of its efforts on the "ABCS" of heart disease and stroke prevention: **appropriate low-dose Aspirin therapy, Blood pressure prevention and control, Cholesterol prevention and control, and support for Smoking cessation** for those trying to quit and, even more generally, comprehensive tobacco prevention and control efforts. (CDC, 2012)

The American Heart Association projects that by 2030, 40.5% of the U.S. population will have some form of CVD, costing the healthcare system an estimated $1 trillion every year. (AHA, 2012)

Types of Cardiovascular Disease

Arteriosclerosis

Arteriosclerosis is a term used to describe the thickening and hardening of the arteries. Healthy arteries are elastic and will dilate and constrict with changes in blood flow, which allows proper maintenance of blood pressure. Hardened, non-elastic arteries do not expand with blood flow and can increase intrarterial pressure causing high blood pressure. Both high blood pressure and arteriosclerosis increase the risk of an **aneurysm**. With an aneurysm, the artery loses its integrity and balloons out under the pressure created by the pumping heart, in much the same way as an old garden hose might if placed under pressure. If an aneurysm occurs in the vessels of the brain, a stroke might occur. Aneurysms in the large vessels can place a person at risk of sudden death. Maintaining normal elasticity of the arteries is very important for good health. Exercise helps to manage symptoms and the factors that contribute to cardiac risk.

Warning Signs of a Heart Attack:
1. Chest Pain
2. Pain in the arms, the back, neck, or jaw
3. Shortness of breath
4. Cold sweat
5. Nausea
6. Lightheadedness

Atherosclerosis   Atherosclerosis is a type of arteriosclerosis. Atherosclerosis is the long-term buildup of fatty deposits and other substances such as cholesterol, cellular waste products, calcium, and fibrin (clotting material in the blood) on the interior walls of arteries (see Figure 5.7). The leading theory states that plaque develops when the endothelium (a thin layer of cells that line the interior vessel wall) is damaged due to major fluctuations in blood pressure, increased levels of blood triglycerides, cholesterol, and cigarette smoking. Conditions such as these accelerate the development of atherosclerosis. Due to this plaque development, the flow of blood within the artery decreases because the diameter of the vessel is decreased. This may create a partial or total blockage (called an occlusion) that may cause high blood pressure, a heart attack, or stroke. This process can occur in any vessel of the body. If it occurs outside of the brain or heart, it is termed peripheral vascular disease. Within the heart the gradual narrowing of the coronary arteries to the myocardium, or heart muscle, is called coronary artery disease. Atherosclerosis is a disease that can start early in childhood. With a family history of high cholesterol, it is important to check a child's

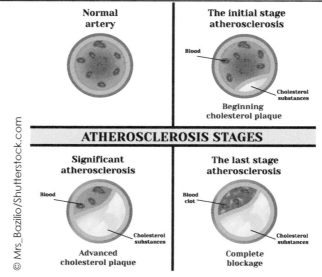

Coronary artery disease occurs when a substance called plaque builds up in the arteries that supply blood to the heart (called coronary arteries). Plaque is made up of cholesterol deposits, which can accumulate in your arteries. When this happens, your arteries can narrow over time. This process is called atherosclerosis.

Increasing lifestyle activity by spending less time on the couch and doing something active daily will have a positive impact on your health.

cholesterol levels early in life. Besides heart disease and stroke, atherosclerosis can lead to kidney disease. The rate of progression of atherosclerosis depends on family history and lifestyle choices. Exercise helps manage symptoms as well as increase coronary collateral circulation. Collateral arteries are the vessels that form preceding the blockage as an artery slowly becomes occluded. Collateral vessels such as these can help lessen the severity of a heart attack when the artery becomes totally blocked. High cholesterol levels can increase risk of atherosclerosis, and low-density lipoprotein cholesterol is thought to contribute to the arterial occlusion. **Triglycerides** are another type of blood fat which at high levels is associated with high risk (see Figure 5.8). Regular physical activity has been shown to lower risk by lowering blood lipid (fat) levels.

Peripheral Vascular Disease

Peripheral vascular disease is simply a term attributed to disease of the peripheral vessels. The lack of proper circulation may cause fluids to pool in the extremities. Associated leg pain, cramping, numbness, tingling, coldness, and loss of hair to affected limbs are common signs. The restrictions in blood flow are typically caused by years of arteriosclerosis and atherosclerosis in the vessels of the extremities. The risk factors are the same as those for cardiovascular disease. One difference is that the disease process may progress extensively before the affected person begins to notice any problems. The heart and brain are much more sensitive to compromised blood flow than are the extremities.

Hypertension

Hypertension, or high blood pressure, is often called the "silent killer" because typically there are no symptoms (Figure 5.8). Because hypertension is asymptomatic, it is important to get your blood pressure checked on a regular basis. High blood pressure is associated with a shortened life span. Interestingly,

Heart Attack: Warning Signs Common in Women

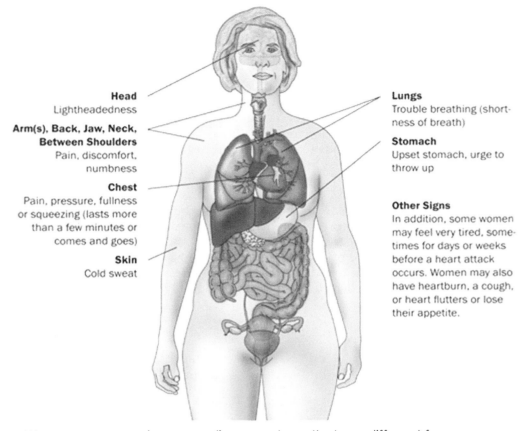

Head
Lightheadedness

Arm(s), Back, Jaw, Neck, Between Shoulders
Pain, discomfort, numbness

Chest
Pain, pressure, fullness or squeezing (lasts more than a few minutes or comes and goes)

Skin
Cold sweat

Lungs
Trouble breathing (shortness of breath)

Stomach
Upset stomach, urge to throw up

Other Signs
In addition, some women may feel very tired, sometimes for days or weeks before a heart attack occurs. Women may also have heartburn, a cough, or heart flutters or lose their appetite.

Women may experience cardiac symptoms that are different from men.
Source: Image courtesy of the Office on Women's Health, U.S. Department of Health and Human Services.

FIGURE 5.8

Blood Pressure is known as the 'silent killer' because many people do not realize that they have high BP. Do you know your BP?

$\dfrac{117}{76}$ **mm Hg**

Read as "117 over 76 millimeters of mercury"

Systolic
The top number, which is also the higher of the two numbers, measures the pressure in the arteries when the heart beats (when the heart muscle contracts).

Diastolic
The bottom number, which is also the lower of the two numbers, measures the pressure in the arteries between heartbeats (when the heart muscle is resting between beats and refilling with blood).

Source: American Heart Association

NHANES data show that a higher percentage of men than women have hypertension until 45 years of age. From 45 to 54 years of age and from 55 to 64 years of age, the percentages of men and women with hypertension are similar. After that, a higher percentage of women have hypertension than men. (AHA, 2016 stats update) High blood pressure causes the heart to work harder. Chronic, untreated hypertension can lead to aneurysms in blood vessels, heart failure from an enlarged heart, kidney failure, atherosclerosis, and blindness. "Based on 2009 to 2012 data, 32.6% of US adults ≥20 years of age have hypertension, which represents approximately 80.0 million US adults. African American adults have among the highest prevalence of hypertension in the world. Among non-Hispanic black men and women, the age-adjusted prevalence of hypertension was 44.9% and 46.1%, respectively." (AHA, 2016 stats update)

When looking at the blood pressure numbers, the top number is the systolic reading, which represents the arterial pressure when the heart is contracting and forcing the blood through the arteries. The bottom number is the diastolic reading, which represents the force of the blood on the arteries while the heart is relaxing between beats. In 2003 new blood pressure guidelines were issued, with a new "prehypertensive" category identified (refer back to Figure 3.15). A blood pressure reading of 115/75 is the new threshold above which cardiovascular complication can occur. The prehypertensive category includes a systolic pressure from 120–139 and a diastolic pressure from 80–89 as a warning zone. If your blood pressure reading is considered prehypertensive, it is time to take action by modifying your lifestyle. Any reading consistently over 139/89 mm Hg is high blood pressure and indicates a high risk. A consistent reading of 180/110 is considered a hypertensive crisis. With persons over 50 years old, a systolic reading of 140 or above is a more important CVD risk factor than the diastolic reading (JNC VII).

Hypertension cannot be cured, but it can be successfully treated and controlled. Most people with hypertension have additional risk factors for cardiovascular disease. Some of the risk factors for high blood pressure include Hispanic or African American heritage, older age, family history, a diet high in fat and sodium, alcoholism, stress, obesity, and inactivity. Exercise has been shown to help symptoms of high blood pressure in mild to moderate hypertension.

> If you don't smoke, don't start. **If you do smoke, get help to quit now!** Many effective programs, nicotine patches, and other medications are available to help you quit. As soon as you stop smoking, your risk of heart disease starts to drop. In time your risk will be about the same as if you'd never smoked.

Anatomy of a heart attack

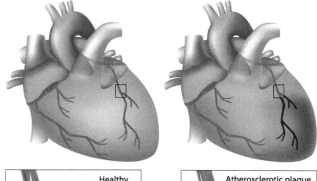

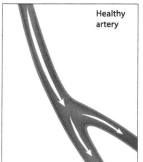
Healthy artery

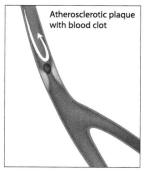
Atherosclerotic plaque with blood clot

Heart Attack

A heart attack or **myocardial infarction** occurs when an artery that provides the heart muscle with oxygen becomes blocked or flow is decreased. The area of the heart muscle served by that artery does not receive adequate oxygen and becomes injured and may eventually die. The heart attack may be so small as to be imperceptible by the victim, or so massive that the victim will die. It is often reported that heart attack victims delay seeking medical help with the onset of symptoms. Every minute counts! In one study, men waited an average of three hours before seeking help. Women waited four hours. It is important to seek medical help at the first sign of a heart attack.

Women who smoke and take oral contraceptives are ten times more likely to have a heart attack (Payne and Hahn). "Smoking and oral contraceptives (OC) appear to act synergistically in increasing the risk of arterial thrombotic disease, particularly in heavy smokers and with old OC formulations," Ojvind Lidegaard reported in 1998. In addition to the classic symptoms of heart attack listed in the box on page 85, women were more likely than men to report throat discomfort, pressing on the chest, and vomiting.

Exercise is the cornerstone therapy for the primary prevention, treatment, and control of hypertension, according to the Position Stand *Exercise and Hypertension* released from the American College of Sports Medicine (ACSM). Adults with hypertension should seek to gain at least thirty minutes of moderate-intensity physical activity on most, if not all, days of the week, but they should be evaluated, treated, and monitored closely.

Each person may experience heart disease in a different way and unfortunately, a fatal sudden cardiac arrest may be the only symptom. Heart attack symptoms for women may be different than the classic symptoms that are commonly known such as chest, jaw, or left arm pain with shortness of breath and weakness. Women may experience more subtle symptoms such as fatigue, depression, back pain, or pain throughout the chest. Don't wait to get help, as time is critical when experiencing a heart attack.

Some findings suggest that **coronary collateral circulation** is increased with regular physical activity (Corbin and Welk). This increased vascularization may decrease the risk of having a heart attack, as well as increase the chances of survival if a heart attack does occur. This happens because the new vessels, which form as a result of exercise, can take over if a major coronary artery is blocked. Since 1951, the death rate from heart attacks has declined by 51 percent, yet more Americans die from coronary artery disease than from any other disease. Both treatment and prevention for heart attacks has increased due to revolutionary new surgical treatments, new drugs, and new information about the etiology of heart disease. Many of the drugs reserved for treating cardiac patients in the past are now used as aggressive prevention in high-risk patients.

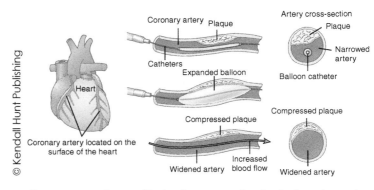

Coronary artery with balloon angioplasty treatment

Stroke

Do you know the warning signs of a stroke? There is a public awareness campaign to increase knowledge of stroke warning signs and symptoms (see box below).

Stroke, or more recently called "**brain attack**," is the fifth leading cause of death affecting 795,000 Americans per year and 80% of stroke deaths are preventable (AHA, 2016). This occurs when the vessels that supply the brain with nutrients become damaged or occluded and the brain tissue dies because of insufficient oxygen. The cerebral artery, the main supply of nutrients to the brain, can be narrowed due to atherosclerosis. The conditions that precipitate stroke may take years to develop. Stroke has the same risk factors as heart disease. Hypertension is the most notable risk factor. Like heart disease, conditions favorable to stroke also respond favorably to exercise. Ischemic (thrombosis and embolism) strokes are the most common form of stroke (87 percent) and occur as a result of a blockage to the cerebral artery (AHA, 2016). The process is similar to that which occurs in a heart attack. Intracerebral hemorrhage, or aneurysm, in which the vessel may rupture and cause bleeding inside the head and result in pressure on the brain, are 10 percent of strokes. Three percent of strokes are caused by hemorrhage. The least common form of stroke results from compression that can occur as a result of a hemorrhage or brain tumor. African Americans have the highest risk at 44% (AHA). African Americans also have a high incidence of stroke risk factors such as high blood pressure and they tend to develop high blood pressure at an earlier age (AHA, 2016). On the average, someone in the United States has a stroke every forty seconds, and every four minutes someone dies of a stroke (AHA, 2016). One-third of

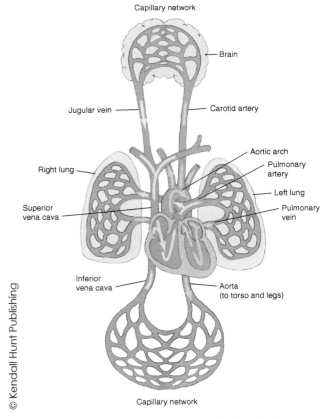

The circulatory system: a network of arteries, capillaries, and veins

all stroke victims die, one-third of stroke victims suffer permanent disability, and one-third of stroke victims gradually return to their normal daily routines (Bishop and Aldana). Stroke is also a leading cause of serious disability. Various studies have shown significant trends toward lower stroke risk with moderate and high levels of leisure time physical activity.

Acting F.A.S.T. Is Key for Stroke

Acting F.A.S.T. can help stroke patients get the treatments they desperately need. The most effective stroke treatments are only available if the stroke is recognized and diagnosed within 3 hours of the first symptoms. If you think someone may be having a stroke, act F.A.S.T.[1] and do the following simple test:

F—Face:	Ask the person to smile. Does one side of the face droop?
A—Arms:	Ask the person to raise both arms. Does one arm drift downward?
S—Speech:	Ask the person to repeat a simple phrase. Is their speech slurred or strange?
T—Time:	If you observe any of these signs, call 9-1-1 immediately.

Note the time when any symptoms first appear. Some treatments for stroke only work if given in the first 3 hours after symptoms appear. Do not drive to the hospital or let someone else drive you. Call an ambulance so that medical personnel can begin life-saving treatment on the way to the emergency room.

Signs of a stoke could be sudden numbness or weakness in one side of the body, sudden confusion, sudden trouble seeing, sudden trouble walking or loss of balance or a sudden severe headache with no known cause.

Make sure you know the risk factors for having a stroke. Do you know the signs and symptoms of a brain attack? Although it is much more common to suffer a stroke as you age, a stroke is possible at any age. If you suspect someone is having a stroke, alert medical personnel immediately. Time to treatment is critical.

Risk Factors for Cardiovascular Disease

Controllable Risk Factors

- ***Cigarette Smoking***—Smokers have two to four times the risk of developing cardiovascular disease than do nonsmokers (AHA, 2016). Cigarette smoking is the most "potent" of the preventable risk factors. Former U.S. Surgeon General C. Everett Koop claims that cigarette smoking is the number one preventable cause of death and disease in the United States and the most important health issue of our time. Women who smoke have a 25% higher risk of developing heart disease than do men (AHA, 2016). Smoking accounts for 50 percent of the female deaths due to heart attack before the age of 55 (Rosato).

- **Hypertension**—The AHA (2016) reports that approximately 76.4 million American adults and children have high blood pressure. Reports from the Harvard Alumni Study show that subjects who did not engage in vigorous sports or activity were 35 percent more likely to develop hypertension than those who were regularly active. Untreated hypertension damages your arteries and can lead to many health complications besides heart disease. Hypertension is the most important modifiable risk factor for stroke.
- **Cholesterol**—Dietary cholesterol contributes to blood serum cholesterol (cholesterol circulating in the blood), which can contribute to heart disease. Every 1 percent reduction in serum cholesterol can result in a 2–3 percent reduction in the risk of heart disease (AHA, 2016). To lower cholesterol, reduce intake of dietary saturated fat, increase consumption of soluble fiber, maintain a healthy weight, do not smoke, and exercise regularly.
- **Inactivity**—Physical inactivity can be very debilitating to the human body. The changes brought about by the aging process can be simulated in a few weeks of bed rest for a young person. Aerobic exercise on a regular basis can favorably influence the other modifiable risk factors for heart disease. Consistent, moderate amounts of physical activity can promote health and longevity. The Surgeon General's report (Satcher, 1996) states that as few as 150 extra calories expended daily exercising can dramatically decrease CVD risk.
- **Obesity**—Highly correlated to heart disease, mild to moderate obesity is associated with an increase in risk of CVD. Fat distribution can also predict higher risk. A waist-to-hip ratio that is greater than 1.0 for men and greater than 0.8 for women constitutes a higher risk because abdominal fat is more easily mobilized and dispersed into the bloodstream, thereby elevating serum cholesterol levels. A BMI over 30 is considered obese.
- **Diabetes**—At least 68% of people age 65 or older with diabetes die from some form of heart disease: and 16% die of stroke (AHA, 2016). Exercise is critical to help increase the sensitivity of the body's cells to insulin.

Health Risks of Obesity
Each of the diseases listed below is followed by the percentage of cases that are caused by obesity.

Colon cancer	10%
Breast cancer	11%
Hypertension	33%
Heart disease	70%
Diabetes	90%
(Type II, non-insulin-dependent)	

As these statistics show, being obese greatly increases the risk of many serious and even life-threatening diseases.

Famed television host **David Letterman** was not overweight when he had quintuple bypass surgery at age 52 in 2000. Although Mr. Letterman didn't look like the typical person who has a heart attack, he had several risk factors going against him. He had a family history—his father, Harry, died of a heart attack in his 50's. Mr. Letterman had high cholesterol. Most likely his job would be considered high stress. David Letterman credits Dr. Wayne Isom, who operated on his heart, with saving his life. In an interview with another talk show host, Larry King (who coincidentally also was operated on by Dr. Isom for quadruple bypass surgery) asked Dr. Isom what was important in avoiding heart disease. Besides exercise, controlling stress, managing weight, and eating well, Dr. Isom said that attitude is very, very important. Post-heart surgery, the patient must decide for himself that he is going to get well. An important part of cardiac rehabilitation is a *positive attitude*.

Uncontrollable Risk Factors

- *Age*—Risk of CVD rises as a person ages.
- *Gender*—Men have a higher risk than women until women reach postmenopausal age. Remember that CVD is an equal opportunity killer!
- *Heredity*—A family history of heart disease will increase risk.

Contributing Risk Factors

- *Stress*—Although difficult to measure in concrete form, stress is considered a factor in the development and acceleration of CVD. Without stress-management techniques, constant stress can manifest itself in a physical nature in the human body. Stress contributes to many of today's illnesses.
- *Triglycerides*—Most of the fat in the human body is stored in the form of triglycerides. Elevated triglyceride levels are thought to increase CVD risk by being involved in the plaque formation of atherosclerosis.

Obesity

Since 1979 the World Heath Organization (WHO) has classified obesity as a disease. "Obesity is a complex condition, one with serious social and psychological dimensions, that affects virtually all age and socioeconomic groups and threatens to overwhelm both developed and developing countries. "In 2014, more than 1.9 billion adults aged 18 years and older were overweight. Of these over 600 million adults were obese" (WHO, 2016). "Globesity" may be the new term coined for the world's heavy populations. While malnutrition still contributes to an estimated 60 percent of deaths in children ages 5 and under globally, in the United States the excess body weight and physical inactivity that leads to obesity cause more than 112,000 deaths each year, making obesity and being overweight together the second leading cause of death in our county.

Figure 5.9 shows the prevalence of obesity among adults aged ≥20 years, by race/ethnicity and sex in the United States during 2009–2010, according to the National Health and Nutrition Examination Survey. Among adults aged ≥20 years in 2009–2010, 35.5% of men and 35.8% of women were obese. Among men, 38.8% of non-Hispanic blacks, 37.0% of Hispanics, and 36.2% of non-Hispanic whites were obese. Among women, 58.5% of non-Hispanic blacks, 41.4% of Hispanics, and 32.3% of non-Hispanic whites were obese.

Obesity causes, contributes to, and complicates many of the diseases that afflict Americans. Obesity is associated with a shortened life, serious organ impairment, poor self-concept, and a higher risk of cardiovascular disease and diabetes, as well as colon and breast cancer. Additional obesity and overweight related issues are osteoarthritis, sleep apnea, gallbladder disease, insulin resistance, potential pregnancy and/or menstrual complications, surgical risk and social discrimination. These factors can affect the quality of a person's life in a negative manner.

Fat distribution is related to health risk (Canoy, 2007). "Apples" describe male-fat patterned distribution with fat accumulating mostly around the torso. "Pears" describe female-fat patterned distribution with fat accumulating mostly on the hips and upper thighs (see Figure 5.10). Apples have a higher health risk especially if they have visceral fat located around internal organs.

Examples of Lifestyle Activity: Looking for Opportunities to Expend More Calories

- Taking the stairs instead of the elevator.
- Parking farther from your destination to increase walking distance.
- Walking rather than riding.
- Vacuuming with vigor, taking big lunging steps.
- Doing sit-ups during the commercials of your favorite program.
- Playing Frisbee or planting a garden instead of watching TV.

FIGURE 5.9

Prevalence of Obesity Among Adults Aged ≥20 Years, by Race/Ethnicity and Sex—National Health and Nutrition Examination Survey, United States, 2009–2010

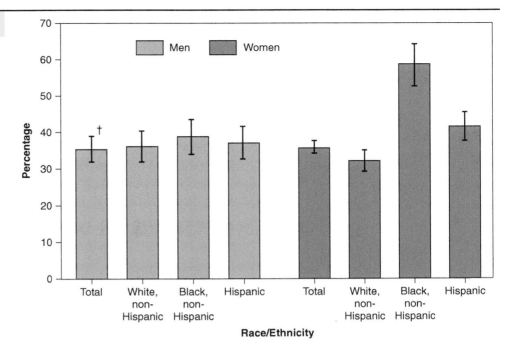

Source: National Health and Nutrition Examination Survey, 2009–2010.

FIGURE 5.10

Body Shape and Associated Health Risk

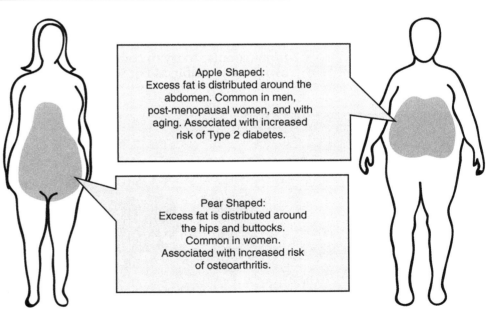

Apple Shaped:
Excess fat is distributed around the abdomen. Common in men, post-menopausal women, and with aging. Associated with increased risk of Type 2 diabetes.

Pear Shaped:
Excess fat is distributed around the hips and buttocks. Common in women. Associated with increased risk of osteoarthritis.

Source: From National Institute of Diabetes and Kidney Disease.

Teens, Sleep, and Blood Pressure In the News

A new study finds that teens who get too little sleep or erratic sleep may elevate their blood pressure. "Our study underscores the high rate of poor quality and inadequate sleep in adolescence coupled with the risk of developing high blood pressure and other health problems which may lead to cardiovascular disease," says Susan Redline, M.D., professor of medicine and pediatrics and director of University Hospital's Sleep Center at Case Western Reserve University in Cleveland, Ohio. Researchers say technology in bedrooms (phone, games, computers, music) may be part of the problem (AHA, 2008).

Childhood Obesity

We are a society of excesses. Unfortunately, everyone seems to be getting bigger—all ages, sexes, races independent of socioeconomic status, gender, or locale. The increase in overweight children causes the most concern. For some parents, childhood obesity has become a bigger concern than smoking or drug abuse. In the last 30 years, school age children (ages 6–11) have increased obesity rates from 4% to 20%. "According to 2011 to 2012 data from NHANES (NCHS), the overall prevalence of obesity. . . for children aged 6 to 11 years, prevalence was 17.7%. . ." (AHA, 2016 stats update).

The causes of **childhood obesity** are complex. As with adult obesity, the bottom line is that if there is a caloric intake surplus, weight will be gained. Infants can be overfed, toddlers can be pacified with candy, and teenagers love soft drinks and junk food. Overweight parents are more likely to have overweight children because the children learn eating and activity patterns from parents. To try to combat childhood obesity, adults should look at their own lifestyle habits: 44 oz sodas several times a day, fast food throughout each week, and lots of time spent playing video games, watching hours of Netflix, or staring at smart phones continuously will increase the risk of obesity for children and adults alike. These behaviors are not the way to encourage kids to become healthy. Simple things such as eating balanced meals together at home, recreating as a family, and not having junk food always accessible at home are good places to start. Childhood obesity can have a negative impact on overall health risk including psychosocial consequences. Perhaps as individuals, families, schools, communities, and as a nation we should emphasize being more active. Overweight by some arbitrary standard may or

may not mean cardiovascular or diabetic risk. Sedentary living, however, almost always predicates poor health in the future, if not sooner. "School aged youth should participate daily in 60 minutes or more of moderate to vigorous physical activity that is developmentally appropriate, enjoyable, and involves a variety of activities" (*Journal of Pediatrics*, 2005). How ironic that we should have to tell our kids to go out and play! Adults would do well to follow this same advice.

In regards to aging, if a young adult is overweight then the odds are he or she will be overweight or obese in middle age and older. Established patterns in life are difficult to change. Tim Spector (St Thomas Hospital in London, UK) reported in *The Lancet* that obesity may accelerate the aging process. Spector found dramatic differences in obese and lean women in the length of the telomeres on the end of their white blood cell chromosomes (see information regarding telomeres in Chapter 6). The difference was over 8 years of aging. Spector also found that smokers were biologically older than non-smokers by 4.6 years, according to telomere length. Losing weight or quitting smoking can slow the loss of telomere length. Poor lifestyle choices can have a synergistic effect and contribute to aging, however it is prudent to focus on the fact that positive lifestyle choices also can have a positive synergistic effect on both quality of life and the aging process.

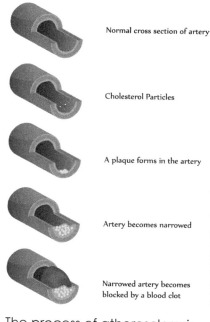

Normal cross section of artery

Cholesterol Particles

A plaque forms in the artery

Artery becomes narrowed

Narrowed artery becomes blocked by a blood clot

The process of atherosclerosis can start at an early age

The Surgeon General Encourages Americans to **Know Their Health History**—In the fall of 2008 the acting Surgeon General encouraged all Americans to take advantage of family gatherings to speak with family members to discuss, identify, and make a record of health problems that seem to run in the family. Doing this can offer insight into your health risk. Check out the Web-based tool "My Family Health Portrait" at www.hhs.gov/familyhistory/

Causes of Obesity

Is it your genes or your fast-food lunches every day? Most likely it is both. Since you cannot change who your parents are, change your lifestyle habits. *Physical inactivity is certainly a major, if not the primary, cause of obesity in the United States today* (Wilmore, 1994). Most often caloric intake exceeds caloric expenditure. Glandular disorders affect 2 percent of the obese population. Genetically we are predisposed to a certain somatotype, fat distribution, size, and weight.

In every person, body weight is the result of many factors; genetic, metabolic, behavioral, environmental, cultural as well as socioeconomic influences (Surgeon General, 2005). An individual's lifestyle choices can help to modify these tendencies. Nineteen out of twenty overweight teenagers will be overweight adults (Texas A&M University Human Nutrition Conference, 1998).

Let's Move! America's Move to Raise a Healthier Generation of Kids

The health of American children should be a bipartisan initiative in every administration

Today's kids live differently than kids raised a generation ago. Most children, 30 years ago, walked to and from school, had homemade meals at home, and maybe one snack a day (3–6 snacks are common today). Fast food meals were a rarity. Kids played at recess and had gym class. Today, budget cuts require gym class, librarians, and after-school activities to be cut. Sweetened drinks are the norm for many kids and can be a source of extra calories. Parents are busy and the average American child spends 7.5 hours with electronic devices for entertainment. Less than 1/3 of high school students get the recommended amount of daily physical activity. In the last 30 years, our society has changed dramatically.

With the Let's Move! Campaign, the goal is to end the epidemic of childhood obesity in one generation. Mrs. Obama hopes kids can put "play" back into their lives by having the children experience "that exercise and eating good stuff" can be fun. The first lady quoted a young 7-year-old Penacook, New Hampshire resident, Caitlyn Habel, remarking that, "I like being able to play games before school because it's really fun and it helps me wake up my heart." 3/9/12 (whitehouse.gov/the press-office)

It has taken 3 decades to create an environment where childhood obesity rates have tripled. Programs such as Let's Move! strive to work with schools, families, communities, and the corporate sector to change the circumstances for this generation and also for generations to come. So choose to get involved in your community. Ask a kid to help you plant a community garden!

"The physical and emotional health of an entire generation and the economic health and security of our nation is at stake." —First Lady Michelle Obama at the Let's Move! Launch on February 9, 2010.

Olivier Douliery/MCT/Newscom

Physiological Response to Obesity

For an obese person, more blood vessels are needed to circulate blood. The heart has to pump harder, therefore increasing blood pressure. Extra weight can be tough on the musculoskeletal joints, causing problems with arthritis, gout, bone and joint diseases, varicose veins, gallbladder disease, as well as complications during pregnancy. Obese individuals often are heat intolerant and experience shortness of breath during heavy exercise. Obesity increases most cancer risks (Bishop and Aldana, 1999).

Activity Permissive Learning Environment: An Active Mind Requires an Active Body

One simple thing can help a child build and maintain healthy bones, muscles, reduce risk of injury, weight gain and chronic diseases, reduce feelings of depression and anxiety and promote feelings of well-being. What is that one thing? PURPOSEFUL MOVEMENT! Instead of hearing "sit down, be still" during class, Activity Permissive Learning Environments (APLE) encourage movement. They encourage movements like standing, rocking, fidgeting and walking. We now have scientific evidence that our bodies are so connected to our minds that our ability to focus on difficult cognitive tasks is directly linked to adequate physical activity. Active workstations reduce disruptive behavior problems and increase students' attention. When students are learn at a desk which allows them to stand with a footstool and also to have a seated option (called stand-biased workstations), not only does learning improve but so does their health.

"After adjusting for grade, race and gender, the group of children that had stand-biased desks for two consecutive years had a decreased BMI percentile change of 5.24 compared to the group that had standard desks for both years. The difference is statistically significant with a p-value of 0.037. This may be the most profound health outcome discovered by our team working with these 500 elementary school students. BMI can be impacted by small daily movements and those small daily movements can be directly enhanced by school design. Students that moved more at the standing desks compared to other more traditional desks also improved their step count by more than 2,000 steps per day." ~Mark Benden

Technology-Induced Inactivity is a term that Dr. Mark Benden at the TAMU Ergonomics Center has coined to refer to our progressive dependence on machines for acts of daily living. Savvy school districts should make sure kids are active every day – perhaps someday soon college campuses will also have stand-based work stations in every classroom.

Contributed by Mark Benden. Copyright © Kendall Hunt Publishing Company.

Photo courtesy of Stand2Learn

Stand2Learn Desks being used in College Station, Texas

"Standing for eight hours a day adds up to 160 calories, the equivalent of a half-hour walk. Over weeks and years, the energetic difference between mostly sitting and standing is staggering."
Daniel Lieberman,
The Story of the Human Body

Cancer

Cancer is characterized by the uncontrollable growth and spread of abnormal cells. Cancer cells do not follow the normal code of DNA that is encrypted in noncancerous cells.

Who Gets Cancer?

"Cancer is the second most common cause of death in the US, exceeded only by heart disease, and accounts for nearly 1 of every 4 deaths" (American Cancer Society, *Cancer Facts and Figures 2016*). Possibly in the future people will be able to go to the doctor for a simple blood test to determine whether they will have cancer or not. Unfortunately there seems to be no rhyme or reason for some cancer cases. Lifestyle choices, as well as heredity and also luck, play a big role in a person's risk of developing cancer. Even personality can influence if a person is prone to cancer. With health promotion and prevention, fewer people may develop cancer, and more cancer patients may survive.

Can Cancer Be Prevented?

It is theorized that 80 percent of cancers can be prevented with positive lifestyle choices. Avoiding tobacco and over-exposure to sunlight are two major examples. Eating a varied diet, consuming antioxidants, having a positive attitude, and participating in regular physical activity are simple choices that can have a large impact on cancer prevention. Cancer is the second leading cause of death in the United States, accounting for nearly 1 in 4 deaths (AHA, 2016).

Does Exercise Help?

Recognition of the potential of exercise to prevent cancer came in 1985 when the American Cancer Society began recommending exercise to protect against cancer. Regular activity has been shown to reduce risk of colon cancer (see Table 5.1). Active people have lower death rates from cancer than inactive people—50 to 250 percent lower. Colon, breast, rectal, and prostate cancers each have an established link with inactivity.

Can You Make a Difference?

Get involved in your local school district as an activist for good health. When school budgets are tight, P.E. teachers are often the first to be let go. Often we think one person can't make a difference. Molly Barker didn't let that stop her from forming a grassroots organization that targets the emotional and the mental fitness as well as developing the physical fitness of young girls. The program, called **Girls on the Run**, is a twelve-week program that culminates in the participants running or walking a 5-km road race. The road race is secondary to what the girls experience in the twelve weeks leading up to the race. Positive preteen emotional development is the focus. The girls might warm up by running/walking around a track, and then have focused girl talk. They discuss positive people in their lives. Issues such as pressures to look a certain way, anorexia, bullying, nutrition, the role of women in society, and what makes each girl special are contemplated as a group. *Girls on the Run* is now in over one-hundred cities across Canada and the United States. One person can make a difference. Be a good role model for your kids, your siblings, your relatives, for any children that you come in contact with. Like Molly Barker, choose to be involved not only with your own health, but also with the health of your community.

TABLE 5.1 ♦ Physical Activity and Cancer

Cancer Type	Effect of Physical Activity
Colon	Exercise speeds movement of food and cancer-causing substances through the digestive system, and reduces prostaglandins (substances linked to cancer in the colon).
Breast	Exercise decreases the amount of exposure of breast tissue to circulating estrogen. Lower body fat is also associated with lower estrogen levels. Early life activity is deemed important for both reasons. Fatigue from therapy is reduced by exercise.
Rectal	Similar to colon cancer, exercise leads to more regular bowel movements and reduces "transit time."
Prostate	Fatigue from therapy is reduced by exercise.

Exercising early in life also seems to have an impact in reducing risk of breast cancer in post-menopausal women. A study at the USC Norris Cancer Center reported that one to three hours of exercise a week over a woman's reproductive lifetime (between the teens and age 40) may result in a 20 to 30 percent risk reduction for breast cancer. Exercise that averaged four or more hours per week resulted in a 60 percent reduction! A woman starting to exercise in her 20's or 30's can also experience reduced risk. Active females, such as a dancer or track athlete, may put off the age of onset of menstruation, and if they continue to be active, they may experience earlier menopause than their inactive counterparts. This results in a lower lifetime exposure to estrogen, which also reduces cancer risk. Ironically lower estrogen levels may contribute to osteoporosis.

It is also thought that exercise can boost immunity that can help kill abnormal cancer cells (Bishop and Aldana). Dr. Steven Blair at the Institute for Aerobics Research in Dallas, Texas, has done long-term epidemiological studies that show rate of death due to cancer is significantly lower in patients with elevated levels of fitness. It must also be noted that people who are active tend to also participate in other healthy behaviors, such as eating a varied diet low in fat and high in fiber. These other behaviors may also influence cancer risk and help those with cancer lead more fulfilling and productive lives. The American Cancer Society reports that people with healthy lifestyles (non-smokers, regular physical activity, and sufficient sleep) have the lowest cancer mortality rates.

> "Exercise is a known remedy for the weakness and low spirits that cancer patients experience during their recovery. It boosts energy and endurance, and also builds confidence and optimism. But, within the past five years, several medical investigations have revealed a surprising new fact: Exercise may also help prevent cancer" (Rosato, 1994).

Diabetes

Diabetes is a disorder that involves high blood sugar levels and inadequate insulin production by the pancreas or inadequate utilization of insulin by the cells. "A total of 1.7 million new cases of diabetes (type 1 or type 2) were diagnosed in the US adults (greater than or equal to) 20 years of age in 2012" (AHA 2016 Stats Update). Type II diabetes will be discussed in this chapter.

"Between 2001 and 2009, the prevalence of type 2 Diabetes in youths increased by 30.5%" (2017 AHA update)

© Lapina/Shutterstock.com

Who Gets Diabetes?

Eighty percent of the adults who develop Type II diabetes are obese (Surgeon General, 2005). The mortality rate is greater in diabetics with CVD—68% of people with diabetes die from some form of CVD. Each year, 1.6 million new cases of diabetes are diagnosed (AHA, 2012). Diabetes is the seventh leading cause of death in people over 40 (Corbin and Welk, 2009). Due to the surge in childhood obesity in the past several decades, children are more at risk for diabetes. Diabetes is one of the most important risk factors for stroke in women.

Can Diabetes Be Prevented?

Research shows that changing lifestyle habits to decrease risk for heart disease also decreases risk for diabetes. "According to research, a seven percent loss of body weight and 150 minutes of moderate-intensity physical activity a week can reduce the chance of developing diabetes by 58 percent in those who are at high risk. These lifestyle changes cut the risk of developing type II diabetes regardless of age, ethnicity, gender, or weight." Type II diabetes may account for 90–95 percent of all diagnosed cases of diabetes (AHA, 2012).

Does Exercise Help?

Exercise plays an important role in managing this disease, as exercise helps control body fat and improves insulin sensitivity and glucose tolerance. Exercise does not prevent Type II diabetes; however, exercise does help manage the disorder.

Aging and Diabetes

Having diabetes is an additional challenge to the aging adult. There is even more reason to stay vigilant about eating well, staying active and monitoring blood glucose. Having a diabetes management checklist including medication dosage, medical appointments, blood glucose measurements, meal planning and exercise is recommended. According to the AHA 2016 update, of adults over 65 with diabetes, 68% die of some form of CVD and 16% die of stroke.

Diabetic Walkers Gain Fitness

Diabetics who **walked moderately for thirty-eight minutes** (4,400 steps or 2.2 miles) did not lose weight; however, they showed significant effects: risk of heart disease decreased; cholesterol improved; triglycerides improved; and they saved $288.00 in health costs per year.

© Tyler Olson, 2012, Shutterstock, Inc.

Diabetics who **walked ninety minutes** (10,000 steps or 5 miles) saw bigger benefits: the number of walkers needing insulin therapy decreased by 25 percent; those receiving insulin therapy reduced the dosage by an average of eleven units per day; cholesterol, triglycerides, blood pressure, and heart disease risk decreased; and they saved over $1,200.00 per year.

Diabetics in the control group that **walked 0 minutes** saw health care costs rise $500.00; insulin use, cholesterol, blood pressure, triglycerides, and heart disease risk all increased. This study was conducted for two years. (Sullivan et al., 2009)

Metabolic Syndrome

Moderate and vigorous activity is associated with a lower risk of developing **metabolic syndrome**. Metabolic syndrome is a "cluster" of cardiovascular risk factors including overweight or obesity (waist circumference above 102 cm for men or above 88 cm for women), high blood pressure (above 130/85 mm Hg or current drug treatment for hypertension), elevated triglycerides (150 mg/dL or higher), low levels of high-density lipoprotein (below 40 mg/dL in men and below 50 mg/dL in women or undergoing drug treatment for reduced HDL-C), and high fasting glucose levels (100 mg/dL or higher) (AHA, 2016). Having three or more of these risk factors puts you at higher risk of developing CVD or diabetes. In studies done at the Cooper Institute in Dallas, the risk of metabolic syndrome for men with moderate fitness was 26 percent lower, and for men with high fitness the risk was 53 percent lower compared to their lower fitness counterparts. For women the risk was 20 percent and 63 percent lower, respectively. It is clear that to prevent metabolic syndrome, improving cardiovascular fitness through regular physical activity is critical. Also called Syndrome X, the prevalence of metabolic syndrome goes up with age. This set of symptoms is very similar to prediabetes.

Nonalcoholic fatty liver disease (NAFLD), also called hepatic steatosis, is characterized by excess fat in the cells of the liver which is not caused by alcohol. Excess consumption of fat and sugar in the diet and a sedentary lifestyle are considered to be the cause. The liver plays an important role as a filter for your blood and is the second largest organ in your body. NAFLD is characterized by overweight, obesity, diabetes, high cholesterol, or high triglycerides, and therefore it is also associated with metabolic syndrome. Abdominal fat is called visceral fat. Excess visceral fat increases the amount of fatty acids that the fat cells secrete, and the fatty acids are dumped through a circulation portal to the liver. If the liver becomes swollen, scarring or cirrhosis may occur which over time could lead to liver failure. Although NAFLD may be asymptomatic, excess fatigue can be a sign of NAFLD and a blood test indicating high liver enzymes may indicate further testing. Both prevention and treatment currently consist of eating a healthy diet and exercising to maintain a healthy weight.

Low Back Pain

Low back pain is characterized by chronic discomfort in the lumbar region of the back. Chronic back pain may be the result of an injury; however, back pain is most often due to a lack of fitness. The National Safety Council data indicates that the back is the most frequently injured of all the body parts, with the injury rate double that of other body parts. Intervertebral disks can suffer degeneration from overuse, which is more common in men than in women. Backache is the second leading medical complaint when visiting a physician for people under the age of 45 (ACSM, 2015).

© Syda Productions/Shutterstock.com

Who Suffers from Low Back Pain?

More than eight out of ten Americans will suffer some back-related pain at some point in their lifetime (Corbin and Welk, 2009). Low back pain is epidemic throughout the world and is the major cause of disability in people aged 20 through 45 in the United States. Ninety percent of back injuries occur in the lumbar region (Donatelle and Davis, 2007). Thirty to 70 percent of all Americans have recurring back problems; two million Americans cannot hold a job as a result. Back pain is the most frequent cause of inactivity in individuals under the age of 45 (Corbin and Welk, 2009). Improper lifting, faulty work habits, heredity, diseases such as scoliosis, and excess weight are other causes of low back pain. Undue psychological stress can cause back pain via tight muscles and constricted blood vessels (Hoeger et al., 2009).

© Marcin Balcerzak/Shutterstock.com

Can Low Back Pain Be Prevented?

Lack of activity is the most common reason for low back pain, so movement is critical to good back health. Staying active, using common sense regarding lifting heavy objects, and managing weight all are important in low back pain prevention. Decrease occupational risks. Use caution, as it is often employees new to a job who injure their back. Another factor in low back pain is poor posture while sitting, standing, or walking. If your job requires extensive hours of sitting, consider a stand up desk. Try using a footstool and adjusting the height of the desk so your forearms are at about 90 degrees. This option allows you to burn more calories and helps to prevent "sitting disease" a 21st century phenomenon. If you must sit for long periods of time, try getting up briefly to move and stretch. Some office workers have light weights at their desk and take a five minute muscle break each hour. Another option is to consider trying office yoga.

Does Exercise Help?

Exercise helps with enhancing posture, balance, strength, and flexibility. Strengthening abdominal muscles, which are the complimentary muscle group to the lower back, helps support the spine. Stretching the hip flexors and the hamstrings are important to help tilt the anterior portion of the pelvis back. Low back pain and tight hamstrings are highly correlated. Excess weight around the torso and abdominal region pulls the pelvis forward, causing potential strain in the lumbar region. In general, strengthening the "core" (all the muscles from the shoulders and the hips) helps prevent back pain. **Sarcopenia** is the loss of skeletal muscle mass and functional strength often associated with aging. Around 50 years of age, muscle deteriorates about 5% every decade thereafter. The upside is that "mature" muscle responds positively to a regular strength training and flexibility program to help manage weight over a lifetime.

Osteoporosis

Osteoporosis is a disease characterized by low bone density and structural deterioration of bone tissue, which can lead to increased bone fragility and increased risk of fractures to the skeletal structure. Osteoporosis is sometimes called the "silent disease" because there are often no symptoms as bone density decreases. In a 2001 article, the *Dallas Morning News* called osteoporosis an "epidemic of young women with old bones." Many young women delay the onset of menstruation due to high activity levels, which in turn lowers body fat and estrogen levels. Your physician may recommend a bone mineral density test. The test is noninvasive, painless, and safe.

How much calcium does a college student need? **1,300 mg daily**

- Good sources of calcium: low-fat dairy products, dark green leafy vegetables, broccoli, tofu, sardines, and salmon.
- Calcium-fortified foods: cereals, breads, orange juice, and some antacids.

Bone is living, growing tissue. With adequate nutrition and activity, bone formation continues to occur throughout a lifetime. Old bone is removed through **resorption**, and new bone is formed through a process called **formation**. Bones need to be fed and cared for just as the rest of our body. Childhood and teenage years are when new bone is developed more quickly than the old bone is resorbed. Bones become stronger and denser until peak bone mass is attained at approximately age 30. Thereafter, bone loss exceeds bone formation. **Osteopenia** is low bone mass that precedes osteoporosis. Note that weak, porous and brittle bones are a condition, not a disease. Adequate calcium intake, minimal exposure to sunlight for vitamin D, and regular physical activity are critical for young adults because the higher peak bone mass is at age 30, the less likely it is that osteoporosis will develop in later years.

Who Gets Osteoporosis?

"In the United States today, more than 53 million people either already have osteoporosis or are at high risk due to low bone mass" (NIH, 2016). Considered to afflict mostly women, this disease can affect males as well. Of the women with osteoporosis, 80 percent are post-menopausal. One out of two women and one out of eight men over 50 will get osteoporosis in their lifetime.

Weight-bearing exercise helps both prevent and treat osteoporosis.

Risk increases with age. Have you observed older women who seem to slump? Many women with low bone density have **kyphosis** (also called dowager's hump), or a rounding of the upper back. The head tilts forward because often the cervical vertebrae in the upper spine actually suffer compression fractures. This keeps older women from being able to stand up straight or to get a full breath. Small, thin-boned women are at higher risk, and there may also be a genetic factor. If there are people in a family with weak, thin bones then relatives with the same body type may have an inherently higher risk. Post-menopausal Caucasian and Asian women are at the highest risk. It is unknown why these particular groups are more susceptible to osteoporosis. African Americans have bone that is 10 percent more dense than Caucasians (Greenberg et al.). Others at risk include those with poor diets, especially if calcium and vitamin D are low over a long period of time. It is estimated that 75 percent of adults do not consume enough calcium on a daily basis. An inactive lifestyle contributes greatly. A history of excessive use of alcohol or cigarette smoking can also increase risk.

Another growing group of high-risk individuals is the eating disordered. Many active young women suffer stress fractures, which can be a sign of osteoporosis. If a person is extremely active with a low percentage of body fat, then hormone levels may be askew. Prolonged **amenorrhea** (absence of menstruation) can signal low body fat or an eating disorder. If symptoms such as amenorrhea, disordered eating, or abuse of exercise are suspected, then it would be prudent for the physician to order or for the athlete to consider asking for a bone density test.

Can Osteoporosis Be Prevented?

The good news is that osteoporosis can be both prevented and treated. Regular physical activity reduces the risk of developing osteoporosis. A lifetime of low calcium intake is associated with low bone mass (www.osteo.org). Adequate calcium intake is critical for optimal bone mass. Growing children, adolescents, and pregnant and breast-feeding women need more calcium. It is estimated by the National Institutes of Health that less than 10 percent of girls age 10–17 years are getting the calcium they need each day. A varied diet with green leafy vegetables and plenty of dairy will help ensure good calcium intake. Many calcium-fortified foods are now available. A varied diet will also ensure adequate intake of vitamin D, which aids in prevention.

It is also advisable to limit caffeine and phosphate-containing soda, which may interfere with calcium absorption. Prolonged high-protein diets may also contribute to calcium loss in bone. A high-sodium diet is thought to increase calcium excretion through the kidneys. For post-menopausal women, some physicians consider hormone replacement therapy to help strengthen bones, unless there is a CVD risk. Weightbearing exercise such as walking, running, tennis, and basketball is an excellent way to strengthen bones to help prevent osteoporosis.

Does Exercise Help?

The stress caused by working against gravity during activity strengthens and causes bones to be more dense, just as any other living tissue. Weight-training is highly recommended to keep the bones strong and to build bone mass. Consider the muscle atrophy experienced when a person is confined to bed rest, or a limb that is in a cast for a period of time. Bones deteriorate just as muscles deteriorate without the stimulation of movement. An interesting current topic of study is the effect of zero gravity in space on bone mass. It appears that even a short duration in space can impact bone density (see "Spaceflight Is Bad to the Bone" box below).

Physical activity is presented as the only known intervention that can potentially increase bone mass and strength in the early years of life and reduce the risk of falling in older populations according to a new Position Stand from the American College of Sports Medicine (ACSM, 2014).

Spaceflight Is Bad to the Bone

In the 1980's, NASA scientists observed a dramatic spike in calcium excreted by Space Lab astronauts after the first week of living in the weightless environment of space. Researchers later confirmed that Space Shuttle and early ISS crew members lost bone mineral density (BMD) at a rate 10-fold faster than does the average post-menopausal woman. Studies conducted by Dr. Susan Bloomfield at Texas A&M University demonstrate that this bone loss is not uniform across the skeleton but focused in trabecular ("spongy") bone sites (e.g., in the ends of the long bones, inside spinal vertebrae). This is the same type of bone that is affected most dramatically in osteoporotic patients here on Earth. Sophisticated engineering analyses called finite element modeling using computed tomography (CT) scans of the femoral neck (near the hip joint, site of hip fractures) in ISS crew members revealed a stunning result: the average loss of mechanical strength of the femoral neck in healthy male astronauts over a 6-month mission equaled 25-50% of the loss accrued by Caucasian women over a lifetime of aging! This raises great concern about the increased risk of a hip fracture should that astronaut fall soon after returning to Earth or while working on the distant surface of Mars. Not eating enough calories might be another potential contributor to bone loss in astronauts. Restricting caloric intake by 40% causes reductions in trabecular bone formation rate similar in magnitude to that observed with the mechanical unloading of microgravity. This finding has important implications for the many Americans who attempt long-term restriction of caloric intake to achieve weight loss. Interestingly, Scott Smith of NASA's Nutritional Biochemistry Laboratory at JSC has determined that ISS crew members who regularly engage in vigorous resistance training and eat all assigned food, assuring adequate caloric and Vitamin D intake, experience no losses of femoral BMD. The main challenge for future 3-year exploration missions to destinations like Mars is that space for exercise equipment will be highly limited, so strategic combinations of lower intensity exercise and pharmacological agents may be necessary to minimize fracture risk for astronauts.

Bloomfield, S.A., M.R. Allen, H.A. Hogan, and M.D. Delp. Site- and compartment-specific changes in bone with hindlimb unloading in mature adult rats. Bone 31: 149–157, 2002.

Keyak, J.A., A.K. Koyama, A. LeBlanc, Y. Lu, and T.F. Lang. Ruduction in proximal femoral strength due to long-duration spaceflight. Bone 44:449–453, 2009.

Baek, K., A.A. Barlow, M.R. Allen, and S.A. Bloomfield. *Food restriction and simulated microgravity: effects on bone and serum leptin.* J. Appl. Physiol. 104: 1086–1093. 2008.

Smith, S.M., M.A. Heer, L.C. Shackelford, J.D. Sibonga, L. Ploutz-Snyder, and S.R. Zwart. *Benefits for bone from resistance exercise and nutrition in long-duration spaceflight: Evidence from biochemistry and densitometry.* J. Bone Miner. Res. 27: 1896–1906, 2012.

References

AHA, 2016 stats update - sourced from National Center for Health Statistics. Mortality multiple cause micro-data files, 2013. Public-use data file and documentation. NHLBI tabulations.http://www.cdc.gov/nchs/data_access/Vitalstatsonline.htm#Mortality_Multiple. Accessed May 19, 2015.

Alters, S. and Schiff, W. *Essential Concepts for Healthy Living* (5th ed). Sudbury, MA., Jones and Bartlett. 2009.

American College of Sports Medicine (ACSM). *Exercise and Hypertension.*

American College of Sports Medicine *Strength Training for Bone, Muscle and Hormones* Current Comment, 2014

American Heart Association (AHA). *Poor Teen Sleep Habits May Raise Blood Pressure, Lead to CVD.* News release December 10, 2008.

American Heart Association (AHA). *Heart Disease and Stroke Statistics—2016 Update.* 2016. www.aha.com

Benden, Mark, CPE, PhD Director, TAMU Ergonomics Center, College Station TX 77843

Bergland, Christopher, 4 *Lifestyle Choices That Will Keep You Young*, The Athlete's Way http://www.psychologytoday.com/em/133701

Canoy, M. P. et al. Abdominal Fat Distribution Predicts Heart Disease, *Circulation*, 2007. Castelli, W. P., Chair, Women, smoking and oral contraceptives; Highlights of a consensus conference, Montreal, November 1997.

Center for Health and Health Care in Schools, School of Public Health and Health Services, George Washington University Medical Center. *Childhood Overweight: What the Research Tells Us.* September 2007 Update. *www.healthinschools.org*

Corbin, C. and Welk G. *Concepts of Physical Fitness* (15th ed). New york: McGraw-Hill. 2009.

Crivello, Joseph, *Human Anatomy and Physiology, A Functional Approach*, Kendall Hunt Publishing Co. Dubuque, Iowa, 2014.

Donatelle, R. J. and Davis, L. G. *Access to Health* (10th ed). Boston: Benjamin Cummings. 2007.

Gaesser, G. Obesity, Health, and Metabolic Fitness, *www.thinkmuscle.com/articles*

Gibbs, W. W. Obesity: An Overblown Epidemic? *Scientific American*, May 23, 2005.

Hoeger, W. W. K., Turner, L. W., and Hafen, B. Q. *Wellness Guidelines for a Healthy Lifestyle* (4th ed). Belmont, CA: Thomson Wadsworth. 2009.

http://www.cancer.org/research/cancerfactsstatistics/cancerfactsfigures2016/index

https://www.niams.nih.gov/health_info/Bone/Osteoporosis/osteoporosis_hoh.asp#11

http://www.who.int/mediacentre/factsheets/fs311/en/

Current Recommendations to Decrease Osteoporosis Risk

- Engage in daily weight-bearing aerobic activity
- Weight training (the ACSM recommends ten–twelve reps, two sets two times weekly)
- Vitamin D, 10 micrograms/day ages 51 to 70 and 15 micrograms/day after age 70 (also a well balanced diet and adequate exposure to sunlight)
- 1200 mg Calcium daily

Jiantao Ma, Shih-Jen Hwang, Alison Pedley, Joseph M. Massaro, Udo Hoffmann, Raymond T. Chung, Emelia J. Benjamin, Daniel Levy, Caroline S. Fox, Michelle T. Long. Bi-directional analysis between fatty liver and cardiovascular disease risk factors. *Journal of Hepatology*, 2016; DOI: "http://dx.doi.org/10.1016/j.jhep.2016.09.022"10.1016/j.jhep.2016.09.022.

Juraschek SP, Blaha MJ, Blumenthal RS, Brawner C, Qureshi W, Keteyian SJ, Schairer J, Ehrman JK, Al-Mallah MH. Cardiorespiratory fitness and incident diabetes: the FIT (Henry Ford ExercIse Testing) project. Diabetes Care. 2015;38:1075–1081. doi: 10.2337/dc14-2714.

Lumey LH, Stein AD. Offspring birth weights after maternal intrauterine undernutrition: a comparison within sibships. *Am J Epidemiol* 1997; 146: 810–819.

National Institutes of Health. Osteoporosis and Related Bone Disease, http://www.osteo.org

Ochoa, L. W., editor. Women's Health and Wellness, an Illustrated Guide (26th ed).

Paffenbarger, R. et al. Physical Activity and Physical Fitness as Determinants of Health and Longevity. In C. Bouchard et al. *Exercise Fitness and Health.* Champaign, IL: Human Kinetics Publishers. 1990.

Payne, W. A. and Hahn, D. B. *Understanding Your Health* (6th ed). St. Louis, MO: Mosby. 2000.

Powers, S. K. and Dodd, S. L. *Total Fitness and Wellness.* San Francisco: Pearson Benjamin Cummings. 2014.

Satcher, D. *Surgeon General's Report on Physical Activity and Health.* Atlanta, GA: CDC. 1996.

Sesso, H. D. and Paffenbarger, R. S. The Harvard Alumni Health Study, Harvard School of Public Health. Boston: 1956.

Seventh Report of the Joint National Committee on Prevention, Detection, Evaluation, and Treatment of High Blood Pressure (JNC vII). *Hypertension,* December 2003.

Skokie, IL: Lippincott Williams & Wilkins. 2002.

Speigelman, Bruce, et al., *A PGC1-α-dependent myokine that drives brown-fat-like development of white fat and thermogenesis Nature* 481, 463–468 Published 11 January 2012.

Sullivan, P. W. et. al. Obesity, Inactivity, and the Prevalence of Diabetes and Diabetes-related Cardiovascular Comorbidities in the U.S., 2000–2002, *Diabetes Care,* 28: 1599–1603, 2009.

Surgeon General's Call to Action to Prevent and Decrease Overweight and Obesity, www.surgeongeneral.gov

Surgeon General's Report on Bone Health and Osteoporosis: What It Means to You. Washington, DC: U.S. DHHS. October, 2004.

The Heart Truth for Women: Women and Heart Disease, *www.hearttruth.gov*

Wilmore, J. H. Exercise, Obesity, and Weight Control, *Physical Activity and Research Digest.* Washington D.C.: President's Council on Physical Fitness & Sports. 1994.

World Health Organization (WHO). *Controlling the Obesity Epidemic.* Geneva: Author December 2016.

Chapter 6
Aging and Longevity

© Rawpixel.com/Shutterstock.com

OBJECTIVES

Students will be able to:

- Identify key concepts and findings related to the aging process.
- Determine wellness behaviors that enhance longevity and quality of life.
- Examine how inflammation contributes to conditions associated with aging.

Adaptation of *Health and Fitness: A Guide to a Healthly Lifestyle,* 5th Edition, by Laura Bounds, Gayden Darnell, Kirstin Brekken Shea, and Dottiede Agnor. Copyright © 2012 by Kendall Hunt Publishing Company.

The life expectancy of this baby is almost double that of a baby born one hundred years ago.

Social support, whether with family or friends, plays a significant role in the health of people of all ages.

Gerontologists are scientists who study aging. Aging happens to everyone, but not everyone responds in the same way. Gerontologists are interested in finding out why we age differently: is it nature or nurture or something different? The fact is, people are living longer than ever before and population projections suggest that in 2060, the number of people living that are over 65 years will almost equal the number of people under the age of 15 years. (Uhlenberg, 2013) In this chapter we will look at some factors that impact living long and living well.

In 1997 Jeane Calmaut died at the age of 122.5 years. The French woman is the longest living person in documented history. According to Jan Vijg at Albert Einstein College of Medicine, Jeanne Calmaut was the exception, as maximum human lifespan is expected to be 115 years of age.

The life expectancy for someone born at the beginning of the twenty-first century is almost double the life expectancy of those born at the beginning of the twentieth century. The Centers for Disease Control and Prevention (CDC) has determined that *lifestyle is the single largest factor affecting longevity of life.* "If exercise could be packed into a pill, it would be the single most widely prescribed, and most beneficial, medicine in the nation" (National Institute on Aging). Wellness across the lifespan is dependent on many factors. Meeting all the needs to sustain life is the minimum, with quality and quantity of life determined by many factors. Maintaining a sense of purpose, staying active, staying connected socially, getting adequate rest and nutrition, and being engaged in lifelong learning can help—from childhood through the end of life—to live life well. "Further progress against infectious and chronic diseases may continue boosting average life expectancy, but not maximum lifespan," said Dr. Vijg. "While it's conceivable that therapeutic breakthroughs might extend human longevity beyond the limits we've calculated, such advances would need to overwhelm the many genetic variants that appear to collectively determine the human lifespan. Perhaps resources now being spent to increase lifespan should instead go to lengthening healthspan—the duration of old age spent in good health." Scientists are interested in what influences our **healthspan**. Health span is characterized by maximizing the number of years of our life that we live in good health and good function.

Aging

Although aging is a completely natural and inevitable process, some people age more gracefully than others. As the typical American's lifespan expands, quality of life for many is compromised due to habits and lifestyle choices made earlier in life. Ensure your independence as you age by choosing how you live your life now. Balancing work, family commitments, and leisure time can be stressful. Stress takes a toll on our bodies, our minds, and our relationships. Take time to consider how well are you managing the stress in your life.

Everyone experiences age-related decline regarding the biological functions of the body. Chronological age is our true age in years. Biological age can be different depending on our lifestyle choices. **Biological age** can be younger than chronological age with good nutrition, adequate rest on a regular basis, effective stress-management, and consistent exercise. Biological age can be older than chronological age when unhealthy habits are the norm: poor diet, inadequate sleep, excessive alcohol use, smoking, and obesity. You are in charge of your biological age. What will your biological age be ten, twenty, and thirty years from now? How about fifty years from now? It is interesting to note that physiological changes with aging are similar to those changes seen with inactivity or prolonged weight-lessness, such as experienced by the astronauts (Bloomfield et al., 2017). An integrative biology professor at Berkeley, 78-year-old Marian Diamond, lists five **essentials for staying mentally vigorous:**

1. diet,
2. exercise,
3. challenge,
4. novelty,
5. love.

These five essentials seem to be critical to maintain quality of life at retirement age, but perhaps they are essentials for us all, at any age (Springen and Seibert).

Lack of activity can accelerate age-related muscle and bone loss. However, staying active can do the opposite. Participating in resistance training as an older adult can impact age-related declines often seen in cognition and memory. "Our research found that resistance training could positively affect cognition, information processing, attention, memory formation and executive function" (Chang et al., 2012). *It is clear that as more people live longer, it is possible to live a long healthspan as well as lifespan, but this is not the norm.* Disability in later years is common due to hypokinetic (a disease characterized by sedentary living) conditions such as obesity, high blood pressure and high levels of blood sugar.

Live Long and Live Well to 100 in a Blue Zone

In 2004, Gianni Pes and Michel Poulain completed demographic work identifying a geographic region with the largest proportion of men living past 100. On their map they drew a blue circle to identify the region and thus was born the concept of the Blue Zones. The first region identified was Sardinia in Italy. Dan Buettner, photographer for National Geographic, joined Pes and Poulain and helped identify other regions in the world where it was common to live past 100 years of age and to also live well. Okinawa (Japan), Nicoya (Costa Rica), Icaria (Greece), and Loma Linda (Seventh Day Adventists in California) joined Sardinia (Italy) as being the blue zone "hotspots". Lessons learned from studying these people may be surprising to some. There are nine commonalities that all the Blue Zone residents have:

- they move naturally,
- they have a sense of purpose each day,
- they "downshift" or have routines for daily relaxation,
- they follow the 80% rule, eating only until they fill about 80% full,
- they have a plant-based diet with occasional meat,
- they drink moderately, typically red wine,
- they belong to a faith group,
- they put their families first,
- and they have a tribe or sense of community with social circles that support them.

These attributes together have been termed the "Power 9" by Buettner in his book on the Blue Zones.

The Longevity Project

In 1921, Stanford University psychologist Lewis Terman recruited 1500 of the brightest boys and girls living in the area. Some of the original members in the study are still alive today. He studied many aspects about them, their families, and their environment. Then he followed them continuing to collect

Just 15 Minutes Makes a Difference

© marilyn barbone/Shutterstock.com

"A meta-analysis of 9 cohort studies, representing 122,417 patients, found that as little as 15 minutes of daily moderate to vigorous PA [physical activity] reduced all-cause mortality in adults ≥60 years of age. This protective effect of PA was dose dependent; the most rapid reduction in mortality per minute of added PA was for those at the lowest levels of PA. These findings suggest that older adults can benefit from PA time far below the amount recommended by the federal guidelines." (Hupin, 2015)

Thumbs up to an active life!

information on their lives until his death in 1956. Howard Friedman and Leslie Martin are health scientists who picked up where Dr. Terman left off. They looked at careers, relationships, personality traits and different experiences. This 8 decades long study of people has revealed some interesting ideas about longevity, and the story about Dr. Terman's study is told in the book called *The Longevity Project*, written by Friedman and Martin. They found that all stress isn't bad for health, and that being happy and gregarious doesn't equate to a long life. Positive social relationships were associated with a longer life and physical activity was important, but more important was having an activity that they enjoyed. Careful, dependable people that were planners lived longer than cheerful always optimistic people. A strong indicator of long life was conscientiousness. "The findings clearly revealed that the best childhood personality predictor of longevity was conscientiousness – the qualities of a prudent, persistent, well-organized person, like a scientist-professor – somewhat obsessive and not at all carefree."(The Longevity Project, 2011)

The *Gallup-Healthways Wellbeing Index,* started in 2009, focuses on 5 different areas: financial, social, physical, community and purpose. The index is a scientific survey that tracks well-being of individuals and organizations. Each day 500 people 18 or over are interviewed to gather data for the Wellbeing Index. Having a sense of security, having supportive relationships and love in your life, enjoying good health with enough energy to accomplish daily tasks, and enjoying what you do and where you live are critical to a sense of well-being according to the Wellbeing Index. The Wellbeing Index measures personal perception of well-being, but also gives insight into the people at the community, state and national levels.

Albert Lea, Minnesota

Healthways has partnered with Dan Buettner of Blue Zones LLC to bring about a higher quality of life for people living in communities signing on to the *Blue Zones Vitality Project*. The first city to sign onto the project was Albert Lea, Minnesota. The goal was not to directly challenge the Albert Lea citizens to change, but to change their environment so that they might modify their behaviors to create healthy habits. Restaurants changed their menus for healthier options and schools no longer sold candy as fundraisers. The city linked residential, shopping, and school areas with sidewalks for pedestrians. Parents formed groups that escorted the children to and from school on foot or bicycle. Hundreds of townspeople volunteered to take personal measures to make positive changes together. The results were impressive. Walter Willet reports in Newsweek that in half a year, the city of 18,000 residents had lost an average of 2.6 pounds (increasing their life expectancy by 3.1 years) and health care claims dropped by 32% for city and school employees. Due to peer pressure and perhaps social media, many originally skeptical residents jumped onto the bandwagon and began to make positive changes in their lives as well. The challenge is to have college campuses, companies, city parks, urban areas and as much of the built environment as possible be movement friendly. We read about an example of changing habits and health by changing the environment in the previous chapter with schoolchildren using stand-biased desks. As more communities benefit from healthy "makeovers," the hope is that this type of healthy transformation will work in larger towns.

Community

In modern American culture it is not uncommon for children to move away from home and raise families far away from the grandparents. Distance can make relationships difficult, and particularly challenging when an aging parent needs assistance. Elders may face loneliness, loss of purpose and depression. When elders stay connected and involved both physical and mental health can be positively impacted. In Hispanic and Italian cultures there is a deep emphasis on family, often with grandparents living in the house with their married children and helping to care for grandchildren. These grandparents stay integrated in the family, often teaching the grandkids life lessons and about family history. In Asian cultures elders are venerated. Respect for a person only increases with age, and it is considered an honorable duty to care for parents as they age. The 60th and 70th year birthdays are special life events celebrated by the community. In Greek, "old man" is a reverent word indicating deep respect. In countries such as China, there are very few nursing homes, and there is a negative social stigma associated with sending one's relatives to live elsewhere.

A strong sense of community was found to be one of the most integral parts of living well and aging well in the Blue Zones.

If family is far away, an older adult is more likely to be isolated, so encouraging them to stay active and engaged will help to maintain a healthy life. Joining a club, volunteering, learning a new language and staying active are just a few of the options. College Station's Jesse Coon was a great example of how it should be done-aging well (see "It's Never Too Late" inset).

It's Never Too Late

He was a world champion. Jesse Coon of College Station, Texas, passed away on July 30, 2005, after a long, full, and active life. He was 94. Coon started swimming competitively at the ripe old age of 64, and he started breaking world records in his early 80's.

The former physics professor at Texas A&M University broke five world records at his last major swim meet in Munich, Germany, in the 90 through 94 age group. His stroke? The butterfly. When competing, Coon worked out in the pool ninety minutes five times per week. Jesse Coon was an active sailor and he mowed his own lawn.

Not all mature Americans need to be world record holders to benefit from a more active lifestyle. Recent studies indicate that regular exercise and physical activity can reduce or slow down the biological process of aging. Older adults can experience increased life satisfaction, happiness, and self-esteem, along with reduced stress with a regular activity. A friend noted that it never occurred to Jesse that he was old. He celebrated life and always had a positive attitude. Coon himself said "the older you get, the more important it is to exercise." Coon is an example not only to others of the gray-haired set, but to all of us of all ages.

Epigenetics: Are Your Genes Malleable?

The concept of **epigenetics** introduces the possibility that how we live our lives can alter the expression of our genes, and perhaps the genes of our children. The term **brain plasticity** refers to the brain as an organ that can change and grow and develop. The brain changes as we learn new things, as we grow, and in response to injury and stress. Just as skeletal muscle grows stronger with physical training and with proper nutrition, the brain "muscle" also grows with necessary nutrients provided by exercise, nutrition, and new experiences. **Neurogenesis** is the growth of new brain cells. DNA controls the process of neurogenesis, and a protein called brain-derived neurotrophic factor (BDNF) acts as a catalyst for creating new neurons. BDNF has been shown to be decreased in studies on Alzheimers patients. David Perlmutter, M.D., author of *Neurogenesis: How to Change Your Brain* writes, "Fortunately, many of the factors that influence our DNA to produce BDNF factors are under our direct control. The gene that turns on BDNF is activated by a variety of factors including physical exercise, caloric restriction, curcumin and the omega-3 fat, DHA. This is a powerful message. These factors are all within our grasp and represent choices we can make to turn on the gene for neurogenesis." This is indeed a powerful and exciting message that our lifestyle changes can actually transform our life.

Epigenetics is the study of functional changes in the genome that do not result in changes in the DNA. The Greek prefix "epi" implies changes in gene function that are "on top of" or "in addition to" genetics. You can think of your genes as being malleable where their expression can be turned up or down and in some case off and on by environmental conditions.

Epigenetics changes, for example, have been observed in rats given dietary supplements. These supplements alter the expression of particular genes that affect fur color, weight, and propensity to develop particular cancers. The Overkalix Study looked at physiological effects of environmental factors on the children and grandchildren of Swedish men and women exposed to famine in the late 1800s and early 1900s. Mortality risk ratios were determined for the children and grandchildren. The grandfathers' food supply (famine or normal) was linked to the mortality rate of the grandsons but not the granddaughters. However, the grandmothers' food supply was related to the mortality rate of the granddaughters. Lumley, L.H., et. al., determined that The nutrition of the grandmother during her pregnancy influences the mother's nutrition in utero which in turn influences the grandchild's birth weight.

There are also numerous studies looking at identical twins. Why do identical twins become more different as they age? Factors like diet, exercise, substance abuse, stress, and exposure to toxins are thought to modify gene expression. In other words, environment and lifestyle choices can make a difference in the expression of the genetic blueprint that identical twins start with. More research is needed into this fascinating area of study. One thing is certain, that the human body is a complex organism with many factors influencing growth, development, health and aging.

This should be good news! You do not have to accept that because a disease, mental health issue, personality characteristic, or any other trait that runs in your family that you are stuck with it. You can't change the genes you were born with, but you might be able to change your gene expression.

Telomeres, the DNA protein "caps" on the end of our chromosomes, are the subject of numerous studies. Often compared to the plastic end on a shoelace which keeps the lace from fraying, telomeres inhibit chromosomal fraying. Obesity, chronic stress, smoking, depression and aging have been associated with shortened telomeres. A recent study in the Proceedings of the National Academy of Sciences found an association with chronic social stress in children and telomere length erosion (Mitchell, March 2014.) Molecular biologist and 2009 Nobel Laureate Elizabeth Blackburn identified the enzyme telomerase, which is responsible for lengthening and repairing telomeres. Dr. Dean Ornish, UCSF clinical professor of medicine, directed a 5 year study that followed 35 men with early stage prostate cancer to explore how specific comprehensive lifestyle changes could impact telomere length and telomerase activity. The findings were published in the journal *The Lancet Oncology.* "Our genes, and our telomeres, are not necessarily our fate," said Ornish. "These findings indicate that telomeres may lengthen to the degree that people change how they live. Research indicates that longer telomeres are associated with fewer illnesses and longer life." The participants in the study made lifestyle changes not only to their diet and activity levels, but they also made time for relaxation and community.

The study found these four lifestyle changes changed the participants lives: (1) eating a whole food plant based diet, high in fruits and vegetables and high in unrefined grains and low in fat and refined carbohydrates, (2) moderate exercise such as walking 30 minutes on most days of the week, (3) managing stress with a practice of mindfulness, meditation, and a discipline such as yoga, and finally (4) having a strong social support-a network of friends and family or a supportive community-these things can lengthen your telomeres and perhaps lengthen your life as well. This is exciting research noting that not only can we stop telomere shortening, but we can actually increase telomere length with the significant but doable lifestyle changes noted in the study.

Four Lifestyle Choices That Keep You Young and Will Change Your Life

1. Plant-based diet (high in fruits, vegetables and unrefined grains, and low in fat and refined carbohydrates)
2. Moderate exercise (walking 30 minutes a day, six days a week)
3. Stress reduction (gentle yoga-based stretching, mindfulness, breathing, meditation)
4. Social support network (friends, family, sense of community)

These provocative findings are not really a fountain of youth . . . but maybe? Juan Carlos Izpisua Belmonte at the Salk Institute in La Jolla, California has attempted to reverse aging by reprogramming the epigenome in mice. The Salk team saw improved organ health and a clock "reset" on the aging process by genetically engineering the mice. The Yamanaka (named for the Japanese discoverer) genes were only turned on by a chemical that was given to the mice in their water. The mice lived about 30% longer than expected. This is not possible in humans, but studies such as this can help to better understand the human aging process. "Dr. Izpisua Belmonte believes these beneficial effects have been obtained by resetting the clock of the aging process. The clock is created by the epigenome, the system of proteins that clads the cell's DNA and controls which genes are active and which are suppressed." (NYT, 2016)

The fact remains that it is our choice how we live. Lifestyle choices impact the epigenetic marks that control cell maintenance. These epigenetic marks are described as molecular caps that chemically change the proteins around the chromosomes. We are impacted by these choices throughout our lifespan-from before we are born until the day we die. Choices have consequences, but our lives are in flux. It is never too late to make better choices in order to live life well.

Inflammation and Aging

Inflammation part of the body's immune response. **Acute inflammation** in response to an injury or wound is the body setting in motion the process of self-healing. The traditional response is to use methods to reduce swelling such as non-steroid anti-inflammatory drugs or to apply a cold compress to reduce swelling. Researchers at the Cleveland Clinic in Ohio found that the inflammatory cells called macrophages produce a high level of insulin-like

Photo courtesy of Zane Biggs

Pickleball is growing in popularity around the country.

Go4Life, launched by the U.S. Surgeon General and the National Institutes for Health, is a program targeting mature Americans. http://go4life.nis.gov/ is the website which encourages older Americans to make exercise a priority. Tips for success, workouts, videos, and success stories are available. Share with your favorite elder-and be sure and do the activity with them!

growth factor-1 (IGF-1) which increases the rate of muscle repair (Zhoa, 2010). The macrophages can do their job more efficiently when inflammation is allowed to progress. This insight into how inflammation helps healing may change conventional treatment-or at least inform practitioners to use therapies that don't eliminate the benefits of inflammation.

Chronic inflammation is long term and is present in some conditions such as asthma, Crohn's disease, and rheumatoid arthritis. Some long term inflammation is caused by an overactive immune reaction and the end result can be damage to the cells involved. Sleep quality influences inflammation, as a study at Emory University in Atlanta indicated: "Poor sleep quality and short sleep duration are associated with higher levels of inflammation."(Morris, 2010) It is not uncommon for sleep to be disrupted as person ages-and authors of this study suggest that sleep disturbance may increase cardiovascular risk through inflammation. Studies have shown that obese men have more inflammatory markers than their normal weight counterparts. Another study showed that inflammatory markers in women dropped when they lost weight. (McTierman, 2012) Some cancers are associated with inflammation, and the authors determined that losing weight through exercise and diet can not only help with obesity, but can reduce risk of cancer directly lowering inflammation. Non pharmaceutical means of treating chronic inflammation that are being studied now are ginger, turmeric, fish oil (Omega-3 fatty acids), green tea, and tart cherries.

Dementia is a neurodegenerative condition associated with memory, learning, problem-solving and behavior changes over time. **Alzheimer's disease** is the most common form of dementia afflicting 10% of the population over age 65. A study published in *Brain* indicates that inflammation in the brain drives Alzheimer's. The scientists at the University of Southampton suggest that blocking a protein that regulates immune cells in the brain could be a way to stop progression of Alzheimer's disease. (Olmos Alonzo, 2016)

Autopsies of Alzheimer's victims show plaques and tangles in the brain that are characteristic of the disease. The plaques are amyloid protein clumps and the tangles are a build-up of a protein called tau that twists and impairs the nerves cells in the brain. The tau protein is involved in spatial cognitive issues like remembering your address or knowing how to walk the correct route in order to get back home-tasks that may challenge dementia patients. Tau pathology interferes with the grid cells, the nerves that act as the brain's GPS. (Duff, 2017) Essentially, as the tau protein tangles increase, the brain's GPS system becomes less effective. Researchers hope that this research may help not only with treatment in the future but also with the development of early detection testing for Alzheimer's disease.

It is possible that the immune system changes with age and that this can cause susceptibility to diseases of aging. Many chronic infections and diseases impact the immune system. **Immunosenescence** is the term used to describe loss of immune functions in people 65 years and older. (Larbi, 2013) Inflammation has been identified with many of the diseases of aging. A 2013 study published in *Cell Metabolism* found that immune sensor NIrp3 inflammasone is a "common trigger of this inflammation" and can result in diseases related to insulin resistance, bone loss, and cognitive decline. "This is the first study to show that inflammation is causally linked to functional decline in aging," said lead author Vishwa Deep Dixit, professor of comparative medicine and immunobiology at Yale School of Medicine. "There are multiple cellular triggers of inflammation throughout the body, but we've pinpointed NIrp3 as the specific sensor that activates inflammation with age." Dixit indicates that if they can identify the triggers of aging that cause inflammation, then "turning off" those triggers may reduce the number of people succumbing to said diseases. In mice studies, Dixit's team showed that with lower NIrp3 activation, the mice were protected from diseases associated with aging such as "dementia, bone loss, glucose intolerance, cataracts, and thymus degeneration." The mice also had more endurance after the NIrp3 activation. Additional studies are needed, but there is hope that immunotherapy with NIrp3 could extend healthspan by dampening the inflammation process.

Senescent: growing old; aging

Studying Human Longevity

The Human Genome consists of approximately 25,000 genes. It would be ideal to isolate and study a specific gene responsible for longevity in human beings, but finding, isolating and studying those genes is a very complex task. Longevity studies on humans are inefficient and complicated due to lifespan, so short lived animal models (i.e. worms, flies) are used. Many genes associated with aging in the animal models have been identified so scientists look for human genes that have a similar function. Is living to 100 years a variant of a particular gene or the normal expression of the gene? Or is it a combination of the expression of dozens of genes together? The longevity genes that have been identified so far influence one of three different pathways in the cell: (1) insulin/IGF-1, (2) sirtuins, or (3) mTOR. The insulin/IGF-1 pathway is related to aging in roundworms via a specific gene called age-1 (discovered in the 1980's). When the gene was turned off by the scientists, the worms lived longer. In human studies, this leads to excitement regarding aging and diseases like diabetes. As metabolism regulators, the sirtuin genes are present in every cell in every species. In the 1990's MIT researchers genetically engineered yeast cells adding an extra copy of a sirtuin-like gene which resulted in

Have you released any Irisin lately?

Called the "exercise hormone," irisin was first reported on in January 2012 issue of the Journal Nature by Bruce Spiegelman and colleagues at the Dana-Farber Cancer Institute in Boston. Irisin is released by skeletal muscle as a response to endurance exercise, and is thought to be how muscle helps regulate the activity of adipose tissue. "Irisin increases adipocyte mitochondrial biogenesis, and the expression of uncoupling proteins, leading to greater mitochondrial heat production and energy expenditure." (Crivello, 2014) Spielgelman and colleagues discovered in 2013 that when Irisin is released during aerobic activity, new growth of brain neurons (neurogenesis) occurs and genes involved in learning and memory are activated. In 2014, a research team in the UK at Aston University lead by Dr. James Brown found that Irisin is related to the molecular benefits of exercise on telomere length, indicating that irisin may be involved in slowing the aging process (Christopher Bergland, The Athlete's Way).

Creativity and Aging

Typically mental processes begin to slow down with age; however, some characteristics such as creativity can flourish with age. There are many examples of great creative accomplishments by elderly artists. Michaelangelo completed his final frescoes for the vatican's Pauline Chapel at 75. Georgia O'Keeffe painted into her 90's despite failing eyesight. Benjamin Franklin invented bifocal glasses at 78 to correct his poor vision. Folks that have lived longer and have had more experience tend to be more comfortable in their own skin. Because mature adults seldom experience the adolescent need to "fit in," they are more likely to have the freedom to express themselves. This may enhance creative endeavors. So look forward to good health and artful aging in your golden years.

"Real Age"

Dr. Michael Roizen has developed a "real" age test. Log on to www.realage.com to take the free test. According to Roizen, exercising regularly can make your "real" age as much as nine years younger.

"Those who think they have no time for bodily exercise will sooner or later have to find time for illness." Edward Stanley (1826–1893)

an increased lifespan of yeast, flies, and worms. They have yet to be successful in rodents-but the research on the sirtuin pathway is exciting. mTOR stands for "mammalian target of rapamycin" and this pathway influences aging in animal models by controlling the rate of protein synthesis. Pharmacologically or genetically adding rapamycin improved lifespan and healthspan of the yeast, worms, and flies as well as the mice.

The genetics of aging is indeed an exciting but complex realm. Researchers use two main approaches to studying human longevity. One type of study is the **candidate gene approach.** Healthy centenarians are evaluated to determine if they have a variant of a gene that is similar to the longevity genes identified from animal models. These are then compared with the genetic make-up of those cells in individuals who live an average lifespan. "In one NIA-funded project, researchers studied 30 genes associated with the insulin/IGF-1 pathway in humans to see if any variants of those genes were more common in women over 92 years old compared to women who were less than 80 years old. Variants of certain genes—like the *FOXO3a* gene—predominated among long-lived individuals, suggesting a possible role with longer lifespan." (National Institute on Aging, 2015)

Genetically similar Sardinians in Italy live in one of the originally identified Blue Zones, and they have been studied with the second approach called the **genome-wide associated study (GWAS).** In the GWAS studies, researchers are hoping to identify new genes not previously associated with aging by looking for similar traits in long lived people. According to Biology of Aging (NIH), with this approach, scientists scan the entire genome looking for variants that occur more often among a group with a particular health issue or trait. From the Sardinian study, they found 7 new genes not previously associated with lipids in the blood. Since high cholesterol is a major contributor to cardiovascular disease, identifying these variants could possibly inform scientists about how aging and heart disease are related, or how certain individuals are less susceptible to CVD due to their genetic make-up.

Many factors affect the outcome of who we become as individuals and how we interact with our environment. Who we are and how long we will live is a combination and influence of both nature and nurture. There is no fountain of youth and no magic pill, and there is no recipe for success because we are all individuals with different parents, different life experiences and we make different choices in life. Perhaps we can strive to be worried less about the past and the future, and to focus on making positive choices for the present moment. Establish meaningful relationships. Eat well most of the time, drink in moderation if at all, and make sure you move every day. Do things that you enjoy to enhance your health. Live your life with purpose and be conscientious. These are the lessons learned from those who live long and live well.

Basketball: Fitness, fun and competition at any age!

Louisiana

The Tigerettes Basketball team, age 65+
The Tigerettes are five-time women's basketball gold medalists from Baton rouge, Louisiana. Off the court, they are charming Southern belles and caring grandmothers. On the court, they transform into winner-take-all competitors who will dive, push, and elbow their way to another title. Learn more about the Tigerettes through the pBS documentary age of Champions by visiting http://ageofchampions.org.

It is never too late to start exercising, but it is *always* too soon to stop!"
-Walter Bortz

Eleven Essential Elements to HEALTH AND HAPPINESS

1. NORMAL NUMBERS NOW

2. CRITIQUE CALORIC CONSUMPTION

3. MAKE MOVEMENT MANDATORY

4. HALT HARMFUL HABITS

5. METICULOUSLY MANAGE MONEY AND MINUTES

6. GRACIOUSLY GIVE YOUR GIFTS

7. FORGIVE: FAMILY, FRIENDS, FOES - OURSELVES

8. PASSIONATELY PURSUE PURPOSE AND PRIORITIES

9. STIFLE STRESS / SEVER SUFFERING

10. PERIODICALLY PAUSE, PONDER, PLAN, AND PRAY

11. SEEK AND SECURE SUPPORT

living **WELL** aware ™

PATRICIA J. SULAK, MD

www.livingWELLaware.com

Dr. Patricia Sulak, author of "Should I Fire my Doctor?" and Living Well Aware at Texas A&M University: *"It's a fact: All diseases can be prevented or improved with a healthy lifestyle. I can handle whatever comes my way if I'm in an optimal wellness state."*

References

Adrián Olmos Alonso et al., *Pharmacological targeting of CSF1R inhibits microglial proliferation and prevents the progression of Alzheimer's-like pathology,* Brain, doi:10.1093/brain/awv379, online January 2016.

Biology of Aging, National Institutes on Aging, Publication No. 11-7561, Nov. 2011.

Dixit, VD et al., *Canonical Nlrp3 inflammasome links systemic low-grade inflammation to functional decline in aging. Cell Metabolism,* Vol. 18, Issue 4 doi.

Duff, Karen et al., *Tau pathology induces excitatory neuron loss, grid cell dysfunction and spatial memory deficits reminiscent of early Alzheimer's disease,* Neuron, published online 19 January 2017.

Fernandez, Elizabeth, *Lifestyle Changes May Lengthen Telomeres, A Measure of Cell Aging* http://www.ucsf.edu/news/2013/09/108886/lifestyle-changes-may-lengthen-telomeres-measure-cell-aging retrieve June 2014.

Healthways-Gallup Wellbeing index Healthways, Inc., Franklin, TN 1(800) 327-3822 https://www.nytimes.com/2016/12/15/science/scientists-say-they-can-reset-clock-of-aging-for-mice-at-least.html?_r=1

Hupin D, Roche F, Gremeaux V, Chatard JC, Oriol M, Gaspoz JM, Barthelemy JC, Edouard P. Even a low-dose of moderate-to-vigorous physical activity reduces mortality by 22% in adults aged ≥60 years: a systematic review and meta-analysis. *Br J Sports Med.* 2015;49:1262–1267. doi: 10.1136/bjsports-2014-094306.

Larbi, A. et al., The Immune System in the Elderly: A Fair Fight Against Diseases? Aging Health. 2013;9(1):35–47.

Lu, H et al., Macrophages recruited via CCR2 produce insulin-like growth factor-1 to repair acute skeletal muscle injury FASEB J. doi:10.1096/fj. 10-171579.

Mitchell, et. al., *Social disadvantage, genetic sensitivity, and children's telomere length,* Proceedings of the National Academy of Sciences, vol. 111 no. 16.

Morris, A. et al., *Sleep Quality and Duration are Associated with Higher Levels of Inflammatory Biomarkers: the META-Health Study, Circulation,* 23 November 2010; 122: Abstract: A17806.

Neurogenesis: How to Change Your Brain http://www.huffingtonpost.com. dr-david-perlmutter-md/neurogenesis-what-it-mean_b_777163.html#es_share_ended retrieved June 2014.

Poulain, Michel et al., "Identification of a geographic area characterized by extreme longevity in the Sardinia island: the AKEA study". Experimental Gerontology. 39 (9): 1423–1429. doi:10.1016/j.exger.2004.06.016.

Springen, K. and Seibert S. Artful Aging, *Newsweek,* January 17, p. 57. 2005.

The Biology of Aging; NIH National Institute on Aging 31 Center Drive, MSC 2292, Bethesda, MD 20892 January 2015

Uhlenberg, Peter. Generations, Spring, 2013 pp. 12-18; American Society on Aging.

Vijg J, Campisi J. *Puzzles, promises and a cure for ageing.* Nature 454:1065-1071.

Willet, Walter and Underwood, Anne. Newsweek, Crimes of the Heart; Feb 15, 2010 pp 43-43.

Chapter 7
Exercise Science

© videodoctor/Shutterstock.com

OBJECTIVES

Students will be able to:

♦ Identify and explain key components necessary to safely maintain or improve cardiovascular fitness, muscular fitness, and flexibility.

♦ Explain the importance of cardiovascular conditioning for health maintenance and disease prevention.

♦ Integrate body measurements and fitness values to determine current health status.

♦ Recognize and explain the importance of having strong core musculature to overall health.

♦ Identify the key components of a cardiovascular and/or a muscular training program.

Adaptation of *Health and Fitness: A Guide to a Healthly Lifestyle*, 5th Edition, by Laura Bounds, Gayden Darnell, Kirstin Brekken Shea, and Dottiede Agnor. Copyright © 2012 by Kendall Hunt Publishing Company.

"Physical Fitness is not only one of the most important keys to a healthy body, it is the basis of dynamic and creative intellectual activity. The relationship between the soundness of the body and the activities of the mind is subtle and complex. Much is not yet understood. But we do know what the Greeks knew: That intelligence and skill can only function at the peak of their capacity when the body is healthy and strong; that hardy spirits and tough minds usually inhabit sound bodies."

—President John F. Kennedy,
"The Soft American," Sports Illustrated,
December 26, 1960

Why Is Physical Activity Important?

Just like a car can rust and fall into disrepair when it isn't run for long periods of time, the human body can deteriorate and fall into disrepair when it isn't taxed beyond a resting state. Every system in the body, from the large muscles to the mitochondria in the cells, "runs" more optimally when the brain and the body are stimulated. Activities like walking, running, dancing, and playing tennis work the muscles and in turn the actions of the muscles stimulate bones to increase in density. The heart and the entire cardiorespiratory system increase activity to elevate heart rate, blood pressure and cardiac output to meet the demand for increased oxygen to the working muscles. Capillary circulation increases. The contractility of the cardiac (heart) muscle increases. Positive impact is seen in attitude, self-esteem, ability to focus, and decreased risk of depression. The list goes on and on. We live better and most of us feel better when involved in some sort of moderate activity on most days of the week. Cars run better when driven, and people live better when active. For all ages, in all walks of life, regular activity can enhance quality of life. This chapter discusses options when considering your personal fitness program.

Clinical, scientific, and epidemiological studies indicate that physical activity has a positive effect on the delay in development of cardiovascular disease (ACSM). In a landmark report in 1996, the Surgeon General recommended that all Americans accumulate thirty minutes of activity on most, if not all, days of the week. Recent recommendations state that thirty minutes might not be enough. The 2015–2020 Dietary Guidelines recommend most Americans should be active at least 150 minutes per week. In 2002, the Institute of Medicine issued a statement that all Americans, regardless of age, weight, size and race, should achieve a total of sixty minutes of moderately intense physical activity daily. In December 2003, the National Sports and Physical Education (NASPE) changed the previous recommendation (1998) to be increased to "at least sixty minutes, and up to several hours of physical activity per day" for children 5 to 12 years of age.

In 2007 the American College of Sports Medicine (ACSM) and the American Heart Association (AHA) together released updated physical activity guidelines that emphasize thirty minutes of moderate activity five times weekly for most

Americans. An alternative would be three twenty minute vigorously intense bouts of activity. In 2011 ACSM updated its position stand on physical activity guidelines to include functional fitness activities, or neuromuscular training involving multiple joints and planes of movement such as yoga or tai chi. Strength training two or three days a week along with regular flexibility training is also recommended. (ACSM, 2011) Both ACSM and AHA endorse recommendations by the Institute of Medicine that in order to lose weight when these guidelines are already being met, "an increase in activity is a reasonable component of a strategy to lose weight." *For individuals that are overweight and want to avoid becoming obese, exercise sessions of forty-five to sixty minutes may be prudent. Formerly obese individuals who are trying to avoid regaining weight should consider up to ninety minutes of aerobic activity on most days of the week.*

How do we define moderate or vigorous activities? Examples of each follow. **Moderate activities** (You can still speak while doing them) are activities like line dancing, biking with no hills, gardening, tennis (doubles), manual wheelchair wheeling, walking briskly, and water aerobics. **Vigorous activities** are aerobic dance or step aerobics, biking hills or going faster than ten miles per hour, dancing vigorously, hiking uphill, jumping rope, martial arts, racewalking, jogging or running, sports with continuous running such as basketball, soccer and hockey, swimming laps, and singles tennis. With vigorous activities it would be difficult to carry on a conversation due to the intensity of the exercise. Try to do all of these activities for a minimum of ten minutes at a time. It is important to recognize that moderate activity is beneficial to everyone, while vigorous activity may not be appropriate for everyone.

Regardless of recommendations, children, adults, and the elderly all benefit from regular, consistent physical activity (see Figure 7.1). Choosing to seek opportunities to move such as walking, biking, swimming, gardening, and other activities can impact risk of disease as well as quality of life. In this chapter, we will discuss why you should exercise and give suggestions to help ensure your success.

Health Benefits of Physical Activity—A Review of the Strength of the Scientific Evidence	
Adults and Older Adults	**Children and Adolescents**
Strong Evidence	**Strong Evidence**
• Lower risk of:	• Improved cardiorespiratory endurance and muscular fitness
• Early death	• Favorable body composition
• Heart disease	• Improved bone health
• Stroke	• Improved cardiovascular and metabolic health biomarkers
• Type 2 diabetes	**Moderate Evidence**
• High blood pressure	• Reduced symptoms of anxiety and depression.
• Adverse blood lipid profile	
• Metabolic syndrome	
• Colon and breast cancers	
• Prevention of weight gain	
• Weight loss when combined with diet	
• Improved cardiorespiratory and muscular fitness	
• Prevention of falls	
• Reduced depression	
• Better cognitive function (older adults)	
Moderate to Strong Evidence	
• Better functional health (older adults)	
• Reduced abdominal obesity	
Moderate Evidence	
• Weight maintenance after weight loss	
• Lower risk of hip fracture	
• Increased bone density	
• Improved sleep quality	
• Lower risk of lung and endometrial cancers	

Source: U.S. Department of Health & Human Services.

FIGURE 7.1

Evidence abounds that everyone, all ages, can benefit from an enhanced quality of life with regular physical activity

METs: Sample Physical Activities Defined by Level of Intensity

Moderate Activity* 3.0 to 6.0 METs** (3.5 to 7 kcal/min)	**Vigorous Activity*** Greater than 6.0 METs** (more than 7 kcal/min)
• Walking at a moderate or brisk pace of 3 to 4.5 mph on a level surface inside or outside, such as walking to class, work, or the store • Using crutches • Hiking • Stationary bicycling—using moderate effort • Water aerobics • Yoga • Ballroom dancing • Tennis—doubles • Playing Frisbee • Swimming—recreational • Saddling or grooming a horse • Raking the lawn • Moderate housework: scrubbing the floor • Waiting tables or institutional dishwashing	• Racewalking and aerobic walking—5 mph or faster • Jogging or running • Mountain climbing, rock climbing, rappelling • Step aerobics • Calisthenics—push-ups, pull-ups, vigorous effort • Tennis—singles • Soccer • Racquetball • Water polo • Running • Skipping • Jumping rope • Shoveling heavy snow • Farming—forking straw, baling hay, cleaning barn, or poultry work

The following is in accordance with CDC and ACSM guidelines.

Source: U.S. Department of Health and Human Services, Public Health Service, Centers for Disease Control and Prevention, National Center for Chronic Disease Prevention and Health Promotion, Division of Nutrition and Physical Activity. *Promoting physical activity: a guide for community action.* Champaign, IL: Human Kinetics, 1999.

* For an average person, defined here as 70 kilograms or 154 pounds.

** The ratio of exercise metabolic rate. One MET is defined as the energy expenditure for sitting quietly, which, for the average adult, approximates 3.5 ml of oxygen uptake per kilogram of body weight per minute (1.2 kcal/min for a 70-kg individual). For example, a 2-MET activity requires two times the metabolic energy expenditure of sitting quietly.

To compute the amount time needed to accumulate 150 kcal, do the following calculation: 150 kcal divided by the MET level of the activity equals the minutes needed to expend 150 kcal. For example:

150 ÷ 3 METs = 50 minutes of participation. Generally, activities in the moderate-intensity range require 25–50 minutes to expend a moderate amount of activity, and activities in the vigorous-intensity range would require less than 25 minutes to achieve a moderate amount of activity.

Swimming is an excellent lifetime fitness activity.

Activity More Important than Weight Loss

Increasing lifestyle activity by spending less time on the couch and doing something daily will have a positive impact on your health. Being overweight and obese is associated with complications and high risk factors such as hypertension, high blood cholesterol, and diabetes. *A growing body of evidence, however, indicates physical inactivity is more critical than excess weight in determining health risk.* Longitudinal studies such as the ongoing research by epidemiologist Steven Blair, previously of the Cooper Institute in Dallas, Texas, and information from the ongoing Harvard alumni study indicate that lifestyle is more significant than weight. Fitter people have lower death rates regardless of body weight. Indeed, the mortality rate for low fit males is more than 20% higher than for those that are high fit. While this effect is smaller for women, the decrease in mortality rate for high fit females is more than 6% compared to those who are low fit. Previously sedentary Harvard alumni (Sesso and Paffenbarger, 1956) who became active reduced their all-cause mortality rate by 23 percent. The alumni who lost weight (but were not active) did not improve their mortality rate. Improvements in metabolic fitness (glucose

Waist Measurement as Risk Indicator

Recent evidence from a study done at the University of Manchester in the United Kingdom indicates that **abdominal obesity** is a strong independent risk factor for heart disease. "A large waist with large hips is much less worrisome than a large waist with small hips." The conclusion of the study determined that the simple waist-to-hip ratio is a strong predictor of heart disease (AHA, 2011).

tolerance, blood pressure, and cholesterol) are often seen with just moderate amounts of physical activity. The good news is that overweight Americans don't need to go on a crash diet, buy a gym membership, or totally give up Twinkies. Increasing lifestyle activity and walking regularly, spending less time on the couch, and doing something active daily can have a positive impact on health.

Fitness or Fatness

Dr. Steven Blair is convinced we are too focused on obesity and overweight. Physical activity is much more crucial than a high BMI. People who are active, yet have a high BMI, have lower death rates than those who have a normal BMI but are sedentary. It is clear that if a sedentary person begins an exercise program, blood glucose and cholesterol could improve, yet that person might not lose any weight. *"Fitness is a more important indicator of health outcomes than fatness"* says Steven Ball, University of Missouri exercise physiologist.

Cardiovascular Fitness

Cardiovascular fitness refers to the ability of the heart, lungs, circulatory system, and energy supply system to perform at optimum levels for extended periods of time. **Cardiovascular endurance** is defined as the ability of the body to perform prolonged, large-muscle, dynamic exercise at moderate to high levels of intensity. The word **aerobic** means "in the presence of oxygen" and is used synonymously with *cardiovascular* as well as *cardiorespiratory* when describing a type of exercise.

2011 American College of Sports Medicine Exercise Recommendations:

Cardiovascular Activity:

- At least 30–60 minutes of moderate level activity a minimum of 5 days a week.
- OR, at least 20–60 minutes of vigorous activity 3 days a week.
- Shorter sessions of at least 10 minutes at a time are acceptable with the goal of 150 minutes of moderate intensity exercise a week.
- Progress slowly to avoid injury.
- Persons unable to meet these minimums will benefit from some activity.

Five components of **health-related fitness**:

1. cardiovascular fitness,
2. muscular strength,
3. muscular endurance,
4. flexibility, and
5. body composition.

© Pete Niesen/Shutterstock.com

Athletes typically have high levels of skill-related fitness.

Physical inactivity is listed as the fourth leading preventable risk factor for global mortality rates-*World Health Organization*.

Complete fitness is comprised of health-related fitness and skill-related fitness. **Health-related fitness** consists of cardiovascular fitness, muscular strength, muscular endurance, flexibility, and optimal body composition. The components of health-related fitness affect the body's ability to function efficiently and effectively. Optimal health-related fitness is not possible without regular physical activity. Most health clubs and fitness classes focus primarily on the health-related fitness components. **Skill-related fitness** includes agility, balance, coordination, reaction time, speed, and power. These attributes are critical for competitive athletes. Skill-related fitness is not essential in order to have cardiovascular fitness. Balance is, however, important for seniors. Staying active helps seniors maintain strength and balance, which can be critical in avoiding injuries.

Cardiovascular fitness is often referred to as the most important aspect of physical fitness because of its relevance to good health and optimal performance. **Muscular fitness** is critical because of its effect on efficiency of human movement, functional stability, and basal metabolic rate. **Flexibility** is important for everyone, athletes and non-athletes alike, especially as a person ages. Knowing how to exercise correctly for effectiveness and reduced risk of injury is also important. Physically active individuals can expect to experience a positive impact on glucose regulation, blood pressure, blood cholesterol, bone density, body weight, and their outlook on life. Small amounts of activity for sedentary individuals can have a positive impact on overall health risk. For those who are overweight or obese, a loss of 5 to 10 percent of body weight can have a significant impact on **body composition** and overall health risk.

Exercising with friends can be enjoyable and help to keep you motivated and committed to your fitness program.

How important is participation in physical activity in achieving and maintaining good health? Since 1992, the American Heart Association has considered **inactivity** as important a risk factor for heart disease as high blood cholesterol, high blood pressure, and cigarette smoking. The U.S. Centers for Disease Control and Prevention (CDC) and the American College of Sports Medicine (ACSM) reported that 300,000 lives are lost each year due to inactivity (AHA, 2015). In 1996 the U.S. Surgeon General's Report made several definitive statements regarding physical activity and its impact on one's health. Evidence is mounting that physical activity is an integral part of good health. Lack of exercise has spawned a whole new field of study termed **inactivity physiology.**

How Aerobic Exercise Helps Cardiovascular Fitness

There are many benefits associated with aerobic exercise. When one is aerobically fit, there is an overall reduction in the risk of coronary artery disease, i.e., stroke, blood vessel diseases, and heart diseases. Related to this reduction, there is a decrease in resting **heart rate** due to the improved efficiency of the heart. There is also an increase in **stroke volume.** The amount of blood pumped by the left ventricle of the heart with each beat is increased (stroke volume) which in turn increases total cardiac output. Cardiac output ($\dot{Q}$) is the total volume of blood pumped during one minute.

A decrease in systolic blood pressure, which is the highest arterial blood pressure attained during the heart cycle, and a decrease in diastolic blood pressure, or lowest arterial pressure attained during the heart cycle, also

$\dot{Q}$=SV x HR Cardiac output is the stroke volume times the heart rate during a one minute interval

© Kochergin, 2012, Shutterstock, Inc.

occurs. There is also an increase in collateral circulation, which refers to the number of functioning capillaries both in the heart and throughout the body. Increased capillarization is an adaptation to regular aerobic activity. Delivery of oxygen to the working muscles and removal of metabolic wastes is more efficient with increased collateral circulation. In addition to the specific physiological changes just listed, other benefits of a mental, emotional, and physical nature will increase with regular aerobic exercise. You will recall from Chapter 5 some of the potential benefits that have been documented when aerobic fitness levels increase are:

- a decrease in percent body fat,
- an increase in strength of connective tissues,
- a reduction in mental anxiety and depression,
- improved sleep patterns,
- a decrease in the speed of the aging process,
- an improvement in stress management,
- an increase in cognitive abilities.

Exercise and the Heart

Stress and the Heart
A strong heart will be more efficient than a weak heart when demands are imposed on it through stress. Exercise makes the heart stronger. Sympathetic nerve stimulation is responsible for the fight-or-flight response experienced as a result of emotional or physical stress. High fitness levels decrease the impact of this stress on the heart.

Heart rate becomes elevated during exercise because of the increase in demand for oxygen in the muscle tissues. Oxygen is attached to hemoglobin molecules and is transported in the blood. The heart pumps at a faster rate to meet the increased demand for oxygen. The heart is a muscle, and like other muscles, it becomes stronger due to the stress of exercise. Through regular exercise, the heart will increase slightly in size and significantly in strength, which results in an increased stroke volume. The primary difference is seen in the increased thickness and strength of the left ventricle wall. As a result of exercise, blood plasma volume increases, which allows stroke volume to increase. These two factors will cause resting heart rate to decrease, exercising heart rate will become more efficient, and there will be a quicker recovery to a resting heart rate after exercise ceases. Lack of exercise can contribute to many cardiovascular diseases and conditions, including **myocardial infarction,** or heart attack; **angina pectoris,** a condition caused by insufficient blood flow to the heart muscle that results in severe chest pain; and **atherosclerosis,** a build-up of fatty deposits causing blockage within the blood vessel.

Closely associated with the function and efficiency of the heart is the function and efficiency of the **circulatory system**. Blood flows from the heart to arteries and capillaries where oxygen is released and waste products are collected and removed from the tissues. The deoxygenated blood then makes the return trip to the heart through the venous system. As a result of aerobic exercise, blood flow to the skeletal muscles improves due to an increase in stroke volume, an increase in the number of capillaries, and an increase in the function of existing capillaries. This provides more efficient circulation both during exercise recovery and during daily activities.

Blood flow to the heart muscle is provided by two coronary arteries that branch off from the aorta and form a series of smaller vessels. With regular aerobic activity, the size of the coronary blood vessels increase and collateral circulation improves. These small blood vessels can supply oxygen to the cardiac muscle tissue when a sudden block occurs in a major vessel, such as during a heart attack. Often the degree of developed collateral circulation determines one's ability to survive a myocardial infarction, or heart attack. It appears that a regular exerciser might have a higher chance of surviving a heart attack due to collateral circulation within the heart, as the smaller collateral vessels take over when the primary artery becomes occluded, or blocked.

The lungs, air passages, and muscles involved in breathing that supply oxygen and remove carbon dioxide from the body are known as the **respiratory system**. During exercise, **pulmonary ventilation**, which is the movement of gases into and out of the lungs, increases in direct proportion to the body's metabolic needs. At lower exercise intensities, this is accomplished by increases in respiration depth. At higher intensities, the rate of respiration also increases. Although fatigue in strenuous exercise is frequently referred to as feeling "out of breath" or "winded," it appears that the normal capacity for pulmonary ventilation does not limit exercise performance (McArdle, Katch, and Katch). In a normal environment, one inhales sufficient amounts of oxygen. The breathing limitation is in the efficiency of the oxygen exchange at the cellular level. *The primary benefit of aerobic exercise to the respiratory system is an increase in strength and endurance of the respiratory muscles, not an increase in lung volume.* Maximal pulmonary ventilation volumes are dependent on body size (Wilmore and Costill). Muscles that elevate the thorax such as the diaphragm are referred to as muscles of inspiration. Muscles of expiration, including the abdominal muscles, depress the thorax. Regular aerobic training will result in an increase in both the strength and endurance of these muscles, and will also result in more efficient respiration.

Aerobic and Anaerobic Exercise

Aerobic exercise is activity that requires the body to supply oxygen to support performance over a period of time. Aerobic exercise is characterized by the use of the large muscle groups in a rhythmic mode with an increase in respiration and heart rate. *Aerobic* literally means "with oxygen." Walking, the most common form of exercise in the United States, is an aerobic activity. Other aerobic exercises include running, swimming, biking, cardiokickboxing, rowing, jump-roping, and any activity that fits the above criteria. As with most exercise, the rate of energy expenditure varies with an individual's skill level and intensity of exercise. *Aerobic activities of low intensity are ideal for the beginning or sedentary exerciser because they can be maintained for a longer period of time and have been shown to be effective in promoting weight loss and enhancing cardiovascular health.* Many activities are too intense to be maintained more than a few minutes; these activities are considered anaerobic.

Anaerobic literally means "in the absence of oxygen." **Anaerobic exercise** is exercise performed at intensity levels so great that the body's demand for oxygen exceeds its ability to supply it. Anaerobic activities are usually short in duration, high intensity, and result in the production of blood lactate. The energy for anaerobic activity is primarily from carbohydrates stored within the muscles, called **glycogen,** which is in limited supply. Fatigue rapidly sets in when glycogen stores are depleted. Examples of anaerobic activities include strength training, sprinting, and interval training. Sprinting requires so much energy that the intensity of the activity cannot be maintained for a long period of time. Anaerobic training can enhance the body's ability to cope with the effects of lactic acid and fatigue, thus promoting greater anaerobic fitness.

Bicycling is an aerobic exercise that uses the large muscle groups in a rhythmic mode with an increase in respiration and heart rate.

Interval training has been used for years, but now there is a new name for it–boot camp. The concept is simple: work for a shorter amount of time, but work harder. Working with a coach or personal trainer is recommended so that you also work smarter. Interval training involves high intensity cardiovascular exercise alternating between short rest or active rest periods. People who tend to get bored just running for 40 minutes often enjoy the variety and change in routine. The increased challenge of a 20 to 40-minute interval workout means increased energy expenditure. It is common to see the acronym **HIIT**, for high intensity interval training. Research indicates that 3 times per week is likely best for this type of training to limit injury and in order to allow for full recovery between sessions (Kravitz). The basic variables manipulated when designing an interval training program include:

1. Duration (time/distance) of intervals
2. Duration of rest/recovery phase
3. Number of repetitions of intervals
4. Intensity (speed) of intervals
5. Frequency of interval workout sessions

Working hard with other people can be motivating due to the supportive and/or competitive nature in a class. A December, 2016 study reported in PLOS ONE compared HIIT training with moderate aerobic training. For six weeks, three days a week, the HIIT group did ten sets of high intensity training on a stationary bike for one minute followed by one minute of rest. The aerobic group cycled for 28 minutes at 70 to 75% peak heart rate with no breaks. The study's authors looked at enjoyment of exercise and exercise workload. The HIIT group had a 10% higher enjoyment score, and the HIIT group also increased their workload twice as much as the moderate intensity group. Dr. Jennifer Heisz, lead author in the study, suggests that there may be an association between enjoyment and improved fitness: "It appears that the stronger you get, the more you enjoy the workout. This may make you more motivated to continue." (Harvard Health, 2017) A fringe benefit of interval training is that you will not only become more aerobically fit, but you might get stronger, faster, and more powerful.

HIIT may cause you to work harder, but it also may make working out more fun, according to a December, 2016 study (*PLOS ONE*). Compared to moderate intensity exercisers, a HIIT group improved twice as much and enjoyed the activity more. The anaerobic energy system is trained as well as the aerobic energy system in an interval type class. Due to increased caloric expenditure in a high intensity class, participants may experience weight loss success. Use caution, as the injury risk may also increase with HIIT; listen to your body. Remember to warm up thoroughly, progress slowly, and stretch after activity.

Exercise Prescription, or How to Become FITT

To improve cardiovascular fitness, one must have a well-designed regimen of cardiovascular exercise. In order for improvement to occur, specific guidelines must be adhered to when designing a personal exercise program. As will be discussed later, the following guidelines apply not only to aerobic exercise, but to other components of physical fitness as well. The **FITT** acronym is easy to remember when identifying an appropriate cardiovascular exercise prescription: **frequency, intensity, time,** and **type.**

Frequency

Frequency refers to the number of exercise sessions per week. The American College of Sports Medicine recommends exercising for at least 30 minutes five days per week at a moderate to vigorous level of intensity, or engaging in 20 minutes of vigorous activity three or more days per week.

For individuals with a low level of aerobic fitness, beginning an exercise program by working out two times a week will result in an initial increase in aerobic fitness level. However, after some time, frequency and/or intensity will need to be increased for improvement to continue.

Intensity

Intensity refers to how hard one is working, and it can be measured by several techniques. These techniques include **measuring the heart rate while exercising (Figure 7.2)**, **rating of perceived exertion (RPE)**, exercise METs, and the **talk test**. To use heart rate as a measure of intensity, one's target heart rate range needs to be calculated before exercising. **Target heart rate range** is the intensity of training necessary to achieve cardiovascular improvement (see Figure 7.3). Calculation of target heart rate range using the Karvonen formula is done by multiplying maximum heart rate (220 minus one's age) by a designated intensity percentage. The American College of Sports Medicine guidelines for intensity recommends working between 55 and 90 percent of maximum heart rate, or between 50 and 85 percent of heart rate reserve (maximum heart rate minus resting heart rate). For individuals who are very unfit, the recommended range is 55 to 64 percent of maximum heart rate or 40 to 49 percent of heart rate reserve (Pollock, Gaesser, Butcher, Despres, Dishman, et al., 1998). Use of a heart rate monitor is also useful for specific heart rate and intensity feedback. Programs can be designed using heart rate to alleviate boredom and increase efficiency of the workout.

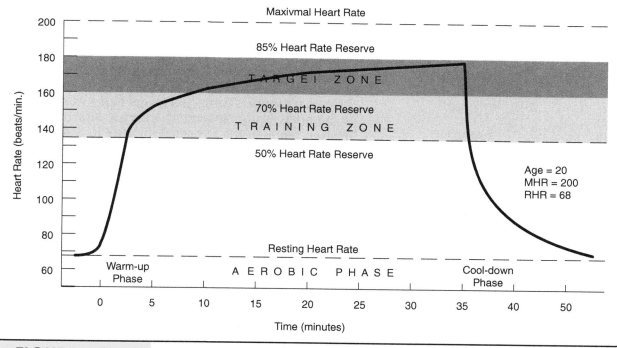

FIGURE 7.2

Cardiovascular Exercise Prescription Guidelines Tracking the Heart Rate Response through a Typical Cardiovascular Exercise Session

FIGURE 7.3

Target Heart Rate Zones for Individuals of Ages 20 through 70. The zones cover 70–90 percent of maximum heart rate, which is indicated above the zones for selected ages

Source: From Total Fitness and Wellness, 5th Edition, by Powers and Dodd, Pearson Benjamin Cummings Publishers.

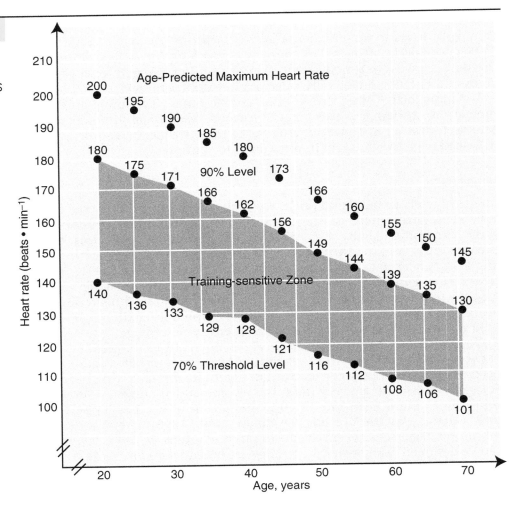

TABLE 7.1 ♦ The Borg RPE Scale

Score	Degree of Exertion
6	No exertion at all
7	Extremely light
8	
9	Very light
10	
11	Light
12	
13	Somewhat hard
14	
15	Hard (heavy)
16	
17	Very hard
18	
19	Extremely hard
20	Maximal exertion

Source: © Gunner Borg, 1970, 1985, 1998.

Another technique for measuring exercise intensity is through subjective self-evaluation or a psychophysiological scale of how hard one is working. The body and the mind are called on to perceive one's effort. Gunner Borg designed the **Rating of Perceived Exertion Scale (RPE)** (see Table 7.1) in the early 1950s. It is a numbered scale from 6 to 20, with the lowest numbers being "very, very light" exercise, the highest numbers being "maximal" exercise, and the numbers in between representing a gradual increase in exercise intensity, from low to high. Using this scale, a rating of 10 corresponds roughly to 50 percent of maximal heart rate and a rating of 16 corresponds roughly to 90 percent of maximal heart rate. A person estimates his or her exercise intensity level by taking into consideration or "perceiving" how they feel, how much sleep they have had, whether or not they have eaten, whether or not they are ill, and so on. This scale is a useful tool for estimating exercise intensity when exact measures are not needed, and it is often used in a clinical setting as well as fitness classes and health clubs. Perceived exertion is also useful when a person is taking medication that can alter the heart rate. When using RPE, it is important to remember there is no right or wrong rating.

A third measure of intensity when exercising is using **metabolic equivalents** or **METs**. "The amount of oxygen your body consumes is directly proportional to the amount of energy you expend during physical activity. At rest, your body uses approximately 3.5 ml of oxygen per kilogram (2.2 lb) of body weight per minute (ml/kg/min). This resting metabolic rate is referred to as 1.0 MET." (Wilmore, 1994) Refer to page 122 for sample activities for moderate (3–6 METs) and vigorous (greater than 6 METs) activities. Using METs as an intensity measure is only an approximation since metabolic efficiencies vary from person to person; it doesn't take into account environmental changes or changes in physical conditioning.

A fourth, and probably the easiest, technique to measure exercise intensity is the **talk test.** If you are exercising and must laboriously breathe rather than participate in a conversation, the exercise intensity is too high and training heart rate has probably been exceeded. Exercise at this intensity will be difficult to maintain for long periods of time. On the other hand, if you are able to sing, intensity level is probably insufficient for improvement in your fitness level.

Time

The third factor to be considered when designing a cardiovascular exercise workout is **time,** or duration. For benefits to be accrued in the cardiovascular system, exercise duration should be a minimum of twenty minutes of continuous exercise or several intermittent exercise sessions of a minimum of ten minutes each. Some beginning exercisers may not be capable of exercising continuously for twenty minutes at a prescribed intensity. While a minimum of twenty minutes is recommended, a duration of ten minutes can certainly be beneficial to people who are at a low fitness level and just beginning an exercise program. Duration and exercise intensity are interdependent, having an inverse relationship. As exercise effort increases, duration typically decreases. Distance runners exert a moderate effort for a long period of time, called long slow distance training. Sprinters exert a maximal effort for a brief period of time. Duration at a lower intensity is optimal for beginning exercisers. Exercise intensity levels should remain within recommended guidelines, while maximum duration is only limited by the participant's available fuel for energy and mental determination to keep going.

Type

Another factor that should be considered in determining a cardiovascular exercise prescription is **type,** or mode, of exercise. The choice of exercise modality is up to each individual, but one must keep in mind the specific requirements of cardiovascular exercise: use the large muscle groups via continuous and rhythmic movement, and exercise for a duration of twenty to thirty minutes or more in the target heart rate range a minimum of three to five times per week. Common types of aerobic exercise include running, walking, swimming, step aerobics, cross-country skiing, biking, or using a machine such as a rower, stairstepper, or treadmill. However, these are certainly not the only types of exercise available. Any exercise that meets the requirements of intensity and duration is acceptable. Some sports can provide aerobic exercise, depending on the nature of the sport, the position being played, and the skill level of the player. For example, an indoor soccer player could get an aerobic workout by playing a game, provided there is constant movement and training heart rate was maintained in the target heart rate range. Many sports provide an excellent way for people to expend a lot of energy and burn a significant number of calories, but the "play some and rest some" nature often prevents them from being good aerobic exercise. In order to achieve longterm cardiovascular fitness, it is good to pick a variety of activities, and to find activities that are pleasurable to the individual.

Components of an Exercise Session

The sequence of a cardiovascular workout should be as follows: warm-up, optional dynamic stretching, workout, cool down, and static stretch for increased flexibility.

To achieve long-term cardiovascular fitness, find an activity that you enjoy doing.

Warm-Up

A good cardiovascular workout follows a specific sequence of events. First and foremost, to prepare the body and increase the comfort level for a cardiovascular workout, a warm-up is crucial. The purpose of the warm-up is to prepare the body and especially the heart for the more vigorous work to come. The warm-up should increase body temperature, increase heart rate, increase blood flow to the muscles that will be used during the workout, and include some rhythmic movement to prepare muscles that may be cold and/or tight. A warm-up should raise the pulse from a resting level to a rate somewhere near the low end of the recommended heart rate training zone. Beginning vigorous exercise without some kind of warm-up is not only difficult physically and mentally, but it can also contribute to musculoskeletal injuries.

Dynamic Movement

It is important to warm up the muscles that will be used during the workout. Focus on moving the large muscles that will be used in your activity. A brisk walk, a light jog, easy leg swings—these are all examples of stretching with movement or dynamic movement. Dynamic movements are preferable to holding a static stretch as part of the warm up. A dynamic movement is a controlled moving stretch such as leg swings with the hips stabilized or any gentle movements that move the muscles around the joints that will be used in the activity. A brisk walk, light jog, or walking toe touches are examples of dynamic movement. Many athletes choose to go through rhythmic limbering, with dynamic movements focusing on functional movement patterns that will be used in the race, sport, or fitness class rather than holding a static stretch.

Activity

When doing cardiovascular exercise, the aerobic component should be from fifteen minutes to sixty minutes, depending on the individual's fitness level and goals. A gradual increase in intensity and duration is recommended for beginners. It is important to pay attention to your body's signals to slow down or perhaps stop.

Cooldown and Stretch

After an aerobic exercise session, heart rate should be lowered gradually by slowly reducing the intensity of the exercise. Sudden stops are not recommended and can lead to muscle cramps, dizziness, and blood pooling in the legs. After a gradual cooldown such as walking, static stretching of the muscle groups is needed and highly recommended. *When muscle core and body core temperature are elevated, it is an optimal time to stretch for increased flexibility.* Warmer muscle core temperature increases the pliability of the muscle and connective tissue, allowing it to lengthen better.

Static stretching is great after your workout when your muscle core temperature is elevated.

Rest and Recovery

An often overlooked yet critical component of any fitness program is rest and recovery. Jeff Galloway, Olympic runner and author of *Galloway's Book of Running*, believes that rest is the most integral part of any athletic program. Whether running, doing HIIT, or heavy weight training, fueling your body pre and post workout will ensure better training and better training leads to better performance. Dr. Mark Kovacs, a Fellow with the ACSM, has developed an easy to remember program to optimize recovery: R^4–Rehydrate, Refuel, Rest, and Repair.

Rehydrate with water. If the exercise duration is longer than 60 minutes, or if exercise was in extreme heat and humidity, carbohydrate and electrolyte replacement drinks may be considered.

Refueling can be with a variety of foods, smoothies, or protein drinks. Lean protein (15–25 grams post activity meal is appropriate) and high complex carbohydrate foods are ideal. If consuming protein, whey protein is absorbed faster than other types of protein and a recent study indicates that muscle protein synthesis is increased if amylopectin and chromium complex are added to the whey protein. (Ziegenfuss, 2017) Unless you are training for muscle hypertrophy, chocolate milk has been shown to be a great aid in recovery from exercise with both available protein and carbohydrate. Some studies have also shown that consuming tart cherry juice can aid in endurance running recovery by reducing muscular swelling. "Ingesting tart cherry juice for 7 days prior to and during a strenuous running event can minimize post-run muscle pain." (Kuehl, 2010) Consuming more than 2 drinks of alcohol can also impact recovery–negatively.

Rest is necessary to allow the body to respond to the stress of the exercise stimulus. The sleep state is restorative to all the body systems; sleep deprivation has been shown to disrupt cognitive function and metabolic function. Sleep disturbances such as sleep apnea, jet lag, insomnia or poor quality sleep due to use of technology prior to sleeping can negatively impact recovery from exercise. Long naps may also be contrary to the quality and quantity of restorative nature of sleep by disrupting circadian rhythms. Try to stick to short power naps of 20-30 minutes.

Repair will happen physiologically if the above criteria are met, but it can be enhanced and post-exercise discomfort can be reduced with many different modalities. Both ice and heat have been shown to help immediately after exercise, with cold therapy more beneficial 24-48 hours post workout. Manual therapies like massage, foam rolling, soft tissue work and joint mobilization are helpful. Self-myofascial release is beneficial because it can be done at home simply by rolling on a lacrosse or tennis ball. Physical therapists can apply electrical muscle stimulation to ease pain. Active recovery with a different low intensity activity is also advised.

My Workout Considerations

Goals: What is my purpose in exercising? There is a big difference between getting up at 5:00 am to run alone, body-building for 3 hours at a time in the gym, rock-climbing, or joining a Zumba class.

Activity: Do something you like to do-enjoyment is key to sticking with the activity.

Equipment: What do I need to be successful in my chosen activity? Examine the quality of your equipment to ensure safety. Wear the right footwear for your activity.

Time: Workout when it is convenient. If you don't have time, make time. You are worth the effort. Regular exercise often enhances sleep quality-so getting up 30 minutes earlier can actually help you get more from your sleep.

Intensity: If you have only a short amount of time, increase exercise intensity. This is the basis of interval type classes like Tabata and Cross-Fit. It is a good mix up of longer endurance activities along with shorter higher intensity activities.

Warm up: Warm up prepares you both physically and mentally. Rehearse movements to be used-like a swimmer will swing his arms and rotate his trunk. Besides joint and muscle warm up, think of moving the whole body to increase respiration and heart rate. The more vigorous the activity, the more complete the warm-up should be.

Be safe: Work hard, train safe. If it hurts, likely your body is signaling you to stop. Consult a personal trainer if you are unsure about your exercise.

Focus: Consider leaving your phone in your locker. Focus on what you are doing in the moment.

Afterwards: Let your heart rate drop gradually. When your muscles are warm is the best time to stretch for increased flexibility. Hold your stretch, breathe, and relax.

Eat: Fuel your body to get the most out of your exercise, eating a light snack or meal that has protein and carbohydrate. After activity replace muscle glycogen with again, complex carbohydrates and protein and plenty of fluids.

Drink: Water! Before, during and after.

Rest: Rest is the most significant part of an exercise program, allowing the body to adapt and recover from the stress of exercise.

Variety: Try new things to challenge yourself and avoid boredom.

Commit: Put your workout time on the calendar. Inform family and friends of your intention and ask for their support to help you follow through.

Evaluating Cardiovascular Fitness

There are many ways to measure a person's level of cardiovascular fitness. Over time, the body adapts to regular activity by not working as hard when given the same workload. An example would be running the mile. A person may have a goal of running the mile in eight minutes. At first an eight-minute mile may be a challenge, but with continuous practice, an eight-minute mile can be achieved, and may actually become easier. The body has adapted by allowing the pace to be maintained with less apparent effort. Working heart rate, the heart rate during activity, is lower. Oxygen delivery is increased to the working muscles. Respiration rate is less as the respiratory muscles become stronger. Muscles become stronger with use, creating ease of movement. Body composition typically becomes more favorable, which contributes to efficiency of movement. Powers and Howley have shown that in general twelve to fifteen weeks of endurance exercise results in a 10 percent to 30 percent improvement in VO2 Max. You will recall VO2 Max (discussed in the biometrics section of Chapter 3) is the measure of how efficient our body is at utilizing oxygen when exercising. While a direct measure is expensive, cumbersome, and is done in a laboratory, VO2 can be estimated with submaximal testing. The 1.5 mile run, a one mile walk, and cycle and swim tests can estimate VO2 measurements.

Recovery heart rate is taken after an exercise session is completed. The time it takes for your heart rate to return to its normal resting rate is called the heart rate recovery period. The higher a person's level of cardiovascular fitness, the less time it will take after exercise for the heart rate to return to a pre-exercise level. One minute after the cessation of exercise, a conditioned male heart rate should have returned to below 90, and a female heart rate to below 100 beats per minute. Five minutes post exercise, it is desirable for both male and female heart rates to be below 80 beats per minute. This is an indication not only of one's fitness level, but also of the adequacy of a cooldown period. Heart rate recovery time is a great tool to use to track individual progress during training.

"Fitness isn't just for highly skilled athletes. It is for all of us. It's our natural state of being, particularly when we are young. Being out of shape is really being out of sorts with ourselves."
—Kenneth H. Cooper, M.D.,
The Aerobics Way

Principles of Fitness Training—The Rules

There are specific principles that can be applied to any exercise program. Understanding and applying these exercise principles will increase your chance of success in achieving your exercise goals.

Overload and Adaptation

The principle of overload and adaptation states that in order for a body system to become more efficient or stronger, it must be stressed beyond its normal working level. In other words, it must be overloaded. When this overload occurs, the system will respond by gradually adapting to this new load and increasing its work efficiency until another plateau is reached. When this occurs, additional overload must be applied for gain. The cardiovascular system can be overloaded in more than one way. For example, a person has been running for a few months and is running a distance of three miles in thirty minutes. The runner never goes farther than three miles and never runs faster than a ten-minute per mile pace. For this individual, some techniques of overloading would be: to increase distance, to run the same distance at a faster pace, or to add hills or sprint segments to the run. In terms of weight training, any time a person adds more weight to the bench press or increases the number of repetitions, that person is using the principle of overload. *In order for improvements to be realized, overload must occur.* The principle of overload and adaptation applies to muscular strength, cardiovascular and muscular endurance, and flexibility training.

Photo courtesy of Kirstin Brekken Shea

Getting stronger with weight training is an example of the principle of overload and adaption.

Specificity

The principle of specificity refers to training specifically for an activity, or isolating a specific muscle group and/or movement pattern one would like to improve. For example, a 200-m sprinter would not train by running long, slow distances. Likewise, a racewalker would not train for competition by swimming. Workouts must be specific to one's goal with respect to the type of exercise, intensity, and duration. The warm-up should also be specific to a particular activity. The more intense the activity, the longer the warm up. A sprinter may warm up for 30–40 minutes doing a variety of drills and running prior to a 100 meter run. Cross training, defined as using several different types of training, has recently increased in popularity. The benefits of cross training are to prevent injury from overuse and to decrease boredom. The principle of specificity does not negate participation in cross training activities; rather, it indicates that the primary training protocol should be in one's chosen activity.

Individual Differences

The principle of individual differences reminds us that individuals will respond differently to the same training protocol. Some individuals may be what is called a "low responder" to an exercise stimulus. It is not clear why individuals vary in response to exercise, but initial fitness level, age, gender, genetic composition, and previous history will also cause individual responses to specific activities to differ. Coaches, athletic trainers, and personal trainers should be especially aware of this principle when designing workouts in order to achieve maximum performance levels. It is also critical that individuals realize that body type is genetically determined. Body fat distribution and metabolism are individual. Lifestyle and activity can affect one's physique; however, a large-framed person will never be a small-framed person and vice versa. Focusing more on enhanced health rather than trying to change one's body type is prudent.

Reversibility

The inevitable process of losing cardiovascular benefits with cessation of aerobic activity is known as the reversibility principle. The old adage "if you don't use it you lose it" applies here. Physiological changes will occur within the first two weeks of detraining and will continue for several months. Bed rest causes this detraining process to greatly accelerate. Consider the muscle atrophy that occurs with disuse when a cast is removed from a body part that has been immobilized for several weeks. The reversibility principle is clearly the justification for off-season programs for athletes and immediate initiation of physical rehabilitation programs for individuals with limited mobility or for those individuals recovering from injury.

Muscular Fitness

Muscular fitness includes two specific components: muscular strength and muscular endurance. **Muscular strength** is the force or tension a muscle or muscle group can exert against a resistance in one maximal effort. **Muscular endurance** is the ability or capacity of a muscle group to perform repeated contractions against a load, or to sustain a contraction for an extended period of time. Muscular fitness is improved with progressive resistance training (PRT).

2011 American College of Sports Medicine Exercise Recommendations:

Muscular Fitness:

- Adults should train each major muscle group 2-3 days each week using a variety of exercises and equipment
- 2–4 sets of each exercise will help adults improve strength.
- Perform 8–12 repetitions deliberately and in a controlled manner.
- A single set of repetitions can improve strength and size, especially in novice exercisers.

Benefits of Muscular Fitness

Several **physiological adaptations** occur as a result of resistance training. *Strength gains can be seen within the first six weeks, with little or no change in muscle size, and are attributed to neural changes.* These changes include decreased activation of antagonistic muscles, learning how to perform the activity, changes in activation of the motor unit, improved recruitment patterns of muscle fibers, change in the gain of the muscle spindle and Golgi tendon organ, and reduction in the sensitivity of force-producing limiting factors.

As strength training activities continue, hypertrophy, or an increase in the size of the muscle fibers, occurs. Another result from training is an increase in the amount of energy available for contraction. Carbohydrates are stored in the form of **glycogen** in the muscle and can be used as the primary energy source for contraction. These muscle glycogen stores increase

Top Ten Reasons to Work Your Muscles

1. *Gain lean body mass and lose body fat.* For each pound of muscle you gain, you'll burn 35 to 50 more calories daily.
2. *Get strong.* Extra strength makes it easier to carry suitcases and accomplish some daily activities, such as lifting children or groceries.
3. *Build denser bones.* Weight training can increase spinal bone mineral density by 13 percent in six months.
4. *Reduce risk of diabetes.* Weight training can boost glucose utilization in the body by 23 percent in four months and lower the likelihood of developing diabetes.
5. *Fight heart disease.* Strength training reduces harmful cholesterol and lowers blood pressure.
6. *Beat back pain.* In a twelve-year study, strengthening the low-back muscles had an 80 percent success rate in eliminating or alleviating low-back pain.
7. *Move easier.* Weight training can ease arthritis pain and strengthen joints, so you feel fewer aches.
8. *Improve athletic ability.* Whatever your sport, strength training may improve proficiency and decrease risk of injury.
9. *Feel younger.* Even men and women in their 80's and 90's can make significant gains in strength and mobility with weight training.
10. *Boost your spirits.* Strength training reduces symptoms of anxiety and depression and instills greater self-confidence.

as a result of training. Bone and connective tissue also undergo changes with resistance training, including an increase in bone matrix, an increase in **bone mineral density,** and an increase in mass and tensile strength of ligaments and tendons. These increases help prevent injury and decrease the chance of development of osteoporosis after middle age. More muscle mass increases an individual's basal metabolic rate, which is why weight training is excellent for "dieters," or those wanting to reduce their percentage of body fat. "An increase in one pound of muscle elevates basal metabolic rate by approximately 2–3 percent" (Powers and Dodd, 2009). Current research at the University of Birmingham is focused on determining the role of active levels of vitamin D as well as body fat and lean body mass in developing strength. The studies point to associations between active vitamin D and lean mass, however there appear to be gender differences. (Science Daily, 2017)

Along with the physiological adaptations previously discussed come benefits that improve the quality of one's life. These benefits of muscular fitness include:

- an increase in muscular strength,
- power and endurance,
- a higher percentage of muscle mass,
- improved posture,
- increased metabolic rate,
- improved ease of movement,
- increased resistance to muscle fatigue,
- increased strength of tendons, ligaments, and bones,
- decreased risk of low back pain,
- increased energy and vitality,
- Improved balance and coordination.

2011 American College of Sports Medicine Exercise Recommendations:

(New) Neuromotor Exercise:

- Also called functional training
- Recommended 2–3 days per week
- 20-30 minutes per day for neuromotor exercise
- Great for adults as well as seniors
- Neuromotor exercise involve motor skills such as balance, agility, coordination, gait and also proprioception.
- Tai Chi and Yoga are examples of this type of exercise.

Neuromotor Exercise and Functional Training

For a number of years progressive resistance training (PRT) has been the gold standard to improve muscular strength and muscular endurance. More recent studies, however show that strength gains do not always result in functional strength gains (Latham, 2004). The data indicate that power (strength and speed) training is more effective in improving function. Functional training is exercise based on real life movement. ACSM added neuromotor exercise two or three times a week as a recommendation when they updated their 1998 position stand in 2011. Challenging motor skills like balance and coordination incorporated into an activity provide stimuli for the body's neuromuscular control mechanisms, and ultimately may provide injury prevention. These activities are appropriate for adults of any age.

In the past decade the trend in training in the weight room has been away from large seated stationary machines (i.e. *Universal, Nautilus*). Seated machines typically isolate one muscle group per exercise. Muscular endurance often refers to a specific muscle group such as training the biceps brachai when doing a biceps curl. Functional movement usually involves gross motor, multi-planar, multi-joint movements which place demand on the body's core-from the hips to the sternum. Functional training typically requires a stabilizing challenge and a balancing challenge when increasing the complexity of the movement while also mimicking how we move in our daily lives. This is especially true for the athlete, in personal training and in group exercise. The actions done by an athlete in his/her sport are functional. Functional exercises such as a medicine ball warm up, a full squat with military press, wood choppers, kettle bell swings or a walking lunge with a twist require attention in order to be executed correctly. It is important to focus on stabilizing the hips, engaging the core, keeping the spine neutral and breathing throughout the range of motion.

Many athletes now focus on a variety of different exercises to increase stabilization and strength of the core musculature. In the past, the focus

was often mostly on doing numerous crunches to strengthen the abdominals. Examples of the functional approach for abdominal training would be to do some standing cable rows in the transverse plane, bird dogs in the quadraped position, side plank or hip bridges with abdominal bracing. Abdominal bracing is tensing the muscles of the abdomen as if you were anticipating getting hit in the stomach. The resulting contraction serves to stiffen the spine to help stabilize and support the back. Abdominal bracing is taught both as a therapeutic technique and also as a tool to use in exercise to prevent low back pain.

What Makes up the "Core?"

A strong core reduces the risk of injury and increases the efficiency of movement. Training the core can lead to an increase in balance and coordination, as well as gains in strength, power, endurance, and ultimately performance.

Bird dog exercise for strengthening the core

- ***Pelvic floor muscles***—The pelvic floor muscles run collectively from the pubic bone to the tailbone. Contraction of these muscles contributes to spinal stability, which is the foundation from which we move.
- ***Abdominal wall***—The rectus abdominus, the internal and external obliques, and the transverse abdominus together are responsible for spinal flexion, extension, and rotation, as well as for assisting in stabilization.
- ***Back muscles***—The erector spinae and multifidus produce spine extension, lateral flexion, and rotation. The interconnections of these muscles help contribute to stability of the lower back and pelvis.
- ***Hip muscles***—The adductor and abductor muscles of the hip, when in balance, provide optimum stability and mobility to the hip and lumbopelvic area.
- ***Lats and glutes***—Both of these muscle groups attach to the spine or pelvis, so each has an important role in the stability and mobility of the trunk.

Just as the nutritionists cannot agree on what exactly we should be eating, the experts cannot agree on which muscles exactly make up the core. In general terms, you can focus on the muscles that support the spine as being the core. The muscles in the core play an important role in stabilization, muscle balance, and proper alignment, as well as strength and flexibility.

Effective Training

The following are general definitions regarding the use of weight training for developing an exercise protocol to increase *muscular endurance* (Cissik, 2015).

Planks are a great functional exercise when done with correct form.

- **Frequency** refers to how often one should lift, with the recommendation being three nonconsecutive days per week.
- **Load** defines the amount of weight lifted. This will vary with each individual, with the recommended amount being a weight that will allow twelve to fifteen repetitions with good form. If form is compromised, the load should be decreased.

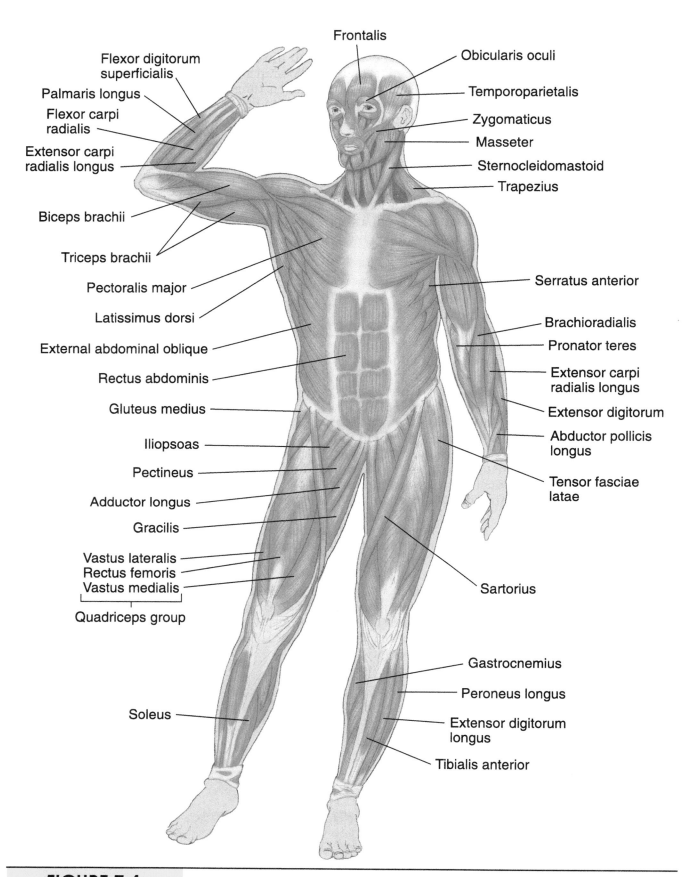

FIGURE 7.4a

Major Anterior Muscles in the Human Body

Source: Kendall/Hunt Publishing Company.

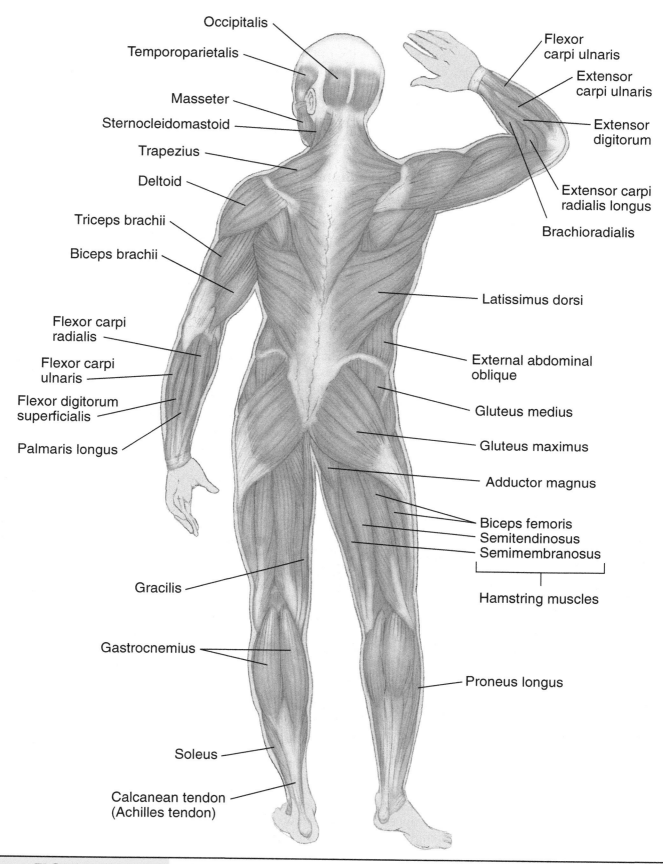

FIGURE 7.4b

Major Posterior Muscles in the Human Body

Source: Kendall/Hunt Publishing Company.

- **Repetition** is simply the performance of a movement from start to finish one time.
- **Set** is the specific number of repetitions performed without resting. Twelve to fifteen repetitions per set are recommended while performing two to three sets of each exercise. Each exercise session should contain eight to ten different exercises, with at least one being a full-body exercise.
- **Recovery** is the amount of time between each set. Thirty seconds is considered the optimum amount; however, taking more time is not detrimental.
- **Repetition-maximum** (also called one rep max) is the maximum amount of weight that can be lifted one time without compromising form.
- **Intensity** is the stress level of the exercise and is expressed as a percent of a one repetition-maximum. The recommended intensity level is less than 70 percent of a one repetition-maximum.

Training for the Best Results

The exercise prescription for developing muscular strength is more intense than for endurance. The number of repetitions decreases from eight to one, with the number of sets increasing from three to five. The percent of the one repetition maximum that should be lifted increases to 80 to 100 percent. Due to the increase in intensity, the rest period is extended, lasting three to five minutes. Exercise prescription will vary depending on one's goals and objectives for training (see Figure 7.5 p. 148). It is common now for personal trainers to perform a functional movement screen (FMS) in order to assess flexibility, mobility, strengths, and weaknesses. After assessment the best training routine with necessary modifications and appropriate progression can be established depending on the client's goals.

Muscle soreness often accompanies resistance training and will occur at various times during the training process. Muscle soreness that begins late in an exercise session and continues during the immediate recovery period is known as acute muscle soreness. This soreness will last only a brief period of time and is typically gone within twenty-four hours, while **delayed-onset muscle soreness** begins a day or two after the exercise session and can remain for several days. Eccentric contraction seems to be the primary cause of delayed-onset muscle soreness. According to Wilmore and Costill (1999), the causes of delayed-onset muscle soreness include structural damage to muscle cells and inflammatory reactions within the muscles. Muscle soreness can be prevented or minimized by: reducing the eccentric component of muscle action during early training, starting training at a low intensity and gradually increasing it, or beginning with a high-intensity, exhaustive bout, which will cause much soreness initially, but

Always focus on correct form when doing resistance exercise.

© Supri Suharjoto, 2012, Shutterstock, Inc.

will decrease future pain. During delayed-onset muscle soreness, strength production is reduced by as much as 50 percent during the first five days and a reduction in strength can occur for as long as fourteen days. The best technique for prevention of delayed-onset muscle soreness is to maintain an appropriate training program. A diet rich in Vitamin E, an antioxidant, may also help to reduce damage to muscle fiber membranes by helping to heal the cell plasma membrane.

Dr. Paul McNeil, cell biologist at the Georgia Regents University, found that Vitamin E is essential for rapid cell membrane repair and "ultimately cell survival." (Labazi, 2015)

As with any type of training program, watch for signs of **over-training** called burn-out. With muscular fitness training, these indicators include a decrease in physical performance, weight loss, increase in muscle soreness, increase in resting heart rate, sleeplessness, nausea after a workout, constant fatigue, and decreased interest in exercise.

True or False? Weight Training Myths

1. **Myth:** Weight training causes one to lose flexibility.
   Fact: Resistance training will increase muscle size, but it does not necessarily make one less flexible. In fact, proper strength training can actually increase flexibility when a full range of motion is used.
2. **Myth:** Resistance training or "spot reducing" is beneficial in reducing deposits of fat from specific areas on the body, such as in the hips, thighs, and waist.
   Fact: Resistance training focuses on the muscles used. Fat is not removed from one area of the body by working the muscles in that area. Creating a caloric deficit consistently, through diet, exercise, or a combination of both, loses fat. The location of fat deposits is determined genetically. The majority of women tend to be "pears" with fat deposits collecting on the hip and thigh region. The majority of men tend to be "apples" with fat deposits collecting around the torso. Abdominal fat has been shown to indicate an increased health risk.
3. **Myth:** Fat will be converted to muscle with resistance training.
   Fact: Fat is not converted to muscle with exercise, nor is muscle converted to fat through disuse. Muscle cells and fat cells are different entities. The size of muscle cells can be increased with resistance training. Fat cell size is increased with sedentary living combined with a poor diet.
4. **Myth:** Dietary supplements will make one bigger and stronger.
   Fact: A balanced diet and hard work in the weight room will increase muscle size and strength. Most dietary supplements will only cause the manufacturer's wallet to become bigger. Often when a person spends money on a supplement believing that supplement to work, the placebo effect might result in some apparent short-term improvement.
5. **Myth:** Performance-enhancing drugs such as steroids, growth hormones, diuretics, and metabolism boosters will help make one fit.
   Fact: These drugs are extremely dangerous and potentially fatal. They can contribute to aesthetic changes, but can also have a negative impact on health. Some fitness enthusiasts have lost their lives searching for a short-cut to health by using supplements.
6. **Myth:** Women will become masculine in appearance by participating in resistance training activities.
   Fact: Masculinity and femininity are determined through hormones, not through resistance training. Resistance training will cause an increase in muscle tone, which is perceived to increase the attractiveness of both males and females.
7. **Myth:** Kids should not weight train.
   Fact: Pre-adolescent children can and should use their body as resistance. Swinging on the monkey bars or climbing a tree are good examples of using one's body as resistance; push-ups, sit-ups, and tumbling activities are also great. Teaching 11- to 13-year-olds proper technique and form lifting light weight with proper supervision helps lay a strong foundation for future training. Proper training can improve flexibility, as well as strengthen muscles and the skeletal structure. Body composition and self-esteem are also usually enhanced with a training program, which can be a positive outcome with childhood obesity on the rise.

FIGURE 7.5

Beginning Strength
Training Guidelines

It is important to learn proper form and technique when weight training.

Preparation:

- Establish goals. Why do you want to weight train? Your goals will affect the way you train.
- Don't train on an empty stomach; fuel your body and brain before working out with a healthy snack.
- Consume a balanced diet daily.
- Stay hydrated with water before, during, and after the workout.
- Dress properly in loose clothing and wear non-slip athletic shoes.
- Commit to a regularly scheduled training time weekly for best results.
- Get instruction in a safe, effective, and balanced program.
- Adjust the weight machine to your body height.
- Prepare your after workout snack: replace muscle glycogen with protein and complex carbohydrates.

Lifting:

- Always warm up; try ten minutes of cardiovascular activity or calisthenics followed by joint-specific movements for the body parts you will target.
- Progress slowly; use common sense when overloading.
- Work all the major muscle groups; avoid focusing on just one or two areas of the body.
- Consider balance—working opposing muscle groups (biceps-triceps, hamstring-quadriceps, lower backabdominals).
- Work the larger muscle groups first, progressing to the smaller muscles.
- Complete multi-joint exercises before doing singlejoint exercises (squats before leg curls).
- Keep the weights as close to the body as required for proper form and technique.
- Use a full range of motion for each exercise.
- Make sure stretching needs are appropriate to the individual; only stretch the muscle, not the ligaments or joint capsule.

- Maintain good posture throughout each movement.
- Movement should be slow and controlled, with a smooth rhythm.
- Breathe, exhaling on the exertion phase.
- Avoid breath holding during heavy lifting.
- Expect some soreness; excessive muscle soreness may be a sign of overuse or injury.
- Allow forty-eight hours of recovery for a particular body part after heavy lifting; light activity is fine during recovery.
- Get plenty of rest, water, and good nutrition to allow for muscle repair and recovery.
- Enlist a workout buddy to help with technique, motivation, and safety.
- Use a workout log to track your progress, recording weight, sets, and repetitions.

Safety:

- Learn the rules at your facility.
- Don't overtrain; listen to your body.
- Never sacrifice form for additional repetitions or weight.
- When squatting, maintain a natural lordotic curve in your spine; descend until the thighs are parallel to the floor.
- Use collars or other locking devices to keep the plates on the bars when using free weights.
- Use experienced spotters for heavy lifting.
- Always lift free weights with a partner.
- Avoid locking out or hyperextending any joints while lifting.
- Don't lift if you are too fatigued to maintain good form.

Etiquette:

- Practice good weight room etiquette; don't drop or bang the weights.
- Always re-rack free weights.
- Use a towel to wipe equipment when you are done at an exercise station.
- Be considerate of others who are waiting to use the equipment.

Flexibility

Can you touch your toes? Think of how much your flexibility has changed in the last ten years. How much more will it change in the next ten years? Truly, if you don't stretch or if you are not active, flexibility will be lost. Why is this a concern? Loss of flexibility with age or injury can greatly affect a person's quality of life. Simple activities such as putting on your socks, or bending to lift a toddler can be painful or worse, impossible. Individuals who are active tend to be more flexible simply because they tend to use a full range of motion in their

Yoga is gaining in popularity in the United States. Most forms of yoga encourage the buildup of heat within the body to facilitate movement and internal focus. Relaxation is a common goal of most yoga participants, yet most experience enhanced flexibility and increased strength as a fringe benefit. One style of yoga, Bikram yoga, advocates practicing yoga in rooms with temperatures as high as 105 degrees. The premise is that the heat will allow the tendons, ligaments, and muscles to loosen up more and stretch further. A common yoga truism is that even steel, when heated hot enough, will bend.

Practicing yoga can help alleviate symptoms deriving from many different medical conditions: musculoskeletal issues like sciatica, respiratory conditions such as asthma, auto-immune conditions like rheumatoid arthritis, digestive issues such as irritable bowel syndrome, and all stress-related disorders. Although it doesn't cure many diseases, the practice of yoga and conscious breathing may improve your outlook and your emotional well-being.

activity. Active individuals are also more likely to engage in health-enhancing behaviors. Several factors can have an impact on the amount of flexibility a person can achieve, including gender, age, genetic composition, activity level, muscle core temperature, and previous or current injury. Old injuries often hamper flexibility for adults later in life, therefore affecting future activity.

Flexibility is defined as the range of motion around a joint. Flexibility is also specific to individual joints. For instance, an individual may have complete range of motion in the wrist but be very limited or stiff in the shoulder. An individual could be very flexible on the right side of the body, and inflexible on the left side. Flexibility exercises should be included in all exercise programs regardless of the objectives. The benefits of maintaining flexibility include having the ability to perform daily activities without developing muscle strains or tears and being able to participate in sports with enhanced performance. Consider a swimmer who increases shoulder flexibility is able to reach further, pull more water, and thus swim faster.

The athlete, whether serious about competition or a weekend recreator, will have a greater ability to perform particular sports skills with an increased range of motion. Consider a football coach encouraging his receivers to bench press as much as possible. That receiver can be very strong in the weight room; however, if he cannot apply that strength on the football field, he will not be an effective player. Athletes should train for **functional strength.** Training for functional strength means being able to transfer strength of the movement to enhance a desired performance or to improve movement in everyday living. This often involves coordination, speed of movement and range of motion. A wide receiver should train to jump high and extend from his shoulders to catch a pass. Strength without flexibility is

"Yoga isn't about touching your toes, it is about touching your soul."—M.C. Yogi, Eight Limbs, Mantra, Beats, and Meditations.

2011 American College of Sports Medicine Exercise Recommendations:

Flexibility:

- Flexibility exercises are more effective when muscle core temperature is elevated through light to moderate cardiorespiratory or muscular endurance exercise.
- Perform flexibility exercises 2–3 times per week or more to improve range of motion.
- Hold each stretch for 10–30 seconds to the point of tightness or slight discomfort; repeat each stretch to accumulate 60 seconds per stretch.
- Static, dynamic, PNF, or ballistic are all effective types of stretching.

limiting. It is especially important to include flexibility exercises in a muscular fitness workout. Flexibility also helps to prevent injuries through a reduction in strains and muscle tears. Refer to the discussion of fascia in Chapter 10.

Stretching exercises are identified through four specific categories: **ballistic, static, dynamic,** and **PNF.**

© Marcos Mesa Sam Wordley/Shutterstock.com

1. **Ballistic** stretching involves dynamic movements, or what is commonly referred to as "bouncing." Ballistic stretching is not recommended for the general population as a means to improve flexibility. An exception is athletes who have ballistic movement in their sport. This type of stretch actually stimulates receptors in the muscle that are designed to help prevent injury due to over-extending the muscle. Thus, the ballistic stretch can cause the muscle to contract rather than relax, and can contribute to muscle soreness. A more appropriate type of muscular stretching for the general population is identified as static stretching.

2. **Static** stretching involves slowly moving the joint to the point of mild discomfort in the muscle and maintaining that angle for approximately thirty seconds before allowing the muscle to relax. The entire procedure should be repeated several times for maximum benefit. As previously noted, a warmup is highly recommended prior to stretching for injury prevention and to facilitate the stretch. A warm environment and a warm muscle will greatly enhance the stretch. If the stretch hurts the muscle or the joint, then stop. Learn to distinguish between the mild tensions needed to overload from pain, indicating a potential injury.

3. **Dynamic** stretching is active stretching, moving a body part through a range of motion in a controlled manner. Athletes use sport specific dynamic stretching to increase blood flow by elevating the heart rate and moving large muscle groups that will be used in their sport. Soccer teams often have players line up and do rhythmic movements that focus on hips, legs, and back such as walking lunges, walking and touching their toes, or jogging with hip circles.

4. A fourth type of stretching activity is called **proprioceptive neuromuscular facilitation** or **PNF.** This activity requires a partner to provide resistance. The basic formula for this activity is to isometrically resist against a partner using the muscle groups surrounding a particular joint, causing contraction, and then relaxing the same muscle group. For example, in stretching the hamstring, both the hamstrings and the quadriceps will be contracted and then relaxed. This contraction and relaxation process will increase the range of motion in the hamstrings. When stretching with a partner, communication is essential to avoid injury to the joint.

Other Exercise Considerations

Injuries

Although injuries do occur during exercise, the benefits of regular exercise far out-weigh the risk of injury. In most cases, proper training, clothing, and equipment will prevent injuries. Avoiding injury requires common sense and moderation. One should not attempt to self-diagnose, nor try to "train through the pain." Pain is a signal that something is wrong, and activity should be stopped until the source of the pain is identified and a trained medical professional can advise you. Some common injuries resulting from exercise include joint sprains, muscle strains, and other musculoskeletal problems. Knowing how to treat an acute, or immediate, injury is important (see Table 7.2). **RICE** most injuries, such as a twisted ankle: Rest, Ice, Compression, and Elevation.

> Time, Inc reported (Aug. 5, 2002) that tai chi is the perfect exercise for seniors. **Tai chi** is an ancient martial art involving graceful movement performed slowly with great concentration and focus on breathing. The atmosphere is non-competitive, and participants are encouraged to progress at their own pace. The Oregon Research Institute reports that studies show older men and women who are inactive yet relatively healthy attain many benefits from participation in tai chi.

RICE
R—Rest the injured limb, preventing further injury.
I—Ice will help reduce swelling by reducing circulation and easing pain. Apply ice in thirty-minute periods several times per day. A Styrofoam cup with frozen water can be used as an ice rub. A bag of frozen peas also works well!
C—Compression will help reduce swelling and fluid collection at the injury site. An elastic bandage works well to wrap the injured limb.
E—Elevating the injured limb will reduce swelling. Ideally, raise the injured area above the heart. Placing the injured area on pillows on a stool is helpful.

Of course, using proper equipment, wearing proper clothing and shoes, and practicing correct technique are essential for injury prevention. Weight-bearing forms of exercise will obviously cause more stress on the joints, but also have benefits that non-weight-bearing activities do not have, such as increasing strength of the bones and other connective tissues.

Proper Footwear

It many seem trivial, but proper footwear is critical to success in weight bearing exercise. Shoe technology has come a long way in the past decade. Sport-specific shoes are highly recommended to avoid injury and to enhance performance. Unfortunately, the consumer pays for the research and technology, as well as the logo on the shoes. A good cross trainer shoe is the way to go if you like to do a variety of activities. Cross trainers are not, however, recommended for aerobic dance or running. Running shoes are also not appropriate for "studio activities" such as aerobic dance, step aerobics, BOSU activities, as

Table 7.2 ♦ Reference Guide for Exercise-Related Problems

Injury	Signs/Symptoms	Treatment*
Bruise (contusion)	Pain, swelling, discoloration	Cold application, compression, rest
Dislocations, fractures	Pain, swelling, deformity	Splinting, cold application, seek medical attention
Heat cramps	Cramps, spasms and muscle twitching in the legs, arms, and abdomen	Stop activity, get out of the heat, stretch, massage the painful area, drink plenty of fluids
Heat exhaustion	Fainting, profuse sweating, cold/clammy skin, weak/rapid pulse, weakness, headache	Stop activity, rest in a cool place, loosen clothing, rub body with cool/wet towel, drink plenty of fluids, stay out of heat for two to three days
Heat stroke	Hot/dry skin, no sweating, serious disorientation, rapid/full pulse, vomiting, diarrhea, unconsciousness, high body temperature	Seek immediate medical attention, request help and get out of the sun, bathe in cold water/spray with cold water/rub body with cold towels, drink plenty of cold fluids
Joint sprains	Pain, tenderness, swelling, loss of use, discoloration	Cold application, compression, elevation, rest, heat after thirty-six to forty-eight hours (if no further swelling)
Muscle cramps	Pain, spasms	Stretch muscle(s), use mild exercises for involved area
Muscle soreness and stiffness	Tenderness, pain	Mild stretching, low-intensity exercise, warm bath
Muscle strains	Pain, tenderness, swelling, loss of use	Cold application, compression, elevation, rest, heat after thirty-six to forty-eight hours (if no further swelling)
Shin splints	Pain, tenderness	Cold application prior to and following any physical activity, rest, heat (if no activity is carried out)
Side stitch	Pain on the side of the abdomen below the rib cage	Decrease level of physical activity or stop altogether, gradually increase level of fitness
Tendinitis	Pain, tenderness, loss of use	Rest, cold application, heat after forty-eight hours

*Cold should be applied three or four times a day for fifteen to twenty minutes. Heat should be applied three times a day for fifteen to twenty minutes.

well as court activities like tennis or racquetball. Running shoes have little lateral support and the higher flared heel can actually cause a person participating in step aerobics to be more prone to twisting an ankle or knee joint. Some steps also have a rubber top which can grip the waffle sole of the running shoe and increase the risk of injury.

In any athletic shoe, fit and comfort are of the utmost importance. It is worth going to a store staffed by knowledgeable personnel. Often they can give you good insight into the type of shoe that is most appropriate for your foot and your gait.

Christopher McDougall's 2009 publication *Born to Run* started a discourse between runners regarding what is the best way to run—wearing $160.00 state-of-the-art running shoes or running barefoot? The barefoot crowd claims that a barefoot runner has a more natural gait, striking with the mid or forefoot first. Shoes with cushioning and a high heel cause the runner to strike the ground with the heel first. Vibram's successful FiveFingers brand popularized the minimalist shoe movement in California and first-place runners in marathons have been seen wearing them. Barefoot runners using the FiveFingers shoe can "feel" the road and may run with a more natural gate and yet still have protection from irritants on the ground like small shards of glass. There are 2 categories of minimalist shoes—the FiveFingers type that fits snug on your foot, and a minimalist running shoe (a cross between a traditional running shoe and being barefoot) which has just a bit of structure and support. If you decide to try the minimalist route, progress slowly and use caution. (Ellingson)

Environmental Conditions

Take into consideration environmental conditions such as temperature, air pollution, wind-chill, altitude, and humidity that can affect one's health and safety. Dressing appropriately is important when exercising in extreme weather conditions.

When exercising in the cold weather, layering of clothes is advised. There are new fabrics that can wick away moisture from the body better than fabrics such as wool, polypropylene, and cotton. Avoid cotton as a base layer in cold weather because if it gets wet with perspiration it will stay wet and make you colder. The Dupont company pioneered such a fabric called ComfortMax (Powers and Dodd, 2009). This is an advantage because moisture from perspiration can be transferred away (called "wicking") from the body, allowing evaporation to occur. This type of fabric is excellent as a first layer when skiing, jogging, or hiking in cold weather. Outer layers are ideally a waterproof shell that has mesh or zippered compartments to "breathe" and can be peeled off as needed. It is advisable to limit exercise time in extremely cold weather to avoid hypothermia.

Exercising in the heat can be a challenge (see Figure 7.6). It is important to acclimate to the heat and humidity, especially when moving from an area that is cool and arid. Gradually increase duration and intensity when exercising in a new type of environment. Especially in the Southern states, heat injuries are a real concern. **Heat cramps**, **heat exhaustion**, and **heat stroke** can all occur with prolonged exposure to the heat. Heat stroke is a life-threatening condition, and necessitates hospitalization. Heat exhaustion is more common, with individuals typically suffering from dehydration. In order for the body to effectively cool, evaporation of sweat needs to occur. *In a humid environment when perspiration drips off of a person, evaporation is not occurring, and therefore cooling is not taking place.* A hot and humid environment is especially risky to the very young, the old, and those with low cardiovascular fitness levels.

Heat injuries are much less likely to occur if a person is adequately hydrated. Proper hydration is necessary

Proper footwear is critical to success in weight bearing exercise. Sport-specific shoes help prevent injury and enhance performance.

Guidelines for Exercising in the Heat

1. Stay hydrated with cool water (cool water is absorbed best in the gut) before, during and after activity.
2. Dress appropriately in clothes that can wick moisture away from the body.
3. Limit exposure time.
4. Exercise with a buddy, or let someone know your plan and stick to it.
5. Wear lightweight sunglasses for eye protection against sun glare, dust and debris in the air. (Important if you exercise near a construction site or near traffic.)
6. Exercise in the coolest time of the day if possible.
7. Stop activity if you experience nausea, dizziness, or extreme headache.
8. Monitor your heart rate, staying within your target heart rate zone.
9. Check the heat index to make sure it is safe to exercise.

for the body to function properly. Water aids in controlling body temperature, contributes to the structure and form of the body, and provides the liquid environment for cell processes. When the thirst mechanism is activated, dehydration has already begun. It is important to pre-hydrate, drink before thirst occurs, and especially drink before exercising. The standard recommendation is to drink at least eight eight-ounce glasses of water a day. Exercise increases the body's demand for water due to an increase in metabolic rate and body temperature. Therefore, this amount should be increased. Drinking water every waking hour is a good habit for individuals who exercise on a regular basis. Hydration is very critical in a humid environment. Before, during, and after aerobic exercise, increase the amount of water consumed. *Water is necessary for the efficient functioning of the body; thus, the importance of hydration cannot be overstated.* Electrolyte levels, especially calcium, sodium, and potassium, are critically important in muscle contraction and should also be carefully maintained. This may be accomplished through re-hydrating with sports drinks. Sports drinks are useful for glycogen replacement when the duration of an activity is sixty to ninety minutes or longer or if the athlete is in a tournament with multiple events.

Hyponatremia

Avoiding dehydration is critical when exercising, especially in the heat and high humidity. There is, however, a possibility of over-hydration, which can be just as critical. Due to the popularity of marathon and triathlon training programs, more people are participating in longer road races. There are more marathon walkers than ever before. A walker can be on the course for a much longer time than a runner—perhaps six or seven hours. If the walker is hydrating the entire time, it is possible to over-hydrate. This over-hydration can lead to a condition called **hyponatremia**, also called **water intoxication**. Hyponatremia is characterized by a low sodium concentration in the blood. Hyponatremia is seen in some medical conditions such as certain forms of lung cancer. Exercise-associated hyponatremia involves excess ADH

FIGURE 7.6

Heat and Humidity Chart

Apparent temperature (what it feels like)

Air temperature (F°)		70°	75°	80°	85°	90°	95°	100°	105°	110°	115°
Relative Humidity	0%	64°	69°	73°	78°	83°	87°	91°	95°	99°	103°
	10%	65°	70°	75°	80°	85°	90°	95°	100°	105°	111°
	20%	66°	72°	77°	82°	87°	93°	99°	105°	112°	120°
	30%	67°	73°	78°	84°	90°	96°	104°	113°	123°	135°
	40%	68°	74°	79°	86°	93°	101°	110°	123°	137°	151°
	50%	69°	75°	81°	88°	96°	107°	120°	135°	150°	
	60%	70°	76°	82°	90°	100°	114°	132°	149°		
	70%	70°	77°	85°	93°	106°	124°	144°			
	80%	71°	78°	86°	97°	113°	136°				
	90%	71°	79°	88°	102°	122°					
	100%	72°	80°	91°	108°						

Apparent temperature:	Heat stress risk with exertion:
90°–105°	Heat cramps and heat exhaustion possible.
105°–130°	Heat cramps or heat exhaustion likely; heat stroke possible.
130° and above	Heat stroke highly likely with continued exposure.

To determine the risk of exercising in the heat, locate the outside air temperature on the top horizontal scale and the relative humidity on the left vertical scale. Where these two values intersect is the apparent temperature. For example, on a 90°F day with 70 percent humidity, the apparent temperature is 106°F. Heat cramps or heat exhaustion are likely to occur, and heat stroke is possible during exercise under these conditions.

Source: Adapted from U.S. Department of Commerce, National Oceanic and Atmospheric Administration, Heat index chart, in *Heat wave: A major summer killer.* Washington, D.C.: Government Printing Office, 1992.

(antidiuretic hormone) being secreted from the pituitary gland. The longer a person sweats, the higher the risk of hyponatremia due to lost electrolytes. Hyponatremia can be life-threatening, and unfortunately the hyponatremia symptoms mimic the symptoms of heat illness (fatigue, light headedness, nausea, cramping, headache, dizziness). If you treat a hyponatremia victim the same way you would a heat illness victim, you could accelerate their decline.

The best way to avoid hyponatremia, or dehydration for that matter, is to be aware of fluid loss and fluid intake. When training, weigh yourself pre- and post-activity to determine fluid loss from your workout. After approximately sixty minutes of activity, it is best to rehydrate in part with sports drinks that contain electrolytes such as sodium and chloride. "Fluid consumption that exceeds sweating rate is the primary factor leading to exercise-associated hyponatremia. Women are at a greater risk than men to develop exercise associated hyponatremia." (ACSM, 2007) It is also prudent to eat a normal diet including salt-containing foods unless you are restricted by your physician from sodium in your diet. When competing in races, avoid ingesting aspirin, ibuprofen, or acetaminophen, which can interfere with kidney functioning. As with other things in life, balance is the key.

Illness

Use common sense when ill. If you have cold symptoms with no fever, then possibly a light workout might make you feel better. If fever is present, you have a headache, extreme fatigue, muscle aches, swollen lymph glands, or if you have flu-like symptoms, then bed rest is recommended. Marathon efforts of high intensity and long duration have been shown to temporarily suppress the immune system. Mild to moderate exercise has been shown to enhance the immune system and to reduce risk of respiratory infections (ACSM, 1989).

Adverse Effects of Dehydration

Exercise in the heat can be extremely dangerous, depending on exercise intensity, ambient temperature, relative humidity, clothing, and state of hydration (water content of the body). Although some forms of heat injury can occur prior to significant weight loss due to sweating, the table in this box shows how weight loss during exercise can be a predictor of some of the dangers associated with exercise in the heat. The loss of body weight during exercise in the heat is simply due to water loss through sweating. Thus, prolonged, profuse sweating is the first warning signal of impending dehydration.

% Body Weight Loss	Symptoms	% Body Weight Loss	Symptoms
0.5	Thirst	6.0	Impaired temperature regulation, increased heart rate
2.0	Stronger thirst, vague discomfort, loss of appetite	8.0	Dizziness, labored breathing during exercise, confusion
3.0	Concentrated blood, dry mouth, reduced urine output	10.0	Spastic muscles, loss of balance, delirium
4.0	Increased effort required during exercise, flushed skin, apathy	11.0	Circulatory insufficiency, decreased blood volume, kidney failure
5.0	Difficulty in concentrating		

Source: From Total Fitness and Wellness, 5th Edition, by Powers and Dodd, Benjamin Cummings Publishers.

Allergies and asthma can make exercising a challenge. If you suffer from either or both conditions, take precaution when exercising. Dealing with asthma and allergies does not preclude exercising outdoors-it means you have to be prepared and manage your symptoms. People who suffer from allergies have an immune system that responds to triggers in the environment.

If you're interested in training for a 5K or 10K fun run, visit Smart Coach at runnersworld.com. You will find a beginning runner's training guide that includes free advice according to your personal fitness and training level.

The Biggest Risk to Exercise Is Not Starting!

The internal conditions of the body before and during exercise are even more crucial than exercising with the proper external conditions. Eating a regular meal immediately before exercising will usually result in poor performance, stomach cramps, and sometimes even vomiting. The days of a steak and potato pre-game meal are gone. It is important to fuel your body with high quality protein, low fat, and high complex carbohydrate foods prior to competition; however, even more important is fueling your body on a daily basis. *Everyday good nutrition will cause an athlete to perform better in practice, thereby optimizing training that may result in a better performance in competition.* This is also sound advice for non-athletes trying to stay active. The recommendations for individuals involved in a regular exercise program are: 55 to 60 percent of total calories consumed should be from carbohydrates, 25 to 30 percent from fat, and 12 to 15 percent from protein. Individuals who are involved in a high-intensity muscular training program should consume a higher amount of protein and less fat for muscle growth and maintenance. Adequate hydration is also critical and can make a difference in the quality of exercise and performance.

Staying active has clearly been shown to enhance a person's quality of life. **Exercise is for everyone; it is never too early or too late to start.** Most people know that they would benefit from participating in an exercise program, but for many it is difficult to get started. Find an activity you enjoy. Make a plan. Write it down. Get a workout buddy. Start slowly, and listen to your body. Pain is usually a signal that something is wrong. The old adage 'no pain, no gain' can cause beginners to become frustrated. Balance activity, leisure time, and rest each week. With consistency, activity can have a positive impact on reducing risk for many conditions associated with too little activity, called hypokinetic conditions. And most importantly, you should experience increased stamina, enthusiasm, and enhanced mental well-being in your daily life.

References

American College of Sports Medicine (ACSM). *Exercise and the Common Cold.* 1989.

American College of Sports Medicine. *Perceived Exertion* Current Comment, 2014.

ACSM/AHA Joint Position Stand "Exercise and Acute Cardiovascular Events: Placing Risks into Perspective." *Medicine and Science in Sports and Exercise.* 2007.

ACSM Exercise and Fluid Replacement Postition Stand; Medicine & Science in Sports & Exercise: February 2007 - Volume 39 - Issue 2 - pp 377-390 doi: 10.1249/mss.0b013e31802ca597

American Heart Association. *Heart and Stroke Statistical Update.* Dallas: American Heart Association. 2012.

Bishop, J. G. and Aldana, S. G. *Step Up to Wellness.* Needham Heights, MA: Allyn & Bacon. 1999.

Circulation is available at http://circ.ahajournals.org. © 2016 American Heart Association, Inc. https://doi.org/10.1161/CIR.0000000000000440

Circulation. 2016;134:e262- e279; Originally published August 15, 2016 Sedentary Behavior and Cardiovascular Morbidity and Mortality: A Science Advisory From the American Heart Association

Cissik, J. M. *The Basics of Strength Training.* New York: McGraw-Hill Companies, Inc. 1998.

Corbin, C. B. and Lindsey, R. *Concepts of Fitness and Wellness: Active Lifestyles for Wellness* (15th ed). McGraw Hill. 2009.

Corbin, C. et al. Physical Activity for Children: A Statement of Guidelines for Children Age 5–12, NASPE. Dec. 2003.

Ellingsen, Jan, The Basics of Barefoot/Minimalist Running Jan. 2012, REI expert advice online. www.physicalactivityplan.org

Evans, W. J. Vitamin E, Vitamin C, and Exercise. *American Journal of Clinical Nutrition,* Vol. 72, 647s-652s. August 2000.

Fox, E., Bowers, R., and Merle, F. *The Physiological Basis for Exercise and Sport* (5th ed). Madison, WI: WCB Brown & Benchmark Publishers. 1989.

Galloway, Jeff. *Galloway's Book of Running.* Shelter Publications, Bolinas, California (2002)

Garber, C.E., Blissmer, B., Deschenes, M.R., et al. Quantity and Quality of Exercise for Developing and Maintaining Cardiorespiratory, Musculoskeletal, and Neuromotor Fitness in Apparently Healthy Adults: Guidance for Prescribing Exercise. America College of Sports Medicine, Indianapolis, IN. Medicine and Science in Sports and Exercise. 2011 July; 4(7): 1334–1359

Haskell WL, Lee I-M, Pate RP, Powell KE, Blair SN, Franklin BA, Macera CA, Heath GW, Thompson PD, Bauman A. Physical activity and public health: updated recommendation for adults from the American College of Sports Medicine and the American Heart Association. *Circulation.* 2007;116: 1081–1093.

Haskell, W. L. et al. Physical Activity and Public Health: Updated Recommendations for Adults from the American College of Sports Medicine. *Medicine and Science in Sports and Exercise* 39 (8):1424–1434 Belmont, CA: Wadsworth/Thompson Learning. 2007.

Healthier U.S. Initiative; www.whitehouse.gov

http://www.health.harvard.edu/exercise-and-fitness/hit-workouts-may-boost-exercisemotivation

http://journals.lww.com/acsmmsse/Fulltext/2016/03000/Nutrition_and_Athletic_Performance.25.aspx

Journal of Obesity Vol 2012, Article ID 480467. doi:10.1155/2012/480467

Kuehl KS[1], Perrier ET, Elliot DL, Chesnutt JC. *Efficacy of tart cherry juice in reducing muscle pain during running: a randomized controlled trial.* J Int Soc Sports Nutr. 2010 May 7;7:17. doi:10.1186/1550-2783-7-17.

Latham, N.K., et al. 2004. Systematic review of progressive resistance strength training in older adults. *The Journals of Gerontology Series A: Biological Sciences and Medical Sciences, 59A* (1), M48–M61.

McArdle, W. D., Katch, F. I., and Katch, V. L. *Exercise Physiology: Energy, Nutrition, and Human Performance.* Baltimore: Williams and Wilkins. 1999.

McGill, S. Low Back Disorders: Evidence-Based Prevention and Rehabilitation. Champaign, IL: Human Kinetics, 2002.

Mohamed Labazi, Anna K. McNeil, Timothy Kurtz, Taylor C. Lee, Ronald B. Pegg, José Pedro Friedmann Angeli, Marcus Conrad, Paul L. McNeil. The antioxidant requirement for plasma membrane repair in skeletal muscle. Free Radical Biology and Medicine, 2015; 84: 246 DOI:10.1016/j.freeradbiomed.2015.03.016

Pate, R., Pratt, M., Blair, S., Haskell, W., Macera, C., et al. Physical Activity and Public Health: A Recommendation from the Centers for Disease

Control and Prevention and the American College of Sports Medicine. *Journal of the American Medical Association, 273:* 402–407. 1995.

Payne, W. A. and Hahn, D. B. *Understanding Your Health* (6th ed). St. Louis, MO: Mosby. 2000.

Physical Activity and Health: A Report of the Surgeon General. Atlanta: U.S. Department of Health and Human Services, Centers for Disease Control and Prevention, National Center for Chronic Disease Prevention and Health Promotion. 1996.

Pollock, M. L., Gaesser, G. A., Butcher, J. D., Despres, J-P., Dishman, R. K., et al. ACSM Position Stand on the Recommended Quantity and Quality of Exercise for Developing and Maintaining Cardiorespiratory and Muscular Fitness, and Flexibility in Adults. *Medicine & Science in Sports & Exercise, 30:* 975–991. 1998.

Powers, S. K., and Dodd, S. L. *Total Fitness and Wellness* (5th ed). San Francisco: Pearson Benjamin Cummings. 2009.

Powers, S. K., and Howley, E. T. *Exercise Physiology: Theory and Application to Fitness and Performance* (6th ed). New York: McGraw-Hill Companies, Inc. 2006.

Rosato, F. *Fitness to Wellness: The Physical Connection* (3rd ed.) Minneapolis: West. 1994.

Sabo, E. *Good Exercises for Bad Knees.* www.healthology.com; Retrieved June 14, 2005.

Schuna JM Jr., Johnson WD, Tudor-Locke C. Adult self-*reported and objectively monitored physical activity and sedentary behavior: NHANES 2005-2006. Int J Behav Nutr Phys Act. 2013;10:126. doi: 10.1186/1479-5868-10-126.*

Sharkey, B. J. *Fitness and Health.* Champaign, IL: Human Kinetics Publishing. 1997.

Sieg, K. W., and Adams, S. P. *Illustrated Essentials of Musculoskeletal Anatomy.* Gainesville, FL: Megabooks Inc. 1985.

T. N. Ziegenfuss,[1] H. L. Lopez,[1] A. Kedia,[1] S. M. Habowski,[1] J. E. Sandrock,[1] B. Raub,[1] C. M. Kerksick,[2] and A. A. Ferrando[3] *Effects of an amylopectin and chromium complex on the anabolic response to a suboptimal dose of whey protein.* J Int Soc Sports Nutr. 2017; 14: 6. Published online 2017 Feb 8. doi: 10.1186/s12970-017-0163-1

University of Birmingham. "Increased levels of active vitamin D can help to optimize muscle strength." ScienceDaily. ScienceDaily, 15 February 2017. www.sciencedaily.com/releases/2017/02/170215145953.htm.

Why We Are Losing the War on Obesity; Health Annual Editions 05/06, 26th edition, McGraw-Hill/Dushkin.

Wilmore, J. H. and Costill, D. L. *Physiology of Sport and Exercise.* Champaign, IL: Human Kinetics Publishing Company. 1999.

Chapter 8
Nutrition and Metabolism

© 2012, Shutterstock, Inc.

OBJECTIVES

Students will be able to:

- Define the essential nutrients (carbohydrates, fats, proteins, vitamins, and minerals) and describe their roles in daily nutrition.
- Introduce and explain the USDA Food Guide Pyramid.
- Introduce guidelines for food labeling and explain how food labels describe the nutritional values of food.
- Define the four styles of vegetarianism.
- Discuss the roles of organic and functional foods.

Adaptation of *Health and Fitness: A Guide to a Healthly Lifestyle,* 5th Edition, by Laura Bounds, Gayden Darnell, Kirstin Brekken Shea, and Dottiede Agnor. Copyright © 2012 by Kendall Hunt Publishing Company.

"A man's health can be judged by which he takes two at a time—pills or stairs."

—Joan Welsh

Good, sound nutritional choices are necessary for maintaining a healthy lifestyle. Making the effort to obtain the essential nutrients through daily dietary intake is not something in which most Americans are proficient. In general, Americans eat too much salt, sugar, and fat and do not consume the recommended daily allowance (RDA) of vitamins and minerals.

Poor dietary habits, along with being physically inactive, are major factors that result in Americans becoming increasingly overweight and obese. As noted in Chapter 5, being overweight or obese is a major risk factor for chronic health problems such as hypertension, cardiovascular disease, diabetes, and certain types of cancers. With this in mind, the importance of building a knowledge base that will allow an individual to develop sound, life-long nutritional habits and practices becomes clear.

Once an individual has made the effort to gather information that will allow him or her to make good nutritional choices, he or she must then make a concentrated effort to obtain the essential macronutrients and micronutrients through their daily food selections. **Macronutrients** provide energy in the form of calories. Carbohydrates, fats, and proteins make up the sources of macronutrients. **Micronutrients**, which include vitamins and minerals, regulate bodily functions such as metabolism, growth, and cellular development. Together, macronutrients and micronutrients are responsible for the following three tasks that are necessary for the continuance of life:

1. growth, repair, and maintenance of all tissues,
2. regulation of body processes, and
3. providing energy.

Because nutrition information is often filled with scientific terminology and unfamiliar jargon, it is many times misleading or appears to be overly complicated. Several government agencies, such as the U.S. Department of Agriculture (USDA) and the U.S. Department of Health and Human Services (DHHS), have teamed up in an effort to simplify and streamline nutritional information widely available to the general public in an effort to decrease the amount of misinformation on nutrition and increase the prevalence of practical, easy-to-apply, user-friendly information.

Dietary Guidelines for Americans

In 1980 the *Dietary Guidelines for Americans* was first published as a scientifically-based health promotion that attempted to reduce an individual's risk for chronic diseases through diet and increased levels of physical activity. The USDA and the DHHS have updated and republished these *Dietary Guidelines* every five years since their inception in 1980.

The most current version of the *Dietary Guidelines* was published in early 2015 (https://health.gov/dietaryguidelines/2015/guidelines/chapter-1/key-recommendations/). Despite the 2015 report containing more scientific and technical information than it has in the past, it continues to be an excellent source to aid in the building of a nutritious and healthy diet for the general population.

The recommendations stated by the *Dietary Guidelines* are interrelated and depend on each other. Therefore, it is the intent of the *Guidelines* to be used together in planning a healthy diet. However, it is still possible to achieve health benefits if just some of the recommendations are followed.

The following is a list of the key recommendations of the *Dietary Guidelines*.

Key Recommendations

Consume a healthy eating pattern that accounts for all foods and beverages within an appropriate calorie level.

A healthy eating pattern includes:[2]

- A variety of vegetables from all of the subgroups—dark green, red and orange, legumes (beans and peas), starchy, and other
- Fruits, especially whole fruits
- Grains, at least half of which are whole grains
- Fat-free or low-fat dairy, including milk, yogurt, cheese, and/or fortified soy beverages
- A variety of protein foods, including seafood, lean meats and poultry, eggs, legumes (beans and peas), and nuts, seeds, and soy products
- Oils

A healthy eating pattern limits:

- Saturated fats and trans fats, added sugars, and sodium

Key Recommendations that are quantitative are provided for several components of the diet that should be limited. These components are of particular public health concern in the United States, and the specified limits can help individuals achieve healthy eating patterns within calorie limits:

- Consume less than 10 percent of calories per day from added sugars[3]
- Consume less than 10 percent of calories per day from saturated fats[4]
- Consume less than 2,300 milligrams (mg) per day of sodium[5]
- If alcohol is consumed, it should be consumed in moderation—up to one drink per day for women and up to two drinks per day for men—and only by adults of legal drinking age.[6]

[2]Definitions for each food group and subgroup are provided throughout the chapter and are compiled in Appendix 3. USDA Food Patterns: Healthy U.S.-Style Eating Pattern.

[3]The recommendation to limit intake of calories from added sugars to less than 10 percent per day is a target based on food pattern modeling and national data on intakes of calories from added sugars that demonstrate the public health need to limit calories from added sugars to meet food group and nutrient needs within calorie limits. The limit on calories from added sugars is not a Tolerable Upper Intake Level (UL) set by the Institute of Medicine (IOM). For most calorie levels, there are not enough calories available after meeting food group needs to consume 10 percent of calories from added sugars and 10 percent of calories from saturated fats and still stay within calorie limits.

[4]The recommendation to limit intake of calories from saturated fats to less than 10 percent per day is a target based on evidence that replacing saturated fats with unsaturated fats is associated with reduced risk of cardiovascular disease. The limit on calories from saturated fats is not a UL set by the IOM. For most calorie levels, there are not enough calories available after meeting food group needs to consume 10 percent of calories from added sugars and 10 percent of calories from saturated fats and still stay within calorie limits.

[5]The recommendation to limit intake of sodium to less than 2,300 mg per day is the UL for individuals ages 14 years and older set by the IOM. The recommendations for children younger than 14 years of age are the IOM age- and sex-appropriate ULs (see Appendix 7. Nutritional Goals for Age-Sex Groups Based on Dietary Reference Intakes and Dietary Guidelines Recommendations).

[6]It is not recommended that individuals begin drinking or drink more for any reason. The amount of alcohol and calories in beverages varies and should be accounted for within the limits of healthy eating patterns. Alcohol should be consumed only by adults of legal drinking age. There are many circumstances in which individuals should not drink, such as during pregnancy. See Appendix 9. Alcohol for additional information.

Essential Nutrients

It is necessary for an individual to ingest more than forty different nutrients in order to maintain good health. Because no single food source contains all of these nutrients, variety in one's diet is essential. Eating a wide variety of foods will help ensure adequate intake of carbohydrates, fats, proteins, vitamins, and minerals.

Carbohydrates

Carbohydrates should be the body's main source of fuel. Between 45 and 65 percent of an individual's diet should be composed of carbohydrates. Of this 45 to 65 percent, 35 to 55 percent of total daily caloric intake should be from complex carbohydrates, leaving simple carbohydrates to account for less than 10 percent of the daily carbohydrate intake.

Complex carbohydrates are relatively low in calories (4 calories per gram), nutritionally dense, and are a rich source of vitamins, minerals, and water. Complex carbohydrates provide the body with a steady source of energy for hours. The best sources of complex carbohydrates are breads, cereals, pastas, and grains.

Dietary fiber, also known as roughage or bulk, is a type of complex carbohydrate that is present mainly in leaves, roots, skins, and seeds and is the part of a plant that is not digested in the small intestine. Dietary fiber helps decrease the risk of cardiovascular disease and cancer, and may lower an individual's risk of coronary heart disease. Table 8.1 lists good sources of dietary fiber.

Dietary fiber is either soluble or insoluble. **Soluble fiber** dissolves in water. It helps the body excrete fats and has been shown to reduce levels of blood cholesterol and blood sugar, as well as helping to control diabetes. Water-soluble fiber travels through the digestive tract in gel-like form, pacing the

TABLE 8.1 ♦ Good Sources of Dietary Fiber

Fruits	Grams	Grains	Grams
1 medium apple	4–5	1 bagel	1
1 banana	3	1 whole-grain slice of bread	1–3
1 cup blueberries	5	4 graham crackers	3
10 dates	7	1 bran muffin	2
1 orange	3	hot dog/hamburger bun	1
1 pear	5	1 cup cooked oatmeal	7–9
1 cup strawberries	3	1/2 cup Grape Nuts cereal	3.5
1 watermelon slice	2–3	1 cup Nature Valley granola	7.5
		3/4 cup Shredded Wheat cereal	4
Vegetables	**Grams**	1 cup cooked macaroni	1
1 artichoke	4	1 cup cooked rice	2.5–4
1 raw carrot	2	1 cup cooked spaghetti	1–2
1/2 cup cream style corn	6	**Other**	**Grams**
1 cup chopped lettuce	1		
1/2 cup green peas	6	1 cup almonds	15
1 cup cooked spinach	6	1 cup cashews	8
1 cup cooked squash	5–6	1 cup shredded coconut	11
1 tomato	2	1 tbsp peanut butter	1
Legumes	**Grams**		
1 cup cooked black beans	15		
1 cup cooked green beans	3		
1 cup pork and beans	18		
1 cup cooked blackeyed peas	11		
1 cup kidney beans	20		
1 cup cooked navy beans	16		
1 cup cooked pinto beans	19		

absorption of cholesterol, which helps prevent dramatic shifts in blood sugar levels. Soluble fiber is found primarily in oats, fruits, barley, and legumes.

Insoluble fiber does not dissolve easily in water; therefore, it cannot be digested by the body. Insoluble fiber causes softer, bulkier stool that increases peristalsis. This, in turn, reduces the risk of colon cancer by allowing food residues to pass through the intestinal tract more quickly, limiting the exposure and absorption time of toxic substances within the waste materials. Primary sources of insoluble fiber include wheat, cereals, vegetables, and the skins of fruits.

The recommended daily intake of fiber is 25–30 g per day. Health disorders associated with low fiber intake include constipation, diverticulitis, hemorrhoids, gall bladder disease, and obesity. Problems associated with ingesting too much fiber include losses of calcium, phosphorous, iron, and disturbances of the gastrointestinal system.

Simple carbohydrates are sugars that have little nutritive value beyond their energy content. Sugars that are found naturally in milk, fruit, honey, and some vegetables are examples of simple carbohydrates. Foods high in simple sugars are sometimes dismissed as "empty calories." Examples of these foods include candy, cakes, jellies, and sodas.

Fats

Fats are the body's primary source of energy, and supply the body with 9 calories of energy per gram ingested. While many Americans consume too many of their daily calories from fats (37 to 40 percent), dietary fat is not necessarily a "bad" component of an individual's diet at moderate levels of consumption. At moderate amounts, between 20 and 35 percent of daily calories, fat is crucial to good nutrition.

Fat has many essential functions: providing the body with stored energy, insulating the body to preserve body heat, contributing to cellular structure, and protecting vital organs by absorbing shock. Fat not only adds flavor and texture to foods and helps satisfy an individual's appetite because it is digested more slowly, it also supplies the body with essential fatty acids and transports fat-soluble vitamins A, E, D, and K. Fat is also necessary for normal growth and healthy skin, and is essential in the synthesis of certain hormones.

There are different types of dietary fat. **Saturated fats** are found primarily in animal products such as meats, lard, cream, butter, cheese, and whole milk. However, coconut and palm oils are two plant sources of saturated fat. A defining characteristic of saturated fats is that they typically do not melt at room temperature (an exception being the above mentioned oils that are "almost solid" at room temperature). Saturated fats increase low-density lipoproteins (LDL) or "bad cholesterol" levels and in turn increase an individuals risk for heart disease and colorectal cancer.

Trans fat is different from other types of fat in that it typically does not occur naturally in plant or animal products. While a small amount of trans fat is found naturally, the majority of trans fat is formed when liquid oils are made into solid fats (i.e., shortening and some margarines). Trans fat is made during hydrogenation—when hydrogen is added to vegetable oil. This process is used to increase the shelf life of foods and to help foods maintain their original flavor. Many fried foods and "store bought" sweets and treats have high amounts of this type of fat. While most individuals consume four to five times more saturated fat than trans fat, it is important to be aware of the amount of trans fat in one's diet because it raises LDL, "bad," cholesterol and increases the risk of coronary heart disease. Starting January 1, 2006, the Food and Drug Administration (FDA) requires all foods to list the amount of trans fat contained in the product on the Nutrition Facts panel. The exception to this new requirement is that if the total fat in a food is less than 0.5 g per serving and no claims are made about fat, fatty acid, or cholesterol content, trans fat does not have to be listed.

Unsaturated fats are derived primarily from plant products such as vegetable oils, avocados, and most nuts, and do not raise the body's

TABLE 8.2 ◆ What Is Your Upper Limit on Fat for the Calories You Consume?

Total Calories per Day	Saturated Fat in Grams	Total Fat in Grams
1,600	18 or less	53
2,000*	20 or less	65
2,200	24 or less	73
2,500*	25 or less	80
2,800	31 or less	93

*Percent Daily Values on Nutrition Facts Labels are based on a 2,000 calorie diet. Values for 2,000 and 2,500 calories are rounded to the nearest 5 grams to be consistent with the Nutrition Facts Label.

blood cholesterol. Unsaturated fats include both monounsaturated and polyunsaturated fats. **Monounsaturated fats** are found in foods such as olives, peanuts, canola oil, peanut oil, and olive oil. **Polyunsaturated fats** are found in margarine, pecans, corn oil, cottonseed oil, sunflower oil, and soybean oil (see Table 8.3).

Fats become counterproductive to good health when they are consumed in excess. Too much fat in many Americans' diets is the reason Americans lead the world in heart disease. Excess fat intake elevates blood cholesterol levels and leads to atherosclerosis. Diets with excess fat have attributed to 30 to 40 percent of all cancers in men and 60 percent of all cancers in women, and have also been linked to cancer of the breast, colon, and prostate more frequently than any other dietary factor.

By following the guidelines listed in Table 8.2 of this chapter, the level of saturated fat and trans fat consumed each day can be limited to 10 percent of that day's total calories.

Protein

Even though **proteins** should make up only 10 to 35 percent of total calories ingested, they are the essential "building blocks" of the body. Proteins are needed for the growth, maintenance, and repair of all body tissues, that is, muscles, blood, bones, internal organs, skin, hair, and nails. Proteins also help maintain the normal balance of body fluids and are needed to make enzymes, hormones, and antibodies that fight infection.

Proteins are made up of approximately twenty amino acids. An individual's body uses all twenty of these amino acids in the formation of different proteins. Eleven of the twenty are **non-essential amino acids**—they are manufactured in the body if food proteins in a person's diet provide enough nitrogen. Nine of the twenty are **essential amino acids**—the body cannot produce these, and thus must be supplied through an individual's diet. All amino acids must be present at the same time for particular protein synthesis to occur.

The suggested RDA of protein for adults is 45 through 65 g per day (intake should not exceed 1.6 g/kg of body weight (1kg. = 2.2 lbs). A few exceptions to

TABLE 8.3 ◆ Composition of Oils (%)

Type	Sat	Poly	Mono
safflower	9	75	16
sunflower	10	66	24
corn	13	59	28
soybean	14	58	28
sesame	14	42	44
peanut	17	32	51
palm	49	9	42
olive	14	8	78
canola	7	35	58

TABLE 8.4 ◆ Percentage of Fat Calories in Foods

Type of Food	Less than 15% of Calories from Fat	15%–30% of Calories from Fat	30%–50% of Calories from Fat	More than 50% of Calories from Fat
Fruits and Vegetables	Fruits, plain vegetables, juices, pickles, sauerkraut		French fries, hash browns	Avocados, coconuts, olives
Bread and Cereals	Grains and flours, most breads, most cereals, corn tortillas, pitas, matzoh, bagels, noodles, and pasta	Corn bread, flour tortillas, oatmeal, soft rolls and buns, wheat germ	Breakfast bars, biscuits and muffins, granola, pancakes and waffles, donuts, taco shells, pastries, croissants	
Dairy Products	Nonfat milk, dry curd cottage cheese, nonfat cottage cheese, nonfat yogurt	Buttermilk, low-fat yogurt, 1% milk, low-fat cottage cheese	Whole milk, 2% milk, creamed cottage cheese	Butter, cream, sour cream, half & half, most cheese, (including part-skim and lite cheeses)
Meats		Beef round; veal loin, round, and shoulder; pork tenderloin	Beef and veal, lamb, fresh and picnic hams	All ground beef, spareribs, cold cuts, beef, hot dogs, pastrami
Poultry	Egg whites	Chicken and turkey (light meat without skin)	Chicken and turkey (light meat with skin, dark meat without skin), duck and goose (without skin)	Chicken/turkey (dark meat with skin), chicken/turkey bologna and hot dogs, egg yolks, whole eggs
Seafood	Clams, cod, crab, crawfish, flounder, haddock, lobster, perch, sole, scallops, shrimp, tuna (in water)	Bass and sea bass, halibut, mussels, oyster, tuna (fresh)	Anchovies, catfish, salmon, sturgeon, trout, tuna (in oil, drained)	Herring, mackerel, sardines
Beans and Nuts	Dried beans and peas, chestnuts, water chestnuts		Soybeans	Tofu, most nuts and seeds, peanut butter
Fats and Oils	Oil-free and some lite salad dressings			Butter, margarine, all mayonnaise (including reduced-calorie), most salad dressings, all oils
Soups	Bouillons, broths, consomme	Most soups	Cream soups, bean soups, "just add water" noodle soups	Cheddar cheese soups, New England clam chowder
Desserts	Angel food cake, gelatin, some new fat-free cakes	Pudding, tapioca	Most cakes, most pies	
Frozen Desserts	Sherbert, low-fat frozen yogurt, sorbet, fruit ices	Ice milk	Frozen yogurt	All ice cream
Snack foods	Popcorn (air popped), pretzels, rye crackers, rice cakes, fig bars, raisin biscuit cookies, marshmallows, most hard candy, fruit rolls	Lite microwave popcorn, Scandinavian "crisps," plain crackers, caramels, fudge, gingersnaps, graham crackers	Snack crackers, popcorn (popped in oil), cookies, candy bars, granola bars	Most microwave popcorn, corn and potato chips, chocolate, buttery crackers

Source: American Heart Association/USDA.

FIGURE 8.1

Daily Diet Recommendations based on a 2,000-calorie pattern of a 19-Year-Old Female Who Does Less Than Thirty Minutes of Physical Activity a Day.

Go to MyPyramid. gov to get your personalized diet recommendation.

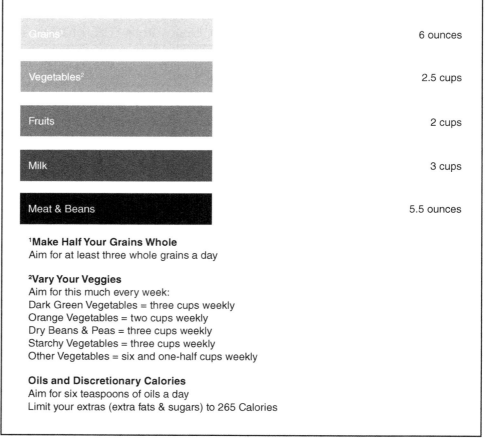

Grains[1]	6 ounces
Vegetables[2]	2.5 cups
Fruits	2 cups
Milk	3 cups
Meat & Beans	5.5 ounces

[1]Make Half Your Grains Whole
Aim for at least three whole grains a day

[2]Vary Your Veggies
Aim for this much every week:
Dark Green Vegetables = three cups weekly
Orange Vegetables = two cups weekly
Dry Beans & Peas = three cups weekly
Starchy Vegetables = three cups weekly
Other Vegetables = six and one-half cups weekly

Oils and Discretionary Calories
Aim for six teaspoons of oils a day
Limit your extras (extra fats & sugars) to 265 Calories

Source: From www.mypyramid.gov

this rule should be noted: Overweight individuals need slightly less than the calculated "norm," and women who are pregnant or lactating need slightly more protein per pound of body weight than the calculation indicates.

It is inadvisable to consume more protein than the daily recommended dosage (45–65 g/day), particularly in the form of protein supplements. Excessive protein supplementation can damage the kidneys, increase calcium excretion, negatively affect bone health, inhibit muscle growth, and can be detrimental to endurance performance.

Individuals who are trying to maximize muscular strength, endurance, and growth should take in the recommended 1.5 g of protein per kilogram of body weight, as well as an additional 500 calories of complex carbohydrates. The recommended protein and additional complex carbohydrates will work together to provide the extra nutrients and glucose needed for the increased muscular work load.

Vitamins

Vitamins are necessary for normal body metabolism, growth, and development. They do not provide the body with energy, but they do allow the energy from consumed carbohydrates, fats, and proteins to be released. Although vitamins are vital to life, they are required in minute amounts. Due primarily to adequate food supply, vitamin deficiencies in Americans are rare. However, there are some situations that may alter an individual's requirements, including pregnancy and smoking. Non-smokers need to consume 60 mg of vitamin C each day; a smoker must ingest 100 mg of vitamin C each day in order to gain the same nutritional benefits. A man or a non-pregnant woman should consume 180–200 mcg of folic acid, while a pregnant woman should consume approximately 400 mcg of folic acid per day.

Choose Sensibly for Good Health

- Choose a diet that is low in saturated fat and cholesterol and moderate in total fat.
- Choose beverages and foods to moderate your intake of sugars.
- Choose and prepare foods with less salt.
- If you drink alcoholic beverages, do so in moderation.

Fats and Oils

- Choose vegetable oils rather than solid fats (meat and dairy fats, shortening).
- If you need fewer calories, decrease the amount of fat you use in cooking and at the table.

Meat, Poultry, Fish, Shellfish, Eggs, Beans, and Nuts

- Choose two to three servings of fish, shellfish, lean poultry, other lean meats, beans, or nuts daily. Trim fat from meat and take skin off poultry. Choose dry beans, peas, or lentils often.
- Limit your intake of high-fat processed meats such as bacon, sausages, salami, bologna, and other cold cuts. Try the lower fat varieties (check the Nutrition Facts Label).
- Limit your intake of liver and other organ meats. Use egg yolks and whole eggs in moderation. Use egg whites and egg substitutes freely when cooking since they contain no cholesterol and little or no fat.

Dairy Products

- Choose fat-free or low-fat milk, fat-free or low-fat yogurt, and low-fat cheese most often. Try switching from whole to fat-free or low-fat milk. This decreases the saturated fat and calories but keeps all other nutrients the same.

Prepared Foods

- Check the Nutrition Facts Label to see how much saturated fat and cholesterol are in a serving of prepared food. Choose foods lower in saturated fat and cholesterol.

Foods at Restaurants or Other Eating Establishments

- Choose fish or lean meats as suggested. Limit ground meat and fatty processed meats, marbled steaks, and cheese.
- Limit your intake of foods with creamy sauces, and add little or no butter to your food.
- Choose fruits as desserts most often.

Following the tips here will help you keep your intake of saturated fat at less than 10 percent of calories. They will also help you keep your cholesterol intake less than the Daily Value of 300 mg/day listed on the Nutrition Facts Label.

TABLE 8.5 ♦ Facts about Vitamins

Vitamin	Functions	Deficiency Problems
Fat Soluble		
Vitamin A	Allows normal vision in the dark; promotes health and growth of cells and tissues; protects health of skin and tissues in the mouth, stomach, intestines, and respiratory and urogenital tract	Night blindness and other eye problems; dry, scaly skin; reproduction problems; poor growth
Vitamin D	Promotes absorption of calcium and phos phorus to develop and maintain bones and teeth	Osteoporosis and softening of the bones, rickets, defective bone growth
Vitamin E	Antioxidant and may protect against heart disease and some types of cancer	Nervous system problems
Vitamin K	Helps blood clotting	Thin blood that does not clot
Water Soluble		
Vitamin C	Helps produce collagen; maintenance and repair of red blood cells, bones, and other tissues; promotes healing; keeps immune system healthy	Scurvy, excessive bleeding, swollen gums, improper wound healing
Thiamin	Conversion of carbohydrates into energy	Fatigue, weak muscles, and nerve damage
Riboflavin	Energy metabolism, changes tryptophan into niacin	Eye disorders, dry and flaky skin, red tongue
Niacin	Helps the body use sugars and fatty acids, produce energy, enzyme function	Diarrhea, mental disorientation, skin problems
Vitamin B6	Converts tryptophan into niacin and serotonin, helps produce other body chemicals such as insulin, hemoglobin, and antibodies	Depression, nausea, mental convulsions in infants; greasy, flaky skin
Folate	Produces DNA and RNA to make new body cells, works with vitamin B12 to form hemoglobin in red blood cells	Impaired cell division and growth, anemia
Vitamin B12	Works with folate to make red blood cells, vital part of body chemicals	Anemia, fatigue, nerve damage, smooth tongue, very sensitive skin
Biotin	Metabolize fats, protein, and carbohydrates	Heart abnor malities, appetite loss, fatigue, depressions, and dry skin
Pantothenic Acid	Metabolize protein, fat, and carbohydrates	Rare

© stocksnapp, 2012, Shutterstock, Inc.

Fat-soluble vitamins, such as A, E, D and K, are stored in the body for relatively long periods of time.

Vitamins are grouped as either fat soluble or water soluble. **Fat-soluble vitamins** are transported by the body's fat cells and by the liver. They include vitamins A, E, D, and K. Fat-soluble vitamins are not excreted in urine; therefore, they are stored in the body for relatively long periods of time (many months), and can build up to potentially toxic levels if excessive doses are consumed over time.

Water-soluble vitamins include the B vitamins and vitamin C. These vitamins are not stored in the body for a significant amount of time, and the amounts that are consumed and not used relatively quickly by the body are excreted through urine and sweat. For this reason, water-soluble vitamins must be replaced daily. Table 8.5 summarizes the functions of vitamins, lists the best sources for each vitamin, and outlines associated deficiency symptoms.

Effect of Excess Amounts	Dietary Sources
Birth defects, headaches; vomiting, double vision; hair loss; bone abnormalities; liver damage	Liver; fish oil; eggs; milk fortified with vitamin A; red, yellow, and orange fruits and vegetables; many dark green leafy vegetables
Kidney stones or damage, weak muscles and bones, exces sive bleeding	Sunlight on the skin, cheese, eggs, some fish, fortified milk, breakfast cereals, and margarine
May interfere with vitamin K action and en hance the effect of some anticoagulant drugs	Vegetable oils and margarine, salad dressing and other foods made from vegetable oils, nuts, seeds, wheat germ, leafy green vegetables
None observed	Green leafy vegeta bles, smaller amounts widespread in other foods
Diarrhea, gastrointestinal discomfort	Citrus fruits, berries, melons, peppers, dark leafy green vegetables, tomatoes, potatoes
None reported	Whole-grain, enriched grain products, pork, liver, and other organ meats
None reported	Milk and other dairy products; enriched bread, cereal, and other grain products; eggs; meat; green leafy vegetables; nuts; liver; kidney; and heart
Flushed skin, liver damage, stomach ulcers and high blood sugar	Poultry, fish, beef, peanut butter, and legumes
Nerve damage	Chicken, fish, pork, liver, kidney, whole grains, nuts, and legumes
Medication in terference, masking of vitamin B12 deficiencies	Leafy vegetables, orange juice and some fruits, legumes, liver, yeast breads, wheat germ, and some fortified cereals
None reported	Animal products and some fortified foods
None reported	Eggs, liver, yeast breads, and cereal
Diarrhea and water retention	Meat, poultry, fish, whole-grain cereals, and legumes; smaller amounts in milk, vegetables, and fruits

Minerals

Minerals are inorganic substances that are critical to many enzyme functions in the body. Approximately twenty-five minerals have important roles in bodily functions. Minerals are contained in all cells and are concentrated in hard parts of the body—nails, teeth, and bones—and are crucial to maintaining water balance and the acid-base balance. Minerals are essential components of respiratory pigments, enzymes, and enzyme systems, while also regulating muscular and nervous tissue excitability, blood clotting, and normal heart rhythm. Table 8.6 outlines the major sources and functions of specific minerals, as well as lists deficiency symptoms for those minerals.

Two groups of minerals are necessary in an individual's diet: macrominerals and microminerals. **Macrominerals** are the seven minerals the body needs in relatively large quantities (100 mg or more each day). These seven minerals are: calcium, chloride, magnesium, phosphorus, potassium, sodium, and

TABLE 8.6 ♦ Facts about Selected Minerals

Mineral	Functions	Deficiency Problems
Calcium	Helps build strong bones and teeth, control of muscle contractions and nerve function, supports blood clotting	Stunted growth in children, bone mineral loss in adults
Fluoride	Formation and maintenance of bones and teeth	Higher occurrence of tooth decay
Iron	Helps carry oxygen to body tissues	Anemia, weakness impaired immune function, cold hands and feet, gastrointestinal distress
Iodine	Component of thyroid hormones that help regulate growth, development, and metabolic rate	Enlarged thyroid, birth defect
Magnesium	Facilitates many cell processes	Neurological disorders, impaired immune function, kidney disorders nausea, weight loss
Phosphorus	Works with calcium to build and maintain bones and teeth, helps convert food to energy	Bone loss, kidney disorders
Potassium	Vital for muscle contractions and nerve transmission, important for heart and kidney function, helps regulate fluid balance and blood pressure	Muscular weakness, nausea, drowsiness, paralysis, confusion, disruption of cardiac rhythm
Sodium	Maintains fluid and electrolyte balance, supports muscle contraction and nerve impulse transmissions	Muscle weakness, loss of appetite, nausea, vomiting
Zinc	Involved in production of genetic material and proteins, ability to taste, wound healing, sperm production, normal fetus development	Night blindness, loss of appetite, skin rash, impaired immune function, impaired taste, poor wound healing

sulfur. In most cases, these minerals can be acquired by eating a variety of foods each day.

While **microminerals** are essential to healthy living, they are needed in smaller quantities (less than 100 mg per day) than macrominerals. Examples of these minerals include chromium, cobalt, copper, fluoride, iodine, iron, manganese, molybdenum, selenium, and zinc.

Antioxidants

Antioxidants are compounds that aid each cell in the body facing an ongoing barrage of damage resulting from daily oxygen exposure, environmental pollution, chemicals and pesticides, additives in processed foods, stress hormones, and sun radiation. Studies continue to show the ability of antioxidants to suppress cell deterioration and to "slow" the aging process. Realizing the potential power of these substances should encourage Americans to take action by eating at least five servings of a wide variety of fruits and vegetables each day (see Table 8.7 on page 173).

There are many proven health benefits of antioxidants. Vitamin C speeds the healing process, helps prevent infection, and prevents scurvy. Vitamin E helps prevent heart disease by stopping the oxidation of low-density lipoprotein (the harmful form of cholesterol); strengthens the immune system; and may play a role in the prevention of Alzheimer's disease, cataracts, and some forms of cancer, providing further proof of the benefits of antioxidants.

Adequate amounts of vitamins, minerals, and antioxidants are crucial to good overall health.

Effect of Excess Amounts	Dietary Sources
Muscle and abdominal pain, calcium kidney stones	Milk and milk products, tofu, green leafy vegetables, fortified orange juice, and bread
Increased bone density, mottling of teeth, impaired kidney function	Fluoridated drinking water, tea, seafood
Liver disease, arrhythmias, joint pain	Red meat, seafood, dried fruit, legumes, fortified cereals, green vegetables
Depression of thyroid activity, sometimes hyperthyroidism	Salt, seafood, bread, milk, cheese
Nausea, vomiting, nervous system depression, coma, death in people with impaired kidney function	Widespread in foods
Lowers blood calcium	Dairy products, egg yolks, meat, poultry, fish, legumes, soft drinks
Slower heart beat, kidney failure	Milk and yogurt, many fruits and vegetables (especially oranges, bananas, and potatoes)
Edema, hypertension	Salt, soy sauce, bread, milk, meats
Nausea and vomiting, abdominal pain	Seafood, meats, eggs, whole grains

TABLE 8.7 ♦ Antioxidants and Their Primary Food Sources

Vitamin A	Fortified milk; egg yolk; cheese; liver; butter; fish oil; dark green, yellow, and orange vegetables and fruits
Vitamin C	Papaya, cantaloupe, melons, citrus fruits, grapefruit, strawberries, raspberries, kiwi, cauliflower, tomatoes, dark green vegetables, green and red peppers, asparagus, broccoli, cabbage, collard greens, orange juice, and tomato juice
Vitamin E	Vegetable oils, nuts and seeds, dried beans, egg yolk, green leafy vegetables, sweet potatoes, wheat germ, 100 percent whole wheat bread, 100 percent whole grain cereal, oatmeal, mayonnaise
Carotenoids	Sweet potatoes, carrots, squash, tomatoes, asparagus, broccoli, spinach, romaine lettuce, mango, cantaloupe, pumpkin, apricots, peaches, papaya
Flavenoids	Purple grapes, wine, apples, berries, peas, beets, onions, garlic, green tea
Selenium	Lean meat, seafood, kidney, liver, dairy products, 100 percent whole grain cereal, 100 percent whole wheat bread

Organic Foods

Organic foods are foods that are grown without the use of pesticides. These chemical-free foods are much more difficult to grow because they are more vulnerable to disease and pests. Thus, they are not "high yield" crops. Due to the fact that they are less common, and harder to grow successfully, they are more expensive. Whether the expense is justified by the improved nutritional quality and overall health benefits is yet to be determined.

Functional Foods

Functional foods are foods that have benefits that go above and beyond basic nutrition. A person's overall health can be greatly affected by the food choices they make. Functional benefits of foods that have been consumed for decades are being discovered and new foods are being developed for their helpful dietary components. Table 8.8 lists examples of functional food components, their sources, and their potential benefits.

Additional health benefits can be attained by eating organic and/or functional foods.

TABLE 8.8 ◆ Examples of Functional Components*

Class/Components	Source*	Potential Benefit
Carotenoids		
Beta-carotene	Carrots, pumpkin, sweet potato, cantaloupe	Neutralizes free radicals, which may damage cells; bolsters cellular antioxidant defenses; can be made into vitamin A in the body
Lutein, zeaxanthin	Kale, collards, spinach, corn, eggs, citrus	May contribute to maintenance of healthy vision
Lycopene	Tomatoes and processed tomato products, watermelon, red/pink grapefruit	May contribute to maintenance of prostate health
Dietary (functional and total) Fiber		
Insoluble fiber	Wheat bran, corn bran, fruit skins	May contribute to maintenance of a healthy digestive tract; may reduce the risk of some types of cancer
Beta glucan**	Oat bran, oatmeal, oat flour, barley, rye	May reduce risk of coronary heart disease (CHD)
Soluble fiber**	Psyllium seed husk, peas, beans, apples, citrus frui	May reduce risk of CHD and some types of cance
Whole grains**	Cereal grains, whole wheat bread, oatmeal, brown rice	May reduce risk of CHD and some types of cancer; may contribute to maintenance of healthy blood glucose levels

TABLE 8.8 ♦ Examples of Functional Components*

Class/Components	Source*	Potential Benefit
Fatty Acids		
Monounsaturated fatty acids (MUFAs)**	Tree nuts, olive oil, canola oil	May reduce risk of CHD
Polyunsaturated fatty acids (PUFAs)—omega-3 fatty acids—ALA	Walnuts, flax	May contribute to maintenance of heart health; may contribute to maintenance of mental and visual function
PUFAs—omega-3 fatty acids—DHA/EPA**	Salmon, tuna, marine, and other fish oils	May reduce risk of CHD; may contribute to maintenance of mental and visual function
Conjugated linoleic acid (CLA)	Beef and lamb; some cheese	May contribute to maintenance of desirable body composition and healthy immune function
Flavonoids		
Anthocyanins—cyanidin, delphinidin, malvidin	Berries, cherries, red grapes	Bolsters, cellular antioxidant defenses; may contribute to maintenance of brain function
Flavanols—catechins, epicatechins, epigallocatechin, procyanidins	Tea, cocoa, chocolate, apples, grapes	May contribute to maintenance of heart health
Flavanones—hesperetin, naringenin	Citrus foods	Neutralize free radicals, which may damage cells; bolster cellular antioxidant defenses
Flavonols—quercetin, kaempferol, isorhamnetin, myricetin	Onions, apples, tea, broccoli	Neutralize free radicals, which may damage cells; bolster cellular antioxidant defenses
Proanthocyanidins	Cranberries, cocoa, apples, strawberries, grapes, wine, peanuts, cinnamon	May contribute to maintenance of urinary tract health and heart health
Isothiocyanates		
Sulforaphane	Cauliflower, broccoli, broccoli sprouts, cabbage, kale, horseradish	May enhance detoxification of undesirable compounds; bolsters cellular antioxidant defenses
Minerals		
Calcium**	Sardines, spinach, yogurt, low-fat dairy products, fortified foods and beverages	May reduce the risk of osteoporosis
Magnesium	Spinach, pumpkin seeds, whole-grain breads and cereals, halibut, brazil nuts	May contribute to maintenance of normal muscle and nerve function, healthy immune function, and bone health
Potassium**	Potatoes, low-fat dairy products, whole-grain breads and cereals, citrus juices, beans, bananas	May reduce the risk of high blood pressure and stroke, in combination with a low-sodium diet

(continued)

TABLE 8.8 ♦ Examples of Functional Components*

Class/Components	Source*	Potential Benefit
Selenium	Fish, red meat, grains, garlic, liver, eggs	Neutralizes free radicals, which may damage cells; may contribute to healthy immune function
Phenolic Acids		
Caffeic acid, ferulic acid	Apples, pears, citrus fruits, some vegetables, coffee	May bolster cellular antioxidant defenses; may contribute to maintenance of healthy vision and heart health
Plant Stanols/Sterols		
Free stanols/sterols**	Corn, soy, wheat, wood oils, fortified foods and beverages	May reduce risk of CHD
Stanol/sterol esters**	Fortified table spreads, stanol ester dietary supplements	May reduce risk of CHD
Polyols		
Sugar alcohols**—xylitol, sorbitol, mannitol, lactitol	Some chewing gums and other food	Applications may reduce risk of dental caries
Prebiotics		
Inulin, fructo-oligosaccharides (FOS), polydextrose	Whole grains, onions, some fruits, garlic, honey, leeks, fortified foods and beverages	May improve gastrointestinal health; may improve calcium absorption
Probiotics		
Yeast, *Lactobacilli*, *Bifidobacteria*, and other specific strains of beneficial bacteria	Certain yogurts and other cultured dairy and non-dairy applications	May improve gastrointestinal health and systemic immunity; benefits are strain-specific
Phytoestrogens		
Isoflavones—daidzein, genistein	Soybeans and soy-based foods	May contribute to maintenance of bone health, healthy brain and immune function; for women, may contribute to maintenance of menopausal health
Lignans	Flax, rye, some vegetables	May contribute to maintenance of heart health and healthy immune function
Soy Protein		
Soy protein**	Soybeans and soy-based foods	May reduce risk of CHD
Sulfides/Thiols		
Diallyl sulfide, allyl methyl trisulfide	Garlic, onions, leeks, scallions	May enhance detoxification of undesirable compounds; may contribute to maintenance of heart health and healthy immune function
Dithiolthiones	Cruciferous vegetables	May enhance detoxification of undesirable compounds; may contribute to maintenance of healthy immune function

TABLE 8.8 ♦ Examples of Functional Components*

Class/Components	Source*	Potential Benefit
Vitamins		
A***	Organ meats, milk, eggs, carrots, sweet potato, spinach	May contribute to maintenance of healthy vision, immune function, and bone health; may contribute to cell integrity
B1 (Thiamin)	Lentils, peas, long-grain brown rice, brazil nuts	May contribute to maintenance of mental function; helps regulate metabolism
B2 (Riboflavin)	Lean meats, eggs, green leafy vegetables	Helps support cell growth; helps regulate metabolism
B3 (Niacin)	Dairy products, poultry, fish, nuts, eggs	Helps support cell growth; helps regulate metabolism
B5 (Pantothenic acid)	Organ meats, lobster, soybeans, lentils Helps regulate metabolism and hormone synthesis	Helps regulate metabolism and hormone synthesis
B6 (Pyridoxine)	Beans, nuts, legumes, fish, meat, whole grains	May contribute to maintenance of healthy immune function; helps regulate metabolism
B9 (Folate)**	Beans, legumes, citrus foods, green leafy vegetables, fortified breads and cereals	May reduce a woman's risk of having a child with a brain or spinal cord defect
B12 (Cobalamin)	Eggs, meat, poultry, milk	May contribute to maintenance of mental function; helps regulate metabolism and supports blood cell formation
Biotin	Liver, salmon, dairy, eggs, oysters	Helps regulate metabolism and hormone synthesis
C	Guava, sweet red/green pepper, kiwi, citrus fruit, strawberries	Neutralizes free radicals, which may damage cells; may contribute to maintenance of bone health and immune function
D	Sunlight, fish, fortified milk and cereals	Helps regulate calcium and phosphorus; helps contribute to bone health; may contribute to healthy immune function; helps support cell growth
E	Sunflower seeds, almonds, hazelnuts, turnip greens	Neutralizes free radicals, which may damage cells; may contribute to healthy immune function and maintenance of heart health

*Examples are not an all-inclusive list.

**FDA approved health claim established for component.

***Preformed vitamin A is found in foods that come from animals. Provitamin A carotenoids are found in many darkly colored fruits and vegetables and are a major source of vitamin A for vegetarians.

Source: Reprinted from International Food Information Council Foundation, 2007–2009. Originally printed in the 2007–2009 Foundation Media Guide on Food Safety and Nutrition.

Water lubricates joints, absorbs shock, regulates body temperature, maintains blood volume, transports fluids throughout the body, and comprises 60 percent of your body.

© Andrei Mihalcea, 2009, Shutterstock, Inc.

Visual Cues for 1 Serving of Grains

© Petr Malyshev, 2012, Shutterstock, Inc.

1 large egg = muffin

© Brent Hofacker, 2012, Shutterstock, Inc.

Handful of rubber bands = ½ cup pasta

© Novitech, 2012, Shutterstock, Inc.

CD = 1 slice bread, waffle, or pancake

© Artur Synenko, 2012, Shutterstock, Inc.

6 in. plate = 1 tortilla

Water

In many cases, **water** is the "forgotten nutrient." Although water does not provide energy to the body in the form of calories, it is a substance that is essential to life. Among other things, water lubricates joints, absorbs shock, regulates body temperature, maintains blood volume, and transports fluids throughout the body, while comprising 60 percent of an individual's body.

While it is clear that adequate hydration is crucial to proper physiological functioning, many people are in a semi-hydrated state most of the time. Whether exercising or not, hydration should be a continuous process. Prolonged periods of dehydration can result in as much as a 10 percent loss of intracellular water concentration and can result in death. Individuals more susceptible to dehydration include: persons who are overweight; deconditioned or unacclimatized to heat; very old and very young; and individuals who do not eat breakfast or drink water.

To ensure proper water balance and prevent dehydration, approximately six to eight eight-ounce glasses of water should be consumed each day an individual is not exercising. When working out, current recommendations for water intake are two to three eight-ounce cups of water before exercising, four to six ounces of cool water every fifteen minutes during the workout, and rehydrating thoroughly after the activity.

The Food Guide Pyramid

The Food Guide Pyramid was originally created in 1992 by the federal government in an attempt to arm more Americans with the knowledge that would allow them to create a healthy, balanced, and tasty diet. Twelve years later, in 2004, the U.S. Department of Agriculture produced an expanded and updated version of that original Food Guide Pyramid (see Figure 8.2). Key to the new pyramid is the acknowledged necessity of balancing what an individual eats with the amount of physical activity in which he or she engages.

To make the pyramid portray the changes deemed necessary by the USDA, to promote optimal health, the pyramid was "flipped" onto its side so that all the food group bands run from the top of the pyramid to its base. The different size of each of the bands indicates how much food should be consumed from each food group. The bands are all wider at the base of the pyramid. This symbolizes the importance of eating, when possible, foods without solid fats and added sugar in each of the six bands or groups within the pyramid.

Grains

The color orange represents grains within the pyramid. When examining options of food choices within this group it is important to not only choose a majority on one's daily calories from grains, but also to remember that it is nutritionally prudent to make half of the grains chosen whole grains. Whole grains are defined by the American Association of Cereal Chemists as "food made from the entire grain seed, usually called the kernel, which consists of the bran, germ, and endosperm (AACC International Board of Directors, 1999) (see Figure 8.3). If the kernel has been cracked, crushed, or flaked, it must retain nearly the same relative proportions of bran, germ, and endosperm as the original grain." Examples of easy-to-find whole grains include brown rice, bulgur (cracked wheat), popcorn, whole rye, wild rice, whole oats/oatmeal, whole-grain barley, and whole wheat. Selections of whole-grain products from this group will help an individual maximize their intake of dietary fiber as well as other nutrients. One serving from the grain group equals one slice of bread, half a bagel or one sixteen-inch tortilla.

FIGURE 8.2

Source: From www.mypyramid.gov.

How many grain foods are needed daily?

The amount of grains you need to eat depends on your age, sex, and level of physical activity. Recommended daily amounts are listed in the chart. Most Americans consume enough grains, but few are whole grains. At least half of all the grains eaten should be whole grains.

		Daily recommendation*	Daily minimum amount of whole grains
Children	2–3 years old	3 ounce equivalents**	1½ ounce equivalents**
	4–8 years old	5 ounce equivalents**	2½ ounce equivalents**
Girls	9–13 years old	5 ounce equivalents**	3 ounce equivalents**
	14–18 years old	6 ounce equivalents**	3 ounce equivalents**
Boys	9–13 years old	6 ounce equivalents**	3 ounce equivalents**
	14–18 years old	8 ounce equivalents**	4 ounce equivalents**
Women	19–30 years old	6 ounce equivalents**	3 ounce equivalents**
	31–50 years old	6 ounce equivalents**	3 ounce equivalents**
	51+ years old	5 ounce equivalents**	3 ounce equivalents**
Men	19–30 years old	8 ounce equivalents**	4 ounce equivalents**
	31–50 years old	7 ounce equivalents**	3½ ounce equivalents**
	51+ years old	6 ounce equivalents**	3 ounce equivalents**

*These amounts are appropriate for individuals who get less than 30 minutes per day of moderate physical activity, beyond normal daily activities. Those who are more physically active may be able to consume more while staying within calorie needs.

What counts as an ounce equivalent of grains?

In general, 1 slice of bread, 1 cup of ready-to-eat cereal, or ½ cup of cooked rice, cooked pasta, or cooked cereal can be considered as 1 ounce equivalent from the Grains Group.

The chart lists specific amounts that count as 1 ounce equivalent of grains towards your daily recommended intake. In some cases the number of ounce-equivalents for common portions are also shown.

		Amount that counts as 1 ounce equivalent of grains	Common portions and ounce equivalents
Bagels	WG*: whole wheat RG*: plain, egg	1 "mini" bagel	1 large bagel = 4 ounce equivalents
Biscuits	(baking powder/ buttermilk—RG*)	1 small (2" diameter)	1 large (3" diameter) = 2 ounce equivalents
Breads	WG*: 100% Whole wheat RG*: white, wheat, French, sourdough	1 regular slice 1 small slice French 4 snack-size slices rye bread	2 regular slices = 2 ounce equivalents

		Amount that counts as 1 ounce equivalent of grains	Common portions and ounce equivalents
Bulgur	cracked wheat (WG*)	½ cup cooked	
Cornbread	(RG*)	1 small piece (2½" x 1¼" x 1¼")	1 medium piece (2½" x 2½" x 1¼") = 2 ounce equivalents
Crackers	WG*: 100% whole wheat, rye RG*: saltines, snack crackers	5 whole wheat crackers 2 rye crispbreads 7 square or round crackers	
English muffins	WG*: whole wheat RG*: plain, raisin	½ muffin	1 muffin = 2 ounce equivalents
Muffins	WG*: whole wheat RG*: bran, corn, plain	1 small (2½" diameter)	1 large (3½" diameter) = 3 ounce equivalents
Oatmeal	(WG)	½ cup cooked 1 packet instant 1 ounce (1/3 cup) dry (regular or quick)	
Pancakes	WG*: Whole wheat, buckwheat RG*: buttermilk, plain	1 pancake (4½" diameter) 2 small pancakes (3" diameter)	3 pancakes (4½" diameter) = 3 ounce equivalents
Popcorn	(WG*)	3 cups, popped	1 mini microwave bag or 100-calorie bag, popped = 2 ounce equivalents
Ready-to-eat breakfast cereal	WG*: toasted oat, whole wheat flakes RG*: corn flakes, puffed rice	1 cup flakes or rounds 1¼ cup puffed	
Rice	WG*: brown, wild RG*: enriched, white, polished	½ cup cooked 1 ounce dry	1 cup cooked = 2 ounce equivalents
Pasta—spaghetti, macaroni, noodles	WG*: whole wheat RG*: enriched, durum	½ cup cooked 1 ounce dry	1 cup cooked = 2 ounce equivalents
Tortillas	WG*: whole wheat, whole grain corn RG*: Flour, corn	1 small flour tortilla (6" diameter) 1 corn tortilla (6" diameter)	1 large tortilla (12" diameter) = 4 ounce equivalents

*WG = whole grains, RG = refined grains. This is shown when products are available both in whole grain and refined grain forms.

FIGURE 8.3

A Grain of Wheat

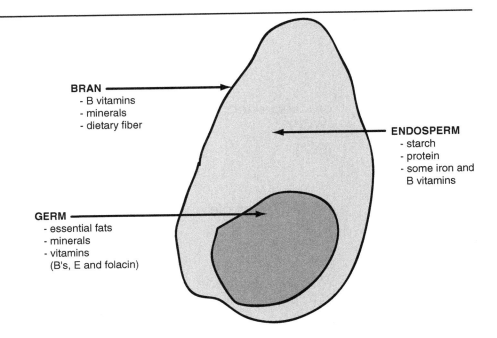

BRAN
- B vitamins
- minerals
- dietary fiber

ENDOSPERM
- starch
- protein
- some iron and
  B vitamins

GERM
- essential fats
- minerals
- vitamins
  (B's, E and folacin)

What Counts as a Whole Grain Serving

- Cheerios – 2/3 cup
- Wheat Chex – 2/3 cup
- Oatmeal (hot, cooked) – 1/2 cup
- Quaker Oatmeal Squares or Toasted Oatmeal Cereal – 1/2 cup
- Grape Nuts – 1/5 cup
- Frosted Mini-Wheats (bite-sized) – 9 biscuits
- 100% whole-grain bread – 1 slice
- 100% whole-grain English muffin – 1 half
- Popcorn (popped) – 2 cups
- Sun Chips or baked tortilla chips – 1 oz. (about 15 chips)
- 100% whole-grain crackers (like Triscuits) – 4 crackers
- Whole-wheat pasta – 1/3 cup cooked
- Brown rice, bulgur, sorghum, or barley – 1/3 cup cooked

© Ljupco Smokovski, 2012, Shutterstock, Inc

tennis ball = 1 serving of vegetable

Vegetables

Green is the color within the pyramid that stands for vegetables. Vegetables are an excellent source of natural fiber, they are low in fat, and provide the body with vitamins, especially vitamins A and C. While all vegetables are good nutritional choices, to maximize the benefits of eating vegetables, one should vary the type of vegetables eaten. It is also important when choosing vegetables to ingest not only a variety of the brightly colored vegetables such as corn, squash, and peas, but also the green and orange vegetables such as carrots, yams, and broccoli. One serving from the vegetable group equals one cup of raw, lefty greens; half cup of other chopped vegetables; or three-quarter cup of vegetable juice.

How many vegetables are needed daily or weekly?

The amount of vegetables you need to eat depends on your age, sex, and level of physical activity. Recommended total daily amounts are shown in the first chart.

Daily recommendation*

Children	2–3 years old	1 cup**
	4–8 years old	1½ cups**
Girls	9–13 years old	2 cups**
	14–18 years old	2½ cups**
Boys	9–13 years old	2½ cups**
	14–18 years old	3 cups**
Women	19–30 years old	2½ cups**
	31–50 years old	2½ cups**
	51+ years old	2 cups**
Men	19–30 years old	3 cups**
	31–50 years old	3 cups**
	51+ years old	2½ cups**

*These amounts are appropriate for individuals who get less than 30 minutes per day of moderate physical activity, beyond normal daily activities. Those who are more physically active may be able to consume more while staying within calorie needs.

What counts as a cup of vegetables?

In general, 1 cup of raw or cooked vegetables or vegetable juice, or 2 cups of raw leafy greens can be considered as 1 cup from the Vegetable Group. The chart lists specific amounts that count as 1 cup of vegetables (in some cases equivalents for ½ cup are also shown) towards your recommended intake:

	Amount that counts as 1 cup of vegetables	Amount that counts as ½ cup of vegetables
Dark Green Vegetables		
Broccoli	1 cup chopped or florets	
	3 spears 5" long raw or cooked	
Greens (collards, mustard greens, turnip greens, kale)	1 cup cooked	
Spinach	1 cup, cooked	
	2 cups raw is equivalent to 1 cup of vegetables	1 cup raw is equivalent to ½ cup of vegetables
Raw leafy greens: Spinach, romaine, watercress, dark green leafy lettuce, endive, escarole	2 cups raw is equivalent to 1 cup of vegetables	1 cup raw is equivalent to ½ cup of vegetables

	Amount that counts as 1 cup of vegetables	**Amount that counts as ½ cup of vegetables**
Red and Orange Vegetables		
Carrots	1 cup, strips, slices, or chopped, raw or cooked	
	2 medium	1 medium carrot
	1 cup baby carrots (about 12)	About 6 baby carrots
Pumpkin	1 cup mashed, cooked	
Red peppers	1 cup chopped, raw, or cooked	1 small pepper
	1 large pepper (3" diameter, 3¾" long)	
Tomatoes	1 large raw whole (3") 1 cup chopped or sliced, raw, canned, or cooked	1 small raw whole (2¼" diameter) 1 medium canned
Tomato juice	1 cup	½ cup
Sweet potato	1 large baked (2¼" or more diameter)	
	1 cup sliced or mashed, cooked	
Winter squash (acorn, butternut, hubbard)	1 cup cubed, cooked	½ acorn squash, baked = ¾ cup
Beans and Peas		
Dry beans and peas (such as black, garbanzo, kidney, pinto, or soy beans, or black eyed peas or split peas)	1 cup whole or mashed, cooked	
Starchy Vegetables		
Corn, yellow or white	1 cup	
	1 large ear (8" to 9" long)	1 small ear (about 6" long)
Green peas	1 cup	
White potatoes	1 cup diced, mashed 1 medium boiled or baked potato (2½" to 3" diameter)	
	French fried: 20 medium to long strips (2½" to 4" long) (Contains added calories from solid fats.)	

Other Vegetables	Amount that counts as 1 cup of vegetables	Amount that counts as ½ cup of vegetables
Bean sprouts	1 cup cooked	
Cabbage, green	1 cup, chopped or shredded raw or cooked	
Cauliflower	1 cup pieces or florets raw or cooked	
Celery	1 cup, diced or sliced, raw or cooked	
long)	2 large stalks (11" to 12" long)	1 large stalk (11" to 12"
Cucumbers	1 cup raw, sliced or chopped	
Green or wax beans	1 cup cooked	
Green peppers	1 cup chopped, raw or cooked	
	1 large pepper (3" diameter, 3¾" long)	1 small pepper
Lettuce, iceberg or head	2 cups raw, shredded or chopped = equivalent to 1 cup of vegetables	1 cup raw, shredded or chopped = equivalent to ½ cup of vegetables
Mushrooms	1 cup raw or cooked	
Onions	1 cup chopped, raw or cooked	
Summer squash or zucchini	1 cup cooked, sliced or diced	

Fruits

Fruits are represented in the pyramid by the color red. Fresh, canned, frozen, or dried fruits are all excellent sources of vitamins and minerals, most notably vitamin C. It is, however, important to watch for heavy, sugary syrups when selecting canned fruits. Fruits canned in lite syrups or the fruit's own natural juice allow an individual to take in the same amount of vitamins and minerals as their heavily syruped counterparts without adding unnecessary and/or unwanted sugar, fat, and calories to their diet. Fruit juices are another important part of many people's diet that should be monitored for "hidden" sugars and calories. When possible, freshly squeezed juices are an ideal alternative. Serving equivalents for the fruit group are: one serving equals one medium apple, banana, or orange; one melon wedge; half cup of chopped berries, or three-quarter cup of fruit juice.

Baseball = 1 serving of fruit

How much fruit is needed daily?

The amount of fruit you need to eat depends on age, sex, and level of physical activity. Recommended daily amounts are shown in the chart.

Recommended amounts are shown in the table below.

		Daily recommendation*
Children	2–3 years old	1 cup**
	4–8 years old	1 to 1½ cups**
Girls	9–13 years old	1½ cups**
	14–18 years old	1½ cups**
Boys	9–13 years old	1½ cups**
	14—18 years old	2 cups**
Women	19–30 years old	2 cups**
	31–50 years old	1½ cups**
	51+ years old	1½ cups**
Men	19–30 years old	2 cups**
	31–50 years old	2 cups**
	51+ years old	2 cups**

*These amounts are appropriate for individuals who get less than 30 minutes per day of moderate physical activity, beyond normal daily activities. Those who are more physically active may be able to consume more while staying within calorie needs.

What counts as a cup of fruit?

In general, 1 cup of fruit or 100% fruit juice, or ½ cup of dried fruit can be considered as 1 cup from the Fruit Group. The following specific amounts count as 1 cup of fruit (in some cases equivalents for ½ cup are also shown) towards your daily recommended intake:

	Amount that counts as 1 cup of fruit	**Amount that counts as ½ cup of fruit**
Apple	½ large (3.25" diameter)	
	1 small (2.5" diameter)	
	1 cup sliced or chopped, raw or cooked	½ cup sliced or chopped, raw or cooked
Applesauce	1 cup	1 snack container (4 oz)
Banana	1 cup sliced	1 small (less than 6" long)
	1 large (8" to 9" long)	
Cantaloupe	1 cup diced or melon balls	1 medium wedge (1/8 of a med. melon)
Grapes	1 cup whole or cut-up	
	32 seedless grapes	16 seedless grapes

	Amount that counts as 1 cup of fruit	Amount that counts as ½ cup of fruit
Grapefruit	1 medium (4" diameter) 1 cup sections	½ medium (4" diameter)
Mixed fruit (fruit cocktail)	1 cup diced or sliced, raw or canned, drained	1 snack container (4 oz) drained = 3/8 cup
Orange	1 large (3-1/16" diameter) 1 cup sections	1 small (2-3/8" diameter)
Orange, mandarin	1 cup canned, drained	
Peach	1 large (2 ¾" diameter) 1 cup sliced or diced, raw, cooked, or canned, drained 2 halves, canned	1 small (2" diameter) 1 snack container (4 oz) drained = 3/8 cup
Pear	1 medium pear (2.5 per lb) 1 cup sliced or diced, raw, cooked, or canned, drained	1 snack container (4 oz) drained = 3/8 cup
Pineapple	1 cup chunks, sliced or crushed, raw, cooked or canned, drained	1 snack container (4 oz) drained = 3/8 cup
Plum	1 cup sliced raw or cooked 3 medium or 2 large plums	1 large plum
Strawberries	About 8 large berries 1 cup whole, halved, or sliced, fresh or frozen	½ cup whole, halved, or sliced
Watermelon	1 small wedge (1" thick) 1 cup diced or balls	6 melon balls
Dried fruit (raisins, prunes, apricots, etc.)	½ cup dried fruit is equivalent to 1 cup fruit: ½ cup raisins ½ cup prunes ½ cup dried apricots	¼ cup dried fruit is equivalent to ½ cup fruit 1 small box raisins (1.5 oz)
100% fruit juice (orange, apple, grape, grapefruit, etc.)	1 cup	½ cup

Milk/Dairy

Milk and other calcium-rich foods such as yogurt and cheese now make up the blue portion of the Food Guide Pyramid. Milk products are not only the body's best source of calcium, they are also an excellent source of protein and vitamin B12. To maximize the benefits of calcium-rich foods and minimize the calories, cholesterol, fat, and saturated fat per selection, low-fat and skim alternatives should be chosen. One serving from the milk group equals one cup of milk or yogurt, or one and a half ounces of cheese.

© Dmitrydesign, 2012, Shutterstock, Inc

6 dice = 1½ oz. cheese = 1 serving of dairy

How Much Food from the Dairy Group Is Needed Daily?

The amount of food from the Dairy Group you need to eat depends on age. Recommended daily amounts are shown in the chart below. See what counts as a cup in the Dairy Group.

Daily recommendation

Children	2–3 years old	2 cups
	4–8 years old	2½ cups
Girls	9–13 years old	3 cups
	14–18 years old	3 cups
Boys	9–13 years old	3 cups
	14–18 years old	3 cups
Women	19–30 years old	3 cups
	31–50 years old	3 cups
	51+ years old	3 cups
Men	19–30 years old	3 cups
	31–50 years old	3 cups
	51+ years old	3 cups

What counts as a cup in the Dairy Group?

In general, 1 cup of milk or yogurt, 1 ½ ounces of natural cheese, or 2 ounces of processed cheese can be considered as 1 cup from the Dairy Group. Additionally, 1 cup of soymilk counts as 1 cup in the Dairy Group.

The chart below lists specific amounts that count as 1 cup in the Dairy Group towards your daily recommended intake.

	Amount that counts as 1 cup in the Dairy Group	**Common portions and cup equivalents**
Milk *[choose fat-free or low-fat milk]*	1 cup milk or calcium-fortified soymilk (soy beverage) 1 half-pint container milk or soymilk ½ cup evaporated milk	
Yogurt *[choose fat-free or low-fat yogurt]*	1 regular container (8 fluid ounces) 1 cup yogurt	1 small container (6 ounces) = ¾ cup 1 snack size container (4 ounces) = ½ cup

	Amount that counts as 1 cup in the Dairy Group	Common portions and cup equivalents
Cheese [choose reduced-fat or low-fat yogurt]	1½ ounces hard cheese (cheddar, mozzarella, Swiss, Parmesan)	1 slice of hard cheese is equivalent to ½ cup milk
	1/3 cup shredded cheese	
	2 ounces processed cheese (American)	1 slice of processed cheese is equivalent to 1/3 cup milk
	½ cup ricotta cheese	
	2 cups cottage cheese	½ cup cottage cheese is equivalent to ¼ cup milk
Milk-based desserts [choose fat-free or low-fat types]	1 cup pudding made with milk	
	1 cup frozen yogurt	
	1½ cups ice cream	1 scoop ice cream is equivalent to 1/3 cup milk
Soymilk	1 cup calcium-fortified soymilk	

Protein/Meats and Beans

Purple is the designated color for meats and beans within the pyramid. Meats and beans are excellent sources of protein, iron, zinc, and B vitamins. It is important to be aware of the fact that many food selections within this food group can be relatively high in fat content, especially saturated fats. Lower fat alternatives within this group that remain a rich source of vitamins and minerals include beans, fish, poultry, and lean cuts of beef. Serving equivalents for the meat and beans group are as follows: one serving equals two to three ounces of cooked lean beef, poultry, or fish; one egg; half cup of cooked beans; or two tablespoons of seeds or nuts.

Visual Cues for 1 Serving of Protein

Deck of cards = 3 oz. meat

How much food from the Protein Foods Group is needed daily?

The amount of food from the Protein Foods Group you need to eat depends on age, sex, and level of physical activity. Most Americans eat enough food from this group, but need to make leaner and more varied selections of these foods. Recommended daily amounts are shown in the chart.

Golf ball = 2 Tb. peanut butter

	Daily recommendation*	
Children	2–3 years old	2 ounce equivalents**
	4–8 years old	4 ounce equivalents**
Girls	9–13 years old	5 ounce equivalents**
	14–18 years old	5 ounce equivalents**
Boys	9–13 years old	5 ounce equivalents**
	14–18 years old	6 ½ ounce equivalents**

Checkbook = 3 oz. thin fish

© Feng Yu, 2012,
Shutterstock, Inc.

Daily recommendation*

Women	19–30 years old	5 ½ ounce equivalents**
	31–50 years old	5 ounce equivalents**
	51+ years old	5 ounce equivalents**
Men	19–30 years old	6½ ounce equivalents**
	31–50 years old	6 ounce equivalents**
	51+ years old	5½ ounce equivalents**

*These amounts are appropriate for individuals who get less than 30 minutes per day of moderate physical activity, beyond normal daily activities. Those who are more physically active may be able to consume more while staying within calorie needs.

What counts as an ounce equivalent in the Protein Foods Group?

In general, 1 ounce of meat, poultry or fish, ¼ cup cooked beans, 1 egg, 1 tablespoon of peanut butter, or ½ ounce of nuts or seeds can be considered as 1 ounce equivalent from the Protein Foods Group.

The chart lists specific amounts that count as 1 ounce equivalent in the Protein Foods Group towards your daily recommended intake:

	Amount that counts as 1 ounce equivalent in the Protein Foods Group	Common portions and ounce equivalents
Meats	1 ounce cooked lean beef	1 small steak (eye of round, filet) = 3½ to 4 ounce equivalents
	1 ounce cooked lean pork or ham	1 small lean hamburger = 2 to 3 ounce equivalents
Poultry	1 ounce cooked chicken or turkey, without skin	1 small chicken breast half = 3 ounce equivalents
	1 sandwich slice of turkey (4½ x 2½ x 1/8")	½ Cornish game hen = 4 ounce equivalents
Seafood	1 ounce cooked fish or shell fish	1 can of tuna, drained = 3 to 4 ounce equivalents
		1 salmon steak = 4 to 6 ounce equivalents
		1 small trout = 3 ounce equivalents
Eggs	1 egg	3 egg whites = 2 ounce equivalents 3 egg yolks = 1 ounce equivalent

	Amount that counts as 1 ounce equivalent in the Protein Foods Group	Common portions and ounce equivalents
Nuts and seeds	½ ounce of nuts (12 almonds, 24 pistachios, 7 walnut halves) ½ ounce of seeds (pumpkin, sunflower or squash seeds, hulled, roasted) 1 Tablespoon of peanut butter or almond butter	1 ounce of nuts or seeds = 2 ounce equivalents
Beans and peas	¼ cup of cooked beans (such as black, kidney, pinto, or white beans) ¼ cup of cooked peas (such as chickpeas, cowpeas, lentils, or split peas) ¼ cup of baked beans, refried beans ¼ cup (about 2 ounces) of tofu 1 oz. tempeh, cooked ¼ cup roasted soybeans 1 falafel patty (2¼", 4 oz) 2 Tablespoons hummus	1 cup split pea soup = 2 ounce equivalents 1 cup lentil soup = 2 ounce equivalents 1 cup bean soup = 2 ounce equivalents 1 soy or bean burger patty = 2 ounce equivalents

Oils

Oils are depicted by the yellow band within the Food Guide Pyramid. As in all other areas of the pyramid, it is important to choose your source(s) of oils carefully. As a general rule, oils such as olive oil, peanut oil, and canola oil contain unsaturated fats. These oils do not raise an individual's blood cholesterol and are therefore a healthier option.

1/2 business card = 1 brownie = 1 serving

How much is my allowance for oils?

Some Americans consume enough oil in the foods they eat, such as:

- nuts
- fish
- cooking oil
- salad dressings

Others could easily consume the recommended allowance by substituting oils for some solid fats they eat. A person's allowance for oils depends on age, sex, and level of physical activity. Daily allowances are shown in the chart.

Daily allowance*

Children	2–3 years old	3 teaspoons
	4–8 years old	4 teaspoons
Girls	9–13 years old	5 teaspoons
	14–18 years old	5 teaspoons
Boys	9–13 years old	5 teaspoons
	14–18 years old	6 teaspoons

Daily allowance*

Women	19–30 years old	6 teaspoons
	31–50 years old	5 teaspoons
	51+ years old	5 teaspoons
Men	19–30 years old	7 teaspoons
	31–50 years old	6 teaspoons
	51+ years old	6 teaspoons

*These amounts are appropriate for individuals who get less than 30 minutes per day of moderate physical activity, beyond normal daily activities. Those who are more physically active may be able to consume more while staying within calorie needs.

How do I count the oils I eat?

The chart gives a quick guide to the amount of oils in some common foods:

	Amount of food	Amount of oil	Calories from oil	Total calories
		Teaspoons/ grams	Approximate calories	Approximate calories
Oils:				
Vegetable oils (such as canola, corn, cottonseed, olive, peanut, safflower, soybean, and sunflower)	1 Tbsp	3 tsp/14 g	120	120
Foods ric in oils:				
Margarine, soft (trans fat free)	1 Tbsp	2½ tsp/11 g	100	100
Mayonnaise	1 Tbsp	2½ tsp/11 g	100	100
Mayonnaise-type salad dressing	1 Tbsp	1 tsp/5 g	45	55
Italian dressing	2 Tbsp	2 tsp/8 g	75	85
Thousand Island dressing	2 Tbsp	2½ tsp/11 g	100	120
Olives*, ripe, canned	4 large	½ tsp/ 2 g	15	20
Avocado*	½ med	3 tsp/15 g	130	160
Peanut butter*	2 T	4 tsp/ 16 g	140	190
Peanuts, dry roasted*	1 oz	3 tsp/14 g	120	165
Mixed nuts, dry roasted*	1 oz	3 tsp/15 g	130	170
Cashews, dry roasted*	1 oz	3 tsp/13 g	115	165
Almonds, dry roasted*	1 oz	3 tsp/15 g	130	170
Hazelnuts*	1 oz	4 tsp/18 g	160	185
Sunflower seeds*	1 oz	3 tsp/14 g	120	165

*Avocados and olives are part of the Vegetable Group; nuts and seeds are part of the Protein Foods Group. These foods are also high in oils. Soft margarine, mayonnaise, and salad dressings are mainly oil and are not considered to be part of any food group.

Daily Activity

The steps along the side of the pyramid symbolize the importance of including exercise into each and every day of a person's life. When daily exercise does not occur, the benefits of even the wisest food or nutrition choices are minimized.

What Happened to the "Fat" Group?

When looking at the new Food Guide Pyramid, it appears that foods like cookies, candies, and sodas found in the former pyramid's "Fat Group" no longer are a part of the pyramid. These foods are typically high in fat, sugars, and "empty" calories, and though they are not mentioned or specifically depicted in the new pyramid, they should only be enjoyed sparingly or in moderation. These foods often taste great but, in general, they provide the body with very little nutritionally.

Due to the fact that one pyramid could not possibly match or meet the needs of all Americans, twelve different pyramids have been created. To determine which Food Guide Pyramid is the best match, you can go to the USDA's Web site at MyPyramid.gov and enter your age, gender, and activity level. This process takes only a few seconds and can personalize the amounts and types of grains, vegetables, fruits, milk products, meats, and beans you should consume each day to maximize your health benefits.

Because an individual's nutritional requirements vary based on their life circumstances, there is a range in the number of servings within each food group. Examples of factors that might influence the number of servings viewed as healthy for an individual could be age, activity level, gender—if the person is a woman, is she pregnant or lactating?

Determining the appropriate number of servings from each of the food groups is extremely important when planning a healthy diet. However, this information is of little practical value unless a person also knows what constitutes an accurate serving size.

FIGURE 8.4

The Healthy Eating Pyramid
© Mountain Brothers/Shutterstock.com

Sugary Drinks, Sweets, Honey
Chocolate, Salt

Alcohol
in moderation

Meat, Poultry, Fish, Beans
Eggs, Milk, Yogurt
Chees, Nuts

Multivitamin
Vitamin D

Vegetable, Fruit

Bread, Cereal
Pasta, Oils
Potatoes
Rice

Daily Exercise, Weight Control

Other Issues in Nutrition

Building a Healthy Plate

MyPlate is an idea based on the 2015 Dietary Guidelines for Americans. The idea behind MyPlate is to simplify the concept of making better/healthier food choices.

MyPlate uses the familiar place setting, using a plate 9 inches in diameter, shown in Figure 8.4 to illustrate the five food groups and the relative proportions in which they should be consumed. When used in conjunction with the ChooseMyPlate.gov website, consumers have access to practical, easy to understand information that will enable them to easily build a healthier diet.

Some select messages ChooseMyPlate uses to help consumers focus in on key behaviors include:

© medejaja/Shutterstock.com

- Balancing Calories
  Eat the right amount of calories for you Everyone has a personal calorie limit. Staying within yours can help you get to or maintain a healthy weight. People who are successful at managing their weight have found ways to keep track of how much they eat in a day, even if they don't count every calorie.

© Kurhan, 2012, Shutterstock, Inc.

Enjoy your food, but eat less.
- Get your personal daily calorie limit at www.ChooseMyPlate.gov and keep that number in mind when deciding what to eat.
- Think before you eat . . . is it worth the calories?
- Avoid oversized portions.
- Use a smaller plate, bowl, and glass.
- Stop eating when you are satisfied, not full.

Cook more often at home, where you are in control of what's in your food. When eating out, choose lower calorie menu options.
- Check posted calorie amounts.
- Choose dishes that include vegetables, fruits, and/or whole grains.
- Order a smaller portion or share when eating out.

Write down what you eat to keep track of how much you eat. If you drink alcoholic beverages, do so sensibly—limit to 1 drink a day for women or to 2 drinks a day for men.

Foods to Increase

© Elena Larina, 2012, Shutterstock, Inc.

Build a healthy plate Before you eat, think about what goes on your plate or in your cup or bowl. Foods like vegetables, fruits, whole grains, low-fat dairy products, and lean protein foods contain the nutrients you need without too many calories. Try some of these options.

Make half your plate fruits and vegetables.
- Eat red, orange, and dark-green vegetables, such as tomatoes, sweet potatoes, and broccoli, in main and side dishes.
- Eat fruit, vegetables, or unsalted nuts as snacks—they are nature's original fast foods.

© Eduardo Alexandre Piccoli, 2012, Shutterstock, Inc.

Switch to skim or 1% milk.
- They have the same amount of calcium and other essential nutrients as whole milk, but less fat and calories.
- Try calcium-fortified soy products as an alternative to dairy foods.

Make at least half your grains whole.
- Choose 100% whole-grain cereals, breads, crackers, rice, and pasta.
- Check the ingredients list on food packages to find whole-grain foods.

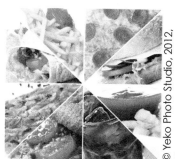

© Yeko Photo Studio, 2012, Shutterstock, Inc.

Vary your protein food choices.
- Twice a week, make seafood the protein on your plate.
- Eat beans, which are a natural source of fiber and protein.
- Keep meat and poultry portions small and lean.

Keep your food safe to eat—learn more at www.FoodSafety.gov.
- Foods to Reduce

*Examples of solid fats and oils

Solid Fats	Oils
Beef, pork, and chicken fat Butter, cream, and milk fat Coconut, palm, and palm kernel oils Hydrogenated oil Partially hydrogenated oil Shortening Stick margarine	Canola oil Corn oil Cottonseed oil Olive oil Peanut oil Safflower oil Sunflower oil Tub (soft) margarine Vegetable oil

Cut back on foods high in solid fats, added sugars, and salt Many people eat foods with too much solid fats, added sugars, and salt (sodium). Added sugars and fats load foods with extra calories you don't need. Too much sodium may increase your blood pressure.

Choose foods and drinks with little or no added sugars.
- Drink water instead of sugary drinks. There are about 10 packets of sugar in a 12-ounce can of soda.
- Select fruit for dessert. Eat sugary desserts less often.
- Choose 100% fruit juice instead of fruit-flavored drinks.

Look out for salt (sodium) in foods you buy—it all adds up.
- Compare sodium in foods like soup, bread, and frozen meals—and choose the foods with lower numbers.
- Add spices or herbs to season food without adding salt.

Eat fewer foods that are high in solid fats.
- Make major sources of saturated fats—such as cakes, cookies, ice cream, pizza, cheese, sausages, and hot dogs—occasional choices, and not every day foods.
- Select lean cuts of meats or poultry and fat-free or low-fat milk, yogurt, and cheese.
- Switch from solid fats to oils when preparing food.*

Physical Activity

Be physically active your way Pick activities that you like and start by doing what you can, at least 10 minutes at a time. Every bit adds up, and the health benefits increase as you spend more time being active.

Note to parents
What you eat and drink and your level of physical activity are important for your own health, and also for your children's health.

You are your children's most important role model. Your children pay attention to what you **do** more than what you **say.**

© Monkey Business images, 2012, Shutterstock, Inc.

You can do a lot to help your children develop healthy habits for life by providing and eating healthy meals and snacks. For example, don't just *tell* your children to eat their vegetables—**show** them that you eat and enjoy vegetables every day.

Reading and Understanding the Nutrition Facts Label

Beginning in May 1993, the federal government has required food manufacturers to provide accurate nutritional information about their products on their product labels. Because food labels are standardized, relatively straightforward, and easy to read, much of the guesswork has been taken out of good nutrition.

Ingredients are listed on food labels by percentage of total weight, in order from heaviest or highest to lowest. By reading the listing of ingredients, an individual can determine whether a food is relatively high in fat, sugar, salt, and so on.

Food labels are legally required to include the number of servings per container, serving size, and the number of calories per serving. They must also list the percentage of the daily value of total fat, saturated fat, and, beginning in January 2006, trans fat. Nutrition Facts Labels must also list the percentage of the daily value of cholesterol, sodium, total carbohydrates (including dietary fiber and sugars), proteins, vitamins, and minerals.

Figure 8.5 and 8.6 on page 199 provides an example of the required changes to the nutrition information found on packaged foods. The updated labels must be in place by July 26, 2018. The updated label will feature a new design, will reflect updated information about the science of nutrition, and will have updated serving sizes and labeling requirements.

The bottom part of Nutrition Facts Labels on larger packages (typically any item that is not packaged for individual sale) contains a footnote with Daily Values (DVs) for 2,000- and 2,500-calorie-a-day diets. Because this information is not about a specific food product, it does not change from product to product. It shows recommended advice for all Americans. In the footnote section of the Nutrition Facts Label, the nutrients that have an upper limit or a set amount one wants to stay below are listed first. These nutrients include total fat, saturated fat, trans fat, sodium, and cholesterol. The amount of dietary fiber listed in this section is a minimum amount that should be consumed each day. The daily value for carbohydrates listed is a recommendation based on a 2,000-calorie-a-day diet, but it can vary slightly depending on the amount of fat and protein consumed.

When an individual takes the time to use the main body of the Nutrition Facts Label in conjunction with the footnote section of the label, he or she can get a very accurate picture of not only what source (carbohydrate, fat, or protein) their calories are coming from, but also how close they are coming to meeting the daily requirements necessary to maintain a high level of health.

Why Is There No Percentage of Daily Value for Trans Fats?

There have been scientific findings and reports that confirm a link between trans fats and an increased risk of coronary heart disease. However, none of the reports have recommended an amount of trans fat that the Food and Drug Administration could use to establish a daily value, and without a daily value, a percentage of that daily value cannot be calculated.

FIGURE 8.5   Original vs. New Format—Infographics to Help Understand the Changes

Nutrition Facts

Serving Size 2/3 cup (55g)
Servings Per Container About 8

Amount Per Serving

Calories 230   Calories from Fat 72

	% Daily Value*
Total Fat 8g	**12%**
Saturated Fat 1g	**5%**
Trans Fat 0g	
Cholesterol 0mg	**0%**
Sodium 160mg	**7%**
Total Carbohydrate 37g	**12%**
Dietary Fiber 4g	**16%**
Sugars 1g	
Protein 3g	

Vitamin A	10%
Vitamin C	8%
Calcium	20%
Iron	45%

* Percent Daily Values are based on a 2,000 calorie diet.
Your daily value may be higher or lower depending on
your calorie needs.

	Calories:	2,000	2,500
Total Fat	Less than	65g	80g
Sat Fat	Less than	20g	25g
Cholesterol	Less than	300mg	300mg
Sodium	Less than	2,400mg	2,400mg
Total Carbohydrate		300g	375g
Dietary Fiber		25g	30g

Nutrition Facts

8 servings per container
Serving size   **2/3 cup (55g)**

Amount per serving
Calories   **230**

	% Daily Value*
Total Fat 8g	**10%**
Saturated Fat 1g	**5%**
Trans Fat 0g	
Cholesterol 0mg	**0%**
Sodium 160mg	**7%**
Total Carbohydrate 37g	**13%**
Dietary Fiber 4g	**14%**
Total Sugars 12g	
Includes 10g Added Sugars	**20%**
Protein 3g	

Vitamin D 2mcg	10%
Calcium 260mg	20%
Iron 8mg	45%
Potassium 235mg	6%

* The % Daily Value (DV) tells you how much a nutrient in
a serving of food contributes to a daily diet. 2,000 calories
a day is used for general nutrition advice.

Source: FDA

Although product labels do have accuracy requirements, mistakes can be made and sometimes do occur. For this reason, it is wise to check the accuracy of food labels. One quick and easy way to do this is to divide the number of servings within the container—does it equal the serving size (Figure 8.7)? For example, you have a product that the Nutrition Facts Label shows having a serving size of one-half cup and the number of servings per container is four. If you open the product and check it, does it contain two cups of that food? If so, the label is correct. Another way to check the accuracy of a nutrition label is to calculate the calories (grams of fat times nine, grams of protein and carbohydrates times four). Does the number calculated match the

Reading labels while grocery shopping is
important in preparing healthy meals.

Source: FDA

FIGURE 8.6

Source: FDA

FIGURE 8.7

What's considered a single serving has changed in the decades since the original nutrition label was created. So now serving sizes will be more realistic to reflect how much people typically eat at one time.

reported calories within 10 to 20 calories? If the numbers are way "off" one should be aware that the label is incorrect. See Figure 8.5 (Nutrition Facts Label) for an example of how to check for label accuracy based on reported calories.

Reported Total Calories per Serving = 250
Reported Calories from Fat = 110

The product contains a total of 12 g of fat. Fat contains 9 calories per gram of fat, so to check for accuracy of reported fat calories, multiply 12 × 9. This equals 108.

To check for accuracy of total number of calories, multiply the total grams of carbohydrates . . . 31 in this product, by 4 (the amount of calories per gram of carbohydrate). This equals 124 calories.

The total grams of protein . . . 5 in this product, by 4 (the amount of calories per gram of protein). This equals 20 calories.

To check for accuracy of the total number of calories per serving, add calories from fat, protein, and carbohydrates. If they are close to the number of calories per serving listed on the Nutrition Fact Label, the label is accurate.

108 + 124 + 20 = 252 actual vs. 250 reported

Both the total calories and fat calories listed on the Nutrition Facts Label were slightly low. Knowing this, an individual can more accurately determine when he or she has reached their nutritional limit.

Vegetarianism

There have always been people who, for one reason or another (religious, ethical, or philosophical), have chosen to follow a vegetarian diet. However, in recent years, a vegetarian diet has become increasingly popular.

Salmon is a good source of Omega-3 fatty acids.

There are four different types of vegetarian diets. **Vegans** are considered true vegetarians. Their diets are completely void of meat, chicken, fish, eggs, or milk products. A vegan's primary sources of protein are vegetables, fruits, and grains. Because vitamin B12 is normally found only in meat products, many vegans choose to supplement their diet with this vitamin.

Lactovegetarians eat dairy products, fruits, and vegetables but do not consume any other animal products (meat, poultry, fish, or eggs).

Ovolactovegetarians are another type of vegetarians. They eat eggs as well as dairy products, fruits, and vegetables, but still do not consume meat, poultry, or fish.

A person who eats fruits, vegetables, dairy products, eggs, and a small selection of poultry, fish, and other seafood is a partial or **semivegetarian.** These individuals do not consume any beef or pork.

Vegetarians of all four types can meet all their daily dietary needs through the food selections available to them. However, because certain foods or groups of foods that are high in specific nutrients are forbidden, it is critical that a vegetarian is diligent in selecting his or her food combinations so that the nutritional benefits of the foods allowed are maximized. If food combinations from a wide variety of sources are not selected, nutritional deficiencies of proteins, vitamins, and minerals can rapidly occur and proper growth, development, and function may not occur. While a vegetarian diet can certainly be a healthy, low-fat alternative to the typical American diet, without diligent monitoring, it is not a guarantee of good health.

For many individuals who choose a vegetarian diet, it is more than simply omitting certain foods or groups of food, it is a way of living that they have embraced.

References

Donatelle, R. J. & Davis, L. G. *Access to Health* (9th ed). Boston: Allyn & Bacon. 2006. Floyd, P. A., Mimms, S. E., and Yelding-Howard, C. *Personal Health: Perspectives & Life-*

styles., Englewood, CO: Morton Publishing Company. 2007.

Hales, D. *An Invitation to Health* (8th ed). New York: Brooks/Cole Publishing Company. 1999.

Hoeger, W. and Hoeger, S. A. *Principles and Labs for Fitness and Wellness* (9th ed). Belmont, CA: Thomson Wadsworth. 2008.

Hoeger, W. W. K. and Hoeger, S. A. *Lifetime Physical Fitness and Wellness: A Personalized Program* (8th ed). Belmont, CA: Thomson Wadsworth. 2005.

Hyman, B., Oden, G., Bacharach, D., and Collins, R. *Fitness for Living.* Dubuque, Iowa: Kendall/Hunt. 2006.

http://www.ific.org/nutrition/functional/index.cfm?rederforprint = 1

Powers, S. K., Todd, S. L. and Noland, J. J. *Total Fitness and Wellness* (2nd ed). Boston: Allyn & Bacon. 2005.

Prentice, W. E. *Fitness and Wellness for Life* (6th ed). New York: WCB McGraw-Hill. 1999.

Pruitt, B. E. & Stein, J. *HealthStyles* (2nd ed). Boston: Allyn & Bacon. 1999.

Robbins, G., Powers, D., and Burgess, S. *A Wellness Way of Life* (4th ed). New York: WCB McGraw-Hill. 1999.

Rosato, F. *Fitness for Wellness* (3rd ed). Minneapolis: West. 1994.

Webmaster@noah.cuny.edu

http://www.cfsan.fda.gov/~dms/transfat.html

http://www.ganesa.com/food/foodpyramid.gif

http://www.healthdepot.com

http://www.health.gov/dietaryguidelines/dga2010.htm

http://www.health.gov/dietaryguidelines/dga2010/document/aim.htm

http://www.health.gov/dietaryguidelines/dga2010/document/choose.htm

http://www.capp.usda.gov/Publications/DietaryGuidelines/2010/PolicyDoc/ExecSumm.pdf

https://health.gov/dietaryguidelines/2015/guidelines/chapter-1/key-recommendations/

http://vm.cfsan.fda.gov/~dms/foodlab.html

http://www.ers.usda.gov/AmberWaves/June05/Features?Will2005WholeGrain.htm

http://www.aaccnet.org/definitions/wholegrain.asp

http://www.capp.usda.gov/Pubications/MyPlate/GettingStartedWithMyPlate.pdf

http://www.choosemyplate.gov/foodgroups/downloads/MyPlate/DG2010Brochure.pdf

Contacts

American Dietetic Association Get Nutrition Fact Sheets at American Dietetic Association Consumer Education Team
216 West Jackson Boulevard
Chicago, IL 60606
(send a self-addressed, stamped envelope), call 800–877–1600, ext. 5000 for other publications or 800–366–1655 for recorded food/nutrition messages

American Obesity Association
1250 24th Street, NW, Suite 300
Washington, DC 20037
800–98–OBESE

Department of Nutrition Sciences University of Alabama at Birmingham
Birmingham, AL 35294
Calorieking.com Fitday.com http://www.caloriesperhour.com/index_food.html

Chapter 9
Scientific Principles of Weight Management

© Sebastian Duda/Shutterstock.com

OBJECTIVES

Students will be able to:

- Identify causes and complications associated with obesity
- Identify factors why the energy balance model doesn't always hold true
- Identify components of healthy eating
- Identify an obesogenic environment
- Identify a healthy Body Mass Index
- Present guidelines for long term weight loss success
- Discuss the importance of activity in weight management
- Recognize the pitfalls of fad dieting

Adaptation of *Health and Fitness: A Guide to a Healthy Lifestyle*, 5th Edition, by Laura Bounds, Gayden Darnell, Kirstin Brekken Shea, and Dottiede Agnor. Copyright © 2012 by Kendall Hunt Publishing Company.

"Thou shouldst eat to live: not live to eat."

~Socrates, 469 BC-399 BC

Why have so many Americans gained so much weight over the last few decades (Figure 9.1)? Approximately two-thirds of adult Americans are overweight, and one-third of children and adolescents are overweight. Even more alarming is the fact that 25% of Americans are clinically obese. This trend is not limited to Americans. A large proportion of developed countries have citizens who are overweight and have obesity related health issues. The reasons for this growing problem are varied and complex. Researchers study environmental, neurological, hormonal, psychological and genetic factors related to overweight and obesity.

"This mystification that obesity is caused by a lack of willpower or just eating the wrong foods is simply a misconception. There is so much social stigma attached to weight that we make a lot of value judgements. The effort in science is to peel back those layers of belief and try to understand things in an experimental, rational mode. Just as we have made progress against heart disease with statins and blood pressure drugs, we will find medications that can safely and substantially lower weight." –Joe Bass, Northwestern

Although the causes of overweight and obesity (see page 210 for a definition of each) are complex and numerous, the risks of being overweight or obese are very real and tangible. An individual who is overweight is at increased risk for conditions such as high blood pressure, high cholesterol, stroke, heart disease, obesity, diabetes, and certain types of cancers. The three largest contributors to overweight are genetics, lack of exercise, and eating choices and behaviors. For most Americans, food is plentiful. Americans are typically not malnourished due to a lack of food, but the World Health Organization predicts that there soon will be a worldwide epidemic of overweight, malnourished people resulting from the unhealthy types of foods that are being eaten. A person living on only fast food that is high in sodium, fat, cholesterol and low in vitamins and fiber can experience a lack of some essential nutrients. Eating a variety of foods such as vegetables, fruits, whole grains, healthy fats, fish, lean cuts of meat and beans are the building blocks of a solid nutritional practice.

Previous chapters emphasized the importance of regular activity for overall health. Exercise can help you get fit, stay fit, and it is a critical aid in efforts to lose weight. Genetics may play a larger role in our weight than previously thought. Studies have revealed the power of the brain and its evolutionary desire to maintain fat mass. Exercise, however, (or the lack of exercise) may be the most significant factor influencing weight. Sobering studies show that most people who successfully lose weight will have gained it back within 2 years. The five percent of the people who successfully maintain weight loss have regular exercise as part

FIGURE 9.1

Percentage of adults who are obese, by state from 1991–2010.

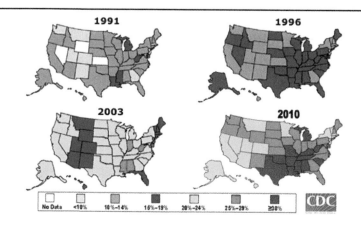

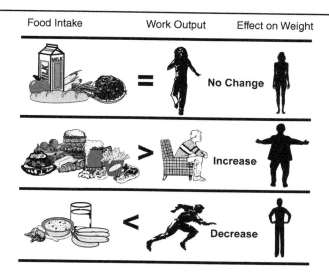

Food Intake   Work Output   Effect on Weight

= No Change

> Increase

< Decrease

FIGURE 9.2
The energy balance model does not always hold true; many other influences can manipulate energy balance.

of their lifestyle. It isn't important to take up running or any activity you are uncomfortable doing. The important thing is to just move.

Current metabolism research challenges the age-old **energy-balance model**, where caloric intake should equal total caloric expenditure in order to maintain weight (Figure 9.2). A person consuming fewer calories than he or she expends should expect to see a net loss when stepping on the scale. Theoretically this model holds true, but as we shall see, this does not hold true for all individuals. The one thing that does hold true is that physical activity mediates positive results both in weight loss efforts and overall health.

Because our society has become increasingly automated, Americans are saving lots of energy in the form of stored fat. "Easier", "automated", "instant", and "remote control" are all terms which describe using less energy. Saving energy relates to moving less, which means saving calories. A person who moves less typically stores more fat. Chapter 5 discusses lifestyle activity, which means looking for opportunities to expend more energy like taking the stairs instead of the elevator. Every time you drive through for fast food, think of all of the energy you are saving. Another culprit in contributing to heavier Americans is the time spent playing electronic games, texting, etc. Balancing sedentary activities with walking, jogging or simply moving is important (Table 9.1). This chapter will explore what effects a person's weight, positive steps to use to try and reduce weight, and pitfalls to avoid when trying to lose weight.

TABLE 9.1 ♦ How Much Physical Activity Do I Need?

It really depends on what your health goals are. Here are some guidelines to follow:

Goal	Physical Activity Level for Adults
Reduce the risk of chronic disease	At least 30 minutes of a moderate intensity physical activity, above usual activity, most days of the week.
Manage body weight and prevent gradual unhealthy body weight gain	Approximately 60 minutes of moderate intensity physical activity most days of the week while not exceeding calorie needs.
Maintain weight loss	At least 60 to 90 minutes of moderate intensity physical activity most days of the week while not exceeding calorie needs. Some people may need to talk to their healthcare provider before participating in this level of physical activity.

Source: cdc.gov

Is One Milkshake Enough?

Research by Eric Stice at the Oregon Research Institute indicates that the "brains of the overweight are wired to feel more pleasure in response to food." (Hurley, June, 2011). Stice tested obese adolescent girls and had them sip on a milkshake while they were having an fMRI scan of their brain. Their brains-specifically the gustatory cortex and the somatosensory regions, showed greater activation than the non-obese control group. This area of the brain is involved with the sensory experience of the pleasure derived from eating food. Interestingly, the brains of the obese adolescent girls showed less activation in a different are of the brain called the striatum. The striatum is part of the cerebrum and gives sensory input to the basal ganglia. The striatum is full of dopamine receptors and is involved in the reward pathway, which affects motivation and behavior. Most of us find pleasure in eating and experience dopamine release as a result. So why would the obese adolescent girls have a decrease in activation of the striatum? It is possible that after years of overeating, part of the brain changed so that when they drank one milkshake, instead of being satisfied it left them hungrier for more. A hypo functioning striatum may attenuate the way dopamine is taken up—much like an addict. "The people who initially find that milk shake enjoyable will want more of it, but in so doing they cause neuroplastic changes that downregulate the reward circuitry, driving them to eat more and more to regain that same feeling they crave." (Stice, 2009)

In a different fMRI study in 2009 Michael Lowe at Drexel University looked at normal weight people. Half of the group were chronic strict dieters while the other half ate whatever they wanted. Both groups had fMRI brain scans immediately after enjoying a milkshake. The non- dieters' brain lit up in the area indicating satisfaction. The chronic dieters' brains activated areas that indicated desire and expectation of a reward. The chronic dieters craved even more. Lowe interpreted his data to suggest that the chronic dieters could be restraining themselves because when given the opportunity, they are more likely to overeat.

(adapted from Dan Hurley "The Hungry Brain" Discover magazine)

Evolution and Genetics

The human body is a marvelously efficient machine. Long ago when humans were hunter-gatherers meals were not a certainty. Often it was feast or famine for long periods of time. When food was available, they had to eat as much as possible. The excess energy they did not utilize was stored as fat which sustained them until the next meal-which could be days off. This mechanism, key for survival in the past, is now what causes some modern day humans to be over-fat. For most Americans, food is abundant and food is good, (think of your favorite meal complete with dessert). It can be challenging to eat good food in moderation.

Hormones, Genes, and Stress

Hormones regulate fat storage in the human body as part of the endocrine system. When we eat more than we need for homeostasis, the excess energy (calories) is stored as fat in our fat cells. These fat cells are called **adipocytes**. Adipocytes do much more than just store fat; adipocytes act as a hormone secreting organ in the endocrine system. The hormones secreted from fat tissue act as mediators involved in inflammation, insulin regulation, appetite regulation and fat storage are called adipokines. **Adipokines** discussed here are **leptin, ghrelin, visfatin, and adiponectin. Leptin** (*leptos* means "thin" in Greek) is a hormone secreted by fat cells. Leptin regulates metabolism and signals satiety to the hypothalamus. The hypothalamus regulates sleep, fatigue, thirst, and hunger cycles, much the same as a thermostat. Basically, leptin signals the brain that the stomach is full. **Ghrelin**, a hormone secreted by our gut, signals hunger to the hypothalamus. **Visfatin** is a hormone secreted by our visceral (abdominal) fat, and is typically elevated in the obese who also have type 2 diabetes and is involved in triglyceride synthesis.

Adiponectin is a hormone involved in inflammation, insulin sensitivity, atherosclerosis and metabolism. Adiponectin levels decrease as obesity increases (Singla, Bardoloi & Parkash 2010). These adipokines work with the brain, the liver, the muscular system and other fat tissue to form a complex mechanism working to manage our metabolism.

Cortisol, released by the adrenal glands which sit atop the kidneys, is the hormone that is released when we experience acute stress. After the stressful incident is over, other stress hormones decrease while cortisol levels remain elevated. Cortisol helps us recover by increasing appetite in order to replace the fat and carbohydrate that was utilized in the stress response. Unfortunately when stressed, many of us crave calorie dense comfort food. When stress becomes chronic, then the constant levels of cortisol present in the body signal it to increase glucose production. The glucose is then turned into fat, and more of that fat is stored in the abdomen. Abdominal fat around the internal organs is called **visceral fat**, and accumulation of visceral fat is considered to enhance health risk, perhaps due to increases in blood pressure and because of increased load on the heart (see Figure 5.4 on page 82). (Koehler, 2016)

Sleep

Good sleep hygiene is important for maintaining a healthy weight. Disruption of your circadian rhythm and sleep cycle can influence your metabolism. "In humans, sleep and feeding are tightly interconnected, and pathological disturbances of either process are associated with metabolism-related disorders," (Alex Keene, Ph.D., of FAU Department of Biological Sciences). Studies on mice, flies, and humans all point to the fact that disrupting your sleep cycle and eating schedule can result in changes in blood sugar levels which may increase the chance of developing diabetes and increase the chance of unwanted weight gain. The hormones leptin and ghrelin are greatly affected by the quality of sleep we get. Lack of sleep or interrupted sleep can cause leptin levels to decrease and ghrelin levels to increase-signaling hunger to the body, potential overeating, and possibly unhealthy weight gain. The message is that how much you eat, what you eat, when you eat, and how much you sleep all have an influence on your blood sugar and weight.

FTO Gene

Unfortunately, the playing field is not even for everyone in terms of managing body weight. A gene called FTO has been identified that is associated with how the brain regulates appetite. Carriers of this gene weigh approximately 2.6 pounds more than a noncarrier, and some people may carry 2 copies of this gene, causing them to be about 5.2 pounds heavier than a noncarrier. A large scale study of more than 38,000 adult Europeans indicated that the FTO genotype is associated with higher body weight, increased BMI, and current research suggests that this genotype is also associated with an increased predisposition to diabetes and obesity (Frayling et al. 2007). The good news is that vigorous physical activity can attenuate the genotype's effect on obesity (Food4Me study, Celis-Morales et. al, 2016). That is, someone with this genotype is not destined to be obese, but can effectively manage their body weight by engaging in vigorous exercise on a regular basis.

Environment

"Genes load the gun, but environment pulls the trigger." Dr. Patrick O'Neil, director of the Weight Management Center at the Medical University of South Carolina is credited with coining this phrase. Evolutionarily speaking, we are programmed to hunt and gather, then eat plenty as the food is available to store energy. Genes may influence tendencies toward overweight slightly, but surely the bigger culprit is the environment we live in. Our **environmental influences** start before we are born. Studies have determined that there is a link between low birth weight babies and obesity later in life. Lack of nutrition in utero may cause newborns to be "programmed" to eat more later in life. Low birth weight babies develop fewer neurons in the part of the hypothalamus associated with food intake. A mom's prenatal nutrition is critical for the developing fetus. Other factors affecting the environment are culture, family, socioeconomic status, education, access to health care and more. These are critical environmental factors that impact health and potential for overweight as a child develops.

Environmental cues to eat are everywhere. In every city, the McDonald's corporation would like to be 4.5 minutes away or less from our location to make fast food convenient for us. Billboards on highways, enticing smells in the mall, television or online advertising constantly bombard all of us with environmental cues to eat. When is the last time you saw a billboard by the side of the highway advertising broccoli? It is usually the calorie-dense high carbohydrate and high fat foods that beckon us to turn at the next exit for a fast food meal. If we happen to be stressed at the time, our brains are hard wired to crave just that type of meal even more. If we skipped breakfast and are experiencing low-blood sugar, then we are more likely to give in to temptation. Every day we are faced with an abundance of easily accessible food sources, but specific characteristics of the environmental situation may increase eating even when we are not hungry. Eating increases when more people are present, when the atmosphere is friendly, when more food options and larger portion sizes are readily available. Beware the food buffet! (Ferriday, D., 2011)

"Few things are more rewarding evolutionarily than calorie-dense food."
–Tracy Bale, University of Pennsylvania neurobiologist.

These environmental cues can affect almost everyone's behavior at times- but studies show some people are more susceptible than others. What can you do to arm yourself against this constant barrage of "eat me" temptations? Plan ahead, manage your time, go to the grocery store and have healthy staples available to you. Keep baggies of nuts and fruit in your backpack, purse or car. Pack your lunch when possible. Drink plenty of water; staying hydrated will help. Get plenty of sleep on a regular basis. If possible when a craving hits, move. Take a walk or call a friend to take the focus off of the food.

"The **obesogenic environment** encompasses the environmental features of modern lifestyles that are postulated to contribute to the increasing prevalence of obesity; in particular, it is thought that the wide availability of food that is energy dense, palatable and inexpensive, combined with increasingly sedentary habits, favor an excess of energy intake over expenditure." (Chaput, J.P., 2011) It is increasingly difficult to eat well and move enough in our modern environment. Obesogenic is a term used to frame the many influential factors that may contribute to our obesity (Figure 9.3). *The Lancet*, a respected medical journal made an observation in an article in 2011: "Perhaps it is our environment that is to blame, and that obesity represents a normal reaction to an abnormal environment." The conditions that surround us may promote obesity; it is incumbent upon us each day to make wise choices with awareness. One approach to combat the obesogenic environment is to get up every day with a plan, knowing that temptations and cues are around each corner.

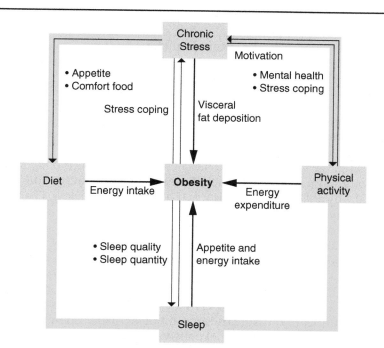

FIGURE 9.3

In the obesogenic environment, there are many environmental, cultural, and lifestyle cues that contribute to overeating.

What Is a Healthy Body Weight?

There is no single ideal body weight; rather there is a range of healthy body weights that are acceptable for a certain height. Activity level, age, eating patterns, body composition, pregnancy or lactation, and gender as well as genetic predisposition can determine weight. You may find that your body seems to change, but it hovers around the same weight. The **set-point theory** postulates that the body regulates metabolism in order to maintain a certain weight, much the same as a thermostat regulates temperature. If fat stores fall below the "set" point, then the body responds by increasing appetite. If we overeat, then appetite may be reduced or all of the calories available may not be stored. The set-point theory proposes that parts of our evolutionary brain want to hang on to fat stores. Set-point gradually creeps up with repeated extreme dieting, this too is a protective mechanism for the species' survival. Studies done on the Biggest Loser contestants show that fast weight loss can disrupt the body's set-point in a negative way. Lowering your set-point is possible, but it takes patience and consistent physical activity.

Body Mass Index or **BMI** is a simple way to determine if your body weight falls within a healthy range. Because BMI is a ratio between weight and height, there are certain populations that cannot use this parameter as a gage of body composition (see margin for BMI for Asian populations). Persons with a large amount of muscle mass will have a higher BMI. Athletes, body builders, pregnant or lactating women, young children or sedentary older populations should not use BMI as a reliable gauge for health risk. Even so, BMI is considered superior to traditional height weight charts. Refer back to Table 3.2 to determine your BMI. A BMI over 25 is considered overweight and a BMI over 30 is considered obese. A higher BMI may indicate you are at an elevated risk for heart disease, Type 2 diabetes and most of the conditions related to obesity.

Underweight is a BMI of 18.5 or below. It is interesting to note that on the catwalks of New York and Paris models now have to weigh in and are unable to participate if they are below a BMI of 18. It is encouraging that the fashion world is participating in increasing awareness regarding the dangers of being too thin.

"If your BMI exceeds 35, you have a 4,000 percent greater chance of developing type 2 diabetes and about a 70 greater chance of getting heart disease than if you have a healthy BMI of 22. These probabilities, however, are altered by physical activity and other factors, including your genes and how much of your fat is visceral or subcutaneous."
–*The Story of the Human Body*, by Daniel Lieberman.

1 kg = 2.2 lbs
1 meter = 39.37 inches

> BMI
> 25–30 =overweight
> 30 and above=obese

> BMI for Asian
> populations
> 23–27.5 = increased
> risk
> 27.5 and greater =
> high risk

$$BMI = \frac{weight\ in\ kilograms}{Height\ in\ meters\ squared}$$

Body composition is one of the five health-related fitness components discussed in Chapter 7. A person's body composition is a measure of health, estimating the amount of fat mass relative to the lean body mass. Lean body mass is comprised of muscle, bone, and internal organs and all other fat-free mass. Body composition is a more accurate indicator of overall fitness rather than using a person's body weight.

The ideal range for college aged females is 18–23 percent body fat and 12–18 percent body fat for college aged men. **Essential fat** is that fat which is necessary for normal physiological functioning. If a female gets below 11–13% essential body fat she typically experiences hormonal disturbances and may experience menstruation cessation. Essential fat for men is around 3% body fat.

There are numerous methods to determine an estimate of percent body fat. Skinfold calipers are commonly used in schools. At health fairs bioelectrical impedance is a simple and inexpensive test to administer. The accuracy of this method is highly questionable due to variations in hydration levels in people throughout the day. The air displacement method uses pressure sensors inside an airtight chamber to measure the amount of air displaced by the person inside the chamber. This is a bulky and expensive container. Hydrostatic weighing is

TABLE 9.2

Estimated Calorie Requirements (in Kilocalories) for Each Gender and Age Group at Three Levels of Physical Activity[a]

Estimated amounts of calories needed to maintain energy balance for various gender and age groups at three different levels of physical activity. The estimates are rounded up to the nearest 200 calories and were determined using the Institute of Medicine equation.

| Gender | Age (years) | Activity Level[b,c,d] | | |
		Sedentary[b]	Moderately Active[c]	Active[d]
Child	2–3	1,000	1,000–1,400e	1,000–1,400e
Female	4–8	1,200	1,400–1,600	1,400–1,800
	9–13	1,600	1,600–2,000	1,800–2,200
	14–18	1,800	2,000	2,400
	19–30	2,000	2,000–2,200	2,400
	31–50	1,800	2,000	2,200
	51+	1,600	1,800	2,000–2,200
Male	4–8	1,400	1,400–1,600	1,600–2,000
	9–13	1,800	1,800–2,200	2,000–2,600
	14–18	2,200	2,400–2,800	2,800–3,200
	19–30	2,400	2,600–2,800	3,000
	31–50	2,200	2,400–2,600	2,800–3,000
	51+	2,000	2,200–2,400	2,400–2,800

[a]These levels are based on Estimated Energy Requirements (EER) from the Institute of Medicine Dietary References Intakes macro- nutrients report, 2002, calculated by gender, age, and activity level for reference-sized individuals. "Reference-size," as determined by IOM, is based on median height and weight for ages up to age 18 years of age and median height and weight for that height to give a BMI of 21.5 for adult females and 22.5 for adult males.

[b]Sedentary means a lifestyle that includes only the light physical activity associated with typical day-to-day life.

[c]Moderately active means a lifestyle that includes physical activity equivalent to walking about 1.5 to 3 miles per day at 3 to 4 miles per hour, in addition to the light physical activity associated with typical day-to-day life.

[d]Active means a lifestyle that includes physical activity equivalent to walking more than 3 miles per day at 3 to 4 miles per hour, in addition to the light physical activity associated with typical day-to-day life.

[e]The calorie ranges shown are to accommodate needs of different ages within the group. For children and adolescents, more calories are needed at older ages. For adults, fewer calories are needed at older ages.

Source: USDA.

popular with laboratories and athletic centers. The clinicians determine how much a person weighs under water, then use that value in a formula. Dual energy X-ray absorptiometry **(DEXA)** is the preferred method in research facilities. Each method has pros and cons-however if measuring percent body fat in a pre and post comparison it is important to replicate the same environment and to use the same technique in the post test as was used for the pretest.

Determining Caloric Needs

Caloric needs are different for every individual. Caloric need is determined by body weight, daily physical activity, and the thermal effect of food, or dietary induced thermogenesis. See Table 9.2 to determine your own daily caloric needs. Notice the different caloric requirement for active individuals compared to sedentary individuals.

Obesity

Overweight, which is defined as an excess of body weight to some height standard, or a BMI of 25–30. **Obesity** is a term that refers to excess fat with an accompanying loss of function and an increase in health problems, or a BMI of 30 or more. **Creeping obesity** is a gradual increase of percent body fat as activity decreases with age. This typically results in a ½ to 1 lb. fat gain per year, with an approximate simultaneous loss of ½ lb. of fat-free mass or muscle. Consider that if you overeat just one-hundred calories per day, you will gain one pound in a month. An extra twelve pounds can sneak up on you in one year. Consider this as you try to avoid the freshman fifteen!

Obesity Prevention

Activity is the optimal way to manage current weight or successfully lose weight. The key is to exercise, maintain a healthy diet throughout your life and avoid gaining excess weight. Participate in planned exercise as well as increase your

Body composition is a more accurate indicator of overall fitness than is a person's body weight.

Some health profesionals think **waist measurement alone** is a valuable indicator of future health risk. High risk for women is a waist measurement over 35", and over 40" for men (National Institute for Health).

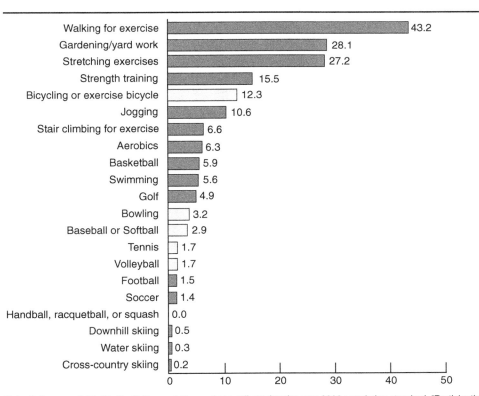

FIGURE 9.4

Most Popular Adult Physical Activities in the United States

Activity	Value
Walking for exercise	43.2
Gardening/yard work	28.1
Stretching exercises	27.2
Strength training	15.5
Bicycling or exercise bicycle	12.3
Jogging	10.6
Stair climbing for exercise	6.6
Aerobics	6.3
Basketball	5.9
Swimming	5.6
Golf	4.9
Bowling	3.2
Baseball or Softball	2.9
Tennis	1.7
Volleyball	1.7
Football	1.5
Soccer	1.4
Handball, racquetball, or squash	0.0
Downhill skiing	0.5
Water skiing	0.3
Cross-country skiing	0.2

Note: Data are weighted to the U.S. population and age-adjusted to the year 2000 population standard. "Participation" in activity reported as being done at least once during the past two weeks.

Source: Centers for Disease Control and Prevention, National Health Interview Survey (NHIS), 1998, Atlanta.

everyday lifestyle activity. Establish support systems to help you with exercise adherence and healthy lifestyle habits.

How Does Activity Help Reduce Obesity?

Those who are successful with weight loss goals are usually committed to a regular exercise routine. People who successfully lose weight are much more likely to maintain the weight loss with a regular exercise routine. Weight gain occurs with inactivity; activity is the best way to reduce the size of fat stores. Even a weight loss such as 10% of your body weight, can suppress your metabolism. Restricting calories while not exercising can result in the loss of lean body mass. Exercising, and especially weight training, can help maintain muscle when dieting. Weight training has been shown to increase a person's confidence and self-esteem, regardless of actual weight loss.

How Do I Lose Weight?

Once you have determined what your daily caloric needs are, then estimate how many calories you are actually eating on a regular basis. The recommended weight loss is ½ to 1 pound per week. Losing weight faster often signifies a short term fix, indicating that the weight loss will be difficult to maintain. Fast weight loss is often followed by fast weight gain. This is called **yo-yo dieting**, and often the weight gain is a bit more than what was initially

Guidelines for a Successful Weight Loss Program

The American College of Sports Medicine has put together the following eleven guidelines in an effort to help individuals recognize potentially successful weight loss programs and avoid unsound or dangerous weight loss programs.

1. Prolonged fasting and diet programs that severely restrict caloric intake are scientifically unsound and can be medically dangerous.
2. Fasting and diet programs that severely restrict caloric intake result in the loss of large amounts of water, electrolytes, minerals, glycogen stores, and other fat-free tissues, but with minimal amounts of fat loss.
3. Mild caloric restriction (500–1,000 calories less than usual per day) results in smaller loss of water, electrolytes, minerals, and other fat-free tissues and is less likely to result in malnutrition.
4. Dynamic exercise of large muscle groups helps to maintain fat-free tissue, including lean muscle mass and bone density, and can result in a loss of body weight (primarily body fat).

5. A nutritionally sound diet resulting in mild caloric intake restrictions, coupled with an endurance exercise program, along with behavior modification of existing eating habits, is recommended for weight reduction. The rate of weight loss should never exceed two pounds per week.
6. To maintain proper weight control and optimal body fat levels, a lifetime commitment to proper eating habits and regular physical activity is required.
7. A successful weight loss plan can be followed anywhere—at home, work, restaurants, parties, and so on.
8. For a plan to be successful, the emphasis must be on portion size.
9. Successful weight loss plans incorporate a wide variety of nutritious foods that are easily accessible in the supermarket.
10. A weight loss plan must not be too costly if it is to be successful.
11. The most essential aspect of a weight loss program is that it can be followed for the rest of an individual's life.

lost. Repeated bouts of weight loss/gain like this can gradually add unwanted excess weight and increase set-point. Yo-yo dieting through the years can make it more difficult to lose weight in the future.

The Weight Loss 'Halo' Effect

Bariatrics is the field of medicine that specializes in treating morbid obesity. A surgeon may perform bariatric surgery to assist in weight loss only after lifestyle changes and other conventional methods are unsuccessful. There is associated short term and long term risks with this type of surgery and this option must be considered carefully. Patti Neighmond reported for NPR on a study directed by Dr. John Morton, Stanford Bariatric Surgery Director. Dr. Morton considers obesity a "family disease." We typically sit around the table together, sharing and learning eating patterns. He noticed that after his patients' surgeries, family members seemed to mimic the patient's new weight loss habits such as eating smaller portions and being more physically active.

The Biggest Loser Loses More than Just Weight

The popular reality show *The Biggest Loser* illustrates, in front of millions of viewers, the fact that extreme lifestyle intervention can inspire dramatic weight loss. Personal trainers as drill sergeants, personalized meal plans, support from others, the pressure and spirit of competition, and the motivation of prize money can all provide impetus for hundreds of pounds lost in a single season. However, losing the weight is only the first step. On *The Biggest Loser* obese adults lose large amounts of weight in just a few months. The environment is extreme, the diet is extreme, the motivation is extreme, but what happens when they go back to the real world? This experience causes extreme drops to the participant's metabolism. The contestants on the Biggest Loser had slow metabolisms when the show ended. For most contestants, maintaining the new weight was next to impossible. Their post-reality show metabolism did not recover, causing them to gain weight even with less daily intake then prior to the show. For those contestants, they did indeed lose out. The important point is that using extreme tactics can result in short term weight loss, but in the long run the weight is likely to return as the brain switches on "survival mode" and slows the metabolism in reaction to the extreme changes. The lesson is that slow, methodical weight loss with diet and behavior modification and regular physical activity as a lifetime habit is a key to long term weight loss success.

Dr. Morton calls this a 'halo' effect; where good habits rub off on family members so much so that in a study of 35 of his bariatric patients one year post-surgery, family members had lost an average of 5% of their body weight. Five percent is enough to significantly enhance health and reduce risk of heart disease and diabetes. Being supportive is positive for the weight loss patient, but due to the 'halo' effect supportive family members often benefit as well (NPR, 2012). In order to change your lifestyle habits to lose weight, you must change your behaviors.

The following are several behaviors you can try in your weight loss war. (1) Plan ahead. Determine what behaviors and everyday patterns seem to sabotage your efforts. Is it the donut cart mid-morning at the office? Is it going through the drive-through at 2:00 a.m. after going out with friends? Anticipate these challenges and have a plan to counteract them. In order to lose a pound, there needs to be an approximate 3500 caloric deficit. (2) Eat fewer calories. Eating 500 calories less per day over the week could theoretically cause a net loss of 3500 calories or one pound. (3) Exercise more. Expending an extra 500 calories per day over one week theoretically may cause a net loss of one pound of body weight. (4) Do both. The best

Being supportive is positive for the weight loss patient, but due to the 'halo' effect, supportive family members often benefit as well.

© Monkey Business Images/ Shutterstock.com

Calorie Intake on the Increase

According to the USDA, the average American consumes almost 2,600 calories a day. This is almost 500 more calories per day than were consumed 30 years ago.

What is even more concerning is that 92% of this increase is in the form of oils, fats, and carbohydrates. This is problematic because the food groups we are eating more of are the same ones found in highly processed foods and fast foods. According to the USDA, between 1977 and 1978, fast food accounted for just over 3% of daily calories consumed by the average American; by 2005 that percentage has increased dramatically to over 13%.

option is to include both caloric restriction and extra activity. Exercise is the key to losing weight, and exercise is also a significant key to maintaining weight loss. The importance of movement illustrates how critical it is to find an activity that you enjoy so that you can embrace it for the rest of your life. (5) Enlist support. Ask your friends and family to support your efforts and to consider accompanying you with your lifestyle changes. (6) Consult a registered dietician; they can check for nutrient adequacy and help you with an individualized program. (7) Focus on portion control; there is strong evidence between portion size and body weight (Academy of Nutrition and Dietetics Evidence Analysis Library, 2015).

Walking is the most popular activity in the United States. See Table 9.3 Countdown to Weight Loss to determine a reasonable schedule for you to lose weight with a walking and caloric reduction program.

If you eat less food than you regularly eat as you might on a calorie restricted diet, the body's natural tendency is to slow the basal metabolic rate up to 30%. Exercise does the opposite-it will maintain or possibly increase your metabolism. Staying active when trying to lose weight is critical because it burns calories, increases metabolism and preserves muscle. Fad diets accompanied by no exercise often result in weight lost with an actual increase in body fat due to the loss of lean body mass.

Dieting or cutting back on calories is considered "severe" when an individual ingests fewer than 800 calories in a day. It is impossible to get all the nutrients you need with less than1000–1200 calories daily. Physiological and psychological problems can result from chronic caloric restriction. Much of the weight lost with severe caloric restriction is in the form of muscle. Cardiac muscle can be weakened to the point that it is no longer able to pump blood through the body-resulting in death. See complications of eating disorders in Chapter 4.

Foods have changed. Fifty years ago foods were less processed. Foods were eaten more in their wholesome state. Portions sizes were smaller than they are today. Today's small McDonald's Happy Meal French fries were the "regular" size when McDonald's opened. A McDonald's Super-Size serving of French fries contains 540 calories with 230 calories coming from fat. It is only in the last 20 years that convenience stores and fast food eateries have offered the 42 ounce size of sweetened soft drinks. A 42 ounce Dr. Pepper has 525 calories. Many in the health industry think that the increase in corn syrup sweetened soft drink consumption has contributed to America's obesity

FIGURE 9.5

Prevalence of respondents eating less or moving more.

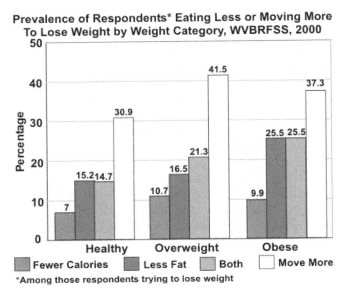

Prevalence of Respondents* Eating Less or Moving More To Lose Weight by Weight Category, WVBRFSS, 2000

*Among those respondents trying to lose weight

Source: www.wvdhhr.org/

TABLE 9.3 ♦ Countdown to Weight Loss

The combination of walking and cutting calories results in greater weight loss than either alone.

			Days to Lose Weight				
If you walk (minutes)	**&**	**If you cut daily calories by**	**5 lb.**	**10 lb.**	**15 lb.**	**20 lb.**	**25 lb.**
30		400	27	54	81	108	135
30		800	16	32	48	64	80
45		400	23	46	69	92	115
45		800	14	28	42	56	70
60		400	21	42	63	84	105
60		800	13	26	39	54	65

Source: cdc.gov

problem, especially childhood obesity. Portion control is a critical component in weight management. Check product labels to determine how much food is considered a serving, as well as how many calories, grams of fat, etc. are in a serving. Many prepackaged foods contain two or more servings-always read the label! See What Counts as a Serving in Chapter 8. Trans-fatty acids have entered the diet via hydrogenation, a process by which liquid oils (which are unsaturated and healthy) are reconstituted to a solid convenient form. As you recall from the nutrition chapter, the problem with ingesting Trans-fatty acids is that it raises LDL-the bad cholesterol and lowers HDL-the good cholesterol. Results from Nurses' Health Study determined that a diet high in Trans-fatty acids increases cardiovascular risk by 50%. A diet high in Trans-fats also may be linked to an increased abdominal fat measurement as well as an increase in the risk of Type 2 diabetes.

Tips for Being a Healthy Eater

1. *Listen to your body.* Try to eat when you feel hunger. Often we react to social, environmental or emotional cues for eating instead of asking ourselves if we are hungry. Sometimes we are simply bored and head for the pantry. Instead of opening the refrigerator, take a walk or call a friend. If you are hungry, eat slowly with mindfulness. Enjoy each small bite. Take your time chewing. Put your fork down between bites. Appreciate your food as you eat it. Eating quickly often leads to over-eating.

2. *Don't "not" eat.* Eating foods and the heat created by the energy cost of digesting them accounts for a significant portion of our metabolism, called **diet-induced thermogenesis (DIT)**. Our daily caloric expenditure is comprised of our basal metabolic rate, the energy expended in physical activity, and also DIT. Thermogenesis can account for 5–15% of total energy expenditure, depending on the macronutrient content of the diet. Very low calorie or fad diets can ultimately lower metabolism by reducing DIT. Klaas Westerterp reports in *Nutrition and Metabolism* (2004) "DIT values are higher for high protein food and alcohol consumption and lower for high fat consumption. Protein induced thermogenesis has an important effect on satiety."

3. *Don't get caught hungry.* If you experience low blood sugar between classes you will surely be tempted to head straight to the vending machine. Consider packing healthy foods in your backpack, desk, or car. When that is not feasible, always carry a baggie full of nuts or trail mix with you just in case you accidentally skip breakfast. Seeds and nuts are a good source of protein and healthful fats. Many centenarians documented in the *Blue Zones Project* (those who live

to be 100 years old and beyond and stay healthy) eat a handful of nuts a day.

4. *The majority of your calories should come from complex carbohydrates*, which is consistent with a plant-based diet. At each meal about 2/3 of your plate should be filled with these types of foods. Vegetables, fruits, beans, and grains are full of nourishing vitamins, fiber, and various bioactive compounds like phytochemicals. Eat these foods in their natural wholesome state when possible. Processed foods contain little fiber and are high in refined sugars. Processed foods can play havoc with our blood sugar, possibly ultimately increasing risk of type 2 diabetes. Dan Buettner cleverly states in his *10 Blue Zones Guidelines* "If it is manufactured in a plant, avoid it. If it comes from a plant, eat it."

5. *Minimize simple and refined carbohydrates.* Read labels to determine if there are hidden sugars in your food or beverage. For some foods the first several ingredients listed on the label are different types of added sugars. Read labels to avoid high fructose corn syrup. High fructose corn syrup is a modified corn syrup (sugar) and is used widely as a sweetener; "The corn lobby disputes it, but nutritionists have long singled out the high- fructose corn syrup used to sweeten soft drinks as one of the reasons so many kids in the U.S. are overweight." (David Bjerklie, Time, 8 Aug. 2005). Another school of thought places the blame on the "low-fat/no-fat" recommendation found in the decades-old USDA Food Guide Pyramid. This guide encouraged consumption of carbohydrates at the base of the pyramid, but it did not differentiate between "good carbs" and "bad carbs."

6. *Eat high quality protein.* Protein can come from animal or plant sources. New buzz- words for choosing meat in your diet are hormone-free, antibiotic-free, grass-fed, and free-range. Minimize consumption of processed meats (hot dogs, sausage, and bacon) which contain additives and preservatives. Fish and seafood are good choices as they are typically low in saturated fat, but high in heart-healthy Omega -3 fatty acids. Salmon and sardines are low-mercury fish choices. Tofu, beans, nuts, and seeds are plant protein. Protein foods provide satiety value. A piece of toast with peanut butter will fill you up more than buttered toast.

7. *All fats are not equal.* Fats that are high in monounsaturated oils are healthy and should be eaten daily. Choose avocado, nuts, and olive oil. Minimize saturated fats, especially if you have high triglycerides and cholesterol in your family history. Coconut oil is an exception as it is extremely high in saturated fat (90%), and will increase total cholesterol, but also increases HDL's-the good cholesterol that is heart-protective. Harvard School of Public Health physician Walter Willett recommends using coconut oil sparingly until more research determines how coconut oil affects heart disease risk. Avoid Trans-fats found in processed foods. Remember to read labels because low fat food options often replace the removed fat with unhealthful additives, sodium and refined carbohydrates.

8. *Enjoy your food.* Most days eat high-quality food in reasonable portions so that an occasional indulgence in a favorite "unhealthy" food won't sabotage your efforts. High- quality food means food that fuels your mind and body. Healthy doesn't mean expensive or tasteless. Why not try new foods on a regular basis with friends, and take turns hosting?

9. *Stay hydrated with plenty of water.* Keep water with you, and refill your glass/bottle throughout the day. Make it a habit to order water when eating out.

10. *Make realistic goals regarding food and your weight.* Focus less on what you cannot eat, and more on what you should eat. Try adding nuts as a snack, or increasing vegetable intake. Changing your behavior one small habit at a time will help develop positive eating habits.

It's All about Balance and Portion Size!

- One small chocolate chip cookie is equivalent to walking briskly for ten minutes.
- The difference between a large gourmet chocolate chip cookie and a small chocolate chip cookie could be about forty minutes of raking leaves (200 calories).
- One hour of walking at a moderate pace (twenty min/mile) uses about the same amount of energy that is in one jelly-filled doughnut (300 calories).
- A fast-food "meal" containing a double-patty cheeseburger, extra-large fries, and a twenty-four-ounce soft drink is equal to running two and one-half hours at a ten min/mile pace (1,500 calories).

(Surgeon General, 2005).

© Moving Moment/Shutterstock.com

© tigermilk/Shutterstock.com

High Fat, Low Fat, No Fat?

For the past several decades the recommendations have been to eat a "heart-healthy low fat diet." Many Americans chose processed low-fat high carbohydrate foods to comply with a low fat diet, and some nutritionists think that Americans are so heavy in part because of increase carbohydrate consumption. Healthy fats are an important part of a healthy diet. Choosing low fat dietary options is not always best. If you opt for low-fat peanut butter, read the label. The full fat version of the same brand will likely have more fat, but less added sugar and sodium. Fat is necessary in the diet and adds satiety value to your food. Monounsaturated fats like olive oil and avocado are rich in healthy fats. You might find satisfaction eating a smaller portion of a higher fat food. "Findings from the Nurses' Health Study and the Health Professionals Follow-up Study failed to find a link between the overall percentage of calories from fat and any important health outcome, including cancer, heart disease, and weight gain. The more important factor is the quality and quantity of the fat you are using. Based on current research, the best bet would be to add liquid fat to your food at the table (olive oil, canola oil, avocado, oils from seeds and nuts) and to minimize the saturated fats found in animal products like butter. However there is a place in a well-rounded diet for some butter. Partially hydrogenated fats like trans-fats typically found in processed foods increase disease risk and should be avoided altogether." *(Walter Willett, Harvard's The Nutrition Source)*

Dietary Supplements

Eating a healthy diet with fruits, vegetables, whole grains, quality proteins and unsaturated fats, as well as restricting refined white flour and sugar is the best method for obtaining an adequate supply of nutrients in your diet. Dietary supplements are popular and provide a means for delivering these nutrients in a more convenient, but often less effective form. It is a good idea to check with a health professional before beginning supplementation.

Taken in concentrations higher than the recommended daily allowance may cause some nutrients have undesirable side effects, some are even toxic.

Unfortunately, some individuals think that one pill is good, so two or more must be that much better. In most cases this is simply not true. Sometimes an excess of nutrient can even be detrimental as in the case of fat-soluble vitamins A, D, E and K. Megadoses of many vitamins, minerals and other supplements can cause kidney and liver damage and interact with other supplements, herbs and drugs. It is possible to interfere with absorption of other nutrients when ingesting megadoses of some supplements. In general, consuming more than the RDA of vitamins and minerals is discouraged. A registered dietician or physician may prescribe supplements for some populations or certain medical conditions (i.e. pregnancy, anemia, elderly, and certain types of vegetarianism).

Energy Drink and Nutrition Bars

Energy drinks and nutrition bars are popular, especially with college students. It is easy to see why-they are relatively inexpensive and they are convenient to put in a backpack. Some drinks and bars are purported to increase energy and alertness, boost academic and athletic performance, and to offer extra nutrition as a supplement. Consuming an occasional energy drink may be ok for most individuals and eating a protein bar is better than skipping breakfast, consuming several bars or energy drinks daily is poor nutritional planning and will take its toll on your long term health. Read the label-extra caffeine and sugars and calories can ultimately cause unwanted weight gain and poor dental health. Large amounts of caffeine can cause you to be "jittery," have headaches, and upset stomach, high blood pressure, or even irregular heartbeats. Remember that people react differently to substances-what your friend can handle (maybe 2 energy drinks) might send you to the emergency room.

Weight Loss Products

Appetite suppressants claim to help diminish a person's appetite, cut cravings, and may increase overall energy and possibly increase metabolism. The dieter must consider the potential negative side effects. Appetite suppressants often contain high levels of caffeine, guarana, or Ma Huang (an herbal form of ephedra) that can cause hypertension, cardiac arrhythmia, myocardial infarction, and /or stroke that can and has led to premature death to the person consuming this type of dietary supplement. Examples of commonly used supplements include Hydroxycut, Xenadrine-EFX, and Trim Spa.

In 1997 fenfluramine and dexfenfluramine (fen/phen) were withdrawn from the market due to a link to the development of a heart valve problem. Serious illness and in some cases death occurred. Even FDA approved drugs need to be used cautiously. In the 1960's and the 1970's amphetamines were often prescribed for weight loss, and in the 1920's weight loss pills were found to contain tapeworm eggs (Hales, 2007). Diet aids and supplements that have gone through rigorous testing and are approved by the FDA still need to be approached with common sense and caution.

Metabolism Boosters are various supplements that speed up or boost an individual's basal metabolism. Most of these types of products claim to act in a way that increases the building of lean muscle mass. Examples of such supplements are creatine phosphate, chromium picolinate, and HMB. Meathin, Microlean and Metabolife (now banned by the FDA) have appetite suppressants as well as metabolism boosters. Long term effectiveness and safety of these types of supplements are unknown.

There are two types of programs, clinical and nonclinical. A clinical program is offered in a health care facility with a team of licensed health professionals (NIDDK, 2006). The following are examples of nonclinical programs: Jenny Craig, Nutrisystem, Weight Watchers, and Slimfast. Jenny Craig and Nutrisystem sell prepackaged foods which are convenient but often costly.

Weight Watchers teaches participants the value of foods on a point system.

The positive aspect of Weight Watchers is that participants are taught how to choose, shop, and prepare foods. Group support is essential and highly recommended after the goal weight is attained. Weight loss maintenance is one the most difficult aspects of dieting, so support from others is often a significant help. Two other programs that offer group support are TOPS (Take Pounds Off Sensibly) and Overeaters Anonymous. Programs such as Slimfast replace one or two meals with shakes or bars. Unless a person learns to make wise choices on their own, it is doubtful weight loss will be maintained.

Fad Diets

Each year billions of dollars are spent in the weight loss industry. Many of these dollars are spent on diet plans that are unhealthy, cannot be maintained long term, or simply do not work. The lure of a quick and easy way to "melt away" the pounds is too tempting for many individuals, and although the diets are more times than not ineffective in the long term weight loss hopefuls are willing to give almost anything a chance. If the diet eliminates entire food groups, promises quick results, or requires you to purchase costly supplements then it is likely not a healthy plan. To avoid the pitfalls of an unsuccessful, unreliable, or even dangerous weight loss plan, take the time to check out as much factual information as possible from a variety of sources.

© Andresr, 2012, Shutterstock, Inc.

The most essential aspect of a weight loss program is that it can be followed for the rest of an individual's life.

Fad Diets

Fad diets are risky because they...

- tend to be very low in calories
- are limited to a few foods, limiting key nutrients and minerals
- produce only short-term, rapid weight loss—not long-term weight management
- ignore the importance of physical activity in healthy weight loss
- increase risks for certain diseases or health complications
- take the pleasure and fun out of eating
- alter metabolism, making it easier to regain the weight after the diet has ceased

Diets That Don't Work

1. **"Magical"/Same Foods Diets** (i.e., grapefruit, cabbage soup, Subway diet)
   - *Pros*—usually the single food is a nutritious food
   - *Cons*—too few calories, risk of overeating, lacking of specific nutrients, lack variety, do not teach healthy eating habits, do not encourage exercise

2. **High-Protein Diets** (i.e., Atkins)
   - *Pros*—weight loss does occur
   - *Cons*—high in saturated fat and cholesterol increasing risk for heart disease; high protein puts strain on liver and kidneys; lacks vitamins, minerals, complex carbohydrates, and fiber; weight loss is water weight, not fat; lack of carbs causes a condition called ketosis with symptoms of nausea, weakness, and dehydration

3. **Liquid Diets** (i.e., Slimfast)
   - *Pros*—drinks have vitamins, minerals, and high-quality protein
   - *Cons*—do not teach new ways of eating, no long-term weight loss, very low in calories

4. **Gimmicks, Gadgets, and Other "Miracles"**
   - *Pros*—none
   - *Cons*—may be harmful, expensive, do not teach healthy eating, do not encourage exercise

What about the popular **high protein low carbohydrate** diets? The Zone, Atkins, Sugar- Busters, Protein Power, the South Beach Diet and more recently the Paleo diet are all examples of this type of diet. Although there are some variation in the diets, all advocate severely limiting carbohydrate foods such as pasta, potatoes, bread, cereals, juices, sweets, and all but the Paleo diet limit fruits and vegetables. Protein rich foods are plentiful such as steak, ham, bacon, eggs, fish, chicken and cheese and some diets allow each to be eaten is unlimited quantities. The Paleo diet encourages plenty of fruits and vegetables but restricts grains and dairy. The Paleo diet mimics how humans probably ate in the beginning-with a hunter/gatherer style. The modern version began in the mid 1980's and picked up a large following around 2008 thanks largely to the online community. A positive is that the diet eliminates refined sugars and processed foods. Some nutritionists cite the lack of whole grains, legumes, and dairy in the diet as faulty. Clean eating is another approach to eating. The eat-clean diet focuses on lean protein, complex carbohydrates, healthy fats, and eliminating overly processed foods and chemically enhanced foods. Water is encouraged while eating six small meals daily.

The basis for the low carbohydrate diet is that during digestion, carbohydrates are converted into glucose, which serves as fuel for every cell within a person's body. When blood glucose levels begin to raise, insulin, the hormone that allows the entry of glucose into the cells, is released. This process lowers the level of glucose in the bloodstream. If the available glucose is not rapidly used for normal cellular functions or physical activity, the glucose is converted to and stored as body fat. Individuals supporting this type of diet believe that if a person eats fewer carbohydrates and more protein, they will produce less insulin, and as insulin levels drop, the body will look to its own fat stores to meet energy needs.

While research has shown that people participating in low carbohydrate-high protein diets do initially lose weight more rapidly than an individual who maintains a more nutritionally balanced diet but decreases calorie intake and increases physical activity, these same studies show that at the one-year mark weight loss for many of the dieters in both groups was not significantly different. Low carbohydrate diets also have the potential to result in the loss of vitamin B, calcium, and potassium. This can lead to osteoporosis, constipation, bad breath, and fatigue. Before starting on this type of diet, consider that because the diet high in protein, and therefore typically high in fat, it may carry an increased risk for heart disease.

An **extremely low carbohydrate diet** of (20 grams or less a day) depletes the body's available source of energy in the form of glucose. The process starts when glycogen levels are low and adipose tissue releases the fat into the blood. The liver produces ketones when its glycogen stores are depleted. In glycolysis, glucose in the blood provides energy, but in the metabolic state of ketosis glucose is not present and ketones in the blood provide the energy. **Ketosis** results from very low carbohydrate diets, extreme exercise, uncontrolled type 1 diabetes, fasting, and starvation states. People in ketosis often have a characteristic acetone (a by-product of ketones-smells like nail polish remover) odor on their breath and in their urine.

Glycemic Load in Foods

A carbohydrate is not always a carbohydrate according to the **glycemic index**. First introduced as a concept in 1981 in the American Journal of Clinical Nutrition by Jenkins, et al., the glycemic index is a numeric value given to foods according to how quickly the foods increase blood glucose-called the postprandial blood glucose effect. It is a tool that consumers can use to help qualify the value of food. Diabetics are familiar with the glycemic index of foods as they need to monitor their carbohydrate intake. Foods are ranked from 1 to 100, with sugar being 100. High glycemic index (GI) foods quickly dump glucose into the bloodstream after consumption.

Harvard Health Publications list the glycemic index and load for 100 common foods here: http://www.health.harvard.edu/diseases-and-conditions/glycemic-index-and-glycemic-load-for-100-foods Consider watermelon which has a high glycemic index (80). But with only six carbohydrates per serving, it has a low glycemic load of five.

Intuitive Eating is not dieting. People using this method are encouraged to listen to the wisdom of their body and to make peace with food. There is no diet, rather they "learn to read, interpret, and follow internal cues regarding the right amount of food for their body." Infants and toddlers are intuitive eaters. A baby will stop nursing when he is full. A toddler asks for food depending on hunger, not because it is lunch time, and she will then stop eating when she is naturally full. The goal is to have a healthy relationship with food. "While intuitive eating may be innate, cultural norms that promote dieting, restriction, supersized portions and hyper-palatable food often hamper our ability to eat intuitively." (Brown, 2017)

Highly processed foods typically have a higher GI. Starch white rice, potatoes, and bread have a high GI. Lower GI foods release glucose slowly. Low GI foods are less processed and may have more fat or fiber which can slow absorption. Another value called the **glycemic load** gives more insight into how quickly, as well as how much, glucose will enter the bloodstream after eating. The glycemic load is determined by multiplying the glycemic index for the food by the grams of carbohydrate in the serving and then dividing by 100. A food that is high for the glycemic index may actually have a low glycemic load. 10 is a low glycemic load and 20 is high. The *Sydney University Glycemic Index Services* in Sydney Australia maintains a large international GI database.

© PEPPERSMINT/Shutterstock.com

Healthy Weight Gain

Although they are in the minority, there are individuals who struggle to gain weight. It is important for individuals who feel that they are "too thin" to recognize that there are healthy and unhealthy ways of accomplishing their goal of weight gain. Over eating all types of foods will simply result in an increase in body fat.

Adding lean body mass through strength training and a slight caloric increase is a much healthier alternative. Chapter 7 outlines the benefits of muscular fitness and presents guidelines helpful for beginning a strength training regimen. Nutrition information in Chapter 8 identified ways to add calories in an appropriate portion and manner to maximize their benefits.

Healthy Food Shopping

Plan your trip to the grocery store or the local farmer's market. Have a list of the ingredients you will need for your recipes. If you have leftovers use them for another meal if possible. Consider cooking more chicken and grains than you would need for one meal and freeze portions for future meals or use a portion in a different preparation the following day. Try not to shop on an empty stomach to avoid the temptation to impulse buy. The National Heart, Lung, and Blood Institute Obesity Guidelines suggest reading labels while shopping – paying particular attention to serving sizes and the number of servings within the container. Take turns preparing meals with your roommate so you don't have to cook every day. Finally, make cooking at home easier and healthier by shopping for healthy refrigerator/freezer/cabinet staples like the list below:

Healthy Kitchen Staples

Cold Items: In-season greens, veggies, fruit and seasonal citrus; frozen vegetables and fruit, olives, refrigerated pickles, plain yogurt (consider full fat version), hard cheeses such as Parmesan, raisins, butter, ghee, tofu; milk, almond milk, soy milk, hummus

Pantry: Onions, garlic, canned tomatoes; dried mushrooms; chili peppers, various mustards, organic low-sodium chicken or vegetable broth, tahini, flaxseed, chia seed, pumpkin seeds, walnuts, pecans, pine nuts, almonds, peanut butter, almond butter, organic popcorn, whole wheat flour, organic spelt flour, unbleached white flour, salsa, pistachios

Grains: Wild or brown rice, quinoa, couscous, chickpeas, lentils, various dried beans, pasta (whole wheat, gluten-free, vegetable, chickpea, shirataki, etc.) steel-cut oats, whole grain preservative free bread, pita bread, barley

Herbs: Parsley, cilantro, mint, basil, oregano, (all of which are easily grown in your garden or window- sill) sea salt, pepper, ginger, cinnamon, cumin, turmeric, chili pepper, paprika, sage, thyme

Liquids/Oils: Tahini, olive oil, extra virgin olive oil, grapeseed oil, unrefined sesame oil, balsamic vinegar, molasses, raw unfiltered honey, red or white wine (for recipes)

Fast Foods/Eating Out

People eat more meals outside the home than ever before and snacking has become the norm. Due to their quick service and relatively low food prices, fast food chains are the most frequent source for meals prepared outside of the home. Each day 50 million people line up inside or drive through outside service lanes of one of the over 160,000 fast food establishments in the country. When meals are prepared with cost and convenience as the primary focus, good nutrition will, in most cases, suffer. A great majority of fast foods are high in fat, calories, and sodium, and low in many of the essential nutrients and dietary fiber.

Super-Size Meals Lead to Super-Size Problems

Most days, you are mindful of what you eat. Occasionally you might be out of your routine or at a celebration involving food-and you may be tempted to go overboard on high-calorie, fatty foods. Can one big meal at your favorite restaurant be so bad? Research shows that it may.

Immediate effects that are most dangerous to people who are at risk or who already have heart disease:

- *Stiffer arteries, reduced blood flow.* Blood vessel dilation and expansion is hampered by a big high fat meal. Large meal digestion forces your heart to work harder, increasing the heart rate, to meet the needs of the digestive tract. Sometimes people who have cardiovascular disease and eat a large meal before exercising will suffer angina or possibly a heart attack.
- *Higher blood pressure.* Norepinephrine is a stress hormone that can be released by a big meal. This hormone raises blood pressure and heart rate.
- *High triglycerides.* Triglycerides are fats in the blood, and any meal elevates levels. A super-size meal loaded with fat or refined carbohydrates boosts levels and keeps them elevated for up to twelve hours.
- *Blood sugar effects.* A diabetic's ability to process glucose can be impaired by a large meal.
- *Heartburn.* The bigger the meal, the more you'll suffer from gastric reflux if you are susceptible to heartburn.

Some studies indicate that taking high doses of Vitamin C and E before eating a fatty meal help maintain arterial blood flow. However, it is not conclusive that these vitamins, or any others, can protect your heart. Another study determined that young, healthy people who ate a super-size meal (1,000 calories worth) and then walked quickly for 45 minutes had the benefit of having their arteries' ability to dilate restored. That being said, exercise is not going to wipe out all the bad effects of chronic overeating.

If you have family or holiday celebration to attend where tempting food will be plentiful, plan ahead. Drink water and have a healthy snack so you are not overly hungry when you arrive. Fill your plate with foods high in water content that will serve to fill you up-fruits and vegetables. Enjoy conversation with others and try to chew your food slowly so that your body has time to

© Jason Stitt, 2012, Shutterstock, Inc.

Everyday choices make a difference!

signal to your brain that you are full. Once you are finished, take a nice walk if you can.

Fast food does not have to mean "junk food." While it may take a little more thought and discretion, quick and healthy alternatives do exist. Depending on what ingredients are used and how the food is prepared, fast foods served in restaurants can be healthy. Most restaurants have nutritional information about the foods they serve posted within the dining area, on the menus or online. By taking a couple of extra minutes to think about their best and most nutritious options, an individual can make dining out more nutritious, filling, and healthy.

Another pitfall of eating meals prepared outside the home is the quantity of food an individual is served. In an effort to be competitive, many restaurants serve well beyond an adequate portion size. To control portion sizes when eating out, order from the senior citizens' or kids' menus, share the entrée with a friend, or take part of the food home for a later meal.

Another way to eat healthy when dining out is to select foods that are steamed, broiled, baked, roasted, or poached rather than foods that are fried or grilled. Asking if the restaurant will trim visible fat off the meat and serve butter, sauces, or dressings "on the side" is also a healthy option.

Fitness or Fatness

Our food choices and habits, our exercise, and our genetic make-up all play a role in our ability to maintain a healthy weight. Managing weight is brought about most successfully by a lifestyle choice, not a short term diet. Even if both of your parents are overweight and you didn't have good nutrition emphasized when you were young, you can make wise choices for yourself today. Make small positive changes to encourage healthful behaviors. If you are overweight or obese, even a small 5% to 10% weight loss can have a favorable effect on your overall health risk.

Tips for Healthy Choices

When dining at a restaurant, ask for a to-go box right away and put ½ of your order in it as soon as it comes.

Order a dinner salad with the dressing on the side, but share the entree with a friend when eating out.

Order water with your meal rather than a soda or sweet tea-save money and calories.

Opt for your traditional foods made in a "light" version.

Use a smaller plate to encourage smaller portions.

Drink a glass of water before your meal.

Eat your salad first.

Eat slowly. Put your eating utensil down and enjoy your meal or converse between bites.

Eat breakfast regularly.

Have healthy snacks in your backpack or briefcase or car always. Try eating fruits for dessert.

Choose healthy fats wisely emphasizing mono and polyunsaturated fats.

Trim off visible fat off meat and take skin off poultry before cooking.

Try to use less refined sugar and processed flour in food preparation. Try whole wheat flour or unbleached white flour.

Wean yourself off of sodas-or try to cut way down on your intake.

Read labels: minimize corn syrup and other added sugars as well as Trans-fat.

Use added fats like salad dressings minimally-try dipping your fork into the dressing before skewering the lettuce.

Avoid supersizing your meal.

Avoid having your favorite foods in the house, or keep them out of sight to avoid snacking when you are not hungry.

Do push-ups or sit-ups or go for a walk when you are craving a particular food.

Before attending a party, eat something small and healthy so you are not tempted to overindulge in party foods.

Bake, broil, steam or grill instead of frying.

Eat high fiber complex carbohydrates daily.

Weight Management References

Al-Suhaimi, E.A., & Shehzad, A. 2013. Leptin, resistin and visfatin: The missing link between endocrine metabolic disorders and immunity. *European Journal of Medical Research,18*, 12.

American Heart Association. Heart Disease and Stroke Statistics. 2016 Update.

Brown, Kelsey 2017. Stop Dieting, Start Intuitive Eating. *IDEA Fitness Journal,* February 2017.

Celis-Morales, C. et. al. 2016. Physical activity attenuates the effect of the FTO genotype on obesity traits in European Adults: The Food4Me study. *Obesity,* 24(4), 962–969.

Chaput JP *et al.* (2011) Modern sedentary activities promote overconsumption of food in our current obesogenic environment *Obes Rev* 12:e12–20 PMID 20576006

Coletta, M., Platek, S., Mohamed, F., van Steenburgh, J., Green, D., & Lowe, M.R. (2009). Brain activation in restrained and unrestrained eaters: An fMRI study. *Journal of Abnormal Psychology, 118,* 598–609.

Corbin, C. and Welk, G. *Concepts of Physical Fitness* (15th ed). Dubuque, IA: McGraw-Hill. 2009.

Donatelle, R. J. *Access to Health* (9th ed). Boston: Allyn & Bacon. 2006.

Ferriday, D. & and Brunstrom, J.M. (2011) 'I just can't help myself': effects of food-cue exposure in overweight and lean individuals. *International Journal of Obesity* 35, 142–149;

Flegal, K. M., Carrol, M. D., Kuczmarski, R. J., and Johnson, C. L. Overweight and Obesity in the United States: Prevalence and Trends, 1960–1994. *International Journal of Obesity and Related Metabolic Disorders* 22:39–47. 1998.

Floyd, P., Mims, S., and Yelding-Howard, C. *Personal Health: Perspectives and Lifstyles*. Morton Publishing Co. 2007.

Frayling, T.M., et. al. 2007. A common variant in the FTO gene is associated with body mass index and predisposition to childhood and adult obesity. *Science*, 316(5826), 889–894.

Gibbs, W. W. Obesity: An Overblown Epidemic? *Scientific American*, May 23, 2005.

Hahn, D. B. and Payne, W. A. *Understanding Your Health*. McGraw-Hill. 2008.

Hales, D. *An Invitation to Wellness* (Instructor Ed.). Thomson-Wadsworth, 2007.

Hoeger, W. W. K. and Hoeger, S. A. *Lifetime Physical Fitness and Wellness: A Personalized Program* (10th ed). Belmont, CA: Wadsworth. 2009.

http://www.cdc.gov/nccdphp/dnpa/healthyweight/physical_activity/index.htm

http://americaninfomaps.wordpress.com/2013/10/03/map-obesity-rates-united-states-by-county/

http://health.heraldtribune.com/2014/07/15/americans-calorie-intake-increased-years/

https://www.nytimes.com/2016/05/02/health/biggest-loser-weight-loss.html?_r=0

http://www.health.harvard.edu/healthy-eating/glycemic_index_and_glycemic_load_for_100_foods

http://www.wisegeek.com/what-is-the-role-of-ghrelin.htm Written By: Sandra Koehler

Hurley, Dan. The Hungry Brain, *Discover*, June, 2011.

Hyman, B., Oden, G., Bacharach, D., and Collins, R. *Fitness for Living*. Dubuque, IA: Kendall-Hunt Publishing Co. 2006.

IUFOST, International Union of Food Science and Technology Bulletin. Trans-fatty Acids, May 2006.

Jenkins D, Wolever T, Taylor R, et al. Glycemic index of foods: a physiological basis for carbohydrate exchange. *Am J Clin Nutr* 1981; 34:362

Lieberman, Daniel E., The Story of the Human Body, Pantheon Books, New York, 2013.

Neighmond, *Patti, Gain together, Lose Together: The Weight-Loss 'Halo' Effect*, Health Blog: NPR http://www.npr.org/blogs/health/2012/03/12, retrieved 3/17/12.

Nordestgaard, B. G., Benn, M., Schnohr, P., Tybjærg-Hansen, A. Nonfasting triglycerides and risk of myocardial infarction, ischemic heart disease, and death in men and women. *JAMA*. 2007; 298(3):299–308, PubMed.

O'Neil, Patrick. Weight Management Center, Medical University of South Carolina. 2009. www.muschealth.com

Powers, S. K., Todd, S. L., and Noland, U. J. *Total Fitness and Wellness* (2nd ed). Boston: Allyn & Bacon. 2005.

Rutter H (2011) Where next for obesity? *Lancet*

Satcher, D. Surgeon General's Report on Physical Activity and Health. Atlanta: U.S. Department of Health and Human Services, CDC. 1996.

Singla, P., Bardoloi, A., & Parkash, A.A. 2010. Metabolic effects of obesity: A review. *World Journal of Diabetes*, 1 (3), 76–88.

Stice, E., Spoor, S., Bohon, C., Veldhuizen, M., and Small, D. (2009) Relation of Reward From Food Intake and Anticipated Food Intake to Obesity: A Functional Magnetic Resonance Imaging Study. *Journal of Abnormal Psychology*, 117, 924–935.

Surgeon General's Call to Action to Prevent and Decrease Overweight and Obesity. 2005. www.surgeongeneral.gov

Texas A&M University, Student Health Services. Fad Diets: Promise or Profit, 77, 2002.

The Center for Health and Healthcare in Schools, School of Public Health and Health Services, George Washington University Medical Center. *Childhood Overweight: What the Research Tells Us.* March 2005 Update. www.healthinschools.org

Westerterp, Klaas R., Diet-Induced Thermogenesis. *Nutrition and Metabolism,* 2004, 18 August

WHO Expert Consultation, Appropriate body-mass index for Asian populations and its implications for policy and intervention strategies. *The Lancet.* 2004;363:157–163.

Wilmore, J. H. Exercise, Obesity, and Weight Control, *Physical Activity and Research Digest.* Washington, DC: President's Council on Physical Fitness and Sports. 1994.

World Health Organization (WHO). Management of Severe Malnutrition: A Manual for Physicians and other Senior Health Workers. Geneva: Author. 1999.

World Health Organization (WHO). Obesity: Preventing and Managing the Global Epidemic — Report of WHO Consultation on Obesity. Geneva, June 1997.

Chapter 10
Complementary Health Approaches

© Luna Vandoorne, 2012, Shutterstock, Inc.

OBJECTIVES

Students will be able to:

♦ Identify components of holistic self-care.
♦ Compare and contrast conventional, complementary and alternative health care systems.
♦ Identify the therapies contained in each major CHA domain.
♦ Identify pros and cons associated with each major CHA practice.
♦ Integrate the benefits of mindfulness into everyday life.
♦ Participate in a self-guided relaxation/meditation practice.

Adaptation of *Health and Fitness: A Guide to a Healthly Lifestyle*, 5th Edition, by Laura Bounds, Gayden Darnell, Kirstin Brekken Shea, and Dottiede Agnor. Copyright © 2012 by Kendall Hunt Publishing Company.

"The doctor of the future will give no medicine, but will interest his patients in the care of the human frame, in diet, and in the cause and prevention of disease."

–Thomas Edison

Complementary Health Approaches

Americans value choice in any venue and healthcare is no different. When buying a car, you want a quality vehicle to meet your needs, a company that can give you a good product, and a salesperson that you trust, and who is dedicated to helping you meet your goals. The same goes for healthcare. You want to find a healthcare option that fits with your healthcare needs, a treatment which will be effective, and a healthcare provider whom you trust and who is dedicated to helping you. With healthcare, you have the option of choosing one or a combination of healthcare approaches and providers to best meet your needs.

There are two main camps of healthcare today. You are probably very familiar with what is called conventional medicine. When you go to a conventional clinic or hospital, doctors and nurses work to diagnose an illness and then treat the symptoms with medication, surgery, or radiation. The roots of **conventional medicine** date back to the mid-1800's with the discovery of the germ and its relationship to illness. While this is the main form of healthcare used in the United States and similar developed nations around the world, more and more people are turning to other types of healthcare that do not fit in the mainstream of conventional medicine.

The other main category of medicine is a group of traditional systems and practices, which are currently called **complementary health approaches** (CHA). The terms complementary and alternative are actually designations of how traditional medical practices, some of which developed thousands of years ago, are used in relation to conventional care. Systems and practices are considered **complementary** when used in conjunction with conventional care and **alternative** when used instead of conventional care. The emphasis in CHA is holistic, in the sense that its purpose is to treat the whole person and support the body's natural ability to heal itself. The increasing use of CHA is expected to continue as people seek out options in healthcare to best meet their needs.

Learning about each form of healthcare, as well as its risks and benefits, will allow you to make the best choices that meet the needs of your health situation.

Medicine has come a long way since the days of the snake-oil salesmen of the early nineteenth century. In the 1800's, homeopaths, midwives, naturopaths, and an assortment of lay healers used herbs and nostrums to combat illness. Thanks to the wonders of modern conventional and emergency medicine, many of the ill and injured can survive what fifty years ago would have meant certain death. This is surely being played out in the modern landscape of the war-torn Middle East. Due to improved body armor, field medical procedures, and medevac capabilities, wounded soldiers are surviving what they would not have survived in the Vietnam War or World War II. Conventional medicine

Alternative practitioners emphasize a wholesome diet rich in organic fruits, vegetables, nuts, seeds, fiber, water, and organically raised meat products.

can work mini-miracles in acute trauma care, the treatment of bacterial infections and life-threatening diseases. Life saving antibiotics and other drugs have revolutionized the medical field. *What conventional medicine has failed to do is prevent the lifestyle-related hypokinetic diseases that plague Western society.* **Conventional** (also called Western, allopathic, or bio-medical) **medicine** developed from the evidence-based scientific method. Traditionally, **alternative medicine** (also called natural, unconventional, or unorthodox in the past) has been based on anecdotal evidence, word of mouth, testimonials, or even the placebo effect. *Part of the attraction of the CHA modalities may be their identification with prevention rather than cure, and consequently CHA has come to be identified with wellness and self-care.*

Today, alternative medicine is also called holistic, complementary, or integrative. Refer back to the wellness dimensions from Chapter 1; a holistic practitioner considers the physical, emotional, mental, social, occupational, environmental, and spiritual factors associated with the individual as a "whole person." "Practitioners of alternative medicine approach healing from a holistic perspective where the primary goal is the creation and maintenance of optimum health in body, mind, and spirit. In addition to the comprehensive care they provide to achieve that goal, they also serve as teachers, instructing their patients in effective methods of selfcare. Such methods not only assist patients in their journey back to wellness, but also help them prevent disease from occurring in the first place "(Goldberg, 2002).

Alternative practitioners emphasize **holistic self-care.** A wholesome **diet** minimizing intake of processed food with foods rich in organic fruits and vegetables, nuts, seeds, fiber, pure water, and organically raised meat products is recommended. **Exercise** is critical to maintaining physical health. Adequate **sleep** is necessary to allow the regenerative processes in the body to work. Keeping the **environment** at home and work healthy may mean adding indoor plants, air filters, humidifiers, and avoiding toxic chemicals and secondhand smoke. Peace of mind and contentment are part of **good mental health.** Spiritual health is also considered an important part of self-care. **Spiritual health** can be gained through prayer, meditation, or even giving of yourself through volunteerism. *In alternative or holistic care, the patient takes an active role and is responsible for looking at all aspects or his/her health.*

How many Americans are using CHA? According to a 2007 National Health Interview Study (NHIS) four out of ten adults use some form of CHA therapy on a regular basis. Twelve percent of children (ages 0–18 years) use CHA (see Figure 10.1). Native Alaskan and American Indians were the most likely to use some form of CHA, followed by white adults. Caucasian college-educated

Mindfulness in Everyday Life

Being mindful means focusing attention on what you're experiencing from moment to moment. It's a daunting challenge in a hectic world, but science has begun to establish that it's a worthwhile habit to cultivate. You can start by getting a sense of how much time you spend not being mindful. See if you recognize any of these statements from a questionnaire developed at the University of Rochester:

- I find it difficult to stay focused on what's happening in the present.
- I snack without paying much attention to what I'm eating.
- It seems I'm "running on automatic" without much awareness of what I'm doing.
- I rush through activities without being really attentive to them.
- I tend to walk quickly to get where I'm going without paying attention to what I experience along the way.
- I find myself listening to someone with one ear and doing something else at the same time.
- I tend not to notice physical tension or discomfort until they really grab my attention.

If these sound familiar, there's plenty of room for increasing mindfulness in your daily life. Take note of times when your thoughts are creating stress or distracting you from the present moment. The Mind/Body Medical Institute suggests that you slow down as you go about everyday activities, doing one thing at a time and bringing your full awareness to both the activity and your experience of it. Here are some tips for integrating mindfulness:

- Make something that occurs several times during the day, such as answering the phone or buckling your seat belt a reminder to return to the present—that is, think about what you're doing and observe yourself doing it.
- Pay attention to your breathing or your environment when you stop at red lights.
- Before you go to sleep, and when you awaken, take some "mindful" breaths. Instead of allowing your mind to wander over the day's concerns, direct your attention to your breathing. Feel its effects on your nostrils, lungs and abdomen. Try to think of nothing else.
- If the present moment involves stress—perhaps you're about to speak in public or undergo a medical test—observe your thoughts and emotions and how they affect your body.
- Find a task you usually do impatiently or unconsciously (standing in line or brushing your teeth, for example) and do it mindfully.

Being mindful doesn't mean you'll never "multitask," but you can make multitasking a conscious choice. It doesn't mean you'll never be in a hurry, but at least you will be aware that you are rushing. Although upsetting thoughts or emotions won't disappear, you will have more insight into them and become aware of your choices in responding to them.

From Harvard Women's Watch, Vol. 11, #6, February 2004.

women in a higher income bracket use CHA more than other segments of the population. However, CHA is practiced by all types of people across racial, cultural, and socioeconomic lines (see Figure 10.2). The most commonly used CHA therapies are non–vitamin, non–mineral, natural products (for instance, fish oil, echinacea, DHA, glucosamine, and ginseng), deep breathing, meditation, yoga, massage, chiropractic care, and diet-based therapies (see Figure 10.3). Chiropractic is used the most by patients with back pain.

Note: The 2007 and 2012 NHIS did not include folk medicine practices (i.e., covering a wart with a penny and then burying it) or religious healing, as in prayer for oneself or for others. The 2002 NHIS did include prayer in its survey.

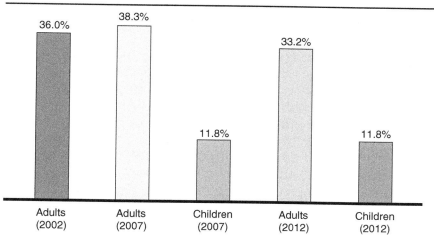

FIGURE 10.1

CHA Use by U.S. Adults and Children

Source: Clarke, T.C., Black, L.I., Stussman, B.J., Barnes, P.M., Nahin, R.L. *CDC National Health Statistics Report Number 78.* Trends in the Use of Complementary Health Approaches Among Children Aged 4–17: United States, National Health Interview Survey, 2007–2012. February 10, 2015.

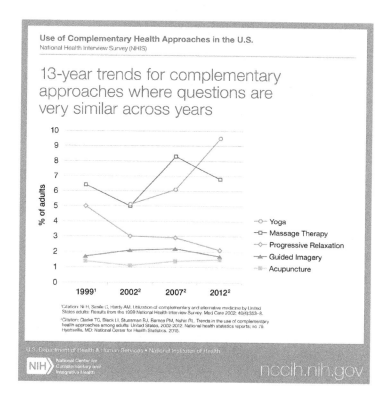

Figure 10.4 shows several accepted and widely used treatments that are rooted in CHA. Indeed, even exercise prescribed as a healing modality was once considered "alternative." "In an age of M.R.I. scans and spinal fusion surgery, a treatment as low tech as exercise can seem to some patients rudimentary or even dangerously illogical" (Ryzik, 2005). Cardiovascular exercise helps with increased circulation and flexibility, and core muscle strength focuses on supporting the spine which can help prevent future pain. Perhaps in the future many more CHA modalities will become mainstream (see Table 10.1).

Why do some people try alternative health care options? Often they are in pain and have not found relief with conventional methods while others choose to try non-invasive or drug-free options. There are five general categories of complementary or alternative therapies we will examine in this

Scientists in the bio-medical research community are recognizing that more and more Americans are choosing complementary and alternative medicine (hereafter referred to as CHA), and therefore funding to test the safety and efficacy of CHA approaches is increasing. In 1991, the National Institutes of Health formed the Office of Alternative Medicine (OAM) to fund research looking into the effectiveness of many complementary and alternative treatments. In 1998 OAM became the National Center for Complementary and Alternative Medicine (NCCAM), and in 2014 it evolved into the **NCCIH**, or the **National Center for Complementary and Integrative Health.** According to large, population based surveys, the use of alternative medicine (unproven practices used in place of conventional medicine) is rare. "Integrative health care, defined as a comprehensive, often interdisciplinary approach to treatment, prevention and health promotion that brings together complementary and conventional therapies, is more common. The use of an integrative approach to health and wellness has grown within care settings across the United States, including hospitals, hospices, and military health facilities." (NCCICH, 2014) *"NCCIH's mission is to define, through rigorous scientific investigation, the usefulness and safety of complementary and integrative health approaches and their roles in improving health and health care."*

FIGURE 10.2

CHA Use by Race/Ethnicity among Adults 2007

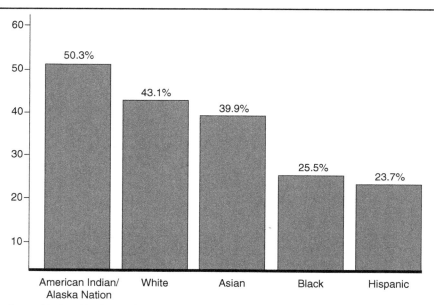

Source: National Institute of Health.

chapter: alternative medical systems, body-based or manipulative therapies, biologically based therapies, mind-body medicine, and energy therapies (see Figure 10.4). It is prudent to do some research prior to spending your time and money on alternative health care. Is insurance coverage important to you? If so, determine if your insurance covers the treatment you are considering. Remember that a treatment may work for someone else, but it may not work for your and your body. Many alternative care therapies are not evidenced-based. That being said, not all evidence-based therapies work for all people. The word natural does not always mean safe. Learn as much about the alternative treatment as you can, and then determine what is best for you.

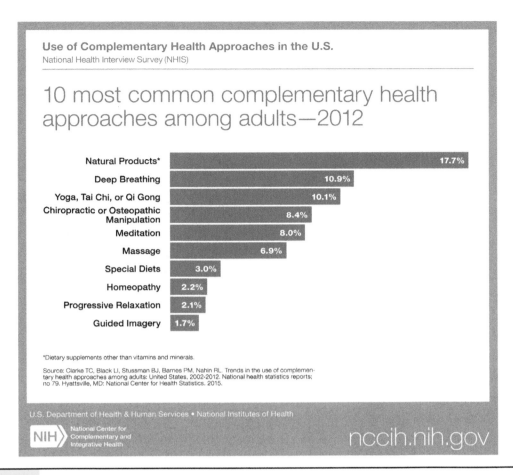

FIGURE 10.3

Ten Most Common CHA Therapies among Adults 2007

Source: Center for Disease Control

TABLE 10.1 ♦ CHA Modalities Now in Mainstream Medicine

Codeine for pain
Digitalis for heart failure
Quinine for malaria
Aspirin for fever
Behavioral therapy for headache
Hypnosis for smoking cessation
Exercise for diabetes
Support groups for breast cancer
Low-fat, low-cholesterol diets

Alternative Healthcare Systems

Alternative healthcare systems are holistic "whole person" systems. Whole person systems refer to treating more than just a patient's symptoms. The CHA practitioner often interviews the patient in an attempt to determine the patient's history, eating habits, lifestyle choices, and so on. Some patients report that they appreciate the fact that their practitioner often regards self-care, positive lifestyle habits, behaviors, quality of life, and the combined role of the mind, body, and spirituality in health, disease, and healing as being very important (WHCCAMP, 2002). Typically the CHA practitioner works out of a small facility

FIGURE 10.4

CHA Domains and Their
Related Pratices

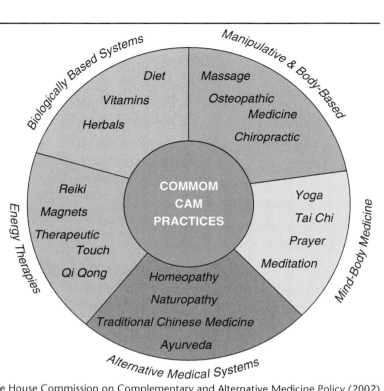

Source: White House Commission on Complementary and Alternative Medicine Policy (2002)

Strengthening and
stretching the body and
mind with yoga.

and spends a fair amount of time with their patient, which may be more attractive to the patient than the short fifteen-minute appointment most people get with their busy conventional doctor. Included in the Alternative Healthcare System domain of CHA is ayurvedic medicine, homeopathic medicine, Native American medicine, and traditional Chinese medicine (including acupuncture and Chinese herbal medicine). Interestingly, the CHA therapies with the most acceptance by the medical community are some of the most infrequently used by patients—hypnotherapy, acupuncture, and biofeedback.

Ayurveda is thought to be the oldest medical system known. In Hindu mythology Ayurveda is considered the medicine of the gods. In Sanskrit, ayurveda is "knowledge of life," with life being defined as mind, body, and spiritual awareness. "Ayurveda is based on the belief that the natural state of the body is one of balance. We become ill when this balance is disrupted, with specific conditions or symptoms indicating a particular disease or imbalance. Ayurveda emphasizes strengthening and purifying the whole person, whereas in conventional medicine, the focus is on a set of symptoms or an isolated region of the body" (Alternative Medicine Foundation, 2005).

Ayurvedic teaching states that every living thing in the universe is made of these five elements: earth, water, fire, air, and space. The elements combine to determine a dosha, or metabolic type. A person's personality and character determine which of three doshas they are: Vata, Pitta, or Kapha. The practitioner can determine which dosha a patient is, then prescribe botanics, exercise, yoga, and massage therapy according to the person's particular dosha type. Ayurvedic practitioners mainly diagnose by observation and by touch. Caution with botanicals is advised as a 2008 study determined that a type of ayurveda that uses Rasa shastra (herbal medicines mixed with minerals and metals) may be cause for concern. Twenty-one percent of the medicines tested (obtained from the Internet) had unsafe levels of lead, arsenic, and mercury (Saper, Phillips, Sehgal, et al., 2008).

Homeopathy is based on a three pronged theory that *like cures like,* treatment is very individualized, and less is more. Homeopathic practitioners give very diluted forms of the substance that causes the symptoms of the disease in healthy people to the ill in the hopes that it will help support the body's natural healing power. The World Health Organization (WHO) has cited

Essential Oils

Essential oils are the natural, aromatic, volatile liquids found in shrubs, flowers, roots, trees, bushes, and seeds. Essential oils are also capable of readily changing from liquid to vapor at normal temperatures and pressures. Each essential oil may consist of hundreds of different and unique chemical compounds that defend plants against insects, environmental conditions, and disease. They also help plants grow, live, and adapt to its environment. Essential oils are extracted from aromatic plant sources by steam distillation. This allows the essential oils to be highly concentrated. It often takes an entire plant to produce a single drop of essential oil.

Essential oils often have a pleasant aroma, and their chemical makeup may provide many health benefits. This is why essential oils have been used throughout history by many cultures for medicinal and therapeutic purposes. Recently there has been a renewed interest in studying the many benefits of essential oils.

Peppermint oil has been shown to have a calming and numbing effect. It has been used to treat headaches, skin irritations, anxiety associated with depression, nausea, and diarrhea. In test tube experiments, peppermint kills some types of bacteria, viruses, and fungus suggesting it may have antibacterial, antiviral, and antifungal properties.

Another common essential oil is lavender oil. Research has confirmed that lavender produces calming, soothing, and sedative effects when its scent is inhaled. Lavender oil may also help alleviate insomnia, anxiety, and fatigue.

Essential oils can be used in a variety of ways. The most common methods of essential oil use are inhalation, topical application, and dietary consumption. Inhaling essential oils can be done by simply smelling them. They may also be dispersed through the air by diffusion.

Many essential oils can be directly applied to the skin. When applying an essential oil directly to the skin it should be diluted with a pure vegetable oil or coconut oil. Dilution may protect against possible skin sensitivities.

Essential oils can be taken internally. Methods of consumption include adding 1–2 drops to a glass of water and drinking, putting 4–6 drops in a capsule and swallowing with water, or adding to your meals when cooking.

Prior to using essential oils it is important to learn about the chemistry and safety of the oils. In order to experience the benefits of essential oils, high quality of pure essential oils must be used. A person will not experience the benefits of essential oils if they use diluted, adulterated, or synthetic oils.

It is important to research the companies that supply the essential oils. Learn how the company selects, grows and harvests its plants. Where the plant is grown, the quality of the

"The competent physician, before he attempts to give medicine to the patient, makes himself acquainted not only with the disease, but also with the habits and constitution of the sick man."

–Cicero

"The art of healing comes from nature and not from the physician. Therefore, the physician must start from nature with an open mind."

—Paracelsus

soil, and time of day that the plant is harvested can all impact the quality and makeup of the essential oil. The distillation process is also important in making high quality essential oils. In order to get the best quality essential oils, proper temperature and pressure, length of time, equipment, and batch size must be closely monitored throughout the distillation process. Like any other product, it is important to fully research and understand essential oils in order to make an informed decision.

Sorting through all the available information on essential oils can be difficult. Ultimately, you are responsible for your healthcare decisions. Using essential oils can be one component of your health care practices. If you are interested in learning more about essential oils, you can consult an aromatherapist or medical practitioner who has experience working with essential oils.

Contributed by Mike Hanik. Copyright © Kendall Hunt Publishing Company.

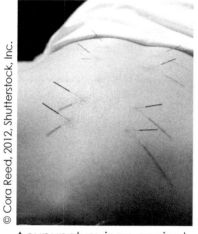

Acupuncture is an ancient medical art using the insertion of very fine needles into the body.

homeopathy as one of the systems of traditional medicine that should be integrated worldwide with conventional medicine in order to provide adequate global care in the twenty-first century (Goldberg, 2002). Homeopaths use low cost herbals, chemicals, and minerals.

Naturopathy is based on the motto "Vis Medicatrix Naturae," which is Latin for *helping nature heal*. Naturopaths emphasize restoring health rather than curing disease. Naturopaths utilize many different healing "tools" found in nature, such as magnets, water, heat, crystals, the sun, herbal medicine, manipulation, light therapy, electrical currents, and more. Naturopaths argue that Americans should return to a more natural and to a simpler way of life. Some naturopaths contend that we should go so far as to cease fluoridation of water and eliminate the addition of preservatives to food. There are three naturopathic training schools in the United States and one in Canada. Although these schools have a four year program emphasizing humanistic medicine, the naturopath is not an M.D.

Traditional oriental medicine (TOM) is a comprehensive system that dates back to the Stone Age. Also called traditional Chinese medicine (TCM), it includes acupuncture, acupressure, herbal medicine (discussed under Biological-Based Therapies), oriental massage, and qigong (discussed under Energy Therapies). Still widely used today, **acupuncture** is an ancient medical art using the insertion of very fine needles on the body in order to affect physiological functioning in the body. The needles are placed on the body at points that correspond to twelve meridians throughout the body. Manipulation of the needles, electrical stimulation, heat, and burning herbs (moxibustion) can be used in acupuncture. Before making a diagnosis, the practitioner talks with, and asks questions about, the patient. Typically the acupuncturist will check the pulse and the tongue of the patient to help diagnose the problem. A reputable acupuncturist will use disposable needles or sterilize reusable needles in an autoclave. With the millions of people treated with acupuncture, there have been relatively few complications reported to the U.S. Food and Drug Administration (FDA). Acupuncturists have a Master of Traditional Oriental Medicine and are required to be state-licensed.

Dry needling is a popular physical therapy approach that differs from acupuncture in that the needle is longer. Acupuncture works along meridian lines, however with dry needling the long thin needle directly targets a **trigger point**, or a chronic pain stimulus. Trigger points are taut bands of skeletal muscle, usually tender to the touch. Trigger points may cause referred pain as well in a different part of the body. A trigger point is often accompanied by musculoskeletal weakness and loss of range of motion in the affected areas. Anecdotal evidence (from this author) supports the effectiveness of relief of pain with dry needling associated with electric muscle stimulation followed by ice modality.

All TOM recognizes an energy force that flows through the body called qi (pronounced chi). Qi consists of the spiritual, physical, mental, and emotional aspects of life. Yin and yang are the vital forces of life that run throughout the twelve meridians within the body. Stimulation of points on the meridians is thought to activate the qi, which restores the body's equilibrium and allows the free flow of qi. The body is considered a flowing, self-healing system. Pain and discomfort can be the result of stagnation of energy which needs to be brought back into balance. Patients may experience calm and peacefulness as well as rejuvenation when their qi has been restored.

U.S. medical doctors became more interested in acupuncture in 1971 when James Reston, a well respected New York Times columnist, had to undergo emergency surgery while in China. Doctors there eased his post-surgery pain with acupuncture. There have been numerous studies done in the United States on the effectiveness of acupuncture. In December 2004 results of the largest randomized, controlled phase III clinical trial of acupuncture ever conducted were published in the *Annals of Internal Medicine.* The study was conducted on 570 patients with osteoarthritis of the knee. The results showed that "acupuncture reduces pain and functional impairment of osteoarthritis of the knee" (NIH, 2004). Dr. Brian M. Berman, M.D. of the University of Maryland School of Medicine directed the study and concluded that acupuncture is an effective complement to conventional arthritis treatment. According to a CDC 2002 survey, 2.1 million Americans have used acupuncture.

Acupressure is similar to acupuncture, but without the needles. The practitioner applies pressure to critical points along the meridian lines to balance yin and yang. There are different pressure points corresponding to specific parts of the body. The pressure releases muscular tension and promotes circulation of blood and qi to promote healing. Gradual steady penetrating pressure for up to three minutes is common (Gach, 1990). Simple acupressure techniques can be practiced on oneself. For example, between the forefinger and thumb is an acupressure point for headaches. **Shiatsu** is a type of acupressure massage using fingers, elbows, fists, and so on to apply pressure to restore the flow of energy in the body.

Can **acupuncture** give the athlete an edge in competition? It is possible that acupuncture treatment can be a positive adjunct to training, just like massage or physical therapy. Needles placed at sites of inflammation may reduce time out of training due to injury or swelling of tissue. There is little research, but Whitfield Reaves (2015) has used pre-performance needling and found personal benefit. Ear (auricular) acupuncture has been used during an athlete's competition, with small "tacks" kept in the ear. Acupuncture points don't work for everyone, but perhaps some sports acupuncture can make your next run a little more enjoyable.

Manipulative and Body-Based Therapies

Manipulative and body-based therapies in CHA use movement or manipulation of part of the body (see Figure 10.5). There are many different types of soft tissue mobilization (STM) therapies available. These therapies are attractive because they are a non-invasive and typically cost-effective treatment option.

Fascia is the sheath of fibrous connective tissue that supports and binds together or separates the internal organs, the musculature and the soft structures throughout the body. Fascia is to the human body like the white fiber is to an orange that connects the slices to the outer peel. Just as we toss the orange peel and white fiber from the orange in the compost and give it little thought, so has the traditional scientific community considered fascia. In the last decade or so, both in the alternative and the scientific camps, more attention and studies are revealing that the fascia within the body may play a significant role in our health. "Most anatomists view connective tissue as something to remove so that joints, muscles, organs and tendons may be studied carefully. In fact, it has now been established that the basic function of joints, muscles, organs and tendons requires a normal, functioning fascial system." (Stecco, 2015)

Massage is an example of STM, however there are new options for a person seeking acute or chronic pain relief. One therapy, called the Graston Technique, involves the practitioner using specially designed stainless steel tools to work the injured area of soft tissue. The tool augments the condition of the connective tissue, giving the therapist information on the adhesion or injury. Many body-based therapies stimulate the injured soft tissue, causing irritation and inciting the inflammatory response. The inflammatory response is considered a self-healing adaptation by the body. Most therapies work with the trigger points in the skeletal muscle or adhesions in the fascia.

Chiropractic is a medical treatment defined as the science of spinal manipulation. Chiropractic is the third most commonly used form of CHA, (following non-vitamin, non-mineral dietary supplements and deep breathing exercises, respectively), in the United States with 18 million Americans visiting the chiropractor each year. A June 2005 Consumer Reports Survey of 34,000 readers reported that of those interviewed with back pain, more went to the chiropractor than used prescription drugs. Practiced in earnest in the United States since 1895, chiropractic can trace its roots back to Galen and Hippocrates who laid their hands on patients for manipulation. Chiropractic

FIGURE 10.5

Diseases/Conditions for Which CHA Is utilized in the U.S.

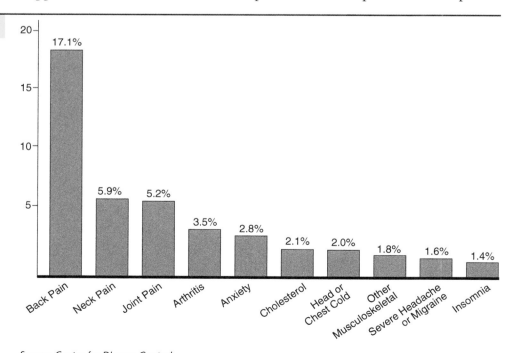

Source: Center for Disease Control

is considered to be the oldest indigenous CHA practices in the United States (NIH Lecture Series, 2002). Chiropractic has been seen in the past to be in competition with conventional medical treatment. Early in the last century, state medical boards used their power to restrict chiropractic practice. The chiropractors successfully brought an antitrust suit against the American Medical Association for allegedly trying to eliminate chiropractic practice in the United States. Today the medical doctors and the doctors of chiropractic enjoy a better working relationship. In April of 2017, The *Journal of the American Medical Association* published a systematic review and meta-analysis on the use of spinal manipulation therapy for low back pain. The conclusion was that chiropractic spinal manipulation was associated with modest improvements in both pain and function. This study prompted the American College of Physicians to include spinal manipulation as a therapy to treat back pain. Chiropractors train for up to six years with in-depth courses in anatomy, physiology, nutrition, and pathology. They also have clinical training.

Chiropractors manipulate the spine, often with high-velocity, low-amplitude spinal adjustments, to align the spine in order to let energy flow through the nervous system. It is unclear exactly how chiropractic works, however scientific evidence supports the use of chiropractic to treat acute or chronic back pain (NIH Lecture Series, 2002). Safety is always a concern, and the apparent risk for lumbar vertebrae adjustment is one in 1 million. Back and head complaints are the most common reason patients visit the physician or chiropractor, which results in $100 billion annually in lost productivity.

Many Americans suffer from neck pain. A recent study looked at the effectiveness of spinal manipulation, home exercise and medication to reduce acute neck pain. The spinal manipulation group received adjustments and mobilization exercises for the spine. The home exercise group received detailed instructions for gentle exercises for the neck and shoulders to be done 6 to 8 times per day. The third group received non-steroidal anti-inflammatory drugs (NSAIDS) as well as acetaminophen. Narcotic medications were an option for those who could not tolerate the NSAIDS. Both the exercises and

Massage involves manipulation of muscle and connective tissue to enhance function and promote relaxation and well-being.

© Alfred Weketo, 2012, Shutterstock, Inc.

Cupping is an ancient Chinese body-based healing therapy being utilized by Olympians like Michael Phelps to speed recovery. The cups cause a suction which breaks subcutaneous capillaries causing the telltale bruising; it is thought that the cupping process causes inflammation and increases blood flow to the affected area. Although there is little science behind it, many Olympians and non-Olympians alike swear by the benefits of cupping.

© Leonard Zhukovsky/ Shutterstock.com

the spinal manipulations groups were equal in improvement with participant rated pain. At 12 weeks, 82% of the exercise and manipulation groups experienced a 50% reduction in pain. Of the medication group, 69% noted improvements of at least 50% reduction in pain. The findings were similar at 26 and 52 weeks. "Additionally, the spinal manipulation group reported greater global improvement, participant satisfaction and function than the medication group" (NCCAM, 2012). The results from this study suggest that movement-based therapies can be effective in chronic pain management, especially before invasive techniques like surgery are considered. The *Clinical Journal of Pain* also reported results from a 2009 study that chronic neck pain patients experienced benefits from therapeutic massage (NCCAM, 2009).

Massage involves manipulation of muscle and connective tissue to enhance function of those tissues and to promote relaxation and well-being. Massage is growing in popularity as the use and acceptance of massage therapy increases. Many Fortune 500 companies are including massage as a benefit for their employees. Even small companies that offer on-site fifteen-minute massage are seeing the benefit in lower employee absenteeism due to headache, fatigue, and back pain (AMTA, 2005). Deep tissue, Swedish, myofascial release, petressage (kneading), sports massage, and trigger point therapy are just a few of the popular types of massage today.

Reflexology is based on the fact that the feet and hands represent a microcosm of the body and that specific parts of the foot and hand correspond or "reflex" to other parts of the body. Working with the feet has been used in many ancient medical practices; however William Fitzgerald developed modern reflexology in the early 1900's in England.

"No illness which can be treated by the diet should be treated by any other means."
—Moses Maimonides
(1135–1204)

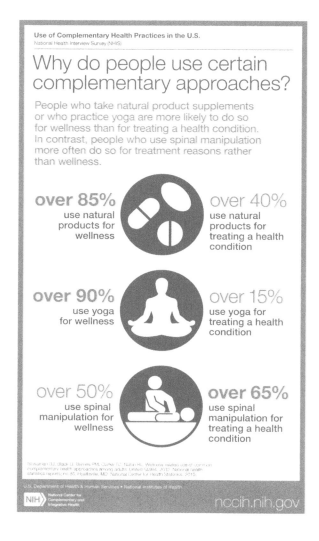

Use of Complementary Health Practices in the U.S.
National Health Interview Survey (NHIS)

Why do people use certain complementary approaches?

People who take natural product supplements or who practice yoga are more likely to do so for wellness than for treating a health condition. In contrast, people who use spinal manipulation more often do so for treatment reasons rather than wellness.

over 85% use natural products for wellness

over 40% use natural products for treating a health condition

over 90% use yoga for wellness

over 15% use yoga for treating a health condition

over 50% use spinal manipulation for wellness

over 65% use spinal manipulation for treating a health condition

nccih.nih.gov

Craniosacral therapy has its origins in the 1800's with Andrew Still M.D. The current form of craniosacral therapy was developed by osteopathic physician John E. Upledger at Michigan State University as a therapy that uses gentle touch to evaluate the physiological functioning of the craniosacral system. The craniosacral system is comprised of the membranes and the cerebrospinal fluid that surrounds and protects the spinal cord. Imbalance in the cerebral and spinal systems may cause sensory or motor dysfunction (IAHE, 2005). As relaxing as a massage, this therapy is typically used by people experiencing chronic pain who have not found relief with other therapies.

Biological-Based Therapies

Biological-based therapies use substances found in nature such as food, vitamins, minerals, herbal products, animal-derived products, probiotics, amino acids, whole diets, and functional foods. Some biological-based therapies are evidenced-based. For example, the FDA now fortifies some foods with folic acid to deter potential neural tube defects in developing fetuses. There are other biological-based therapies that are as of yet unproven. An example is the use of shark cartilage as a treatment for cancer. The consumer should be informed and use common sense and do a little research before spending money and making important decisions regarding healthcare. Drugs are monitored by the FDA, but biological-based systems are measured for truth in advertising by the Federal Trade Commission (FTC). The following biological-based therapies are just a few of the options for consumers today.

Macrobiotics is more than a diet, it is a discipline based on a philosophy of balance in accordance with the universe. It involves managing or changing diet to enhance health or for spiritual benefit. Macrobiotics is characterized by excluding meat and concentrating heavily on whole grains. Besides modifying diet, basic macrobiotic practices emphasize an active life, a positive mental outlook, and regularly eating small portions. There are numerous testimonials from cancer patients that have recovered from a stage IV cancer diagnosis using the macrobiotic diet. The National Cancer Institute has funded a clinical

Many plant extracts can be beneficial, however it is prudent to remember that herbs are drugs and should be consumed only as prescribed.

© Brian Chase, 2012, Shutterstock, Inc.

Use of Complementary Health Approaches in the U.S.
National Health Interview Survey (NHIS)

Most Used Natural Products by U.S. Adults

7.8%	Fish oil/omega 3/DHA, EPA fatty acids
2.6%	Glucosamine and/or chondroitin
1.6%	Probiotics/Prebiotics
1.3%	Melatonin
1.3%	Coenzyme Q10
0.9%	Echinacea
0.8%	Cranberry (pills or capsules)
0.8%	Garlic supplements
0.7%	Ginseng
0.7%	Ginkgo biloba

Citation: Clarke TC, Black LI, Stussman BJ, et al. Trends in the use of complementary health approaches among adults: United States, 2002–2012. National health statistics reports; no 79. Hyattsville, MD: National Center for Health Statistics. 2015.

U.S. Department of Health & Human Services • National Institutes of Health

NIH National Center for Complementary and Integrative Health

nccih.nih.gov

study to determine the effects of a macrobiotic diet on cancer therapy (www
.clinicaltrials.gov/ct/gui/c/alb/show/ NCT00010829). As you recall, evidence-
based science needs clinical trials to provide scientific evidence in order for a
therapy or treatment to have wide acceptance.

Herbals and dietary supplements are a hot trend in the industry, making manufacturers four billion dollars richer each year. Herbal therapy has
been around for several thousand years. It is likely the oldest and most widely
used therapy with roots in traditional Oriental medicine and the ayurvedic tra-
dition. Herbs are substances derived from trees, flowers, plants, seaweed, and
lichen. Herbs are prepared in several different forms: tinctures which contain
grain alcohol for preservation, freeze-dried extracts, and standardized extracts.
Herbs are contained in some manufactured drugs; drugs can also contain a
synthetic copy of the herb. *Many plant extracts can be very beneficial, however
it is prudent to remember that herbs are drugs and should be consumed only as prescribed.* Even if the consumer is using the herbal remedy correctly, there may
be an adverse interaction with food, over-the-counter drugs (OTC), vitamins
and minerals, or prescriptions drugs. Recent studies done by NCCAM (NIH,
2002) found that St. John's wort reduces the action of a common AIDS drug
called Indinavir (see Figure 10.6). St. John's wort, commonly used for mild to
moderate depression, clears 50 percent of all pharmaceutical drugs from the
human body (Markowitz et al., 2003).

An herbalist is a practitioner who bases most of his therapy on the medicinal qualities of plant and herbs. Herbs are prescribed so much in some parts of
Europe that they might not even be considered alternative. There are volumes

FIGURE 10.6

Biologically Based Systems:
St. John's Wort Lowers
Blood Levels of HIV
Protease Inhibitor Indinavir

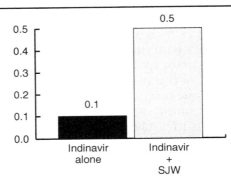

Note: HIV Inhibition threshold = 0.1. Indinavir Level (ug/ml)

Did You Know?

National Consumers League Food and Drug Interaction Brochure

NCL is your consumer healthcare advocate.

Medicines are powerful. The drugs your physician prescribes to
you can help your health. A drug's effectiveness can be rendered
ineffective or enhanced by food, drink, herbs (botanicals), and
other drugs in your diet. Log on to this Web site, write, or call the
NCL to obtain this important food and drug interaction brochure.

www.nclnet.org

National Consumers League (nonprofit membership organization)

1701 K Street, NW, Suite 1200

Washington DC 20006 (202) 835-3323

of testimonials, lots of anecdotal evidence, and many cultural traditions supporting herbal therapy. Gingko biloboa is purported to help with memory. St. John's wort helps with depression (some studies support this, some refute it). Saw palmetto helps manage an enlarged prostate. Butterbur, bee pollen, and stinging nettle may help with allergy symptoms. Evening primrose oil helps to manage PMS. The list is endless! When working with an experienced herbalist it is important to try and regulate the quality of the product you are getting. Using caution, especially when self-prescribing, is important because: safety is assumed, not proven; products are not standardized; products can be contaminated; you may have an allergic reaction, some herbs or certain amounts of the herb can be toxic, and the herbs can interact with drugs. Purity, standardization, and quality of the herbs can be an issue in consistency and the amount of the herb in the product. Another reason to use caution is that sometimes we get the sense that if a little works, perhaps a little more will work better. Toxic levels of drugs and herbs can be dangerous. If your friend takes 200 mg of a drug or herb, then you might do the same with disastrous consequences. You may be a nonresponder for that substance and get no result, or you may tolerate the substance and need a larger amount. Another issue is the amount of product actually contained in the packaging. See Figure 10.7 on ginseng.

An example of an unsafe drug is ephedra, derived from the Chinese herb Ma Huang. Traditionally Ma Huang has been used in China to treat asthma and other ailments associated with respiration. Ephedra was confirmed to be a factor in the death of Orioles pitching prospect Steve Belcher in February of 2003. Steve was taking ephedra to give him energy and to assist him with weight loss. The facts that Steve used ephedra, it was hot, and he was exercising combined to cause his death. The FDA has since banned the use of ephedra. If you are wondering about the safety of a particular herb, a very informative website that contains warnings and safety information is the USFDA Center for Food Safety and Applied Nutrition's Dietary Supplements: Warnings and Safety Information (www.cfsan.fda.gov/~dms/ds-warn.html).

> "Let thy food be thy medicine and thy medicine be thy food."
> —Hippocrates (460–377 B.C.)

Functional foods are foods that contain compounds like phytochemicals that are beneficial beyond basic nutrition, especially when eaten on a regular basis as part of a varied diet. This is a relatively new classification of foods and the specific benefits are still being determined. It is possible that functional foods act synergistically with other foods and antioxidants. Isoflavones in soy products, omega-3 fatty acids in cold water fish, essential fatty acids and fiber in ground flaxseed, and probiotic yeasts found in some yogurts are examples

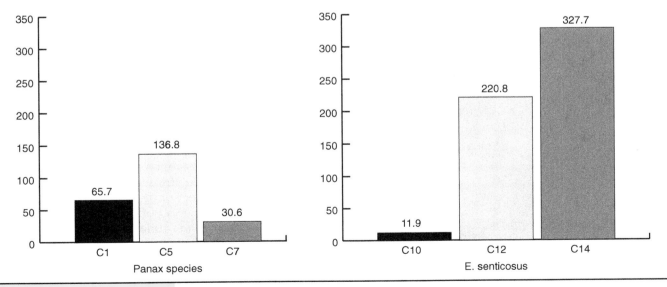

FIGURE 10.7

Variability in Commercial Ginseng Products
Adapted from Harkey, *American Journal of Clinical Nutrition,* 2001.

of other functional foods. If you eat a wholesome diet with plenty of fruits and vegetables and whole grains, then most likely you are getting functional foods in your diet. See Chapter 9 for a complete list of functional foods.

Vitamins and minerals are two of the six essential components for life in the human diet. As with herbs, a little is good but more is not always better. Use caution when megadosing on vitamins and minerals to avoid toxicity and health risks. As always, it is good to consult your physician or an educated CHA practitioner. We will not discuss the particulars of vitamins and minerals here; however, remember that often the best way to get vitamins and minerals is through a daily balanced diet. For those that have chronically deficient diets, a multivitamin and mineral supplement is most likely a good recommendation. For evidence-based information on herbal and supplements, log onto *HerbMed* for herbal information or to *Medline Plus* for other supplement information.

"The revolution we call mind-body medicine was based on this simple discovery: Wherever thought goes, a chemical goes with it. This insight has turned into a powerful tool that allows us to understand, for example, why recent widows are twice as likely to develop breast cancer, and why the chronically depressed are four times more likely to get sick. In both cases, distressed mental states get converted into the bio-chemicals that create disease."

—Deepak Chopra, M.D. (1993)

Mind-Body Medicine

Mind-body medicine taps into the connection between the physical body and the very powerful mind. Mind-body therapies are designed to enhance the mind's capacity to influence the body. Creative therapy involving dance, art, and music, as well as prayer and mental healing, are considered to be in the mind-body category.

Meditation is a way to deal with the effects of chronic stress. The person meditating is able to let go by focusing primarily on taking time (twenty minutes is great) to relax, shutting out external stimuli. There are numerous meditative techniques, and there really is no "right" way to meditate. Almost all techniques involve focus on breathing. The most important factor is to commit the time to just do nothing. This can be a challenge in our busy lives today. Try simply to find a quiet place, eliminate distractions, close your eyes, repeat a word or phrase that is meaningful for you, and say that word over and over with each exhalation. Allow yourself to just let go. "For 30 years, research has told us that meditation works beautifully as an antidote to stress," says Daniel Goleman, author of *Destructive Emotions* (2003). More and more conventional health professionals are recommending meditation as a way to deal with chronic stress as well as chronic pain. Experiencing the calming effect of meditation, if only for ten minutes each day, creates a period of physical relief that can enhance immune function. Over time, the benefits of meditation can have a cumulative effect, improving the well-being of the meditator (Heistand, 2005). With practice, it can calm the body and quiet the mind. The benefits are numerous. Try committing to the Meditation Exercise technique found on page 246 daily for one week to see if it has a positive effect on your life.

© Dallas Events, Inc., 2012, Shutterstock, Inc.

There are numerous meditative techniques. Almost all techniques involve focus on breathing.

Meditation practice can alter brain activity. Andrew Newberg is a University of Pennsylvania neurologist who has studied changes in brain activity during meditation. Using radioactive dye with functional brain imaging, Newberg demonstrated that the brains of Tibetan Buddhist monks blocked out information from the part of the brain that orients the body in space and time. The monks focused their energy inward, while blocking out any external stimuli (Pure Insight, 2005).

Previous studies have determined that meditation has a positive influence on symptoms of stress and anxiety. Another more recent study used brain imaging to look at specifically which regions of the brain were affected by mindfulness meditation. In the study conducted by researchers from University of Massachusetts Medical School and the Bender Institute of Neuroimaging in Germany, the meditation group had increases in gray matter concentration in the left hippocampus. The hippocampus is an area of the brain involved in learning, memory, and emotional control. This is one of the first studies to actually look at what is going on in the brain during meditation.

Applied psycho-neuro-immunology is based on research into psycho-neuroendocrino-immunolgy, the science of how our experiences are encoded neurologically and about how this affects our immune and hormonal systems. How our bodies' encounter, adapt, and react to stress directly affects our immune system. This approach treats the whole body. Our minds can keep us in a dark hole of hopelessness and helplessness with a condition like depression, which can cause a breakdown of our immune system. The reverse can be true as well. "The profound power of the mind that causes this rundown and eventual loss of resistance can also naturally be used positively to tune-up and boost the immune system to maximum level: to repel viruses, bacterium and other micro-organisms and to speed up healing" (AAAPNI).

Prayer and Spirituality—*Newsweek* recently did a cover story on the growth of spirituality in America today (Adler, 2005). The article greatly contrasts with the cover story of a 1966 *Time* article entitled "Is God Dead?" Spirituality is experiencing resurgence among Americans: 55 percent of Americans consider themselves spiritual and religious, and 24 percent consider themselves spiritual but not religious. Young people especially seem to be searching for greater meaning in a rigorous form of faith and prayer. Wanting more than what traditional religious services offer, they want to experience God in their daily lives. Many are drawing on the influence of Eastern religions to enhance their traditional doctrines. Meditations, centering prayer, silent contemplation, as well as disciplines like yoga, are often used in addition to traditional church services (Adler, 2005).

More than half of the medical schools in the country now offer an elective course on "Spirituality and Medicine." Questions abound about the role of prayer in healing the sick. Eighty-four percent of Americans polled believe praying for the sick can improve their chance of recovery (Kalb, 2004). Anecdotal evidence says prayer works. Science demands concrete evidence; however, prayer is hard to measure.

Yoga is a mind/body/spiritual discipline that is rooted in the ancient Hindu religion traced back 5,000 years. Yoga has become popular in the United States in the last several decades. According to the *New York Times,* 16 million Americans currently practice yoga. There are many different styles of yoga—gentle, meditative, powerful, and relaxing yoga to name of few. Movement in yoga can be rigorous and intense, or gentle and calming. Physicians are recognizing the benefits that a yoga practice can have on strengthening the physical body and quieting the mind. In addition to the many physical benefits, the practice of yoga with emphasis on breathing can be a great stress management tool. Movement, breathing, chanting, and sound are a prelude to meditation and conscious relaxation that regular yoga practice can provide. Conscious relaxation gives our minds a break from the daily chatter and unending stimuli to which we are continuously exposed.

Evidence is mounting that spending time with a loved pet has emotional, psychological, and physiological benefits.

Photos courtesy of Kirstin Brekken Shea.

Guided imagery is a concept that has been used successfully with people suffering from post-traumatic stress disorder. Psychologist Kathleen

Meditation Exercise

The most important thing is to allow yourself to do nothing.

Easy steps to meditation:

1. Eliminate distractions.
Turn off the cell phone, decide not to answer the door, let family or friends know you are unavailable for the next ten or fifteen minutes. Go to the bathroom, get a drink of water, and generally take care of any physical distractions that might arise. You might find it helpful to set a timer.

2. Just sit.
Get comfortable—consider sitting on a folded blanket to allow for less stress on the knees. Take a deep breath and allow your spine to extend and your ribs to lift. Maintain a tall posture as you soften your shoulders. Dim lights, a candle, incense, and appropriate music are nice but not necessary.

3. Let go.
Practice silence. Close your eyes and quietly observe the thoughts that come to your mind. Acknowledge them and then let them go. Let go of the outside stimuli so you can focus inward.

4. Listen.
Listen to the sounds of life in and around you. Become receptive to the sounds that are obvious, but also to the sounds that you normally don't hear because your attention is elsewhere. Hear without judgment; just observe. Notice your awareness of the present as it deepens.

5. Use your senses.
Cultivate an awareness of the present moment through sensations. Be attentive to where your body is connecting to the earth. What do you feel? Softness, hardness, coolness, warmth, pressure, and ease. How does your body change with each inhalation and exhalation? Settle into the present moment using your breath and your senses. Begin to focus on your inner self.

6. Simply breathe.
Attend to your breath. Try not to change your breath, just observe it how it is. Use all of your senses to increase awareness of how your body responds to your breath. Relax into your breath. Follow the rhythm of your breath with each inhalation and exhalation. When your mind wanders, just refocus and come back to the breath.

7. Mantra.
Saying a simple word, a phrase, a prayer, or anything meaningful to you over and over again as a mantra can coax you into a contemplative state. Repeat the mantra softly and slowly in an undulating rhythm with your breath, like riding a wave.

8. Practice kindness.
In your quiet state, consider someone who might be in need of some understanding and goodwill. Focus on this person. "In your mind's eye, send this person love, happiness, and well-being. Soften your skin, open the floodgates of your heart, and let gentle goodwill pour forth."

With consistent practice, meditation can make a difference in your life.

Adapted from Meditation 101 by Claudia Cummins, **Yoga Journal.** www.yogajournal.com/practice, 2009

Reyntjiens, Ph.D., reports that imagery was an integral part of her recovery efforts with those recently traumatized by Hurricane Katrina. "As our previous research with imagery has indicated, these simple self-regulation techniques—especially imagery and conscious breathing—are helping to minimize distress, anxiety, hypervigilance, anger, sadness, and insomnia, and allow all of us to be more effective, efficient, kind and caring neighbors in our survival and clean-up efforts" (Naparstek, 2005).

Mindfulness is a concept that includes strategies and activities that help us be more in the present moment. This helps us connect more intently with ourselves, others, and with nature. Peacefulness can be the result of being mindful throughout the day. Mindfulness is often thought of in conjunction with spirituality.

Beginning Your Own Spiritual Journey

Whether a person's quest for spiritual health takes the form of a love for nature, a weekly visit to a place of religious worship, or some other guise, it is clear that spirituality benefits overall health. While it is possible to achieve spiritual health in many ways, the following ideas have helped a number of people on their spiritual path:

Relaxation and Meditation

"There is no greater source of strength and power for me in my life now than going still, being quiet, and recognizing what real power is," says Oprah Winfrey on the segment of her daily television show called "Remembering Your Spirit." Many people take the time to sit quietly and to meditate; for example, more than five million people worldwide practice transcendental meditation, one popular relaxation technique.

Time in Nature

For Henry David Thoreau, who fled civilization to live on Walden Pond, nature was the temple of God and the perennial source of life. A powerfully spiritual moment—and one we have all experienced—is the instant we are confronted with earth's perfection and are filled with awe. The scientist Carl Sagan wrote about his time-in-nature experience: "The wind whips through the canyons of the American Southwest, and there is no one to hear it but us." The crisp, clean smell of the woods after rainfall, the soothing rhythm of crickets on a summer night, the beauty of freshly fallen snow—these experiences inspire unspeakable awe and humility because of the small but rich part that we, as individuals, play in the larger scheme of the universe.

Intimacy with Others

Loving selflessly is part of spiritual experience. Living life with passion and allowing ourselves to "feel" may be the greatest element of the spiritual journey. Experiencing emotion through a poignant musical passage, feeling the grief of a lost love, and surrendering to love's beauty are all part of human spirituality. By giving, sharing, and loving, we become whole and experience all that we are capable of feeling.

Spiritual Readings

Ranging from inspirational self-help books available at the local bookstore to traditional religious works, the written word has provided insight and guidance throughout human history, during its times of joy and darkest moments. For some it's the Bible; for others, it may be the Quran; and for still others, it may be a contemporary book such as *Spiritual Healing: Scientific Validation of a Healing Revolution* by Daniel J. Benor, M.D. (Vision Publications, 2001). To find books that will foster your personal growth and healing, listen to what others recommend and then search for whatever will move you or speak to you.

Prayer

Prayer may be the oldest spiritual practice and the most popular one in America. Almost all world religions include a form of prayer. Says George Lucas, who plays on religious themes such as good and evil in his blockbuster *Star Wars* series, "Religion is basically a container for faith. And faith is a very important part of what allows us to remain stable, remain balanced." The mental and emotional release, along with a sense of connection to a transcendent dimension, may be at the heart of prayer's effectiveness.

From *Psychology Today* (September/October 1999), 48; The Transcendental Meditation Program (see http://www.tm.org).

Feldenkrais method is "a form of somatic education that uses gentle movement and directed attention to improve movement and enhance human functioning. Through this method, you can increase your ease and range of motion, improve your flexibility and coordination, and rediscover your innate capacity for graceful, efficient movement" (The North American Feldenkrais Guild). Feldenkrais is excellent for dancers, athletes, and others, as well as those limited by neuromuscular pain or neurological dysfunction. Moshe Feldenkrais, an Israeli engineer, developed this technique.

"Yoga is the stilling of the restlessness of the mind."
—Yoga Sutras

Somatic movement re-educates the neuromuscular system toward greater health and well-being. Through hands-on movement work by the somatics practitioner, "people can learn to manage stress, relieve back pain, breathe more freely, heal from trauma to the neuromuscular system, and speed recuperation after illness or surgery" (Brockport, 2005). The Feldenkrais method is a type of somatic movement education. Meditation, visualization, craniosacral therapy, and myofascial release techniques are often practiced by the somatic movement practitioner.

Animal-assisted therapy is the use of companion animals to help people with special needs. Evidence is mounting that spending time with a loved pet not only has emotional and psychological benefits, but physiological benefits as well. The act of petting and caring for a loved animal can reduce blood pressure and heart rate and improve survival rates from heart disease (Arkow, www.animal therapy). Close to half of the psychologists responding to a survey indicated prescribing a pet to combat loneliness or depression. According to Phil Arkow, instructor of the Animal Assisted Therapy course at Camden County College in Blackwood, New Jersey, elderly people who have pets visit physicians 16 percent less than those who do not; dog owners in particular make 21 percent fewer visits. "A pet is an island of sanity in what appears to be an insane world. Friendship retains its traditional values and securities in one's relationship with one's pet. Whether a dog, cat, bird, fish, turtle, or what have you, one can rely upon the fact that one's pet will always

remain a faithful, intimate, non-competitive friend—regardless of the good or ill fortune life brings us" (Dr. Boris Levinson, child psychologist).

Energy Therapies

Energy therapies engage the use of energy fields that surround the body and penetrate the body. The science behind energy fields has yet to be proven.

Qigong (pronounced chi-gong) combines movement, meditation, and regulation of breathing to enhance the flow of vital energy (qi), improve blood circulation, and enhance immune function (Donatelle, 2004). Qigong literally means the skill of attracting vital energy. Those that practice qigong call it a "self-healing art" that uses visualization and imagery with movement and meditation.

Reiki (pronounced ray-key) is a type of energy work that utilizes touch and visualization. Reiki is based on ancient Tibetan teachings and is said to date back thousands of years. Today reiki is practiced using the Eastern concept of the five chakras in the body, as well as using the organs and glands from Western anatomy.

Practicing Sheng Zhen style of qigong can balance life energy and open the heart to cultivate health and happiness.

Photo courtesy of Trinity Linh Templin

Therapeutic touch is purported to induce the relaxation response, alleviate pain, and to speed the healing process. In therapeutic touch, the patient is not actually touched. In one study people were wounded on their arms. The control group had conventional therapy, while the other group experienced therapeutic touch. The entire second group experienced quicker healing (Wirth, 1990).

Bioenergy practitioners use psychotherapy, grounding exercise, and deep breathing to assist in releasing muscular tension, pain, and illness. Pain and illness are thought to be caused by suppressed emotions and behaviors (AMFI, 2005).

Ultimately the responsibility lies with the patient to secure quality health care. As time goes on, more CHA modalities will be studied and the results will help guide consumers to which therapies are best for each individual person.

There are many more CHA therapies than are mentioned in this chapter. Conventional physicians and those they work closely with want the same things as most CHA practitioners—for patients to have good health and wellness. "The effectiveness of the healthcare delivery system in the future will depend upon its ability to make use of all approaches and modalities that provide a sound basis for promoting optimal health. People with better health habits have been shown to survive longer and to postpone and shorten disability" (WHCCAMP, 2002). Certainly many CHA practices will be useful in contributing to the nation's health goals. The modern patient is more informed and involved in his or her own health. Most likely the marriage of essential conventional practices with complementary and alternative therapeutics will be the way of the future.

References

Acupuncture Relieves Pain and Improves Function in Knee. *Osteoarthritis NIH News,* December 20, 2004 press release.

Adler, J. In Search of the Spiritual. *Newsweek,* August 29, 2005. Alternative Medicine Foundation www.amfoundation.org

American Massage Therapy Association. www.amtamassage.org Phone (847) 864-0123

Arkow, P. *Animal Assisted Therapy: A Premise and a Promise.* http://www .animaltherapy. net/Premise%20%26%20Promise.html

Association for the Advancement of Applied Psychoneuroimmunology. http://hometown.aol.com/AAAPNI

Barnes, P. M., Bloom, B., and Nahin, R. *CDC National Health Statistics Report #12*. Complementary health approaches Use Among Adults and Children: United States, 2007. December 10, 2008.

Chopra, D. *Ageless Body, Ageless Mind*. Harmony Books. 1993.

Clarke, T.C., Black, L.I., Stussman, B.J., Barnes, P.M., Nahin, R.L. *CDC National Health Statistics Report Number 78*. Trends in the Use of Complementary Health Approaches Among Children Aged 4–17: United States, National Health Interview Survey, 2007–2012. February 10, 2015.

ClinicalTrials.gov; US National Library of Medicine, US National Institute of Health. www. clinicaltrials.gov/ct/gui/c/alb/show/NCT00010829

International Alliance of Healthcare Educators (IAHE). Craniosacral Therapy/Somatoemotional Release: Education for better patient care. 2005. http://www.iahe.come/ html/therapies.cst.jsp

Donatelle, R. J. *Access to Health* (8th ed). Pearson/Benjamin Cummings. 2004. Feldenkrais Educational Foundation of North America (FEFNA) 3611 SW Hood Ave. Suite 100 Portland, OR 97239, USA http://www.feldenkrais.com

Gach, M. R., *Acupressure's Potent Points*. Bantam Books. 1990.

Goldberg, B. *Alternative Medicine, The Definitive Guide* (2nd ed). Berkeley, CA: Celestial Arts. 2002.

Goleman, D. *Destructive Emotion: A Scientific Dialogue with the Dalai Lama*. 2003. Alternative Medicine Foundation Information. How to Assess Credibility on the Web. 2009. www.amfoundation.org/assess.htm

https://nccih.nih.gov/news/press/12172014; NIH complementary and integrative health agency gets new name (12/17/14)

Information on Clinical Trials being conducted; www.clinicaltrials.gov/ct/gui/c/alb/show/NCT00010829

Kalb, C. Faith and Healing, *Newsweek*, November 10, 2004.

Markowitz, J. et al. Effect of St John's Wort on Drug Metabolism by Induction of Cytochrome P450 3A4 Enzyme. *JAMA*, (290),1500–1503. 2003. Naparstek, B. *Health Journeys*. 2005.

National Institutes of Health. NCCAM Online Continuing Education Lecture Series, Manipulative and Body-Based Therapies: Chiropractic and Spinal Manipulation. 2002. http://nccam.org/main.php

Paige, Neil M., Miake-Lye, Isomi, Booth, Marika, et al., Association of Spinal Manipulative Therapy with Clinical Benefit and Harm for Acute Low Back Pain Systematic Review and Meta-analysis. *JAMA*. 2017;317(14):1451–1460.

Psych-Neuro-Immunology http://hometown.aol.com/AAAPNI/

Pure Insight. 2005. http://pureinsight.org/PI/index/html

Reaves, W. Acupuncture and the Athlete, *ACSM Fit Society*, Fall 2008.

Ryzik, M. Z. Exercising That Back Pain Away. *New York Times*, September 15, 2005. Wirth, D. P. The Effects of Non-Contact Therapeutic Touch on the Healing Rate of Full Thickness Dermal Wounds. *Subtle Energies*, Vol. 1, No. 1, 1990.

Saper, R. B., Phillips, R. S., Sehgal, A., et al. Lead, mercury, and arsenic in U.S. and Indian-manufactured Ayurvedic medicines sold via the Internet. *Journal of the American Medical Association*, 300(8):915–923. 2008.

Somatic Movement Studies http://www.brockport.edu/~dance/somatics/techniques.htm, 2005.

Stecco, C. *Functional Atlas of the Human Fascial System* (1st ed). Churchill Livingstone. Elsevier 2015.

USFDA Center for Food Safety and Applied Nutrition's Dietary Supplements: Warnings and Safety Information. www.cfsan.fda.gov/~dms/ds-warn.html

White House Commission on Complementary and Alternative Medicine Policy (WHCCAMP). Final Report. 2002. *(electronic version)*

Chapter 11
Cancer

© fototip/Shutterstock.com

OBJECTIVES

Students will be able to:

♦ Identify genetic and lifestyle causes of cancer
♦ Recognize prevention strategies, risk factors, and screening methods for young adult cancers
♦ Identify new treatment methods for cancer

"Cancer is a word, not a sentence"

– John Diamon

Nearly everyone reading this book will have been affected by cancer in some way; whether personally or through a family member or friend. Cancer is one of the leading causes of morbidity and mortality worldwide, with approximately 14 million new cases in 2012, according to the World Health Organization. Over the next two decades, the number of new causes is expected to increase by 70% (WHO, 2015). Increased exposure to carcinogens (like tobacco), the increasing age of the world's population, viral infections, and lifestyle factors (like lack of physical activity) all contribute to the increased diagnoses. At the same time, massive improvements in cancer detection and treatment are occurring, paving the way for increased life expectancy for those who receive a cancer diagnosis.

Cancer can be classified in two ways: by the location in the body where the cancer first developed, and by the type of tissue in which the cancer originates (histological type). Hundreds of types of cancers are grouped into six main categories based on histological type:

> **Carcinoma:** Cancer of this type begins in the epithelial cells, which cover the inside and outside of the body. This is the most common type of cancer, and includes most types of breast, colon, prostate, skin cancer.
> **Sarcoma:** This type of cancer forms in the supportive and connective tissues such bone, tendons, cartilage, muscle, and fat. The most common cancer of this type is osteosarcoma (cancer of the bone).
> **Lymphoma:** The glands or nodes of the lymphatic system are the origin of lymphoma. The lymphatic system produces disease-fighting white blood cells, or lymphocytes. Abnormal lymphocytes build up in vessels, nodes, and other organs and cause Hodgkin or Non-Hodgkin lymphoma.
> **Myeloma:** This type of cancer occurs in plasma cells. The abnormal cells build up in bone marrow and form tumors in bones throughout the body.
> **Leukemia:** Cancers of this type originate in the blood-forming tissue of bone marrow. Called a "liquid cancer", leukemia makes it difficult for the body to fight infection and control bleeding.
> **Other Types of Tumors:** Tumors, or "solid cancers", can form in various places in the body including the brain and spinal cord (astrocytic tumor), germ cells (cells that form sperm or eggs), and the endocrine system.

(National Cancer Institute, accessed 2016)

Causes of Cancer

Cancer is a complex and ever-changing disease, and despite centuries of research, scientists cannot pinpoint a single "cause" of cancer. Researchers agree that a combination of factors, including genetics, lifestyle choices, infections, and environmental exposures can trigger cancer.

Genetics

Cancer is really a disease of genes; not necessarily genes inherited from family members, but a genetic mutation that alters DNA. Cells become cancer cells because of mutations. More than one mutation is needed for cancer to occur. These mutations can be inherited or acquired:

Inherited gene mutations are present in sperm or eggs. Since all body cells form from the zygote (formed when the sperm fertilizes the egg), this type of mutation is then present in all body cells and passed down to future generations. Inherited mutations are thought to cause only a small fraction of cancers. However, when cells start out with one mutation, it is easier and quicker for enough mutations to build up throughout the lifetime and become cancerous. Family Cancer Syndrome can occur when tumor suppressor gene defects are inherited.

Acquired gene mutations are acquired later in life and affect otherwise healthy genes. These mutations cannot be passed down to the next generation and are the cause of most cancers that occur later in life. Some acquired mutations are the result of environmental exposures and others seem to occur randomly. It is important to realize that genetic mutations actually occur frequently, but most mutated cells are eliminated through apoptosis. But if the cell does not die, it may lead to the development of cancer, especially if the mutation affects a gene involved with cell division.

Lifestyle Choices

Acquired gene mutations can result from cigarette smoke, dietary choices, and lack of physical activity. These factors are all controllable, making cancers caused by lifestyle choices ultimately preventable.

Tobacco in all forms (cigarettes, cigars, smokeless tobacco, and electronic cigarettes) contains carcinogens. Cigarette smoking is the most significant cause of lung cancer, and smoking is also responsible for most cancers of the larynx, mouth, and esophagus. Risk of kidney, cervical, liver, bladder, pancreas, stomach, and colorectal cancer also increases in tobacco users. These risks are not limited to the smoker; environmental tobacco smoke also increases nonsmokers' risk of lung cancer and can increase children's risk of lymphoma, leukemia, liver cancer, and brain tumors.

Dietary choices and their relationship to cancer have received much attention in recent years. According to the National Cancer Institute, one-third of cancer deaths in the United States each year are related to dietary factors including alcohol consumption, caloric balance, food preparation, and types of food.

Alcohol increases cancer risk by impairing the body's ability to break down and absorb nutrients, increasing estrogen levels, and generating reactive molecules that can damage DNA and proteins. Alcoholic beverages may also contain carcinogens, resulting in increased risk for colorectal, breast, liver, esophageal, and head and neck cancers (National Cancer Institute, 2013).

> **Apoptosis:** a genetically directed process of cell self-destruction that is marked by the fragmentation of nuclear DNA, is activated either by the presence of a stimulus or removal of a suppressing agent or stimulus, and is a normal physiological process eliminating DNA-damaged, superfluous, or unwanted cells —called also *programmed cell death* (Source: Mirriam-Webster dictionary)

A Conversation with Dr. Walter Willett about Diet and Cancer

Dr. Walter Willett, chair of the department of nutrition at the Harvard School of Public Health, recently delivered a lecture titled "Diet & Cancer: The Fourth Paradigm" on the NIH campus in Bethesda, MD. An archived videocast of the lecture, sponsored by NCI's Cancer Prevention Fellowship Program, is available online.

How have views on diet and cancer evolved over the last 40 years?

When I started in this area in the 1960s, the thinking revolved around carcinogens in food. These were chemicals produced by high temperatures, such as with barbecuing, that had been shown to cause DNA mutations in animal models and test systems. In fact, this topic has not been totally resolved, but if carcinogens in food were a major problem for humans,

we probably would have seen more evidence than we have. This was the first paradigm.

What were the second and third paradigms?

The second paradigm was the idea that fat in the diet is a major cause of cancer. There was never any strong evidence for this idea, but it was repeated so often that it became dogma in the 1980s and 1990s. For conditions such as heart disease and diabetes, the type of fat in the diet is quite important. But the hypothesis that the percentage of calories from fat in the diet is an important determinant of cancer risk, at least during midlife and later, is not supported by the data.

The third paradigm was that fruits and vegetables dramatically reduce risks of cancer. But, as the prospective data came in, the results just did not support this idea either. That's not to say there's no benefit from fruits and vegetables, but [the benefit is] probably very small and limited to certain foods and certain cancers. Overall, we just don't see a relationship.

That brings us to the fourth paradigm.

The fourth paradigm is that a major cause of cancer is excessive adiposity [obesity]. This paradigm, also referred to as positive energy balance, is here to stay, because the evidence is overwhelming from all types of studies. These findings have coalesced from research over the last 10 to 15 years, but the evidence to support this idea actually goes back to animal studies in the 1930s. In a sense, it was right there in front of us all the time.

Can you put the role of obesity and cancer risk in context?

On a population level, the number of cases of cancer attributable to people being overweight and obese is about equal to the number attributable to current smoking. This is in part because smoking is going down and obesity is going up; in terms of importance within a population, they are in the same ballpark. However, on an individual basis, the cancer risk due to smoking remains substantially higher than that due to obesity.

Are you looking for clues to obesity and cancer in younger people?

Yes, this is one of the new frontiers in cancer research. Until now, we've been looking at a pretty narrow period of life—essentially around the time people are getting cancer. But we have lots of epidemiologic hints that many factors operate earlier in life and maybe even across generations.

What are you learning?

For the first time, we are getting a pretty good look at the diets of adolescents and cancer incidence.

In the Nurses' Health Study 3, we have retrospectively collected details about high school diets from participants, who were 25 to 42 years old at the time of enrollment. They weren't so far beyond their high school diets, so we have some data that is recalled pretty well.

In addition, we collected data from their mothers about their mothers' experiences with the pregnancy resulting in our participant and the participant's infant feeding patterns and diet and activity before age 5. We're just starting to get follow-up from that information. This approach can piece together the lifespan, which I think will be necessary for a thorough look at diet and cancer.

If money weren't a factor, what kind of study would you launch?

The most critical missing elements in the research right now are the dimensions of time—the time when we start the studies, and the length of follow up. The ideal study would start during pregnancy (perhaps even before) and would collect data about maternal diets and then continue to collect data and follow participants—in other words, a birth cohort.

Are these studies under way?

There have been some attempts in this country to develop a birth cohort that was big enough to look at cancer, but the studies sank under the weight of huge budgets. On the other hand, there are more than 300,000 participants in birth cohorts in Scandinavian countries. The next generations of scientists will be the ones to analyze the results in terms of cancer. I've been involved in this work and am hoping to see some of the results myself.

Research is inconclusive on the impact of artificial sweeteners, food preparation techniques such as charring and pickling, and other dietary choices highlighted in current media. However, research does suggest that being overweight or obese, whether it results from a high-fat diet, lack of physical activity, or a combination of factors, does increase cancer risk. Excess weight can stimulate the body to produce more estrogen and insulin, which are hormones that can stimulate cancer growth. Obese people may have an increased risk of cancers of the breast, colon, rectum, esophagus, kidney, pancreas, bladder, and endometrium. On the contrary, observational studies note that adults who maintain a lower weight have decreased risk of colon, breast, and endometrial cancer.

Physical activity promotes overall good health, including decreased cancer risk. Exercising can improve hormone levels and the function of the immune system, both of which protect against cancer. Breast and colon cancers are the most extensively studied with regards to the link with physical activity, with evidence suggesting that 30–60 minutes of physical activity per day helps prevent both.

Infections

Infectious agents, including bacteria, viruses, and parasites, can cause cancer or increase the risk that cancer will form. This can happen because of chronic inflammation or disruption of normal controls of cell growth. Viruses including Human Papilloma Virus (HPV), Hepatitis B, and Hepatitis C are directly linked with cervical, anal, vaginal, vulvar, and penile cancers (HPV) and liver cancer (Hepatitis B and C viruses). Human Immunodeficiency Virus (HIV) weakens the immune system and increases susceptibility to various cancers, and the Epstein-Barr Virus is linked to an increased risk of lymphoma.

Fortunately, vaccines exist for HPV and Hepatitis B, and infections with other agents can help be prevented by avoiding unprotected sex and not sharing needles.

Environmental Exposures

People with direct exposure to carcinogens at the workplace are at high risk for developing cancer on sites including skin, lungs, and nasal passages. Ionizing radiation from x-rays, gamma rays, and other forms of high-energy radiation can damage DNA and cause cancer. These can be released in nuclear accidents and where atomic weapons are made or used. UV radiation from the sun, sunlamps, and indoor tanning booths can also lead to cancer.

The following is Kelli Bevans Joiner's personal story of her diagnosis and treatment of brain cancer while she was a student at Texas A&M. We are profoundly grateful for her openness, honesty, and joyful life.

Growing up in College Station, Texas, I was born an Aggie, daughter of a Texas A&M football player; I bleed maroon. In 2009 I graduated with a nursing license and was accepted to Texas A&M starting fall 2010 as a Community Development major. My life was a balancing act and it got busier when I returned home after a spring break medical mission in Guatemala. Thankfully I had a family physician in College Station because I was running a high fever, fatigued, had an unbearable headache, and something was really wrong. My doctor had me taken to the ER across the street where the health team ordered labs, IVs, and testing. The first red flag was when the results of the CT scan came back with a mass on the right side of my brain. I was immediately taken by ambulance to St. Joseph Hospital in Bryan, Texas. My room in the hospital was full of doctors and nurses. I remember one of the neurosurgeons explaining to my parents that the first step was to have a brain biopsy in order to figure out if I had come in contact with something from traveling to Central America or if something else was going on. The next day after the surgery I was in the ICU, my neurosurgeon stood right in front of me and explained I was diagnosed with a grade II Oligoastrocytoma of the right temporal lobe. This is one of the brain tumors of "gliomas" mixed with abnormal spider like brain cells. Brain tumors are graded on a scale of one to four, with three and four being the most aggressive. The surgeons believed I had that tumor "sitting" in my brain for quite a few years or even longer because the type of brain cancer I had was not very aggressive and a slow growing. We decided it would be okay to finish the spring semester and then after I finished finals I had my first brain surgery the day before my 22nd birthday. Spending my birthday in the ICU was something new but still a celebration of life.

Summer of 2011 was all about recovering and I still worked as a nurse at Beutel. I tried to go back to my normal self but after being diagnosed with brain cancer and having brain surgery,

Photograph by Janet Ni, reprinted by permission.

my mental capacity was not the same. I continued school, work, regular activities along with routine doctors' appointments and MRIs. Fall of 2012 was very difficult. My classes were stressful, I tried to continue work and I was having more seizures than normal. After testing and numerous doctor visits my neurologist diagnosed me with 'Complex Partial Seizures' meaning I would have moments of 'deja veu" tingling sensations throughout my body, my brain felt like it stopped, and I had to remind myself to breathe. One afternoon I finished an exam and I remember I was walking past the Century Tree when my oncologist called to tell me this week's MRI does not look good, it appears cancer cells are growing in the same area where my brain tumor was. I was in shock, sat on the sidewalk and one of my best friends who also works at the clinic came and got me. The next day I met with my oncologist and she referred me to MD Anderson.

The second opinion resulted in those cancer doctors thinking this tumor was growing like a grade III, which is more aggressive than the previous. My doctors immediately put me on chemotherapy.

Some brain cancer patients respond better to a pill form of chemotherapy called Temozolmide, I was prescribed 6 months with one week of taking the temozolmide and then two weeks off. Even though I was in the middle of the fall semester, my health could not be put on hold. My world was spinning and I needed help. Texas A&M Disability Services came to the rescue.

My father went with me to Disability Services and we presented medical documents and letters saying that I could really use some help with my classes in order to graduate and have brain surgery a week later. Disability services set guidelines for my professors to give me some extra time on projects and schedule testing around my treatments. I was fortunate to have the students with the highest academic level give the professors their notes and I would receive them and their lectures on the days I was sick. Reflecting on my college years, that was without a doubt the most stressful and tiring semester of my life. During those months my hair was thinning but I was lucky enough to take senior pictures on campus before it got worse and before my surgery.

The month of May is coincidently the "Brain Cancer" awareness month, my graduation, birthday and a month full of reminders of all the milestones of life we encounter. One week after graduation I was admitted at 5:00 am to prepare for surgery. I was scared for this one and I am the luckiest girl because I was surrounded by my best friends and family. My brain surgery took about 6 hours and this was a more intensive surgery so the surgeon had to drill more into my jaw bone all the way around to the back of my ear. During the surgery I had a mini-stroke (called a TIA), which caused me to have to re-learn how to walk afterwards. In the ICU it was hard for me to chew so I ate a lot of ice cream that week and a half.

Reprinted by permission of Kelli Joiner.

After about two weeks, I had learned how to walk again. I had a follow up appointment with my oncologist a two weeks after my surgery and we got shocking results that the tumor came back as an Anaplastic Astrocytoma, grade III brain tumor. With more aggressive brain tumors it is common to be treated with radiation after surgery. Starting the next day I met my radiologist and got measured and shaped for a molding to go over my head to the top of my chest. Once the molding hardened the doctor marked seven areas around the mask where the radiation beams would hit. My doctors agreed to do 6 weeks of treatment, Monday through Friday every morning. When I check in my nurse takes my temperature and then I get on the radiation table where I lay flat and she clips my plastic mask on to the table tightly over the top of my body. I cannot see the machines during the procedure but I can hear them move around the room and when the light beams are on. I was always tired and sometimes nauseous afterwards. Within about two weeks clumps of hair would fall out when I would wash my hair, and I was bald by the fourth week. Wigs were uncomfortable to wear because my head was so sensitive, especially around the incision site. I wore loose cotton caps or scarves. After treatments my MRI showed the tumor site was scarred but clean of cancer. It has taken time to recover and start a new chapter of normalcy but I am now over three years cancer free. I will always have routine MRIs, take seizure medication, and require rest but I am alive and enjoying life.

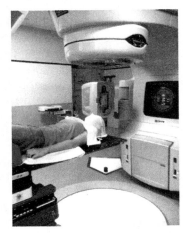

Photograph by Timothy Joiner, reprinted by permission.

Young Adult Cancers

According to the National Cancer Institute, about 5 percent of all cancer diagnoses occur in young adults (ages 15–39). Cancers in this age group may have unique genetic and biological features, making them difficult to diagnose and treat. Young adults with cancer also face challenges due to their age, such as delays in diagnosis and feelings of isolations. People in this age group are often too old for pediatric oncologists, but younger than patients usually treated by other physicians. They may not see other patients their age in the treatment setting. Organizations such as Critical Mass and the 15–40 Connection offer support groups and online assistance. More information about these organizations can be found at the end of the chapter.

While adolescents and young adults can face any type of cancer, some are more common than others in this age group. The National Cancer Institute illustrates the incidence of cancer types in patients ages 15–39 in Figure 11.1.

FIGURE 11.1

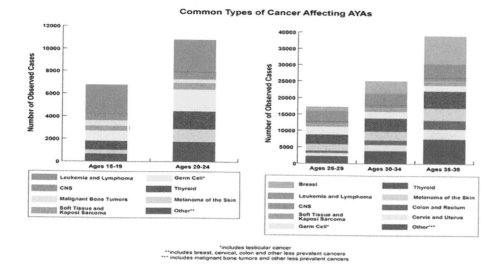

Common Types of Cancer Affecting AYAs

Source: National Cancer Institute at the National Institutes of Health, SEER 18, 2007–2011, ages 15–39

The following sections will describe risk factors, screening methods, and prevention of cancers that are common in young adults or whose screening methods should begin during young adult years. Cervical, breast, testicular, and skin cancers will be discussed. While less prevalent, brain tumors are also included due to the unique symptoms and body awareness that is required for accurate diagnosis.

Cervical Cancer

Cervical cancer types include squamous cell carcinoma, which begins in the thin flat cells that line the cervix and adenocarcinoma, which begins in cervical cells that make mucus. The Centers for Disease Control and Prevention (CDC) reports that almost all cervical cancers are caused by the human papillomavirus (HPV), a virus that can be passes from person to person during sexual contact.

Risk Factors

Long-lasting infection with HPV is the greatest risk factor for cervical cancer. Risk can also be increased by the following:

Smoking: Women who smoke are twice as likely as non-smokers to get cervical cancer (American Cancer Society, 2016). Substances from tobacco by-products can damage the DNA of cervical cells and contribute to the development of cancer, and smoking also decreases the immune system's effectiveness in fighting HPV infections.

HIV infection: The immune system is also negatively impacted by HIV, which is why women with AIDS have a higher risk of cervical cancer. In women with HIV, a pre-cancerous mass in the cervix would develop into an invasive cancer faster than in a woman without HIV.

Long-term use of oral contraceptives: Research suggests that cervical cancer risk is elevated while women take oral contraceptives longer than five years, but the risk returned to normal ten years after use was stopped (National Cancer Institute, 2012).

Multiple full-term pregnancies: Women with three or more full-term pregnancies have an increased risk of developing cervical cancer. The reasons behind this increased risk are not exactly known, but one theory suggests that women with several pregnancies have had unprotected intercourse multiple times, possibly increasing their risk of exposure to HPV. Another possible reason is that pregnant women have suppressed immune systems, which increases susceptibility of contracting HPV.

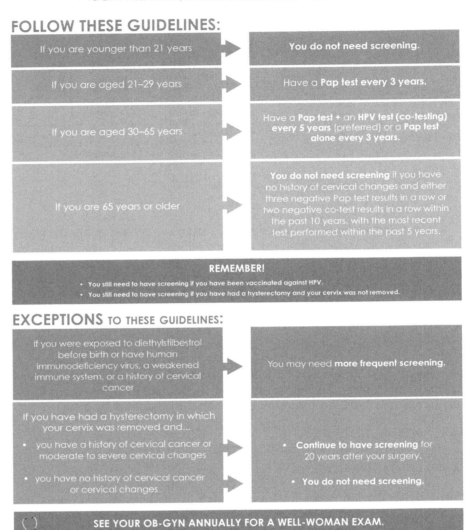

Cervical Cancer Screening

WHAT IS IT?

Your ob-gyn or other health care professional takes a sample of cervical cells and sends them to a lab for testing:

- For a Pap test, the sample is tested to see if abnormal cells are present.
- For an HPV test, the sample is tested for infection with HPV types linked to cancer.

FOLLOW THESE GUIDELINES:

If you are younger than 21 years	→	**You do not need screening.**
If you are aged 21–29 years	→	Have a **Pap test every 3 years.**
If you are aged 30–65 years	→	Have a **Pap test** + an **HPV test (co-testing) every 5 years** (preferred) or a **Pap test alone every 3 years.**
If you are 65 years or older	→	**You do not need screening** if you have no history of cervical changes and either three negative Pap test results in a row or two negative co-test results in a row within the past 10 years, with the most recent test performed within the past 5 years.

REMEMBER!

- You still need to have screening if you have been vaccinated against HPV.
- You still need to have screening if you have had a hysterectomy and your cervix was not removed.

EXCEPTIONS TO THESE GUIDELINES:

If you were exposed to diethylstilbestrol before birth or have human immunodeficiency virus, a weakened immune system, or a history of cervical cancer	→	You may need **more frequent screening.**
If you have had a hysterectomy in which your cervix was removed and... • you have a history of cervical cancer or moderate to severe cervical changes	→	• **Continue to have screening** for 20 years after your surgery.
• you have no history of cervical cancer or cervical changes	→	• **You do not need screening.**

SEE YOUR OB-GYN ANNUALLY FOR A WELL-WOMAN EXAM.

Even if you are not due for cervical cancer screening, you should still see your ob-gyn each year for birth control counseling, vaccinations, health screenings, preconception care, and the latest information about your reproductive health.

Screening

The most common screening technique for cervical cancer is the Pap test, which is conducted during a gynecological exam. This test can detect pre-cancerous lesions, which helps avoid delays in diagnosis. Screening guidelines recommended by the American College of Obstetricians and Gynecologists are illustrated above.

Sometimes, an HPV DNA test can also be done, with or without a Pap test, to help detect cervical changes that can lead to cancer. If the Pap test shows abnormal cells, a biopsy can be used for diagnosis. Sometimes, the biopsy can completely remove the abnormal tissue and is the only treatment needed.

Further testing and treatment is needed in women with large cervical tumors. Screening is especially important because cervical cancer often has no symptoms. Vaginal bleeding, unusual vaginal discharge, pelvic pain, or pain during sexual intercourse may be symptoms of cervical cancer or other conditions.

Prevention

The Pap test is often reported as a way to prevent cervical cancer, but simply getting the test is not a preventive measure. However, by detecting pre-cancerous cells before they develop into invasive cancer, cervical cancer can be stopped before it really starts.

Other prevention methods include avoiding contact with the human papilloma virus (the main cause of cervical cancer) by avoiding sexual activity or using a barrier method of protection like the male or female condom. These do not prevent the transmission of all types of HPV, but can decrease the HPV infection rate by up to 70% (American Cancer Society, 2016). Vaccines are also available that can help protect against certain HPV infections. These vaccines protect against HPV subtypes 16 and 18, as well as some other subtypes. Since vaccines only prevent HPV infection, and they do not treat existing infections, they need to be given before a person is exposed to HPV through sexual activity. The Centers for Disease Control and Prevention (CDC) recommends the HPV vaccine for preteen boys and girls beginning at age 11 or 12, and continues the recommendation for women through 27 years old and men through age 22. The HPV vaccine is a series of 3 shots given over a period of approximately 8 months, and the CDC recommends receiving the full shot series (CDC, 2016).

Breast Cancer

Breast cancer is the second most common cancer in all women. Overall, breast cancer deaths decreased between the years of 2000–2010, partly due to improved testing and targeted breast cancer treatments.

Risk Factors

The main risk factor for breast cancer is being female. Breast cancer is 100 times less common among men than women (American Cancer Society, 2017). Other risk factors that cannot be changed include:

Support from family and friends is important in early detection and treatment of breast cancer.

Age: 2 out of 3 invasive breast cancers are found in women ages 55 and older

Heredity: Inherited breast cancers comprise about 5–10% of cases and are most commonly caused by a mutation in the BRCA1 or BRCA2 gene. Breast cancers related to these mutations occur more often in young women and frequently affect both breasts.

Race and ethnicity: In women under 45 years old, breast cancer is more common in African-American women. This ethnic group continues to be the most likely to die of breast cancer, but white women are slightly more likely to develop it over their entire lifetime.

Starting menstruation before age 12 or menopause after age 55: Longer lifetime exposure to estrogen and progesterone may increase breast cancer risk.

Lifestyle can also increase breast cancer risk, although it is difficult to determine exact causes. The National Cancer Institute identifies obesity and alcohol consumption as breast cancer risk factors, with risk increasing with the amount of alcohol consumed. More research is needed in the areas of high fat diets, products containing estrogen-like properties (such as some plastics, cosmetics, and pesticides), oral contraceptives, secondhand smoke, and shift work that affects melatonin levels. These controllable risk factors are currently considered areas with unclear effects on breast cancer risks. Researchers have also disproved controversial risk factors, such as antiperspirants, bras, abortion, and breast implants. None of these products or events increase breast cancer risk (American Cancer Society, 2016).

Screening

The purpose of screening for breast cancer is to find the cancer before it causes symptoms (like a lump that can be felt). Finding early-stage cancer during the screening process leads to early detection, which is finding and diagnosing a disease before symptoms start. Treatment is more successful when breast cancer is detected at an early stage. Screening guidelines for breast cancer are based on screening technique efficacy, the patient's risk factors, and age. For women under 40 years old with no symptoms and average risk, the National Comprehensive Cancer Network (NCCN) recommends a clinical breast exam every 1–3 years and breast awareness. Breast awareness involves women being familiar with their breasts and promptly reporting changes to a healthcare provider (NCCN, 2016)

For women over 40 years old, the NCCN recommends an annual clinical breast exam and an annual screening mammogram. The American Cancer Society states that screening should continue as long as a woman is in good health and expected to live 10 or more years.

Prevention

Prevention of breast cancer is difficult to determine; therefore the term "protective" factors is more often used. Certain steps can be taken to protect women against or delay the development of breast cancer:

Decreasing the length of time a woman's breast tissue is exposed to estrogen may help prevent breast cancer. Early pregnancy (full term pregnancy before age 20) is more protective than no pregnancy at all or first pregnancy after age 35. Estrogen levels may also be lower when a woman is breastfeeding.

Women who exercise four or more times a week also have a lower risk of breast cancer. The effect is most evident in premenopausal women with low or normal body weight.

Cancer prevention trials continue to be conducted to study ways to lower the risk of developing certain types of cancer, including breast cancer (NCI, 2016).

Testicular Cancer

Testicular cancer is not very common, affecting 1 in 263 males at some point in his lifetime (American Cancer Society, 2017). Males ages 15–34 are most likely to develop testicular cancer. This type of cancer can occur in one or both testicles, and the majority develops in germ cells, which are the cells that make sperm. Treatment is usually highly successful with early detection.

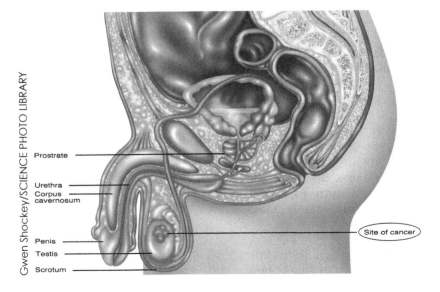

Gwen Shockey/SCIENCE PHOTO LIBRARY

Prostrate

Urethra
Corpus
cavernosum

Penis

Testis

Scrotum

Site of cancer

Risk Factors

Research has not identified specific risk factors that absolutely lead to testicular cancer. Some men will demonstrate several risk factors, while others may have none of them. Possible risk factors include:

Cryptorchidism (undescended testicle): In most males, the testicles descend from the abdomen into the scrotum before birth. Sometimes, a male baby is born with one or both testicles still housed in his abdomen. The body usually corrects this on its own before the child turns one. Other times, a procedure called orchiopexy is performed to surgically move the testicles into the scrotum. Testicular cancer risk is slightly higher in men who were born with one or both testicles undescended.

Orchiopexy may help decrease the risk if it is performed when the child is young, but research has not proven effectiveness of the procedure as a child ages. If testicular cancer does occur, it may occur in either the undescended or descended testicle. Therefore, a factor related to both testicular cancer and cryptorchidism may be present, and lack of testicle descending may not actually cause the cancer.

Family history of testicular cancer: Familial risk of testicular cancer is quite small. Many men who develop it do not have a family history.

HIV infection: Limited evidence exists that indicates a relationship between HIV, especially AIDS infection, with increased risk of testicular cancer. No other viral or bacterial infections are linked to testicular cancer.

Race/ethnicity: A white man's risk of testicular cancer is about 4–5 times that of other ethnicities. Men living in the United States are more likely than citizens of other nations to be diagnosed with testicular cancer.

As with other types of cancer, controversial or disproven risk factors are often highlighted in the media. Horseback riding and other types of strenuous activity have not been proven to increase the risk of testicular cancer (American Cancer Society, 2016).

Screening

Research indicates that young men, despite their heightened risk of testicular cancer, are largely unaware of screening recommendations. Clinical opportunities are also often missed, as healthcare providers are less likely to discuss testicular self-examinations than breast self-examinations (Ugboma & Aburoma, 2011). A painless lump in the testicles is the most common symptom of testicular cancer, and this can be detected by a testicular exam. As the exam is conducted, it is important for men to remember that it is normal for one testicle to be slightly larger than the other and for one to hang lower than the other. If one testicle seems larger than usual, this change is not necessarily cancer. A doctor can perform an examination or an ultrasound to determine if changes are related to other conditions or a developing cancer.

Prevention

Testicular cancer cannot be prevented, which is why screening methods must be promoted to males beginning at age 15.

Treatment and Fertility

Since testicular cancer treatment affects a reproductive organ, young men may be concerned about their ability to produce or ejaculate healthy sperm after treatment.

Although sperm production usually recovers after cancer treatment, patients should speak with their healthcare provider about the preservation and freezing of sperm before treatment begins for future use. According to the Livestrong Foundation, fertility may be decreased during the two years prior to a testicular cancer diagnosis. Even the cancer-free testicle may not function normally. After treatment men often note improved sperm quality within a few years (Livestrong, accessed 2017).

Skin Cancer

Uncontrolled growth of abnormal skin cells causes skin cancer. This growth is usually due to ultraviolet radiation from the sun or tanning beds triggering mutations in skin cells. These cells rapidly multiply and form malignant tumors. Over the past three decades, more people have had skin cancer than all other cancers combined, with 1 in 5 Americans developing skin cancer throughout their lifetime (Skin Cancer Foundation, 2016). The severity of skin cancers depends on the type. Some of the most common types are listed below:

Basal cell carcinoma: The lowest layer of the epidermis, the basal cell layer (Figure 11.2), is home to the most common type of skin cancer. These cancers usually develop on parts of the body most frequently exposed to the sun, such as the neck and head. The cancerous area can be removed, which decreases the likelihood of it spreading. However, once someone has developed basal cell carcinoma, they are more likely to develop growths in other places.

Squamous cell carcinoma: The second most common type of skin cancer grows in the squamous cells (outer layer of the skin, see Figure 11.2). These also occur on parts of the body often exposed to the sun, such as the face, ears, lips, neck, and back of the hands. Squamous cell cancers are more likely than basal cell cancers to grow deeper into the layers of the skin and spread to other parts of the body. This is still uncommon, especially when the cancerous spots are removed (American Cancer Society, 2016).

FIGURE 11.2

EPIDERMIS

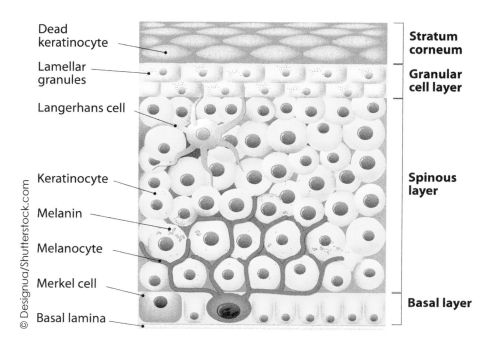

© Designua/Shutterstock.com

Melanoma: This cancer begins in the melanocytes (Figure 11.2), which are cells that make melanin and give skin its brown or tan color. Melanin protects the deeper layers of the skin from the harmful effects of the sun. In most people, melanocytes produce more melanin after sun exposure, causing the skin to darken. Even after cancer develops, these cells still make melanin, which is why the cancerous areas are often brown or black. However, some melanomas do not make any melanin, making those cancerous areas tan, pink, or white. The most common locations for melanoma are the trunk of the body (males), legs (women), neck, face, palms, soles of the feet, and under the nails. Melanoma is much less common than the two other types of skin cancer but it is also more dangerous because of the high likelihood of spreading if not diagnosed early. The number of melanoma cases are increasing each year. (Skin Cancer Foundation, 2016 and National Cancer Institute, 2010).

Risk Factors

According to the Centers for Disease Control and Prevention, the risk factors for all types of skin cancer include:

- A lighter natural skin color.
- Skin that burns, freckles, reddens easily, or becomes painful in the sun.
- Blue or green eyes.
- Blond or red hair.
- Certain types and a large number of moles.
- Family and/or personal history of skin cancer.
- Exposure to the sun through work and play.
- A history of sunburns, especially early in life.
- A history of indoor tanning.

Skin cancers of all types are more common in men than in women, and the risk of melanoma also increases with age.

Genetics determine several of these risk factors, so it is important that individuals limit the risk factors that can be controlled, such as unprotected exposure to the sun and indoor tanning. While everyone's skin can be damaged by the sun's ultraviolet rays, those with skin that burns easily and never or rarely tans are at highest risk (CDC, 2016).

Screening

Changes in the appearance of skin, moles, or other spots on the skin are often the first sign of any type of skin cancer. The US Preventive Services Task Force released a statement in 2016 that included guidelines for self and clinical skin examinations. Patients and clinicians can use the ABCDE rule (Figure 11.3) to look for changes in the skin that are possibly related to cancer:

A = asymmetry (one half of the mole does not match the other half)

B = border irregularity (edges of the mole are ragged, notched, or blurred)

C = color (pigmentation of the mole is not uniform, with varying degrees of tan, brown, or black)

D = diameter of more than ¼ inch (about the size of a pencil eraser)

E = evolving (the mole is changing over time)

(US Preventive Task Force Screening for Skin Cancer, 2016)

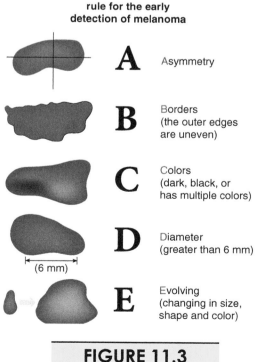

ABCDE
rule for the early
detection of melanoma

A Asymmetry

B Borders (the outer edges are uneven)

C Colors (dark, black, or has multiple colors)

D Diameter (greater than 6 mm)

(6 mm)

E Evolving (changing in size, shape and color)

Modified from © Designua/Shutterstock.com

FIGURE 11.3

Prevention

Avoiding the sun entirely to prevent skin cancer is improbable and impractical. Preventive steps can help ensure an individual's protection from the most harmful rays of the sun while still allowing a normal level of physical activity and time outdoors. The American Cancer Society recommends staying in the shade when the sun's rays are the strongest, which is usually between 10:00 am and 4:00 pm. Clouds, haze, and windows do not block the sun; and snow, sand, and water can reflect rays, intensifying their impact. When individuals do have to be in direct sunlight, protection from clothing and hats can reduce exposure to UV rays. Dark, dry, tightly-woven fabrics are the most effective. For parts of the body not covered by clothing, sunscreen is the next level of defense. Recommendations from the American Cancer Society include using a broad-spectrum sunscreen (protects against UVA and UVB rays) with a Sun Protection Factor (SPF) of at least 30.

The SPF of a sunscreen is often misunderstood by consumers. While higher numbers do offer increased protection, the differences between strengths are slight. SPF specifically refers to the level of protection provided against UVB rays, which are the ones that most frequently cause sunburns. Protection against UVA rays is not rated, even though these rays are linked to skin cancer and aging. The Skin Cancer Foundation explains SPF numbers this way: "An SPF 15 sunscreen blocks 93 percent of UVB radiation, while an SPF 30 sunscreen blocks nearly 97 percent. Furthermore, higher SPF values offer some safety margin, since consumers generally do not apply enough sunscreen. To evaluate SPFs, testers apply two milligrams of sunscreen per square centimeter of skin. But in everyday life, most people apply from only 0.5 to one milligram per square centimeter of skin. Consequently, the actual SPF they achieve is approximately 1/3 of the labeled value." (Skin Cancer Foundation, 2010).

Avoiding indoor tanning beds is also a crucial step in preventing skin cancer. The National Council on Skin Cancer Prevention released a statement in 2014 regarding the risks and regulation of indoor tanning. This group, along with the US Department of Health and Human Services and the World Health Organization, lists indoor tanning devices as a cause of skin cancer and warns that these cause serious health risks not limited to cancer (such as burns and eye damage). Use of indoor tanning beds is closely linked with the development of melanoma, especially if use is frequent and begins before age 30. The American Academy of Dermatology reports that "even one indoor tanning session can increase users' risk of developing squamous cell carcinoma by 67 percent and basal cell carcinoma by 29 percent." (American Academy of Dermatology, accessed 2017)

College students seem to be at increased risk of tanning bed use simply due to the ease of access. A 2014 article in USA Today reported that nearly half of the nation's top colleges offer indoor tanning facilities either on campus or in off-campus housing units. Some of these facilities offer free, unlimited tanning to students (Carlotti, 2014). The temptation to tan is brought on by pressure to have a "glow" for social functions or spring break, and the lack of adult supervision. The Skin Cancer Foundation reports that more than half of US college students have tried tanning devices at least once, despite the well-publicized link between tanning and skin cancer (Skin Cancer Foundation, accessed 2017).

With all of the caution about sun safety, the benefits of sun exposure are often neglected. Lifestyle and environmental factors that reduce outdoor activity are the main causes of vitamin D insufficiency, which affects almost 50% of the world's population. Vitamin D is unique because one of its forms is produced by the body following the skin's exposure to UVB light. This fat-soluble vitamin enhances the absorption of dietary calcium and phosphorus and has significant anti-inflammatory effects. Determining the amount of sun exposure necessary for Vitamin D production is complicated; but a general recommendation from the Vitamin D Council is half the amount of time it would take skin to turn pink. A sunburn is never recommended!

Vitamin D3 supplementation is also available; which has to come in the form of vitamins because just a few foods include a small amount of vitamin D (Nair, R. & Maseeh, A., 2012 and Vitamin D Council, 2017).

Brain Tumors

As mentioned in Kelli Joiner's story at the beginning of this section, brain tumors present many different symptoms, treatment recommendations, and prognoses. The following section offers a generalized discussion of the characteristics of brain tumors and related treatments.

Brain and spinal cord tumors are masses of abnormal cells in the brain or spinal cord that have grown out of control. Unlike other types of cancer, the distinction between benign and malignant is slightly less important in the areas of the brain and spinal cord because of the danger of any type of tumor growing on and destroying normal brain tissue. However, benign tumors cannot spread to distant areas as malignant tumors can.

Symptoms

The American Brain Tumor Association identifies the following as symptoms of brain tumors:

- Headaches
- Seizures
- Sensory (touch) and motor (movement control) loss
- Deep venous thrombosis (DVT, or blood clot)
- Hearing loss
- Vision loss
- Fatigue
- Depression
- Behavioral and cognitive (thinking) changes
- Endocrine dysfunction (hormone/gland changes)
  (American Brain Tumor Association, 2014)

Screening

A neurological exam, brain scans (such as CT or MRI), biopsy, and laboratory tests are used to determine the location and type of brain cancer that may be developing. This information also helps establish the grade of the tumor. The lower the grade, the greater the chance of survival. The World Health Organization published a grading system that was adopted for tumor grades, which can be found in Table 11.1 below:

TABLE 11.1 ♦ Tumor Grades

Grade	Malignancy	Appearance	Reproduction
I	Least malignant	Normal	None; surgical removal
II	Slow-growing	Slightly abnormal	Can spread into nearby tissues
III	Malignant	Actively reproducing abnormal cells	Grow into normal brain tissue
IV	Most malignant	Bizarre appearance	Easily grow into normal brain tissue, form new blood vessels

Glial cells: Cells that nourish, protect, and support neurons.

Treatment

Unless they are completely removed or destroyed, all brain tumors can be life-threatening. The location of the tumor in the brain determines the treatment and prognosis.

The most common brain tumors in adults originate in the layers of tissue that surround the outer part of the brain and spinal cord, the meninges. About 3 out of 10 brain tumors start as gliomas, which is a general term for tumors that start in the **glial cells**. Common examples include astrocytomas and oligodendrogliomas.

A team of highly trained healthcare providers is essential to brain tumor removal and treatment. The team must work closely together and communicate with the patient frequently to monitor progress and make changes as needed. The American Cancer Society identifies these specialties as possible members of a brain tumor treatment team:

- Neurosurgeon—usually the head of the team
- Neurologist
- Medical oncologist
- Radiation oncologist
- Endocrinologist
- Social worker
- Rehabilitation specialist
- Psychologist

Healthcare providers plan the treatment for the greatest possible chance of success with the lowest possible chance of debilitating side effects. Treatment options for all types of cancer depend on the stage and location of the cancer and the patient's age, health status, and personal choices. Often, treatments are combined to increase the chances of success. Brain tumor treatment can be accomplished through surgery, radiation, chemotherapy, targeted therapy, other types of drugs, clinical trials, and complementary/alternative medicine. With brain tumors in particular, monitoring by a team of healthcare providers continues long after the removal and/or treatment of the tumor, with most patients maintaining this relationship the rest of their lives (American Cancer Society, 2017).

War on Cancer—Developments in Treatment

In its "History of Cancer" document, the American Cancer Society reports that the oldest description of cancer came from an Egyptian textbook from around 3000 BC. The author described cases of tumors or ulcers of the breast that were removed by cauterization with a fire drill. The disease was further described with these words: "There is no treatment". (American Cancer Society, 2014).

Since those ancient days, treatments have (thankfully) evolved. While surgery, chemotherapy, and radiation still remain the most common treatments, research constantly strives for more effective and less invasive therapies. One of the newest types of treatment is referred to as precision, or personalized, medicine. As researchers and doctors learn more about the genetic causes of cancer and the actual genetic makeup of tumors (tumor profiling), they can help determine which therapies individual patients will respond best to and which therapies they cannot handle. Personalized medicine is accomplished by analyzing a particular tumor to determine which combination of drugs will work best. This also helps decrease the overall toxicity to patients because the right combination of medicine can be used the first time, without spending time experimenting with different doses (American Cancer Society, 2015).

Today, cancer patients have more treatment options and fewer side effects than patients who lived decades ago. However, precision

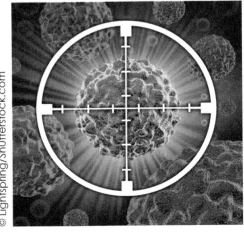

© Lightspring/Shutterstock.com

medicine demands additional research and funding. With continued advancements, the survival rates for all types of cancer have great potential to improve.

"We have two options, medically and emotionally: give up or fight like hell."

– Lance Armstrong

Resources for Young Adults with Cancer

Critical Mass – www.criticalmass.org

15–40 connection – www.15–40.org

Stupid Cancer – www.stupidcancer.org

Livestrong - https://www.livestrong.org/we-can-help/young-adults

Imerman Angels - http://imermanangels.org/

References

American Academy of Dermatology: Indoor tanning (Accessed January 2017). Retrieved from https://www.aad.org/media/stats/prevention-and-care

American Brain Tumor Association: Brain Tumor Symptoms. (2014). Retrieved from http://www.abta.org/brain-tumor-information/symptoms/

American Brain Tumor Association: Tumor Grading and Staging. (2014). Retrieved from http://www.abta.org/brain-tumor-information/diagnosis/grading-staging.html

American Cancer Society: Breast Cancer Risk Factors You Cannot Change (18 August 2016). Retrieved from http://www.cancer.org/cancer/breastcancer/moreinformation/breastcancerearlydetection/breast- cancer-early-detection-risk-factors-you-cannot-change

American Cancer Society: Can Cervical Cancer be Prevented? (2016 December 9) Retrieved from http://www.cancer.org/cancer/cervical-cancer/prevention-and-early-detection/can-cervical-cancer-be- prevented.html

American Cancer Society: Early History of Cancer. (12 June 2014). Retrieved from http://www.cancer.org/cancer/cancer-basics/history-of-cancer/what-is-cancer.html

American Cancer Society: Personalized Medicine: Redefining Cancer and its Treatment. (3 April 2015). Retrieved from https://www.cancer.org/latest-news/personalized-medicine-redefining-cancer-and-its- treatment.html

American Cancer Society: Treating Brain and Spinal Cord Tumors in Adults. (2017). Retrieved from https://www.cancer.org/cancer/brain-spinal-cord-tumors-adults/treating.html

American Cancer Society: What Are Basal and Squamous Cell Skin Cancers? (10 May 2016). Retrieved from http://www.cancer.org/cancer/skincancer-basalandsquamouscell/index

American Cancer Society: What are the Key Statistics About Breast Cancer in Men? (5 January 2017). Retrieved from http://www.cancer.org/cancer/breastcancerinmen/detailedguide/breast-cancer-in-men- key-statistics

American Cancer Society: What are the Key Statistics About Testicular Cancer? (6 January 2017). Retrieved from: https://www.cancer.org/cancer/testicular-cancer/about/key-statistics.html

American Cancer Society: What are the Risk Factors for Cervical Cancer? (2016 December 5). Retrieved from http://www.cancer.org/cancer/cervical-cancer/causes-risks-prevention/risk-factors.html

American Cancer Society: What are the Risk Factors for Testicular Cancer? (12 February 2016) Retrieved from: https://www.cancer.org/cancer/testicular-cancer/causes-risks-prevention/risk-factors.html

American Cancer Society: What Causes Cancer? (2014 June 25). Retrieved from http://www.cancer.org/cancer/cancer-causes.html

Carlotti, P (2014). Tanning beds dangerously accessible on college campuses. *USA Today College.* Retrieved from http://college.usatoday.com/2014/11/06/tanning-beds-dangerously-accessible-on- college-campuses/

Centers for Disease Control and Prevention: HPV Vaccine (2016 December 13). Retrieved from https://www.cdc.gov/hpv/parents/vaccine.html

Centers for Disease Control and Prevention: What are the Risk Factors for Skin Cancer? (25 August 2016). Retrieved from: https://www.cdc.gov/cancer/skin/basic_info/risk_factors.htm

Livestrong Foundation: Male Fertility Preservation. (Accessed January 2017). Retrieved from: https://www.livestrong.org/we-can-help/just-diagnosed/male-fertility-preservation

Nair, R. & Maseeh, A. (2012). Vitamin D: the "sunshine" vitamin. *Journal of Pharmacology and Pharmacotherapuetics.* 3(2): 118–126. DOI: 10.4103/0976-500X.95506

National Cancer Institute: Alcohol and Cancer Risk. (2013 June 24). Retrieved from https://www.cancer.gov/about-cancer/causes-prevention/risk/alcohol/alcohol-fact-sheet

National Cancer Institute: Breast Cancer Prevention – Patient Version (13 October 2016). Retrieved from: https://www.cancer.gov/types/breast/patient/breast-prevention-pdq#section/_12

National Cancer Institute: Oral Contraceptives and Cancer Risk (21 March 2012). Retrieved from https://www.cancer.gov/about-cancer/causes-prevention/risk/hormones/oral-contraceptives-fact- sheet#r15

National Cancer Institute: Skin Cancer (Including Melanoma) – Patient Version (accessed January 2017). Retrieved from: https://www.cancer.gov/types/skin

National Comprehensive Cancer Network: Breast Cancer Screening and Diagnosis (27 July 2016). Retrieved from: https://www.nccn.org/professionals/physician_gls/pdf/breast-screening.pdf

SEER Training Modules, *Cancer Classification.* US National Institutes of Health, National Cancer Institute. Accessed May 2016. Retrieved from https://training.seer.cancer.gov/disease/categories/classification.html

SEER Training Modules, *Cancer Risk Factors.* US National Institutes of Health, National Cancer Institute. Accessed May 2016. Retrieved from https://training.seer.cancer.gov/disease/cancer/risk.html

Skin Cancer Foundation: Does a higher-SPF sunscreen always protect your skin better? (2010). Retrieved from http://www.skincancer.org/skin-cancer-information/ask-the-experts/does-a-higher-spf-sunscreen- always-protect-your-skin-better

Skin Cancer Foundation: Skin Cancer Information (2016). Retrieved from http://www.skincancer.org/skin-cancer-information

Ugboma, H.A.A. & Aburoma, H.L.S. (2011). Public awareness of testicular cancer and testicular self- examination in academic environments: a lost opportunity. *Clinics (Sao Paulo).* 66(7): 1125–1128. DOI: 10.1590/S1807-59322011000700001

U.S. Preventive Services Task Force: Screening for Skin Cancer (July 2016). Retrieved from: https://www.uspreventiveservicestaskforce.org/Page/Document/UpdateSummaryFinal/skin-cancer- screening2

Vitamin D Council: How do I get the vitamin D my body needs? (2017). Retrieved from: https://www.vitamindcouncil.org/about-vitamin-d/how-do-i-get-the-vitamin-d-my-body-needs/

World Health Organization: Cancer. (2015 February). Retrieved from http://www.who.int/mediacentre/factsheets/fs297/en/

Chapter 12
Drug Misuse, Abuse, and Addiction

© Mooid Art/Shutterstock.com

OBJECTIVES

Students will be able to:

- Explain each way drugs can enter the body and how method of exposure affects rate of action, potential for addiction.
- Explain how the brain communicates using neurotransmitters and how drugs interfere with brain communication.
- Identify the dangers of misusing each type of drug.
- Explain the factors related to addiction and current research avenues for addiction treatment.

Adaptation of *Health and Fitness: A Guide to a Healthly Lifestyle*, 5th Edition, by Laura Bounds, Gayden Darnell, Kirstin Brekken Shea, and Dottiede Agnor. Copyright © 2012 by Kendall Hunt Publishing Company.

"Quitting smoking is easy, J've done it hundreds of times."

—Mark Twain

Introduction

A **drug** is defined as a chemical compound or substance that can alter the structure and function of the body. These drugs may be legal or illegal in your community; sold by prescription, over-the-counter, or on the street corner. They may be used responsibly to manage, treat, or cure a medical problem or abused by someone to get high or gain an unfair advantage in the classroom, boardroom, or athletic arena.

America has always had some opposition to the non-medicinal use of drugs. Alcohol and tobacco created outcries throughout the country during colonial times and through the Civil War, which provoked prohibition legislation. Warnings of alcohol and tobacco use did not seem to deter their prevalence in American society.

Early prohibitionists were the precursors to the twentieth century "war on drugs" but it was hard to categorize the variety of substances until Congress passed The Controlled Substance Act in 1970.

Richard Evans, a Professor from the University of Houston, created a model that included teaching students to resist social influences and peer pressure. The slogan "Just Say No" was adopted and The National Institutes of Health supported this model. This program that emerged from the substance abuse model created by Evans, became a campaign throughout college campuses. First Lady, Nancy Reagan, became involved in the program in 1980 during her husband's presidency.

This campaign had a positive outcome with a significant decline in drug use during the late 70's and 80's. However, illicit drug use continues to rise in our country.

The World Health Organization's survey of legal and illegal drug use in 17 countries, including the Netherlands and other countries with less stringent drug laws, shows Americans report the highest level of cocaine and marijuana use.

Despite tough anti-drug laws, the United States has the highest level of illegal drug use in the world.

"Just Say No!" Is it really that simple? The initial decision to use a drug may be a matter of choice, but after the chemistry and structure of the brain is altered by drug abuse, the solution to drug addiction may be more complicated.

Method of Delivery

There are four common ways a drug can enter the body. Chemicals, such as delta-9-tetrahydrocannabinol (THC) from marijuana, are inhaled into the lungs. The drugs that are used each year for a flu vaccine can be **injected** beneath the skin. Prescription antibiotics to treat infection are most commonly **ingested** orally, moving through the digestive system before entering the bloodstream and, eventually, the brain. And hormone therapy can be delivered by **absorption** through the skin. Drugs that are inhaled or injected into the body enter the brain quickly and produce an intense "high" that also dissipates quickly. This short lifespan causes the user to rapidly seek another hit, often increasing exposure to the harmful elements of the drug, as well as the financial cost to maintain the dangerous habit. Drugs that are delivered by ingestion and absorption take a slower route to the brain and generally have a lower addiction risk—one reason this method of delivery is used for addiction treatment medications such as nicotine replacement therapy.

Messaging in the Brain

Your brain is an organ within the central nervous system that is responsible for coordinating and regulating body functions. When you walk, talk, play a game, or learn a new skill your brain is coordinating many body systems to accomplish these tasks. Events such as solving a puzzle, recalling a memory, and understanding a joke are also accomplished in the brain. Let's take a moment to review the ways the brain communicates.

Neuron to neuron: each nerve cell in the brain sends and receives messages in the form of electrical impulses to one another. Similar to having a conversation with a friend or classmate, you talk and listen, sending and receiving messages.

Neurotransmitters: messages between neurons are sent via chemicals called neurotransmitters. Neurotransmitters are released into the space between neurons, called the synapse.

Receptors: to ensure the correct message is transmitted, each neurotransmitter has a specific receptor. Similar to a lock and key, the brain transmits the correct message only after a specific neurotransmitter finds the correct receptor.

Transporters: when a neurotransmitter is released by a cell, transporters recycle it back into the cell, signaling the shut-down of that part of the message, or signal, between neurons.

Drugs, at a most basic level, are chemicals that interfere with messaging in the brain. They may interfere with how messages are sent, received or interpreted. Some drugs, like marijuana and heroin, are so similar that they may fool the brain into believing they are naturally occurring neurotransmitters. They may be similar enough to send the same message, but different enough that the body does not know how to interpret or listen to it, leading to abnormal messaging. As a child, did you ever play the game telephone? Children sit in a circle and whisper the same word from person to person, only to find that the word you began the game with is far different from the word the last person heard. In this childhood game, errors are often made in the interpretation and sending of the message, just as some drugs interfere with the messages the brain is communicating. Other drugs, like amphetamines or cocaine, can cause the nerve cells to release abnormally large quantities of neurotransmitters. In this case, the message is correct, but the volume is drastically different, flooding the communication channels and causing them to malfunction.

Structure and Function in the Brain

Let's take a closer look at structures and functions within the brain which are affected by drugs:

The **brain stem** controls basic autonomic functions that sustain life. For example, when a high volume of alcohol is ingested over a short period of time, there is a risk for alcohol poisoning. Life-sustaining functions, such as respiration, can be depressed, causing breathing to cease and death to occur.

The **limbic system** is the reward circuit, allowing us to feel pleasure. It rewards behaviors that are necessary to our existence, such as food and sex, by making them pleasurable, encouraging us to repeat these behaviors. When drugs are introduced, neurotransmitters such as dopamine may inadvertently reward this behavior by delivering pleasure, (Table 12.1). Can the brain tell the difference between a natural behavior we need to survive, like eating, and a behavior that hurts us, like drug use? Not always. When dopamine is released from drug use it can be two to ten times higher than the amount of reward one might experience from a natural behavior. In some situations, the dopamine is delivered much faster than that from a natural reward, and the pleasure derived from it may also last longer. The experience is much more intense, training our brain to see it as something important, even life-sustaining, and to keep doing it! When a noise is too loud, we seek to turn it down. Similarly, so does the brain. When it is overstimulated by dopamine, it seeks to *turn down the volume* by producing less of the neurotransmitter or providing fewer receptors for it or other neurotransmitters that are affected. The overall impact of this is a person who can no longer feel pleasure as they used to. Eventually, users seek the drug to feel normal, not to feel pleasure, and will likely need more of the drug to reach the desired high, an effect known as **tolerance**.

The **cerebral cortex** is divided into areas that process information from our senses, allowing us to see, hear, feel and taste. The front part of this area, the frontal cortex or forebrain, is where reasoning, thinking, planning and problem-solving takes place. Introducing drugs into this part of the brain is always going to negatively influence decision-making, but is especially risky for those without a fully develop cerebral cortex. Many scientists believe the brain does not fully develop until we reach our mid-to-late twenties.

TABLE 12.1 ♦

Neurotransmitter	Brain Functions	Associated Drugs
Dopamine	Pleasure and reward Movement, Attention, Memory	*All drug abuse directly or indirectly affects the brain's rewards system.* Cocaine. Methamphetamine. Amphetamine
Serotonin	Mood, Sleep, Sexual desire, Appetite	MDMA, LSD, Cocaine
Norepinephrine	Sensory processing, Movement, Sleep, Mood, Memory, Anxiety	Cocaine, Methamphetamine, Amphetamine
Endogenous opioids	Analgesia, Sedation, Rate of bodily functions, Mood	Heroin, Morphine, Prescription painkillers
Acetylcholine	Memory, Arousal, Attention, Mood	Nicotine
Endogenous cannabinoids	Movement, Cognition and memory	Marijuana
Glutamate	increased Neuron activity, Learning, Cognition Memory	Ketamine, Phencyclidine, Alcohol
Gamma- aminobutyric acid (GABA)	Slowed Neuron activity, Anxiety, Memory, Anesthesia	Sedatives, Tranquilizers, Alcohol

National Institute on Drug Abuse

Drug Classification

Drugs, substances, and some specific chemicals used to make drugs are classified into five categories based on acceptable medical use and the drug's abuse or dependency potential (Table 12.2). Schedule I drugs have a very high potential for abuse and no widely accepted medicinal use. Compared with schedule V drugs, which have a very low potential for abuse.

TABLE 12.2 ♦ DEA Schedule of Drugs

Schedule	Definition	Examples
I	Drugs with no currently accepted medical use and a high potential for abuse.	Heroin, LSD, Marijuana, Ecstasy
II	Drugs with a high potential for abuse, with use potentially leading to severe psychological or physical dependence; considered dangerous.	Combination products with less than 15 milligrams of hydrocodone per dosage unit (Vicodin), cocaine, methamphetamine, oxycodone (OxyContin), fentanyl, Adderall, and Ritalin

III	Drugs with a moderate to low potential for physical and psychological dependence. Schedule III drugs abuse potential is less than Schedule I and Schedule II drugs but more than Schedule IV.	Products containing less than 90 milligrams of codeine per dosage unit (Tylenol with codeine), ketamine, anabolic steroids, testosterone
IV	Drugs with a low potential for abuse and low risk of dependence.	Xanax, Valium, Ativan, Ambien, Tramadol
V	Drugs with lower potential for abuse than Schedule IV and consist of preparations containing limited quantities of certain narcotics. Schedule V drugs are generally used for antidiarrheal, antitussive, and analgesic purposes.	Cough preparations with less than 200 milligrams of codeine or per 100 milliliters (Robitussin AC), Lomotil, Motofen, Lyrica, Parepectolin

DEA, https://www.dea.gov/druginfo/ds.shtml

Drugs are often categorized by their effects on the central nervous system.
- **Depressants, tranquilizers** and **sedatives** slow down the central nervous system. In some cases, a drug with this potential can aide in delivering a restful night's sleep, but under other circumstances, such as an overdose of alcohol, the drug can depress and eventually stop vital body systems.
- **Stimulants**, as the name implies, stimulate or increase energy and attention. They also elevate blood pressure, heart rate, and respiration. Common examples include caffeine, nicotine, cocaine, and methamphetamine.
- **Hallucinogens** and **dissociative drugs** are characterized by a profound distortion in one's perception of reality. Examples include LSD, PCP, mescaline, and ketamine.
- **Opioids** are the illicit drug, heroin, and pain killers such as codeine, morphine, fentanyl, oxycodone, and hydrocodone, available by prescription. Opioid pain killers are generally safe, when taken as prescribed, but have a high risk for misuse because of the euphoria experienced along with pain relief.

Commonly Abused Drugs

Alcohol

Ethyl alcohol, or ethanol, is a central nervous system depressant and intoxicating component found in beer, wine, and liquor. The chemical formula is C_2H_5OH.

Ethanol binds directly to neuron receptors and changes neurotransmission. Information is relayed slowly, causing a sedative affects on the brain and body. Long-term abuse irritates and sedates dendrites (nerve endings), causing mood and behavioral changes such as depression, agitation, memory loss, and possibly seizures. With abstinence from alcohol, the dendrites can be repaired and neurotransmitter balance can be restored.

Distributors create ethyl alcohol through a process called fermentation. **Fermentation** is usually the oxidative decomposition of a simple carbohydrate by enzymes in the yeast organism. Depending on the type of beverage, specific yeasts and carbohydrates are used to produce alcohol.

Alcoholic content varies according to the type of drink and the proof of the beverage.

Alcohol slows down the nervous system, impairs vision, and increases the risk of certain cancers, heart, and blood pressure problems.

Types of Drinks

Distilled spirits, or hard liquor, include scotch, gin, rum, vodka, tequila, and whiskey. The alcohol content varies according to the proof of the beverage, which is twice the percent of alcohol. For example, if whiskey is 80 proof, then the beverage is 40 percent alcohol by volume. The average mixed drink contains a 1.0 to 1.5 ounce shot of hard liquor.

Wine usually averages 12 percent alcohol by volume and wine coolers average approximately 5 percent alcohol by volume. The average glass of wine is 4.0 to 5.0 ounces. Wine coolers are usually served in 12 ounce bottles.

Beer is typically served in 12 ounce cans or bottles. The average alcohol content of beer is 4.5 to 5.0 percent by volume. To be considered a beer, the alcohol content must not exceed 5 percent by weight by volume. If the amount of alcohol is greater, it is considered an ale.

12 oz. Beer	5 oz. Wine
× .05	× .12
.60 oz. Alcohol	.60 oz. Alcohol

12 oz. Wine Cooler	1.5 oz Whiskey
× .05	× .40
.60 oz. Alcohol	.60 oz. Alcohol

The alcoholic content of some other typical drinks:

86 Proof Liquor	1 oz.	.43 oz.
Light Beer	12 oz	.46 oz.
Champagne	4 oz.	.58 oz.
Malt liquor	12 oz.	.75 oz.
Margarita	12 oz.	.75 oz.

Blood Alcohol Concentration

Blood Alcohol Concentration (BAC) is a measure of the concentration of alcohol in blood, expressed in grams per 100 ml. For example, 100 mg of alcohol in 10 ml of blood would be reported as .10 percent. The higher the alcohol content of the drink, the higher BAC it will produce. Additional factors influencing a person's BAC are body weight, size of the drink, time spent drinking, and food (Table 12.3). Gender is also a factor in determining one's BAC.

TABLE 12.3 ♦ How to Calculate Your Estimated Blood Alcohol Content/BAC

Showing estimated percent of alcohol in the blood by number of drinks in relation to body weight. This percent can be estimated by:
1. Count your drinks (1 drink *equals* 1 ounce of 100-proof liquor, one five ounce glass of table wine or one 12-ounce bottle of regular beer).
2. Use the chart below and under number of "drinks" and opposite "body weight" find the percent of blood alcohol listed.
3. Subtract from this number the percent of alcohol "burned up" during the time elapsed since your first drink. This figure is .015% per hour. (Example: 180 lb. man—8 drinks in 4 hours / .167% minus (.015 × 4) = .107%

Drinks

Body weight	1	2	3	4	5	6	7	8	9	10	11	12
100 lb.	.038	.075	.113	.150	.188	.225	.263	.300	.338	.375	.413	.450
110 lb.	.034	.066	.103	.137	.172	.207	.241	.275	.309	.344	.379	.412
120 lb.	.031	.063	.094	.125	.156	.188	.219	.250	.281	.313	.344	.375
130 lb.	.029	.058	.087	.116	.145	.174	.203	.232	.261	.290	.320	.348
140 lb.	.027	.054	.080	.107	.134	.161	.188	.214	.241	.268	.295	.321
150 lb.	.025	.050	.075	.100	.125	.151	.176	.201	.226	.251	.276	.301
160 lb.	.023	.047	.070	.094	.117	.141	.164	.188	.211	.234	.258	.281
170 lb.	.022	.045	.066	.088	.110	.132	.155	.178	.200	.221	.244	.265
180 lb.	.021	.042	.063	.083	.104	.125	.146	.167	.188	.208	.229	.250
190 lb.	.020	.040	.059	.079	.099	.119	.138	.158	.179	.198	.217	.237
200 lb.	.019	.038	.056	.075	.094	.113	.131	.150	.169	.188	.206	.225
210 lb.	.018	.036	.053	.071	.090	.107	.125	.143	.161	.179	.197	.215
220 lb.	.017	.034	.051	.068	.085	.102	.119	.136	.153	.170	.188	.205
230 lb.	.016	.032	.049	.065	.081	.098	.115	.130	.147	.163	.180	.196
240 lb.	.016	.031	.047	.063	.078	.094	.109	.125	.141	.156	.172	.188

Source: National Highway Traffic Safety Administration.

Intoxication

Intoxication is defined as a transient state of physical and mental disruption due to the presence of a toxic substance, such as alcohol (Maisto, 2005). As BAC increases, the central nervous system alters behavior and physical function. Change can occur as low as 0.02 BAC in some people, while everyone is impaired to some degree at 0.05 BAC (Table 12.4).

TABLE 12.4 ♦ Blood Alcohol Level and Behavioral Effects

BAC%	Behavioral Effect(s)
0.02–0.03	Alcohol starts to relax the drinker.
0.04	Often drinkers at this stage are relaxed, happier, chatty.
0.05	Skills begin to diminish, as far as judgment, attention, and control. Decision-making ability (such as whether to drive) is impaired, as are sensory-motor skills.
0.08	All states recognize this as the legal point of intoxication. Driving skills and coordination are impaired.
0.10–0.125	Several effects are likely at this point, such as balance, vision, speech, and control problems. Reaction time increases.
0.12–0.15	Peripheral vision is diminished, so less detail is visible. Balance and coordination are problematic. A sense of tiredness, displays of unstable emotions, diminished perception, memory, and comprehension are seen at this level. A person may vomit if not accustomed to drinking or if this BAC level has been reached too quickly.
0.18–0.25	Often the drinker is in a state of apathy and lethargy, and is less likely to feel pain. Vision is certainly diminished in the areas of color, form, motion and dimensions. Drinkers are intense with emotions, confused, dizzy, and disoriented. Walking is often difficult or impossible as muscle coordination is diminished and speech is slurred.
0.25–0.30	Drinkers may lose consciousness during this stage. They have almost completely lost motor functions, have little response to stimuli, can't stand or walk, and experience vomiting and incontinence.
0.30–0.50	Once the BAC reaches 0.45 percent, alcohol poisoning is almost always fatal, and death may occur at a level of 0.37 percent. Unconsciousness, diminished or absent reflexes, lower than normal body temperature, circulatory and respiratory problems and incontinence commonly occur.

Source: Susan J. Hewlings and Dennis M. Medeiros, *Nutrition: Real People, Real Choices,* 2nd Edition. Kendall Hunt Publishing Company, 2011.

Tolerance

Tolerance is when an individual adapts to the amount consumed so that larger quantities are needed to achieve the same effect. This can take place over several months or years of consuming alcohol, depending on the amount consumed and at what age the individual begins to drink. At some point, after a person's tolerance has increased over a period of time, it begins to drop, allowing the effects of alcohol to be felt after only a few drinks. This **reverse tolerance** is caused by the natural aging process or liver disease after years of abusive drinking (Dennis and the Texas Commission of Alcohol and Drug Abuse, 2005).

Digestion and Metabolism

The human body absorbs alcohol quickly (Figure 12.1). From the stomach and small intestine, alcohol enters the blood stream. With a full stomach, alcohol enters the blood stream at a slower rate when compared to an empty stomach.

The liver is the only organ capable of metabolizing alcohol. Ninety percent of alcohol is metabolized through the oxidation process of the liver, at a rate of .015 percent per hour. The lungs and kidneys eliminate the remaining ten percent. For the average individual, the rate of elimination will reduce a given BAC by .015 per hour.

FIGURE 12.1

Alcohol Absorption and Elimination

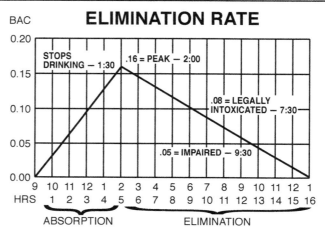

Source: Texas Commission on Alcohol and Drug Abuse

Alcohol dehydrogenase converts alcohol to acetaldehyde. Alcohol is then metabolized at approximately 0.25 to 0.30 ounces per hour, regardless of the blood alcohol concentration. The rate of metabolism is based on the activity of alcohol dehydrogenase, working at its own pace (Ray and Kisr, 1999).

Women do not process alcohol as well as men. There are two biological factors contributing to this principle. Women have a higher percentage of fat mass compared to men. Alcohol is soluble in oils, so molecules permeate the membranes of cells quickly and easily. This results in a faster rate of absorption and a higher BAC for women. Additionally, men produce more alcohol dehydrogenase than women; therefore, men can eliminate alcohol at a slightly faster rate (Dennis and the Texas Commission on Alcohol and Drug Abuse, 2005).

The National Institute on Alcohol Abuse and Alcoholism (NIAAA) found that the earlier young people begin to drink alcohol, the more likely they are to become an alcohol abuser or alcoholic. According to the report:

- Young people who start drinking before age 15 are four times more likely to become an alcoholic than if they start after age 21.
- Forty percent who drink before age 15 become alcohol dependent; 10 percent if they wait until 21.
- Fourteen percent decreased risk of alcoholism for each year drinking is delayed until age 21.

Alcoholism

Alcoholism, also known as alcohol dependence, is a chronic, progressive disease with symptoms that include a strong need to drink and continued drinking despite repeated negative alcohol-related consequences. There are four symptoms generally associated with alcoholism:

1. a craving or a strong need to drink,
2. impaired control or the inability to limit one's drinking,
3. a physical dependence accompanied by withdrawal symptoms such as nausea, sweating, shakiness, and anxiety when alcohol use is stopped, and
4. an increased tolerance.

Can alcoholism be hereditary? Alcoholism has a biological base. The tendency to become an alcoholic is inherited. Men and women are four times more likely to become alcoholics if their parents were (NIAAA, 2008). Currently, researchers are finding the genes that influence vulnerability to alcohol. A person's environment may also play a role in drinking and the development of alcoholism. This is not destiny. A child of an alcoholic parent will not automatically develop alcoholism, and a person with no family history of alcohol can become alcohol dependent.

There are ways to avoid becoming alcohol dependent. It is important to know your limit and stick to it. If choosing to drink, drink slowly and alternate an alcoholic beverage with a non-alcoholic beverage, eat while drinking, and most importantly find more effective ways of dealing with problems instead of turning to alcohol.

If you feel this is a problem, the sooner you stop the better the chances of avoiding serious psychological effects.

- Admit to your drinking—first step in avoiding serious problems.
- Change your lifestyle—try to stay out of situations where alcohol is prominent until you can control your drinking.
- Get involved in self-help groups.

How can you tell if someone has a drinking problem? An individual does not have to be an alcoholic to have problems with alcohol. Problems linked to abuse are neglecting work, school, or family responsibilities. Legal issues such as alcohol violations and drinking-and-driving-related problems can also be a result of alcohol abuse. There are many "red flags" that can point to a problem with alcohol. One way is to answer these questions developed by Dr. John Ewing:

- Have you ever felt you should CUT down on your drinking?
- Have people ANNOYED you by criticizing your drinking?
- Have you ever felt bad or GUILTY about your drinking?
- Have you ever had a drink first thing in the morning to steady your nerves or to get rid of the hangover ("EYE OPENER")?

To help remember these questions, notice that the first letter of each key word spells CAGE. One "yes" answer suggests a possible alcohol problem. More than one "yes" means it is highly likely that a problem exists (Ewing, 1995).

Other signs and symptoms also could indicate that a person could be misusing or abusing alcohol or other drugs. One or two of them does not necessarily point to a problem, but several, combined with the right circumstances, need to be addressed. Some of these signs may include a grade decline or a sudden drop in grades, frequently missing class because of hangovers, binge drinking, legal problems associated with alcohol, or a significant increase in tolerance to alcohol. Other major signs of a drinking problem could be frequently drinking alone, drinking to forget about personal problems, or avoiding activities where alcohol is not available. Another more serious physical sign of alcohol abuse is a **blackout**. This occurs when an individual has amnesia about events after drinking, even though there was no loss of consciousness.

Chronic Effects

Drinking too much alcohol can cause a wide range of chronic health problems including liver disease, cancer, heart disease, nervous system problems, as well as alcoholism.

Although moderate amounts of alcohol may not be harmful, there are some major health issues associated with chronic alcohol use and abuse.

- *Liver disease* is commonly associated with alcohol abuse. The liver has many vital functions in the body. It is a common mistake for people to think that only those individuals who abuse alcohol can harm the liver. Individuals who are heavy social drinkers may run the risk of liver damage as well.
- *Hepatotoxic trauma* or "fatty liver" is the most common alcohol-related disorder causing enlargement of the liver. Some damage can be reversed if alcohol is completely avoided.
- *Alcoholic hepatitis* is an enlarged and tender liver with an elevation of white blood cells. Symptoms can include nausea, vomiting, abdominal pain, fever, and jaundice. If alcohol use continues, this could progress to cirrhosis.
- *Alcohol cirrhosis* results from continued alcohol use and may cause permanent scar tissue to form when the liver cells are damaged. This problem usually occurs in 10 to 15 percent of people who consume large quantities and can develop in as little as five years of heavy drinking.
- *Alcohol pellagra* is a deficiency of protein and niacin. Symptoms may include skin inflammation, gastrointestinal disorders, diarrhea, and mental and nervous disorders.
- *Malnutrition* occurs from a lack of needed nutrients through prolonged alcohol consumption, by depressing the appetite and attacking the lining of the stomach. Heavy drinkers do not get the calories they need, which triggers increased mineral loss and increases fatty acids because of the interference of the transfer of glucose into energy.
- *Polyneuritis* is a condition caused by thiamin deficiency, which causes inflammation of several nerves and causes the drinker to become weak and have a tingling sensation.
- *Cancers*—It is established that 2 to 4 percent of all cancer cases could be caused by alcohol use. Cancer of the upper digestive tract such as mouth, esophageal, pharynx, and larynx can be attributed to alcohol use. Liver cancer as well as breast cancer may be caused by excessive alcohol consumption. Studies indicated that a woman's risk of developing breast cancer increases with age and alcohol consumption (JAMA, 1995).
- *Fetal alcohol syndrome.* The alcohol crosses the placenta but experts don't know exactly how drinking causes problems for the fetus. It may directly affect the fetus or it may be acetaldehyde, the metabolic by-product of alcohol that is harmful to the fetus. Some researchers believe that alcohol effects on the placenta cause blood flow and nutrient deficiencies. Whatever the reason, drinking during pregnancy clearly puts infants at risk for birth defects (Herman, 2003).

Neurological disorders associated with alcohol use are:

- *Wernickes disease* is caused by a thiamine deficiency. Some symptoms include decreased mental functions, double vision, and involuntary oscillation of the eyeballs.
- *Korsakoff's syndrome* is caused by a B complex vitamin deficiency. Symptoms are amnesia, personality alterations, and a loss of reality. This person may become apathetic and have difficulty walking.

Societal Problems

The dangers of alcohol consumption are a major problem in our society. Drinking too much alcohol can cause a range of very serious problems, in addition to the obvious health issues. Alcohol is a contributing factor in motor vehicle accidents, violence, and school/work problems, as well as family problems.

Alcohol Use in College

The legal drinking age in all states is 21 years old, but that does not mean individuals under 21 do not consume alcohol. Studies suggest that substance use, including alcohol, tobacco, and other drug use, is common among college-aged youth. Students who use any of these substances are at significantly greater risk than non-substance using peers to: drive after drinking and with a driver who has been drinking, and are less likely to use a seatbelt. These consistently poor and risky choices increase their risk of being in a motor vehicle crash and having crash-related injuries (Everett, 1999). College students and administrators struggle with the problems associated with alcohol abuse, binge drinking, and drunk driving.

The National Institute on Alcohol Abuse and Alcoholism (NIAAA) reports that 1,825 college students, between the ages of 18 and 24, die annually from alcohol-related unintentional injuries, including motor vehicle crashes. Another 599,000 between the ages of 18 and 24 are injured, assaulted by a drinking student. And approximately 97,000 students are victims of alcohol-related sexual assault or date rape. (NIAAA, 2017)

A Snapshot of Annual High-Risk College Drinking Consequences (NIAAA, 2010)

Academic Problems: About 25 percent of college students report academic consequences of their drinking including missing classes, falling behind, doing poorly on exams or papers, and receiving lower grades overall.

Police Involvement: About 5 percent of 4-year college students are involved with the police or campus security as a result of their drinking, and 110,000 students between the ages of 18 and 24 are arrested for an alcohol-related violation such as public drunkenness or driving under the influence.

Alcohol Abuse and Dependence: 31 percent of college students met criteria for a diagnosis of alcohol abuse and 6 percent for a diagnosis of alcohol dependence in the past 12 months, according to questionnaire-based self-reports about their drinking.

Binge Drinking

The National Institute on Alcohol Abuse and Alcoholism defines **binge drinking** as a pattern of drinking that brings a person's blood alcohol concentration to .08 or above. This typically happens when men consume five or more drinks and women consume four or more drinks in about two hours (NIAAA, 2010). Binge drinkers usually experience more alcohol-related problems than their non-drinking counterparts. These problems affect their health, education, safety, and interpersonal relationships. According to the Harvard School of Public Health College Alcohol Study, these problems include driving after drinking, damaging property, getting injured, missing classes, and getting behind in school work. According to the same Harvard study, one in five students surveyed experienced five or more different alcohol-related problems and more than one-third of the students reported driving after drinking.

The study also found that the vast majority of non-binge drinking students are negatively affected by the behavior of binge drinkers. It was reported that four out of five students who were non-binge drinkers and who lived on campus experienced secondary effects of binge drinking such as being the victim of a sexual assault or an unwanted sexual advance, having property vandalized, and having sleep or study interrupted.

Michael Wagener Story

On August 3, 1999, Michael Wagener, a student at Texas A&M University celebrating his 21st birthday, died as a result of alcohol poisoning. He was an intelligent and insightful young man with many friends and his whole life ahead of him. He was not an alcoholic, nor did he abuse alcohol. Michael was typically a responsible drinker.

On August 2nd, the eve of his 21st birthday, friends joined Michael at a local establishment. While having a few beers, some friends bought him a couple of shots for his birthday. His friends had bought him eight or nine (four-ounce) shots in a matter of thirty to forty-five minutes. Michael had many friends who wanted to share in his celebration; no one wanted him to die.

By the time he was taken home, Michael's body had begun to shut down. He could no longer move and had to be carried into the house. His friends thought they had taken all the precautions: designated driver, turn him on his side in case he vomits. They even stayed the night to ensure his safety.

At 7:00 a.m. his mother called to wish Michael a happy birthday. The call stirred his friends. At 7:10 a.m. the call was made to 911—Michael never woke up. One fun-filled night of celebration turned deadly.

This can happen to anyone. Consuming excessive amounts of alcohol, even one night, can kill you. We often think the only way alcohol can kill is if someone drinks and drives or abuses alcohol for many years. Educating yourself about alcohol will help you make informed decisions and hopefully prevent this tragedy from occurring again.

Alcohol Poisoning

The most serious consequence of binge drinking is alcohol poisoning. Alcohol overdose can be lethal.

The most serious consequence of binge drinking is **alcohol poisoning.** This results when an overdose of alcohol is consumed. When excessive amounts of alcohol are consumed, the brain is deprived of oxygen, which causes it to shut down the breathing and heart rate functions.

Some symptoms of alcohol poisoning are:

- Person does not respond to talking, shouting, or being shaken.
- Person cannot stand up.
- Person has slow, labored, or abnormal breathing—less than eight breaths/minute or ten or more seconds between each breath.
- Person's skin feels clammy.
- Person has a rapid pulse rate and irregular heart rhythm.
- Person has lowered blood pressure.
- Vomiting.

If you think a friend is experiencing alcohol poisoning, do not wait for all symptoms to be present—seek medical attention immediately. Stay with the person until help arrives. Turn the victim onto one side in case of vomiting.

Choking to death on one's own vomit after an alcohol overdose is quite common. Death by asphyxiation occurs when alcohol depresses and inhibits the gag reflex to the point that the person cannot vomit properly. **Do not leave the victim alone.** Be honest in telling medical staff exactly how much alcohol the victim consumed. This is an extreme medical emergency and one that is a matter of life and death. Some states have passed legislation providing limited immunity for a minor who calls 911 for someone who is a possible victim of alcohol poisoning.

> For more information on 911 Lifeline Legislation visit awareawakealive.org

Drinking and Driving

Driving under the influence of alcohol is the most frequently committed and deadliest crime in America. In the Federal Bureau of Investigation's (FBI) Uniform Crime Report, more than 1.4 million people were arrested in 2009 for alcohol-impaired driving. The National Highway Traffic Safety Administration (NHTSA) reported in 2009 that 10,839 people were killed in alcohol impaired driving crashes. This is 32 percent of the nation's total traffic fatalities for the year. The 10,839 deaths in 2009 represent an average of one alcohol-related fatality every 22 minutes (NHTSA, 2011). Even small amounts of alcohol impair driving (Table 12.5).

Drunk driving is no accident; it is a crime. The greatest tragedy is that these crashes are preventable, predictable, and 100 percent avoidable.

Although most drivers involved in fatal crashes have no prior convictions for DUI, about one-third of all drivers arrested for DUI are repeat offenders, which greatly increases their risk of causing a drunk driving accident. As a nation, we have seen a downward trend in alcohol-related fatalities. Today, all states have lowered their legal level of intoxication to .08 BAC. All states have some form of the zero tolerance law, as well as an open container law. These laws, in addition to stricter enforcement of existing laws, have helped in

TABLE 12.5 ◆ The Affects of Blood Alcohol Concentration

Blood Alcohol Concentration (BAC)	Typical Effects	Predictable Effects on Driving
.02%	Some loss of judgment, relaxation, slight body warmth, altered mood	Decline in visual functions (rapid tracking of a moving target), decline in ability to perform two tasks at the same time (divided attention)
.05%	Exaggerated behavior, may have loss of small-muscle control (e.g., focusing your eyes), impaired judgment, usually good feeling, lowered alertness, release of inhibition	Reduced coordination, reduced ability to track moving objects, difficulty steering, reduced response to emergency driving situations
.08%	Muscle coordination becomes poor (e.g., balance, speech, vision, reaction time, and hearing), harder to detect danger, judgment, self-control, reasoning, and memory are impaired	Concentration, short-term memory loss, speed control, reduced information processing capability (e.g., signal detection, visual search), impaired perception
.10%	Clear deterioration of reaction time and control, slurred speech, poor coordination, and slowed thinking	Reduced ability to maintain lane position and brake appropriately
.15%	Far less muscle control than normal, vomiting may occur (unless this level is reached slowly or a person has developed a tolerance for alcohol), major loss of balance	Substantial impairment in vehicle control, attention to driving task, and in necessary visual and auditory information processing

changing behavior. High school and university education programs, such as non-alcoholic activities for prom nights and designated driver organizations, have also contributed in raising awareness to combat such a serious problem.

The NHTSA and the Advertising Council's Innocent Victims public service campaign stresses the need to get the keys from someone who is about to drive. Here are some tips:

- If it is a close friend, try to use a soft, calm approach. Suggest to them that they have had too much to drink and it would be better if someone else drove, or call a cab.
- Be calm. Joke about it. Make light of it.
- Try to make it sound like you are doing them a favor.
- If it is somebody you do not know well, speak to their friends; usually they will listen.
- If it is a good friend, tell them if they insist on driving, you are not going with them.
- Locate their keys while they are preoccupied and take them away. Mostly they will think they lost them and will be forced to find another mode of transportation.
- Avoid embarrassing the person or being confrontational.

Tobacco

The U.S. Surgeon General reported in 1970 that cigarette smoking is dangerous to your health. Over the years we have come to realize just how dangerous. Cigarette smoking is the leading preventable cause of death in the United States, responsible for one in five deaths annually. Through study after study, reports have proven that tobacco use is one of the biggest public health issues that faces the world today (CDC, 2006).

Tobacco Components

The toxic components of tobacco include tar, nicotine, and carbon monoxide. **Tar** is a by-product of burning tobacco. Its composition is a dark, sticky substance that can be condensed from cigarette smoke. Tar contains many potent carcinogens and chemicals that irritate tissue in the lungs and promote chronic bronchitis and emphysema. These substances paralyze and destroy the cilia that line the bronchi, causing "smoker's cough." Long-term exposure of extremely toxic tar to lung tissue can lead to the development of cancer.

Nicotine is a colorless, oily compound that is extremely poisonous in concentrated amounts. This highly addictive drug is a major contributor to heart and respiratory diseases causing short-term increases in blood pressure, heart rate, and blood flow from the heart, resulting in narrowing of the arteries. A strong dependence on nicotine can occur after as little as three packs of cigarettes, and it is more addictive than cocaine or heroin. Because of its addictive effects, the Food and Drug Administration (FDA) has determined nicotine should be regulated.

At first, nicotine acts as a stimulant and then it tends to tranquilize the nervous system. The effects depend largely on how one chooses to smoke. Shallow puffs seem to increase alertness because low doses of nicotine facilitate the release of acetylcholine, which creates feelings of alertness. Long, deep drags tend to relax the smoker because high doses of nicotine block the flow of acetylcholine. Ninety percent of the nicotine inhaled while smoking is absorbed into the body, while 20 to 30 percent of nicotine is absorbed if the smoke is drawn only into the mouth, not the lungs.

Other side effects include inhibiting formation of urine, discoloration of the fingers, dulling the taste buds, and irritating the membranes in the mouth and throat. Because nicotine constricts blood vessels, it causes the skin to be clammy and have a pallid appearance, as well as reducing body temperature (see Figure 12.2 for more effects). The highly addictive nature of nicotine can

One drop of pure nicotine can be fatal. Nicotine poisoning has been reported from accidental ingestion of insecticides by adults, as well as ingestion of tobacco products by children and pets. Death usually results from paralysis and respiratory failure within a few minutes.

FIGURE 12.2

The Health Effects
of Smoking

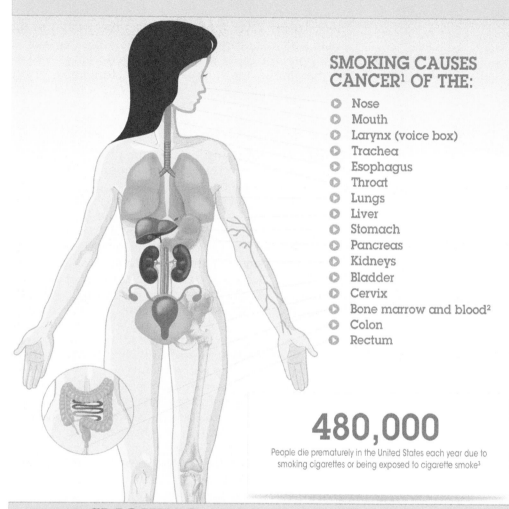

CIGARETTE SMOKE AFFECTS YOUR BODY

SMOKING CAUSES CANCER[1] OF THE:

- Nose
- Mouth
- Larynx (voice box)
- Trachea
- Esophagus
- Throat
- Lungs
- Liver
- Stomach
- Pancreas
- Kidneys
- Bladder
- Cervix
- Bone marrow and blood[2]
- Colon
- Rectum

480,000

People die prematurely in the United States each year due to
smoking cigarettes or being exposed to cigarette smoke[3]

SMOKING ALSO AFFECTS YOUR

AUTOIMMUNE SYSTEM
- Chrohn's Disease[4]
- Rheumatoid Arthritis[5]
- Type 2 Diabetes

HEART
- Plaque Buildup in Your Arteries[6]
- Aneurysms[7]
- Coronary Heart Disease[8]
- Heart Attack[9]
- Peripheral Arterial Disease[10]
- Stroke[11]

BLOOD
- Increased Blood Pressure[17]
- Changes to Blood Chemistry[18]
- Thickened Blood Vessels[19]

VISION
- Macular Degeneration[14]
- Optic Nerve Damage[15]
- Blindness[16]

BONES
- Osteoporosis[12]
- Bone Loss[13]

LUNGS
- Chronic Obstructive Pulmonary Disease[20]
- Emphysema[21]
- Chronic Bronchitis[22]
- Pneumonia[23]
- Asthma
- Tuberculosis

REPRODUCTIVE SYSTEM
- Preterm Birth
- Stillbirth
- Ectopic Pregnancy
- Erectile Dysfunction
- Orofacial Clefts

www.BeTobaccoFree.gov

1 http://cancer.gov/cancertopics/types/commoncancers
2 http://www.cdc.gov/tobacco/data_statistics/sgr/2010/consumer_booklet/pdfs/consumer.pdf
3 http://www.cdc.gov/chronicdisease/resources/publications/aag/osh.htm
4 http://raredisease.info.nih.gov/GARD/Condition/10232/QnA/19275/Crohns_disease.aspx
5 http://www.cdc.gov/arthritis/basics/rheumatoid.htm#4
6 http://www.niams.nih.gov/health_info/bone/Osteoporosis/Conditions_Behaviors/bone_smoking.asp
7 http://www.niams.nih.gov/health_info/bone/Osteoporosis/Conditions_Behaviors/bone_smoking.asp
8 http://www.nhlbi.nih.gov/health/health-topics/topics/sma/
9 http://www.cdc.gov/tobacco/data_statistics/sgr/2010/consumer_booklet/pdfs/consumer.pdf
10 http://www.nhlbi.nih.gov/health/health-topics/topics/sma/
11 http://www.cdc.gov/tobacco/data_statistics/sgr/2010/consumer_booklet/pdfs/consumer.pdf
12 http://www.nhlbi.nih.gov/health/health-topics/topics/sma/
13 http://www.cdc.gov/tobacco/data_statistics/sgr/2010/consumer_booklet/pdfs/consumer.pdf
14 http://www.cdc.gov/tobacco/data_statistics/sgr/2010/consumer_booklet/index.htm
15 http://www.cdc.gov/tobacco/data_statistics/sgr/2010/consumer_booklet/index.htm
16 http://www.cdc.gov/tobacco/data_statistics/sgr/2010/consumer_booklet/index.htm
17 http://www.nei.nih.gov/healthyeyes/eyehealthtips.asp
18 http://www.nei.nih.gov/healthyeyes/eyehealthtips.asp
19 http://www.nei.nih.gov/healthyeyes/eyehealthtips.asp
20 http://www.nhlbi.nih.gov/health/health-topics/topics/copd/
21 http://www.cdc.gov/tobacco/data_statistics/sgr/2010/consumer_booklet/index.htm
22 http://www.cdc.gov/tobacco/data_statistics/sgr/2010/consumer_booklet/index.htm
23 http://www.cdc.gov/tobacco/data_statistics/sgr/2010/consumer_booklet/index.htm

cause withdrawal symptoms to occur quite suddenly. These symptoms include irritability, anxiousness, hostility, food cravings, headaches, and the inability to concentrate.

Carbon monoxide is an odorless, tasteless gas that is highly toxic. It reduces the amount of oxygen the blood can carry, causing shortness of breath. Carbon monoxide ultimately damages the inner walls of the arteries, thus encouraging a buildup of fat on the walls of the arteries; this is called atherosclerosis. Over time, this causes the arteries to narrow and harden, which may lead to a heart attack.

Approximately 1 percent of cigarette smoke and 6 percent of cigar smoke is carbon monoxide. It impairs normal function of the nervous system and is partially responsible for the increased risk of heart attacks and strokes in smokers.

Types of Tobacco Use

Cigarette smoking greatly impairs the respiratory system and is a major cause of chronic obstructive pulmonary diseases (COPD), including emphysema and chronic bronchitis.

Problems associated with cigarette smoking include mouth, throat, and other types of cancer, cirrhosis of the liver, stomach, and duodenal ulcers, gum and dental disease, decreased HDL cholesterol and decreased platelet survival and clotting time, as well as increased blood thickness.

Cigarette smoking increases problems such as heart disease, atherosclerosis, and blood clots. It increases the amount of fatty acids, glucose, and various hormones in the blood, cardiac arrhythmia, allergies, diabetes, hypertension, peptic ulcers, and sexual impotence. Smoking doubles the risk of heart disease, and those who smoke have only a 50 percent chance of recovery. Smokers also have a 70 percent higher death rate from heart disease than non-smokers (CDC, 2006). Smoking also causes cardiomyopathy, a condition that weakens the heart's ability to pump blood.

Life expectancy of smokers parallels smoking habits in that the younger one starts smoking and the longer one smokes, the higher the mortality rate. Also, the deeper smoke is inhaled and the higher the tar and nicotine content, the higher the mortality rate. On average, smokers die 13–14 years earlier than non-smokers (CDC, 2012).

The risk and mortality rates for lip, mouth, and larynx cancers for **pipe and cigar smoking** are higher than for cigarette smoking. Pipe smoke, which is 2 percent carbon monoxide, is more irritating to the respiratory system than cigarette smoking, but for those who do not inhale, the risk for developing cancer is just as likely.

Cigars have recently gained popularity in the United States among younger men and women with approximately 4.5 billion cigars consumed yearly.

Electronic cigarettes, battery-operated devices that deliver nicotine, have become popular in the U.S. over the past 10 years. While the device does create a vapor instead of the smoke that is inhaled from a traditional cigarette, the smoker is still exposed to nicotine and other harmful chemicals. Yet, many believe they are a safer alternative to traditional cigarettes. In reality, a lot is still unknown about the safety of e-cigarettes. As of January 2017, clinical studies focusing on safety have not been submitted to the U.S. Food and Drug Administration, (FDA), and the device remains unregulated. Without regulation of electronic cigarettes, it is difficult for consumers to know exactly which chemicals are in the cartridges they use and how much nicotine a device is delivering to its user.

Clove cigarettes are erroneously believed to be safer because they do not contain as much tobacco. In actuality, clove cigarettes are most harmful because they contain **eugenol**, which is an active ingredient of clove. Eugenol deadens sensations in the throat, which allows smokers to inhale more deeply and hold smoke in the lungs longer.

© Gemenacom, 2014. Used under license from Shutterstock, Inc.

Clove cigarettes also contain twice as much tar, nicotine, and carbon monoxide as most moderate brands of American cigarettes.

Once thought of as a less harmful way to smoke tobacco, **water pipes** have regained popularity in many cities across the United States. In 2005 the World Health Organization (WHO) published its findings emphasizing the harmful effects of waterpipe smoking, also known around the world as narghile, shisha, goza, and hookah. For centuries, smokers have been lead to believe that water pipe smoking is a safer alternative to cigarette smoking, but research shows that this method exposes the smoker to high rates of lung cancer and heart disease, as well as other tobacco-related diseases. There is also a high risk of communicable diseases like tuberculosis and hepatitis because of shared mouthpieces (WHO, 2005).

When smoking tobacco through a water pipe, some nicotine is absorbed as it passes through a water bowl. Because most smokers stop when their nicotine craving has been satisfied, this may actually lead to longer smoking sessions, exposing the user to more smoke over a longer period of time (see Figure 12.3).

Some water pipe products and accessories are marketed and sold with claims of reducing the harmful effects of hookah, but according to the WHO, none have been shown to reduce the smoker's risk of exposure to toxins.

Smokeless tobacco comes in two forms: snuff and chewing tobacco. Snuff is a fine grain of tobacco, and chewing tobacco is shredded or bricked; either choice is placed in the mouth and the user sucks on the tobacco juices, spitting out the saliva. The sucking allows the nicotine to be absorbed in the bloodstream.

The younger someone is when they start smoking, and the longer they continue to smoke, the greater their chance of dying from a smoking-related illness.

Smokeless Tobacco Users

Check Monthly for Early Signs of Disease

The early signs of cancer in the mouth and tongue may be detected by self-examination. Dr. Elbert Glover, director of the Tobacco Research Center at West Virginia University, and the American Cancer Society recommend that the following self-check procedures be conducted every month.

- Check your face and neck for lumps on either side. Both sides of your face and neck should be the same shape.
- Look at your lips, cheeks, and gums. Look for sores, white or red patches, or changes in your gums by pulling down your lower lip. Check your inner cheeks, especially where you hold your tobacco. Gently squeeze your lip and cheeks to check for lumps or soreness.
- Put the tip of your tongue on the roof of your mouth. Place one finger on the floor of your mouth and press up under your chin with a finger from your other hand. Feel for bumps, soreness, or swelling. Check around the inside of your teeth from one side of your jaw to the other.
- Tilt your head back and open your mouth wide. Check for color changes or bumps or sores in the roof of your mouth.
- Stick out your tongue and look at the top. Gently grasp your tongue with a piece of cloth and pull it to each side. Look for color changes. Feel both sides of your tongue with your finger for bumps.

If you use smokeless tobacco and find anything that looks or feels unusual, see your dentist or physician as soon as possible.

From Decisions for Healthy Living by Pruitt, Stein and Pruitt, Addison Wesley Longman Educational Publishers, Inc.

FIGURE 12.3

Comparison of Cigarette Smoking Session and Water Pipe Smoking Session

Cigarette Smoking Session	Water Pipe Smoking Session
8–12 puffs	50–100 puffs
5–7 minutes	20–80 minutes
0.5–0.6 liter of smoke inhaled	.015–1.0 liter of smoke inhaled

Note: Upon analysis, it is possible for a water pipe session to expose the smoker to the equivalent of up to one hundred cigarettes in a single session.

More than $96 billion of total U.S. healthcare costs each year are directly related to smoking. However, this estimate does not take into account the costs related to care for those who are burned in smokingrelated fires, perinatal care for low-birthweight babies born to mothers who smoked during pregnancy, and diseases caused by secondhand smoke. A more accurate estimate of the total cost to the healthcare system is likely more than $193 billion annually.

It can be equally as dangerous and harmful as smoking. Smokeless tobacco is addictive. According to the Centers for Disease Control and Prevention (CDC) estimates, 6.1 percent of high school students are current smokeless tobacco users. Nationally, an estimated 3.5 percent of adults are current smokeless tobacco users. (CDC, 2009).

The National Cancer Institute reports there are three thousand chemical compounds in smokeless tobacco. Nicotine is the addictive drug in all forms of tobacco. Holding one pinch of smokeless tobacco in your mouth for thirty minutes delivers as much nicotine as three to four cigarettes (National Cancer Institute, 2011). There have been at least twenty-eight cancer-causing agents found in smokeless tobacco:

- Nitrosamines—20 to 43,000 more nitrosamines are found in smokeless tobacco. Other consumer products like beer or bacon only contain five parts per billion
- Polonium 210—radioactive particles that turn into radon
- Formaldehyde—embalming fluid
- Cadmium—metallic element; its salts are poisonous
- Arsenic—poisonous element

Immediate effects from chewing tobacco are bad breath and stains on your teeth. Mouth sores also accompany smokeless tobacco users. The complications of long-term use can be very serious. These complications include increased gum and teeth problems, increased heart rate, irregular heartbeat, heart attacks, and cancer. Oral cancer can occur in the mouth, lips, tongue, cheeks, or gums. Other cancer possibilities resulting from smokeless tobacco can be stomach cancer, bladder cancer, and cancer of the esophagus.

Another major problem caused by smokeless tobacco is **leukoplakia**, a precancerous condition that produces thick, rough, white patches on the gums, tongue, and inner cheeks. A variety of cancers such as lip, pharynx, larynx, esophagus, and tongue can be attributed to smokeless tobacco. Dental and gum problems are major side effects as well. Smokeless tobacco used during pregnancy increases the risk for preeclampsia, a condition that includes high blood pressure, fluid retention, and swelling. It also puts the mother and newborn at higher risk for premature birth and low birth weight. In men, smokeless tobacco reduces sperm count and increases the liklihood of abnormal sperm cell. (CDC, 2010).

Environmental Tobacco Smoke

Environmental tobacco smoke (ETS), or secondhand smoke, contains more than 7,000 chemicals, including hundreds that are toxic and 70 carcinogens. Secondhand smoke exposure to non-smoking adults can cause heart disease, a 20–30 percent increased risk of lung cancer, and a 25–30 percent increased risk of heart attacks. Approximately 126 million non-smokers are exposed to secondhand smoke in homes, workplaces, and public places, resulting in an estimated

There is no "risk-free" exposure to secondhand smoke.

© Jonathan Brizendine, 2012, Shutterstock, Inc.

FIGURE 12.4

The benefits you experience when you quit smoking begin almost immediately and continue over many years.

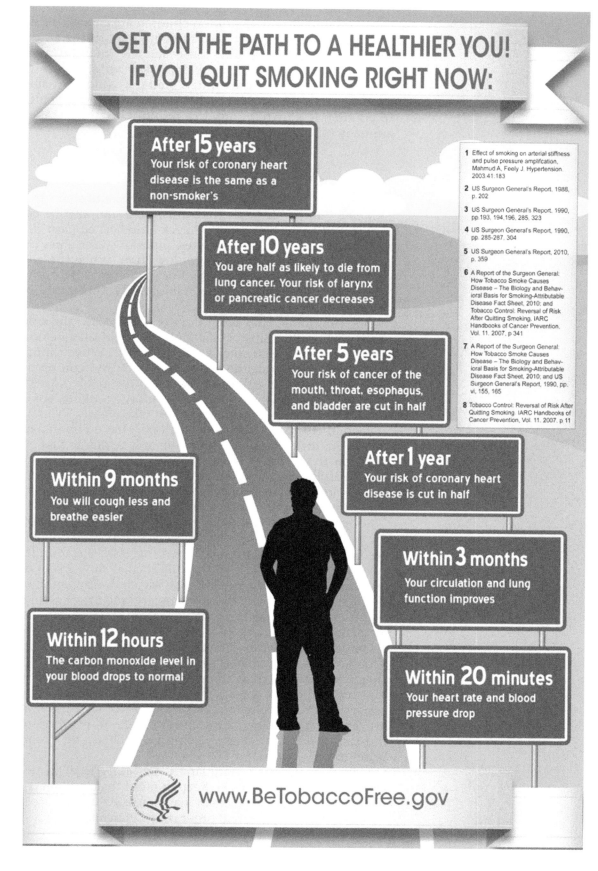

38,000 deaths and healthcare costs exceeding $10 billion annually. To those individuals with existing health issues, second-hand smoke exposure is an extremely high risk. There is no "risk-free" exposure to secondhand smoke; even brief exposure can be dangerous (CDC, 2006).

Secondhand smoke is especially dangerous to infants and children. In the United States, almost 22 million children are exposed to secondhand smoke. Globally almost half of the world's children breathe air polluted by tobacco smoke. This exposure can cause sudden infant death syndrome, acute respiratory infections, ear problems, slow lung growth, and severe asthma attacks. Each year in the United States, secondhand smoke is responsible for an estimated 150,000–300,000 new cases of bronchitis and pneumonia in children less than 18 months, resulting in nearly 15,000 hospitalizations annually (CDC, 2012).

Cannabinoids

Marijuana refers to the dried leaves, flowers, and stems from the hemp plan, *Cannabis Sativa*. Materials from this plant can also be concentrated into a resin called hashish or a sticky, black liquid called *hash oil*. Marijuana can be smoked (inhaled) using cigarettes, pipes or water pipes or it can be infused into foods or brewed into teas for ingestion. When the mind-altering chemical in marijuana, delta-9- tetrahydrocannabinol (THC), is inhaled it enters the bloodstream and travels to the brain quickly. When it is ingested, the drug is absorbed more slowly.

One communication system in the brain, called the endocannabinoid system, functions by using cannabinoid receptors that are normally triggered by naturally occurring chemicals similar to THC. When cannabinoid drugs enter the brain, THC floods the endocannabinoid system, producing the *high* the user feels. The highest concentration of cannabinoid receptors is found in areas of the brain where pleasure, memory, thinking, concentration, sensory and time, and coordinated movement take place.

Beyond effects on the brain, marijuana has additional effects on the body. Damage to the cardiopulmonary system is similar to that of a tobacco smoker: irritation to the lungs, a "smoker's cough," phlegm buildup, and increased risk of respiratory illness and infections. Users also exhibit a 20–100 percent increase in heart rate shortly after use, putting them at increased risk for heart attack in the first hour after smoking marijuana.

Several studies confirm that marijuana users can experience addiction to the drug. Estimates from research suggest approximately nine percent of users become addicted and the likelihood increases the younger you begin to use (about 17 percent) and if you use marijuana daily (25–50 percent). Long-term users trying to quit often experience withdrawal symptoms such as irritability, sleeplessness, decreased appetite, anxiety, and drug cravings.

Currently, legal debate continues from state to state regarding the use of medicinal marijuana. It is categorized as a schedule I drug because there is no widely accepted medicinal use and a rather high rate of abuse and/or addiction. As the *cannabis sativa* plant is grown, there is wide variation in chemicals and potency among producers. Until the FDA can consistently measure and define the chemical makeup of marijuana, it will not likely be approved for medicinal use. Currently, the FDA has approved THC-based drugs to treat pain and nausea. Additional non-psychoactive chemicals from the cannabis plant are also being researched and evaluated for potential benefits.

Recreational use of marijuana is currently legal in seven states and the District of Columbia (2017). Keep in mind that as states continue to vote and pass the legalization of recreational marijuana use, we are likely to see a sharp rise in *impaired* driving and other risky behaviors.

Opioids

Derived from poppy seeds, **opium** is the base compound used for all narcotics. Opiates, which are narcotics, include opium and other drugs derived from opium, such as morphine, codeine, and heroin. Methadone is a synthetic chemical that has a morphine-like action, and also falls into this category of drugs.

Heroin

Heroin is considered a semi-synthetic narcotic because it is derived from a naturally occurring substance in the Oriental poppy plant called opium. It is a highly effective, fast-acting analgesic (painkiller) if injected when used medicinally; however, its benefits are outweighed by its risk of toxicity and high dependence rate. Heroin can be injected, snorted, or smoked. When heroin enters the brain it produces a dream-like euphoria (NIDA, 2010). Abuse is common because this drug creates a strong physical and psychological dependence and tolerance.

The risks of heroin use are increased due to the use of needles for injection. There is an increased likelihood of transmission of communicable diseases like HIV and hepatitis due to the practice of sharing needles. Although abrupt withdrawal from heroin is rarely fatal, the discomfort associated with going "cold turkey" is extremely intense.

Heroin users are at high risk for addiction. Anyone can become dependent, and life expectancy of the heroin addict who injects the drug intravenously is significantly lower than that of one who does not. Overdosing on heroin can result in death within minutes.

Stimulants

Caffeine

Caffeine is a stimulant as well as a psychotropic (mind affecting) drug. Caffeine is generally associated with coffee, tea, and cola, but can also be found in chocolate, cocoa, and other carbonated beverages, as well as some prescription and over-the-counter medications, such as Excedrin®. Approximately 65–180 mg of caffeine are found in one cup of coffee, compared to tea, which contains 40–100 mg per cup, and cola, which contains 30–60 mg per twelve ounce serving. Caffeine is readily absorbed into the body and causes stimulation of the cerebral cortex and medullary centers in the brain, resulting in mental alertness.

Moderation is the key when using caffeine. 300 mg of caffeine is generally considered moderate intake, which is equivalent to approximately three cups of coffee. Some individuals are more sensitive to caffeine than others and may feel the effects at smaller doses.

Caffeine also can cause serious side effects, such as tremors, nervousness, irritability, headaches, hyperactivity, arrhythmia, dizziness, and insomnia. It can elevate the blood pressure and body temperature, increase the breathing rate, irritate the stomach and bowels, and dehydrate the body.

Moderation is the key when using caffeine.

A study by researchers at Duke University Medical Center shows that caffeine taken in the morning has effects on the body that persist until bedtime and amplifies stress throughout the day. In addition to the body's physiological response in blood pressure elevations and stress hormone levels, it also magnifies a person's perception of stress. According to this study, caffeine enhances the effects of stress and can make stress even more unhealthy (Lane, Pieper, Phillips-Butte, Bryant, and Kuhn, 2002).

Excessive amounts of caffeine may increase the incidence of premenstrual syndrome (PMS) in some women and may increase fibrocystic breast disease

How can I reduce my caffeine consumption?

- Keep a log of how much caffeine you consume daily
- Limit your consumption to 200–300 mg/daily
- Substitute herbal tea or decaf coffee
- Stop smoking— caffeine and smoking often go together
- Remember coffee does not help sober up after drinking (McKinley, 2005)

(noncancerous breast lumps) as well. The U.S. Surgeon General recommends that women avoid or restrict caffeine intake during pregnancy. Withdrawal symptoms from caffeine may include headaches, depression, drowsiness, nervousness, and a feeling of lethargy.

In 2015, energy drink and shot sales were over 13 billion in the U.S. College students have been known to use caffeinated products like these for extra energy when studying, driving long distances, or needing more energy in general. A common practice of mixing energy drinks and alcohol is of special concern. Drinking large amounts of caffeine (a stimulant) combined with large amounts of alcohol (a depressant) can cause people to misjudge their level of intoxication. The combination of drugs may mask symptoms such as headache, weakness, and muscle coordination, but in reality visual reaction time and motor coordination are still negatively affected by alcohol. Driving or making any other important decisions under these circumstances can be extremely dangerous.

Cocaine

Cocaine is a naturally occurring psychoactive substance contained in the leaves of the South American coca plant. Crack cocaine, a rock-like crystalline form of cocaine made by combining cocaine hydrochloride with common baking soda, can be heated in the bowl of a pipe, enabling the vapors to be inhaled into the lungs. Cocaine is used occasionally as a topical anesthetic medicinally; however, more commonly it is inhaled (snorted), injected, or smoked illegally. The effects of cocaine use are rapid and short lived (from five to thirty minutes). Snorting enables only about 60 percent of the drug to be absorbed because the nasal vessels constrict immediately. Cocaine use causes dopamine and norepinephrine to be released into the brain, causing a feeling of euphoria and confidence; however, at the same time electrical impulses to the heart that regulate its rhythm are impaired. There is evidence that both psychological and physical dependence on cocaine occurs rapidly.

Today, the smoking of crack cocaine is more prevalent than inhalation. When smoked, the drug reaches the central nervous system immediately, affecting several neurotransmitters in the brain. The effects are short lived (usually around five to ten minutes), leaving the user with feelings of depression. Abuse of this drug can result in convulsions, seizures, respiratory distress, and sudden cardiac failure.

The relatively short-lived "high" from cocaine requires frequent use to maintain feelings of euphoria and is therefore quite costly for the addict. To pay for their habit, addicts will often turn to criminal activities such as dealing drugs, stealing, or prostitution. Crack houses are known for promoting the spread of HIV infection, and thousands of babies are born to crack-addicted mothers. These babies have severe physical and neurological problems, requiring significant medical attention. The cost of this drug is high, not just for the user, but for society as well.

Amphetamines

Amphetamines do not occur naturally and must be manufactured in a laboratory. When used in moderation, amphetamines stimulate receptor sites for two naturally occurring neurotransmitters, having the effect of elevated mood, increased alertness, and feelings of well-being. In addition, the activity of the stomach and intestines may be slowed and appetite suppressed. When amphetamines are eliminated from the body, the user becomes fatigued. With abuse, the user will experience rapid tolerance and a strong psychological dependence, along with the possibility of impotence and episodes of psychosis. When use stops, the abuser may experience periods of depression.

Methamphetamines

An extremely addictive and powerful drug that stimulates the central nervous system is commonly known as "meth." In its smoked form, it is called "crystal," "crank," or "ice." It is chemically similar to amphetamines but much stronger. The effects from methamphetamine can last up to eight hours or in some cases even longer. It comes in many forms and can be injected, inhaled, orally ingested, or snorted.

Methamphetamine is considered to be one of the fastest growing drug in the United States. According to the director of the Substance Abuse and Mental Health Services Administration (SAMHSA), the growth and popularity of this drug is because of its wide availability, easy production, low cost, and highly addictive nature.

Methamphetamine is a psychostimulant but different than others like cocaine or amphetamine. Methamphetamine, like cocaine, results in an accumulation of dopamine. The large release of dopamine is presumed to help the drug's toxic effects on the brain. However, unlike cocaine, which is removed and metabolized quickly from the body, methamphetamine has a longer duration of action, which stays in the body and brain longer, leading to prolonged stimulant effects. Chronic methamphetamine abuse significantly changes the way the brain functions (NIDA, 2010).

Methamphetamine abusers may display symptoms that include violent behavior, confusion, hallucinations, and possible paranoid or delusional feelings, also causing severe personality shifts. These feelings of paranoia can lead to homicidal or suicidal thoughts or tendencies.

Methamphetamines are highly addictive and can be fatal with a single use. The results when overused can cause heart failure and death. Long-term physical effects can lead to strokes, liver, kidney, and lung damage. Abuse can also lead to permanent and severe brain and psychological damage.

Club Drugs

MDMA

MDMA, also known as **ecstasy**, has a chemical structure similar to methamphetamines and mescaline, causing hallucinogenic effects. As a result, it can produce both stimulant and psychedelic effects. In addition to its euphoric effects, MDMA can lead to disruptions in body temperature and cardiovascular regulation causing panic, anxiety, and rapid heart rate. It also damages nerves in the brain's serotonin system and possibly produces long-term damage to brain areas that are critical for thought and memory (NIDA, 2010). Physical effects can include muscle tension, teeth clenching, nausea, blurred vision, and faintness. The psychological effects can include confusion, depression, sleep disorders, anxiety, and paranoia that can last long after taking the drug. It is most often available in tablet form and usually taken orally. Occasionally it is found in powder form and can be snorted or smoked, but it is rarely injected. An overdose can be lethal, especially when taken with alcohol or other drugs, for instance heroin ("H-bomb").

Flunitrazepam

Flunitrazepam is an illegal drug in the United States. In other parts of the world, it is generally prescribed for sleep disorders. The commercial/street name is "Rohypnol."

Flunitrazepam is a tranquilizer, similar to Valium, but ten times more potent, producing sedative effects including muscle relaxation, dizziness, memory loss, and blackouts. A 2-mg tablet is equal to the potency of a six-pack of beer. The effects occur twenty to thirty minutes after use and lasts for up to eight hours.

Rohypnol, more commonly known as "roofies," is a small, white, tasteless, pill that dissolves in food or drinks. It is most commonly used with other drugs, such as alcohol, ecstasy, heroin, and marijuana to enhance the feeling of the other drug. Although Rohypnol alone can be very dangerous, as well as physically addicting, when mixed with other drugs it can be fatal.

It is also referred to as the "date rape" drug because there have been many reported cases of individuals giving Rohypnol to someone without their knowledge. The effects incapacitate the victim, and therefore they are unable to resist an attacker during a sexual assault. It also produces an "anterograde amnesia," meaning they may not remember events experienced while under effects of the drug (NIDA, 2010).

According to the Drug Abuse Warning Network, The Drug Induced Rape Prevention and Punishment Act of 1996 was enacted into federal law in response to the abuse of Rohypnol. This law makes it a crime to give someone a controlled substance without his/her knowledge and with the intent to commit a crime. The law also stiffens the penalties for possession and distribution of Rohypnol and GHB. Used in Europe as a general anesthetic and treatment for insomnia, GHB is growing in popularity and is widely available underground. Manufactured by non-professional "kitchen" chemists, concerns about quality and purity should be considered.

Gamma Hydroxybutyrate (GHB)

GHB is a fast-acting, powerful drug that depresses the nervous system. It occurs naturally in the body in small amounts.

Commonly taken with alcohol, it depresses the central nervous system and induces an intoxicated state. GHB is commonly consumed orally, usually as a clear liquid or a white powder. It is odorless, colorless, and slightly salty to taste. Effects from GHB can occur within fifteen to thirty minutes. Small doses (less than 1 g) of GHB act as a relaxant with larger doses causing strong feelings of relaxation, slowing heart rate, and respiration. It is difficult to estimate a lethal dose, which can lead to seizures, respiratory distress, low blood pressure, and coma.

Dissociative Drugs

Ketamine Hydrochloride

"Special K" or "K" was originally created for use in a medical setting on humans and animals. Ninety percent is legally sold for veterinary use. Ketamine usually comes in liquid form and is cooked into a white powder for snorting. Higher doses produce a hallucinogenic effect and may cause the user to feel far away from their body. This is called a "K-hole" and has been compared to near-death experiences. Low doses can increase heart rate and numbness in the extremities with higher doses depressing consciousness and breathing. This makes it extremely dangerous if combined with other depressants such as alcohol or GHB.

Phencyclidine Hydrochloride

Also known as PCP or angel dust, phencyclidine hydrochloride is sometimes considered a hallucinogen, although it does not easily fit into any category. First synthesized in 1959, it is used intravenously and as an anesthetic that blocks pain without producing numbness. Taken in small doses, it causes feelings of euphoria. The harmful side effects include depression, anxiety, confusion, and delirium. High doses of PCP cause mental confusion, hallucinations, and can cause serious mental illness and extreme aggressive and violent behavior, including murder.

Hallucinogens

Hallucinogens, also called psychedelics, are drugs that affect perception, sensation, awareness, and emotion. Changes in time and space and hallucinations may be mild or extreme depending on the dose, and may vary on every occasion. There are many synthetic as well as natural hallucinogens in use. Synthetic groups include LSD, which is the most potent; mescaline, which is derived from the peyote cactus, and psilocybin, derived from mushrooms, have similar effects.

Lysergic Acid Diethylamide (LSD)

LSD is a colorless, odorless, and tasteless liquid that is made from lysergic acid, which comes from the ergot fungus. It was first converted to lysergic acid diethylamide (LSD) in 1938. In 1943, its psychoactive properties accidentally became known (NIDA, 2009).

Hallucinations and illusions often occur, and effects vary according to the dosage, personality of the user, and conditions under which the drug is used. A flashback is a recurrence of some hallucinations from a previous LSD experience days or months after the dose. Flashbacks can occur without reason, occurring to heavy users more frequently. After taking LSD, a person loses control over normal thought process. Street LSD is often mixed with other substances and its effects are quite uncertain (NIDA, 2009).

Other Compounds/Drugs

Anabolic Steroids

Anabolic androgenic steroids are man-made and very similar to male sex hormones. The word *anabolic* means "muscle building," and *androgenic* refers to masculine. Legally, steroids are prescribed to individuals to treat problems occurring when the body produces abnormally low amounts of testosterone and problems associated with delayed puberty or impotence. Other cases for prescribed steroid use would involve individuals with whom a disease has resulted in a loss of muscle mass (NIDA, 2005).

Although steroids are a banned substance in all professional and collegiate sports, most people who use steroids do so to enhance physical performance in sports or other activities. Some choose to use steroids to improve physical appearance or to increase muscle size and to reduce body fat. Some steroids can be taken orally or injected into the muscle. There are also some forms of steroid creams and gels that are to be rubbed into the skin. Most doses taken by abusers are ten to one hundred times the potency of normal doses used for medicinal purposes.

Consequences from steroid abuse can cause some serious health issues. There can be some problems with the normal hormone production in the individual, which can be very severe and irreversible. Major side effects of steroid abuse can lead to cardiovascular disease, high blood pressure, and stroke because it increases the LDL cholesterol levels while decreasing the HDL levels. There can also be liver damage, muscular and ligament damage, as well as stunted bone growth. In addition to these problems, the side effects for males can be shrinkage of the testes and a reduction in sperm count. For females, steroid use can cause facial hair growth and the cessation of the menstrual cycle.

Research also suggests some psychological and behavioral changes. Steroid abusers can become very aggressive and violent and have severe mood swings. Users are reported to have paranoid and jealous tendencies along with irritability and impaired judgment. Depression has also been linked to steroid use once the individual stops taking the drug, therefore leading to continued use. This depressed state can lead to serious consequences, and in some cases it has been reported to lead to suicidal thoughts (NIDA, 2005).

Inhalants

Inhalants are poisonous chemical gases, fumes, or vapors that produce psychoactive effects when sniffed. When inhaled, the fumes take away the body's ability to absorb oxygen. Inhalants are considered delerients, which can cause permanent damage to the heart, brain, lungs, and liver. Common inhalants include model glue, acetone, gasoline, kerosene, nail polish, aerosol sprays, Pam™ cooking spray, Scotchgard™ fabric protectant, lighter fluids, butane, and cleaning fluids, as well as nitrous oxide (laughing gas). These products were not created to be inhaled or ingested. They were designed to dissolve things or break things down, which is exactly what they do to the body.

Inhalants reach the lungs, bloodstream, and other parts of the body very quickly. Intoxication can occur in as little as five minutes and can last as long as nine hours. Inhaled lighter fluid/butane displaces the oxygen in the lungs, causing suffocation. Even a single episode can cause asphyxiation or cardiac arrhythmia and possibly lead to death.

The initial effects of inhalants are similar to those of alcohol, but they are very unpredictable. Some effects include dizziness and blurred vision, involuntary eye movement, poor coordination, involuntary extremity movement, slurred speech, euphoric feeling, nosebleeds, and possible coma.

Health risks involved with the use of inhalants may include hepatitis, liver and/or kidney failure, as well as the destruction of bone marrow and skeletal muscles. Respiratory impairment and blood abnormalities, along with irregular heartbeat and/or heart failure, are also serious side effects of inhalants. Regular use can lead to tolerance, the need for more powerful drugs, and addiction (NIDA, 2011).

Prescription Drug Abuse

When a drug is prescribed to a patient by a medical professional to treat or manage an illness, condition, or disease, it is viewed by that patient as a literal, or figurative, *life saver*. Those who use medically prescribed drugs from someone else or for an unintended purpose are abusing them. Prescription drug abuse has become a serious epidemic in the United States.

Within the serious, and growing, problem of prescription drug abuse, opioid's account for the highest concentration of issues. The rise in number of prescriptions issued, aggressive marketing of opioids from pharmaceutical companies, and the social acceptance of misuse have all led to an increase of abuse and addiction. Opioid drugs are prescribed to relieve pain. Some examples include hydrocodone, oxycodone, codeine, morphine and fentanyl.

Prescription depressants are sedatives or anxiolytic (anti-anxiety) drugs that depress the central nervous system. Benzodiazepines such as Valium and Xanax and barbituates like Nembutal, Secobarbital, and Phenobarbibtal can be prescribed to releive tension, induce relaxation and sleep, or treat panic attacks. All of these differ in action, absorption, and metabolism, but all produce similar intoxication and withdrawal symptoms.

Prescription depressants can produce both a physical and psychological dependence within two to four weeks. Those with a prior history of abuse are at greater risk of abusing sedatives, even if prescribed by a physician. If there is no previous substance abuse history, one rarely develops problems if prescribed and monitored by a physician. Depressants can be very dangerous, if not lethal, if used in combination with alcohol, leading to respiratory depression, respiratory arrest, and death.

Some of the most commonly abused prescription drugs are pain killers such as morphine, codeine, Oxycodone, Vicodin, and Demerol.

Prescription Opioid Use

Hydrocodone is a narcotic used to relieve pain and suppress cough. This drug, which can lead to both physiological and psychological dependence, saw a dramatic increase in legal sales between 1991 and 2010 with prescriptions topping 100 million (NIDA, 2011). Codeine is a natural derivative of opium. Codeine is medically used as a mild painkiller or a cough suppressant. Although widely used, there is potential for physical dependence. Morphine is the main alkaloid found in opium. It is ten times stronger than opium and brings quick relief from pain. It is most effectively used as an anesthetic during heart surgery, to relieve pain in post-operative patients, and sometimes used to relieve pain for cancer patients. **Oxycodone,** a drug used for moderate to severe pain relief, has a high potential for abuse. Tablets should be take orally, but when crushed and injected intravenously or snorted, a potentially lethal dose is released (FDA, 2004).

According to recent reports from the FDA, a highly abused stimulant among middle and high school students is methylphenidate, commonly known as **Ritalin.** This drug is more powerful than caffeine but not as potent as amphetamines and is prescribed for individuals with attention-deficit/hyperactivity disorders, ADHD, and sometimes to treat narcolepsy. Researchers speculate that Ritalin increases the slow and steady release of dopamine, therefore improving attention and focus for those in need of the increase. "Individuals abuse Ritalin to lose weight, increase alertness and experience the euphoric feelings resulting from high doses" (U.S. Dept. of Justice, 2006). When abused, the tablets are either taken orally or crushed and snorted; some even dissolve the tablets in water and inject the mixture. Addiction occurs when it induces large and fast increases of dopamine in the brain (DOJ, 2006).

Adderall is another stimulant used to treat ADHD as well as narcolepsy. Physical and psychological dependence may occur with this drug. Symptoms of Adderall overdose include dizziness, blurred vision, restlessness, rapid breathing, confusion, hallucinations, nausea, vomiting, irregular heartbeat, and seizures.

Prescription Drug Conclusion

The danger from prescription and over-the-counter drugs is often underestimated by students. Many assume that if the drug is legal and prescribed by a physician, even if for someone else, it must be safe. However, what they fail to realize is that medications and dosages are tailored to each patient and may not be appropriate in the manner they intend to use them.

Addiction and Addiction Research

Have you ever watched someone struggle with a drug addiction from afar, assuming they lacked the self-control or willpower to overcome their addiction? Now that you have a more clear understanding of how drugs interfere with brain communication, I want you to reexamine your beliefs about addiction. **Addiction** is defined as "a chronic, relapsing brain disease that is characterized by compulsive drug seeking and use, despite harmful consequences." In the early stages of drug use, the decision to take drugs is made voluntarily, but as use continues and abuse takes over, physical changes in the brain can be seen. The areas of the brain responsible for judgement, learning and memory, and impulse control are damaged by the drug. Evidence and a better understanding of this damage may help explain to others why an addict continues to use, even through the destruction of his/her health, relationships, and career.

It is difficult to pinpoint why some users may develop a dependence to drugs while others will not. No single factor causes addiction—several factors play a role. "Scientists estimate that genetic factors account for between 40 and 60 percent of a person's vulnerability to addiction, including the effects

The number of prescriptions for opioids, such as hydrocodone and oxycodone products, has escalated from around 76 million in 1991 to nearly 207 million in 2013.

Negative consequences of the increased number of opioid prescriptions:

- Estimated number of emergency department visits involving nonmedical use of opioid analgesics increased from 144,600 in 2004 to 305,900 in 2008.
- Treatment admissions for primary abuse of opiates other than heroin increased from one percent of all admissions in 1997 to five percent in 2007.
- Overdose deaths due to prescription opioid pain relievers have more than tripled in the past 20 years, escalating to 16,651 deaths in the United States in 2010.

FDA Guidelines on How to Use Prescription Drugs Safely:
- Always follow medication directions
- Do not increase or decrease doses without consulting your physician
- Do not stop taking medication on your own
- Do not crush or break pills
- Be clear about the drug's effect on driving and other tasks
- Know the drug's potential interactions with alcohol and other drugs
- Inform your doctor if you have had past problems with substance abuse
- Do not use others' prescription medications, and do not share yours.

Ethical Considerations of Illicit Prescription Use

Gabriel Neal, MD MA (Ethics) FAAFP
Clinical Assistant Professor of Clinical Translational Medicine
College of Medicine, Texas A&M Family Medicine Residency
Texas A&M Health Science Center

The increasing diagnosis of cognitive deficits such as Attention Deficit Disorder over the past two decades has meant that more students are being treated with prescription stimulants (medications that improve cognitive function) such as Ritalin (methylphenidate) and Adderall (amphetamine/dextroamphetamine). While safely treating a cognitive deficit does not raise ethical concern, using the same medications to improve upon normal cognitive function does, and the rise in *illicit* use of prescription stimulants for studying or partying has received significant academic and media attention.1 Surveys of undergraduates suggest that 1–11 % of college students have used prescription stimulants illicitly within the last year,[23] and 13–34% at least once during their lifetime.[45] Students who used prescription stimulants illicitly were significantly more likely to engage in illegal drugs such as marijuana and cocaine as well.[6]

The illicit use of prescription stimulants raises ethical concern in the areas of authenticity (the degree to which a student may take credit for work done) and fairness in the classroom. One may argue that achievements attained by the use of cognitive enhancement are not as authentic as those without enhancement.

A response to the challenge of authenticity is that even with the use of enhancers, some level of study, hard work, and effort is still required, endowing authenticity. Educators will continue to grapple with the issue of authentic student work.

With regard to fairness in the classroom, a student who illicitly uses a prescription to enhance her studying may be able to argue that her ideas are still authentically hers, but it remains to be answered whether it is fair that she use it while other students are denied access to it. In competitive arenas such as the classroom, rules are created to exclude advantages that are of improper magnitude. Consider the use of caffeine. It is well known that caffeine can heighten alertness, but no one complains to the professor if they see someone drinking coffee before an exam. The reason for this is that coffee does not confer benefit of such magnitude that anyone would think it unfair, and caffeine is accessible to any student. But as more potent enhancers emerge, such as prescription stimulants, the rules to ensure fairness may need to be updated. Some have suggested that those using prescription stimulants disclose it when submitting academic work.[7] How professors would grade work differently remains to be seen.

While no one wishes to keep students with legitimate cognitive deficits from receiving proper treatment, students should be concerned about the advantage that illicit use of prescription stimulants offers their classmates; and for those students engaged in illicit use of prescription stimulants, they would do well to consider whether they are cheating themselves out of authentic work and others out of a proper grade.While no one wishes to keep students with legitimate cognitive deficits from receiving proper treatment, students should be concerned about the unfair advantage that illicit use of prescription nootropics offers their classmates; and for those students engaged in illicit use of prescription nootropics, they would do well to consider whether they are cheating themselves out of authentic work and others out of a proper grade.

[1] Smith, M. Elizabeth, and Martha J. Farah. "Are Prescription Stimulants "smart Pills"? The Epidemiology and Cognitive Neuroscience of Prescription Stimulant Use by Normal Healthy Individuals." *Psychological Bulletin* 137 .5 (2011): 717–41. Web.

[2] Boyd, C. J., S. E. Mccabe, J. A. Cranford, and A. Young. "Adolescents' Motivations to Abuse Prescription Medications." *Pediatrics* 118.6 (2006): 2472–480. Web.

[3] Shillington, A. M., M. B. Reed, J.E. Lange, J. D. Clapp, and S. Henry. "College Undergraduate Ritalin Abusers in Southwestern California: Protective and Risk Factors." *Journal of Drug Issues* 36.4 (2006): 999–1014. Web.

[4] Arria, A. M., K. E. O'grady, K. M. Caldeira, K. B. Vincent, and E. D. Wish. "Nonmedical Use of Prescription Stimulants and Analgesics: Associations with Social and Academic Behaviors among College Students." *Journal of Drug Issues* 38.4 (2008): 1045–060. Web.

[5] Desantis, Alan D., Elizabeth M. Webb, and Seth M. Noar. "Illicit Use of Prescription ADHD Medications on a College Campus: A Multimethodological Approach." *Journal of American College Health* 57.3 (2008): 315–24. Print.

[6] McCabe, Sean E, et al. "Non-medical use of prescription stimulants among US college students: prevalence and correlates from a national survey." *Addiction* 100.1 (2005): 96–106. Web.

[7] Farah, M.J., Illes, J., Cook-Deegan, R., Gardner, H., Kandel, E., King P. et al. "Neurocognitive Enhancement: what can we do and what should we do about it?" *Nature Reviews: Neuroscience* 5, May (2004): 421–425.

Contributed by Gabriel Neal, M.D. Copyright © Kendall Hunt Publishing Company.

of environment on gene expression and function." (And the more protective factors a person has may mitigate some of the negative risk factors.) Factors include:

- Environmental factors: if a friend smokes then you will be more likely to smoke and incur the risk for addiction due to regular smoking
- Developmental factors: the earlier the exposure, the higher the risk because the brain is not fully developed
- Genetic, epigenetic, biologic factors: how the brain communicates, genetic predisposition

There are no clear answers to how addictions are formed. Keep in mind, the method of exposure discussed earlier in the chapter makes some drugs more addictive. Drugs that enter the brain quickly, through inhalation and injection, flood the brain with a rush of dopamine causing the high that often also dissipates quickly. Scientists believe that this quick, but short, high leaves the user continually chasing another high.

Also consider, the behavioral addiction that develops with many drugs. For example, cigarette smokers often develop a connection to the smell of a cigarette, feel of the cigarette in their hand, and the accompanying activities where they smoke ("I only smoke when I'm at a bar"). In order to successfully treat this addiction, the user must adequately address the behavioral side of his/her addiction, as well as the physiological symptoms of withdrawal.

The most promising research in addiction treatment is related to non-genetic factors. These strategies focus on continuing to understand how addictive drugs work on the brain and to disrupt a forming addiction. Research into genetic treatments are also continuing, but are much further away. The focus on genetic research is geared toward identifying the most effective treatments and least harmful side effects for an individual, based on genetic makeup.

References

American Heart Association (AHA). *Annual Report.* 2006.

Broadhead, Raymond. (2005). *Synapses and Drugs.* http://outreach.mcb.harvard.edu/lessonplans_S05.htm; Retrieved April 19, 2014.

Center on Addiction and Substance Abuse at Columbia University. Commission on Substances Abuse at Colleges and Universities.

Centers for Disease Control and Prevention. *Behavioral Risk Factor Surveillance System,* 2010.

Centers for Disease Control and Prevention. *National Health Interview Survey,* 2010.

Centers for Disease Control and Prevention. *Smokeless Tobacco,* 2009 and 2010.

Centers for Disease Control and Prevention. *Second Hand Smoke,* 2012.

Centers for Disease Control and Prevention (CDC). Smoking and Tobacco Use. Fast Facts. Atlanta: Author. 2006.

CollegeDrinkingPrevention.gov. *Interactive Body Content.* www.collegedrinkingprevention.gov; Retrieved April 19, 2014.

Dennis, M. E. and the Texas Commission on Alcohol and Drug Abuse. *Instructor Manual, Alcohol Education Program for Minors.* Austin: TCADA. 2005.

Department of Justice. National Drug Intelligence Center. Ritalin Fast Facts, 2006.

Drug Enforcement Agency (2017). Drug Scheduling. Retrieved February 6, 2017, from https://www.dea.gov/druginfo/ds.shtml

Everett, S. A., Lowry, R., Cohen, L. R., Dellinger, A. M. Unsafe motor vehicle practices among substance-using college students. *Accident Analysis,* 1999.

Ewing, J. Detecting Alcoholism: the CAGE Questionnaire. *Journal of the American Medical Association,* 1984.

Herman, A., et al. In an ongoing search to understand the mechanisms of fetal alcohol syndrome. National Institute on Alcohol Abuse and Alcoholism, 2003.

Hewlings, S. J., and Medeiros, D., M. *Nutrition: Real People, Real Choices* (2nd ed). Dubuque, IA:

Hoeger, W. and Hoeger, S. *Principles and Labs for Fitness and Wellness* (5th ed). Englewood, CO: Morton Publishing Company. 1999.

Journal of the American Medical Association. Moderate alcohol intake and lower risk of coronary heart disease, 1994.

Journal of the American Medical Association. Lifetime alcohol consumption and breast cancer risk among postmenopausal women in Los Angeles, 1995.

Kendall/Hunt Publishing Company. 2011.

Lane, J., Pieper, C., Phillips-Butte, B, Bryant, J., and Kuhn, C. Caffeine's Effects Are Long-Lasting and Compound Stress. *Psychosomatic Medicine.* National Institutes of Health, July /August, 2002.

McCusker, R., Goldberger, B., and Cone, E. The Content of Energy Drinks, Carbonated Sodas, and Other Beverages. *Journal of Analytical Toxicology,* Vol. 30, March 2006.

McKinley Health Center. University of Illinois at Urbana-Champaign, 2005.

Mick, Elizabeth. (2005). *The Nervous System Presentation*. http://outreach.mcb.harvard.edu/lessonplans_S05.htm; Retrieved April 19, 2014.

Miller, W., Tonigan, J., Longabaugh, R. Drinking Inventory of Consequences. An instrument for assessing adverse consequences of alcohol abuse. Test manual. Rockville, MD: National Institute on Alcohol Abuse and Alcoholism, 1995.

Miller, E. K., Erickson, C. A., & Desimone, R. Neural mechanisms of visual working memory in prefrontal cortex of the macaque. *Journal of Neuroscience*, 1996.

National Cancer Institute, U.S National Institutes of Health, 2008.

National Highway Traffic and Safety Administration (NHTSA). *Annual Report*. 2010.

National Institute on Alcohol Abuse and Alcoholism. National Institutes of Health. Statistic Snapshot of College Drinking, 2010.

National Institute on Alcohol Abuse and Alcoholism (NIAAA). College Drinking— Changing the Culture. "A Snapshot of Annual High-Risk College Drinking Consequences." 2010.

National Institute on Alcohol Abuse and Alcoholism. National Institutes of Health. Integrative Genetic Analysis Of Alcohol Dependence Using the Genenetwork Web Resources, 2008.

National Institute on Drug Abuse. *Alcohol: Drugs of Abuse*. www.drugabuse.gov/; Retrieved April 19, 2014.

National Institute on Drug Abuse. *Drugs, Brains, and Behavior: The Science of Addiction*. Revised January 2010. www.drugabuse.gov/; Retrieved April 19, 2014.

National Institute on Drug Abuse. *Drug Facts: Marijuana*. Revised January 2014. www.drugabuse.gov/; Retrieved April 19, 2014.

National Institute of Drug Abuse (NIDA). U.S. Dept. of Health and Human Services, 2008.

National Institute on Drug Abuse. Research Report Series: Tobacco/Nicotine. Revised July 2012. www.drugabuse.gov/; Retrieved April 25, 2014.

National Institute on Drug Abuse. The Science of Drug Abuse & Addiction. NIDA Info Facts: Hallucinogens, 2010.

National Institute of Drug Abuse (NIDA). Update on Ecstacy. *NIDA Notes*, Volume 16, Number 5, Dec. 2001.

National Traffic Safety Administration. Traffic Safety Facts. Annual Assessment of Alcohol Related Fatalities, 2012.

NIDA (2007). Impacts of Drugs on Neurotransmission. Retrieved February 8, 2017, from https://www.drugabuse.gov/news-events/nida-notes/2007/10/impacts-drugs-neurotransmission

NIDA (2014). America's Addiction to Opioids: Heroin and Prescription Drug Abuse. Retrieved February 8, 2017, from https://www.drugabuse.gov/about-nida/legislative-activities-testinomy-to-congress/2016/americas-addiction-to-opioids-heroin-prescription-drug-abuse

NIDA (2014). Dr. Joni Rutter Q&A: How Basic Science Is Tackling Addiction. Retrieved February 8, 2017, from https://www.drugabuse.gov/news-events/nida-notes/2014/05/dr-joni-rutter-ga-how-basic-science-tackling-addiction

NIDA (2015). Hallucinogens and Dissociative Drugs. Retrieved January 29, 2017, from https://www.drugabuse.gov/publications/research-reports/hallucinogens-dissociative-drugs

NIDA (2015). Misuse of Prescription Drugs. Retrieved January 29, 2017, from https://www.drugabuse.gov/publications/research-reports/prescription-drugs/stimulants/what-are-stimulants

Ray, O. and Ksir, C. *Drugs, Society, and Human Behavior* (8th ed). New York: WCB McGraw-Hill. 1999.

SAMHSA, National Clearinghouse for Alcohol and Drug Abuse; www.health.org

Taber's Cyclopedic Medical Dictionary – 22ⁿᵈ Ed. (2013)

The International Center for Alcohol Policies. *Annex 1. The Basics about Alcohol.* www.icap.org/; Retrieved April 19, 2014.

The Science of Addiction: Drugs, Brains, and Behavior. National Institute on Drug Abuse, National Institutes of Health, US Department of Health and Human Services, 2010.

U.S. Food and Drug Administration. Prescription Drug Use and Abuse: Complexities of Addiction, 2005.

U.S. Food and Drug Administration. Oxycodone. FDA Statement. Statement on Generic Oxycodone Hydrochloride Extended Release Tablets, 2004.

U.S. Food and Drug Administration, Department of Health and Human Services. FDA Issues Regulation Prohibiting Sale of Dietary Supplements Containing Ephedrine Alkaloids and Reiterates Its Advice That Consumers Stop Using These Products, 2005.

World Health Organization (WHO). *Waterpipe Tobacco Smoking: Health Effects, Research Needs and Recommended Actions by Regulators.* Geneva: Author. 2005.

Chapter 13
Reproduction

© stockyimages/Shutterstock.com

OBJECTIVES

Students will be able to:

- Identify structures and function of the male and female anatomy.
- Outline the process of ovulation and sperm maturation to conception and then to pregnancy.
- Identify the advantages and disadvantages of each method of pregnancy prevention.
- Align pregnancy stages with fetal development.
- Identify symptoms, prevention methods, treatments, and long-term consequences of sexually transmitted infections.

"Most organ systems are crucial for the survival of an individual but not the reproductive system. The overall continuation of the human race, however, depends on the reproductive system functioning properly in a sufficient number of people. The reproductive system is not essential for the survival of an individual and can be nonfunctional in an otherwise healthy individual; in fact, it normally becomes less functional as people age. Hormones produced by the reproductive system are responsible for sex-specific developmental patterns and for differences in behavior. Although most organ systems show little difference between the sexes, reproductive tissues vary significantly by sex. The male reproductive system produces sperm cells and the tissues required to transfer them to the female vagina where they can fertilize eggs. The female reproductive system produces oocytes, or eggs, and tissues that allow for fertilization, fetal development, parturition, and nutrition for the baby after birth.

Even though the male and female reproductive systems show striking differences in structure and function, they also share a number of similarities. Reproductive tissues in both sexes are derived from the same embryonic structures. Reproductive hormones are the same in both sexes, even though they can have different actions, and both have stem cells that are capable of dividing and differentiating into sperm or oocytes."[1]

This chapter will explain the structure and function of male and female anatomy, discuss reproductive hormones, and align pregnancy stages with fetal development. Methods of contraception and sexually transmitted infections will also be explained, in the context of college student health status and decision making.

Male Anatomy

"The external male sexual structures include the penis and scrotum. The **penis** is an organ through which semen and urine pass, and is structured into three main sections: the root, the shaft, and the glans penis (see Figure 13.1). The root attaches the penis within the pelvic cavity at the base, while the shaft, or the tube-shaped body of the penis, hangs freely. The **glans penis** is covered by a loose portion of tissue called the **foreskin**, which may be removed during a surgery known as circumcision. A penis without foreskin is circumcised, while one with the foreskin intact is uncircumcised. Uncircumcised men should gently pull the foreskin back when they bathe to wash the foreskin and tip of the penis. At the base of the glans is a rim known as the corona. On the underside is a triangular area of highly sensitive skin called the frenulum, which attaches the glans to the foreskin. The glans penis is the soft, fleshy, enlarged tissue at the end of the shaft, with the urethral opening at the tip. The **scrotum** is the pouch of skin, which hangs from the root of the penis and holds the two testicles. Covered sparsely with hair, the scrotum is divided in the middle by a ridge of skin, showing the separation of the testes. The surface changes of the scrotum help maintain a moderately constant temperature within the testes (~93 degrees F), which is important for maintaining good sperm production (Crooks and Baur, 2009).

The male internal sexual structures include the testes, epididymus, vas deferens, seminal vesicles, and prostate and Cowper's glands. The **testes** are the reproductive ball-shaped glands inside the scrotum, which are also referred to as testicles. Sperm and hormone production are the two main functions of the testes (Crooks and Baur, 2007). Sperm are formed constantly, beginning during puberty, inside the highly coiled thin tubes called seminiferous tubules within each testis. Between the seminiferous tubules are cells that produce sex hormones. On top of each

1 Source: Crivello, *Human Anatomy and Physiology: A Functional Approach*, Second Edition. Kendall Hunt Publishing Company: 2013.

FRONT VIEW

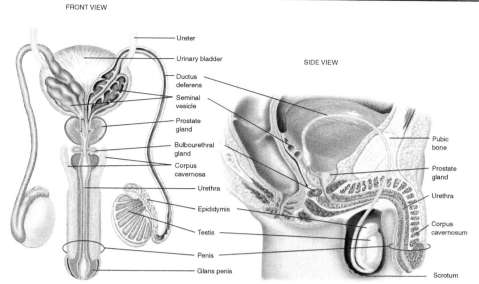

SIDE VIEW

FIGURE 13.1

The Human Male Reproductive System.

From *Biology: Understanding Life,* by Sandra Alters and Brian Alters, John Wiley & Sons, Inc., 2005; permission conveyed through Copyright Clearance Center, Inc.

testis is another tightly coiled tube, the **epididymis**, where nearly mature sperm complete the maturation process (Crooks and Baur, 2009). Mature sperm are stored in the epididymis until they are released during ejaculation. The **vas deferens** is a long tube through which sperm travel during ejaculation. The epididymis is connected to the **seminal vesicle** via the vas deferens, which is responsible for contracting and pushing the sperm to the seminal vesicle. Located beneath the bladder are the two small seminal vesicles, which secrete a fluid that provides nourishment as well as an environment conducive to sperm mobility. After the sperm have combined with the seminal fluid, they reach the prostate where another substance is added. A thin, milky fluid is produced by the prostate and secreted into the urethra during the time of emission of semen, which enhances the swimming environment for the sperm (Crooks and Baur, 2009). Below the prostate and attached to the urethra are the two pea-sized **Cowper's glands**, responsible for depositing a lubricating fluid for sperm and a coating for the urethra. If there are sperm in the urethra from a previous ejaculation, they will mix with the Cowper's fluid and become a pre-ejaculate lubricant fluid. Ejaculation occurs at peak sexual excitement when the prostate muscle opens and sends the seminal fluid to the urethra where it is then forced out through the urethral opening, forming semen."[2]

Each ejaculate contains approximately 5-10 mL of semen, with up to 4 billion total sperm. Many of the sperm are abnormally formed and millions die as they travel through the vaginal and uterine mucus secretions (Crivello, 2013). Sperm can live up to 5 days inside a female (American Pregnancy Association, 2017).

Hormones of the Male Reproductive System

The maturation of sperm in males (spermatogenesis) is regulated by reproductive hormones. These hormones are also involved in puberty, physical development, and sexual response. Three main hormones involved in the male reproductive system are:

> **Follicle-stimulating hormone (FSH)**: stimulates spermatogenesis, which is the process of sperm production.

2 From *Health and Fitness: A Guide to a Healthy Lifestyle,* 5th Edition, by Laura Bounds, Gayden Darnell, Kirsten Brekken Shea, and Dottiede Agnor. Copyright © 2012 by Kendall Hunt Publishing Company.

Luteinizing hormone (LH): stimulates the production of testosterone

Testosterone: assists in spermatogenesis and stimulates the development of male secondary sex characteristics, such as changes in body hair, skeletal muscle mass, fat deposition, voice, and sweat production (SEER Training Modules, 2017).

Age-related changes in the male reproductive system can be caused by a decrease in testosterone production, which begins around age 40. This can lead to a decrease in sperm cell production and an increase in the number of abnormal sperm cells. However, spermatogenesis never completely stops (Crivello, 2013).

Female Anatomy

"The female anatomy consists of multiple integral parts both externally and internally (see Figure 13.2). The **vulva** includes visible external genitalia. The **mons pubis** is the soft fatty tissue covering the pubic symphysis (joint of the pubic bones). This area is covered with pubic hair that begins growing during puberty. The **labia majora** include two longitudinal folds of skin that extend on both sides of the vulva and serve as protection for the inner parts of the vulva. The **labia minora** are the delicate inner folds of skin that enclose the urethral opening and the vagina. These skin flaps, which contain sweat and oil glands, extensive blood vessels, and nerve endings, are hairless and sensitive to touch. When sexually stimulated, the labia minora swell and darken. The **clitoris** is usually the most sensitive part of the female genitalia. The clitoris consists of erectile tissue, which becomes engorged with blood, resulting in swelling during sexual arousal that enables it to double in size. The **clitoral hood** consists of inner lips, which join to form a soft fold of skin, or hood, covering and connecting to the clitoris. The **urethra** is approximately 2.5 cm below the clitoris and functions as the opening for urine to be excreted from the bladder. Because the urethra is located close to the vaginal opening, some irritation may result from vigorous or prolonged sexual activity. The most common problem associated with this is the development of urinary tract infections. The **vagina** is located between the urethral opening and the anus. The **hymen** is the small membrane around the vaginal opening that is believed to tear during initial intercourse, with tampon use, while riding a horse, or other various types of athletic activities. The only function of the hymen is to protect the vaginal tissues early in life. The **perineum** is the smooth skin located between the labia minora and the anus. During childbirth this area may tear or be cut (episiotomy) as the newborn passes out of the vagina. The **anal canal** is located just behind the perineum and allows for elimination of solid waste. The anal canal is approximately an inch long with two sphincter muscles, which open and close like valves.

Internally, just past the vagina, is the cervix, which connects the vagina and the uterus. The uterus is the hollow, pear-shaped muscular organ about the size of a fist when a female is not pregnant. This is the organ in which the fetus develops during pregnancy. The upper expanded portion is referred to as the fundus, and the lower constricted part is the cervix. On each side of the uterus there is a **fallopian tube**, which is quite narrow and approximately four inches in length. Because of the narrow passageway within these tubes, infection and scarring may cause fertility problems. Most women have a right and a left fallopian tube. These tubes extend from the ovaries to the uterus and transport mature ovum. Fertilization usually takes place within the fallopian tubes. The opening between the fallopian tube and the uterus is only about as wide as a needle. On each end of the fallopian tubes are the **ovaries**, where eggs are produced and released usually once a month. Each ovary is about the size

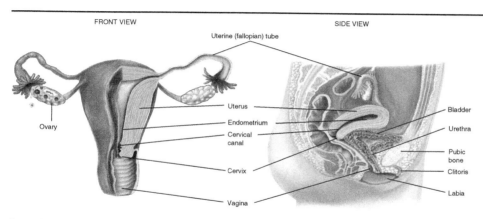

From *Biology: Understanding Life*, by Sandra Alters and Brian Alters, John Wiley & Sons, Inc., 2005; permission conveyed through Copyright Clearance Center, Inc.

FIGURE 13.2

The Human Female Reproductive System.

of a large olive. At birth, a female's ovaries contain 40,000 to 400,000 immature ova, of which approximately 450 will mature and be released during the reproductive years. The ovaries also produce the hormones estrogen and progesterone, both of which help regulate the menstrual cycle (Crooks and Baur, 2009)."[3]

Hormones of the Female Reproductive System

Oogenesis, ovulation, puberty, and the female sexual response are regulated by reproductive hormones. Some of them [these hormones] are similar to the male reproductive hormones, but more are involved in the female process. Figure 13.3 shows the 4 cycles involved in the female reproductive system. This cycle typically lasts 28 days, but can vary from 21–45 days, depending on the woman and factors such as stress and illness.

1. Developing follicles: 0–2 follicles are produced in an ovary each month. When the follicle ruptures, it is forced out of the ovary during ovulation
2. In the beginning of the menstrual cycle, estrogen and progesterone levels are low and almost equal. Around day 7, estrogen begins to increase, which weakens ovarian connective tissue and allows ovulation.
3. Around this same time, the proliferation phase of menstruation is occurring, which is when the lining of the uterus begins to build up in preparation for an implanted fertilized egg
4. Just before ovulation, luteinizing hormone (LH) surges and stimulates a sharp increase in estrogen
5. Follicle stimulating hormone (FSH) also rises and stimulates estrogen production
6. Ovulation, the release of a mature egg out of the ovary, occurs around day 14 of the reproductive cycle
7. and 8. The corpus luteum develops immediately after ovulation in the ovary. It secretes estrogen and progesterone.
9. Another estrogen surge occurs to cause the uterus to grow a functional endometrium and prepare for a pregnancy
10. Progesterone surges, stimulating the endometrium to secrete a protein that prepares it for egg implantation
11. The endometrium becomes twice as thick as normal
12. The pituitary gland decreases FSH and LH levels
13. The corpus luteum becomes inactive, causing the decrease in estrogen and progesterone.

---

3 From *Health and Fitness: A Guide to a Healthy Lifestyle*, 5th Edition, by Laura Bounds, Gayden Darnell, Kirsten Brekken Shea, and Dottiede Agnor. Copyright © 2012 by Kendall Hunt Publishing Company.

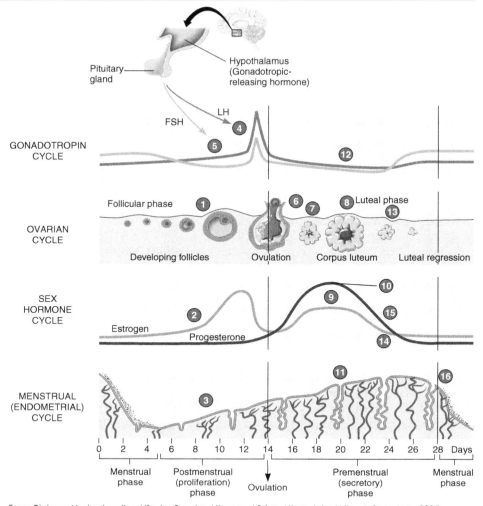

FIGURE 13.3

The Human Menstrual (Reproductive) Cycle.

From *Biology: Understanding Life*, by Sandra Alters and Brian Alters, John Wiley & Sons, Inc., 2005; permission conveyed through Copyright Clearance Center, Inc.

14. and 15. Estrogen and progesterone secretion declines due to the inactive corpus luteum and the decrease in FSH and LH

16. If a fertilized egg has not implanted in the endometrium, the menstrual cycle ends with the sloughing off of the lining, along with blood and other secretions, out of the uterus and through the vagina.

These processes repeat throughout the reproductive years until fertilization or menopause occurs. When a woman reaches her 40s, ovulation occurs less frequently, making the cycles irregular. Less frequent ovulation may be due to women having a limited number of follicles for their lifetime and/or it is caused by follicles being less sensitive to LH and FSH stimulation. This irregular cycle period can last about 10 years, and **menopause** occurs when the menstrual cycle completely stops (Crivello, 2013).

Pregnancy

As an egg travels down the fallopian tube, it has an opportunity to be fertilized by a sperm. If a sperm successfully reaches the egg and penetrates the outer layer, the chromosomes from the egg and sperm come together to form a zygote (as seen in Figure 13.4), which immediately begins dividing. About a week after fertilization, the zygote, now called a blastocyst, can implant in the lining of the uterus (endometrium). Implantation causes the mass of cells to split into two—one half becomes the embryo and the other half becomes the placenta. The placenta is what exchanges nutrients and waste products between the embryo and the mother. At this time, the woman's body also begins secreting **human chorionic gonadotropin (HCG)**, which helps sustain the pregnancy for the first trimester. This hormone is what is detected by home pregnancy tests. The corpus luteum (referenced in Figure 13.3) does not become inactive if the egg is fertilized, so estrogen and progesterone levels remain high to stimulate functional endometrial growth.

Pregnancy is divided into trimesters, each of which lasts approximately 3 months or 13 weeks. The text and pictures below show the fetal development milestones achieved in each trimester.

FIGURE 13.4

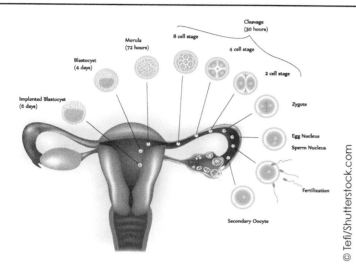

© Tefi/Shutterstock.com

First trimester (week 1-week 12)

At four weeks:

- Your baby's brain and spinal cord have begun to form.
- The heart begins to form.
- Arm and leg buds appear.
- Your baby is now an embryo and one-twenty-fifth inch long.

At eight weeks:

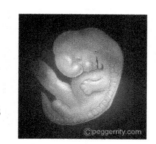

- All major organs and external body structures have begun to form.
- Your baby's heart beats with a regular rhythm.
- The arms and legs grow longer, and fingers and toes have begun to form.
- The sex organs begin to form.

- The eyes have moved forward on the face and eyelids have formed.
- The umbilical cord is clearly visible.
- At the end of eight weeks, your baby is a fetus and looks more like a human. Your baby is nearly 1 inch long and weighs less than one-eighth ounce.

At 12 weeks:

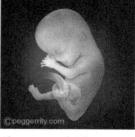

- The nerves and muscles begin to work together. Your baby can make a fist.
- The external sex organs show if your baby is a boy or girl. A woman who has an ultrasound in the second trimester or later might be able to find out the baby's sex.
- Eyelids close to protect the developing eyes. They will not open again until the 28th week.
- Head growth has slowed, and your baby is much longer. Now, at about 3 inches long, your baby weighs almost an ounce.

Second trimester (week 13-week 28)

At 16 weeks:

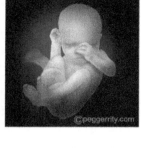

- Muscle tissue and bone continue to form, creating a more complete skeleton.
- Skin begins to form. You can nearly see through it.
- Meconium (mih-KOH-nee-uhm) develops in your baby's intestinal tract. This will be your baby's first bowel movement.
- Your baby makes sucking motions with the mouth (sucking reflex).
- Your baby reaches a length of about 4 to 5 inches and weighs almost 3 ounces.

At 20 weeks:

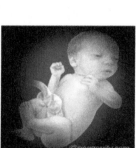

- Your baby is more active. You might feel slight fluttering.
- Your baby is covered by fine, downy hair called lanugo (luh-NOO-goh) and a waxy coating called vernix. This protects the forming skin underneath.
- Eyebrows, eyelashes, fingernails, and toenails have formed. Your baby can even scratch itself.
- Your baby can hear and swallow.
- Now halfway through your pregnancy, your baby is about 6 inches long and weighs about 9 ounces.

At 24 weeks:

- Bone marrow begins to make blood cells.
- Taste buds form on your baby's tongue.
- Footprints and fingerprints have formed.
- Real hair begins to grow on your baby's head.
- The lungs are formed, but do not work.
- The hand and startle reflex develop.
- Your baby sleeps and wakes regularly.
- If your baby is a boy, his testicles begin to move from the abdomen into the scrotum. If your baby is a girl, her uterus and ovaries are in place, and a lifetime supply of eggs have formed in the ovaries.
- Your baby stores fat and has gained quite a bit of weight. Now at about 12 inches long, your baby weighs about 1½ pounds.

Third trimester (week 29-week 40)

At 32 weeks:

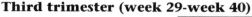

- Your baby's bones are fully formed, but still soft.
- Your baby's kicks and jabs are forceful.
- The eyes can open and close and sense changes in light.
- Lungs are not fully formed, but practice "breathing" movements occur.
- Your baby's body begins to store vital minerals, such as iron and calcium.
- Lanugo begins to fall off.
- Your baby is gaining weight quickly, about one-half pound a week. Now, your baby is about 15 to 17 inches long and weighs about 4 to 4½ pounds.

At 36 weeks:

- The protective waxy coating called vernix gets thicker.
- Body fat increases. Your baby is getting bigger and bigger and has less space to move around. Movements are less forceful, but you will feel stretches and wiggles.
- Your baby is about 16 to 19 inches long and weighs about 6 to 6½ pounds.

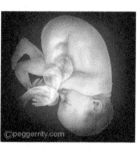

Weeks 37–40:

- By the end of 37 weeks, your baby is considered full term. Your baby's organs are ready to function on their own.
- As you near your due date, your baby may turn into a head-down position for birth. Most babies "present" head down.
- At birth, your baby may weigh somewhere between 6 pounds 2 ounces and 9 pounds 2 ounces and be 19 to 21 inches long. Most full-term babies fall within these ranges. But healthy babies come in many different sizes.

Text and images from the Office on Women's Health, US Department of Health and Human Services, 2017

Multiple Births

Some pregnancies result in multiple births. In 2014, the twin birth rate in the United States was 33.9 twins per 1000 births, which was a new high for the nation. Increased multiple birth rates the past three decades is associated with the expanded use of fertility therapies and older maternal age at childbearing (National Vital Statistics Reports, 2015). The two types of twins are identical and fraternal. **Identical twins** (monozygotic) are formed when one egg that has been fertilized by one sperm splits into two genetically identical halves. Identical twins share 100% of their genetic material, and are essentially natural clones. Almost always, identical twins are the same gender. **Fraternal twins** (dizygotic) more common than identical are formed when two different sperm fertilize two different eggs released by the mother. These twins share 50% of their genetic material and are no more similar or different than regular siblings. Fraternal twins can be the same or different genders (Crivello, 2013).

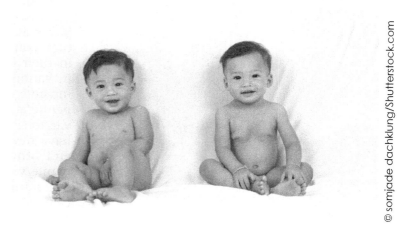

© somjade dachklung/Shutterstock.com

Fetal Vulnerability

During a pregnancy, a number of complex processes allow the original single cell to divide, differentiate, and develop into a baby consisting of several trillion cells (Paulson, 2012). Maternal and environmental factors can negatively impact these processes if the fetus is exposed to **teratogens**, which are agents or factors that interfere with the development of a fetus and cause birth defects. Teratogens can include maternal alcohol consumption (which can cause Fetal Alcohol Syndrome Disorders), high levels of mercury or low levels of iron or folic acid in the mother's diet, and exposure to environmental tobacco smoke. The timing of the influence of teratogens is important to understand. For example, folic acid consumption is most important in the first 28 days after conception to help prevent neural tube defects (Derbyshire, 2012), and adequate iron levels are most crucial during the first trimester to allow normal fetal neural development. (Mehaila et al, 2011). The impact of alcohol on the structures and functions of a developing fetus lasts throughout the pregnancy and is illustrated in Figure 13.5.

FIGURE 13.5

FETAL DEVELOPMENT CHART

This chart shows vulnerability of the fetus to defects throughout 38 weeks of pregnancy.*
• = Most common site of birth defects

PERIOD OF THE OVUM	PERIOD OF THE EMBRYO							PERIOD OF THE FETUS			
Weeks 1-2	Week 3	Week 4	Week 5	Week 6	Week 7	Week 8	Week 12	Week 16	Weeks 20–36	Week 38

Period of early embryo development and implantation.

CNS — heart — eye — heart — eye — ear — palate — ear — limbs — teeth — external genitals — brain

Central Nervous System (CNS)–Brain and Spinal Cord
Heart
Arms/Legs
Eyes
Teeth
Palate
External Genitals

Pregnancy loss

Ears

■ Period of development when major defects in bodily structure can occur.

▨ Period of development when major functional defects and minor structural defects can occur.

Adapted from Moore, 1993 and the National Organization on Fetal Alcohol Syndrome (NOFAS) 2009

*The fetal chart shows the 38 weeks of pregnancy. Since it is difficult to know exactly when conception occurs, health care providers calculate a woman's due date 40 weeks from the start of her last menstrual cycle.

Source: CDC

Decision Making about Sexual Activity

Honest communication is essential in decision making about sexual activity.

The decision to engage in sexual activity is a very personal one, guided by physical, emotional, and spiritual considerations. Individuals find different times in their lives where they are comfortable participating in various sexual activities. These sexual activities can include: oral/penile, oral/vaginal, penile/vaginal, and penile/anal intercourse. The definition of "virginity" is variable; some individuals consider virgins those who have never participated in any type of sexual activity, and others define it as never having participated in penile/vaginal intercourse. When someone considers becoming sexually active, he/she needs to communicate honestly with the partner regarding past experiences, relationship status, and possible risks. All types of sexual activity carry risk of the transmission of sexually transmitted infections (STIs) and penile/vaginal intercourse can cause a pregnancy. When making a decision regarding sexual activity, both partners need ample time to consider the short and long-term implications of the action and consider alternatives.

Decisions about sexual activity are often made in the "heat of the moment." An interesting study examined college-aged males' judgement and decision making under the effect of sexual arousal. The subjects were asked about their willingness to engage in morally questionable behavior to procure sex. They answered these questions in a normal state and again in a sexually aroused state. The arousal state had a significant impact on their answers to the questions, indicating that they were more likely to engage in the questionable behaviors when they were aroused. They were also asked about their willingness to engage in risky sexual behaviors (like engaging in sexual activity without a condom). Again, their answers indicated that they were more likely to engage in risky behaviors when they answered the questions in an aroused state. This research can lead to the conclusion that sexual arousal increases the motivation to have sex, possibly regardless of the morality or risk involved. Certainly, the study is limited only to the responses of the young male participants, but it does suggest that people have a limited insight into the effect of sexual arousal on judgements and decision making (Ariely and Loewenstein, 2006).

Communication with a partner *prior* to sexual activity should include discussions about methods of contraception that can prevent pregnancy and STI protection methods.

Methods of Contraception

Methods of contraception are designed to prevent pregnancy. Some methods also offer sexually transmitted infection (STI) protection. They vary in their effectiveness and convenience, so an individual should choose one that allows the least chance of error and fits with his or her lifestyle. These methods are divided into two categories: non-hormonal and hormonal.

Non-Hormonal

Non-hormonal methods of contraception either prevent sexual activity or form a physical barrier between the partners. These methods include abstinence, fertility-awareness based methods, and male/female barriers.

Abstinence

Abstinence from all types of sexual activity prevents pregnancy and the transmission of STIs. If a couple needs pregnancy prevention only (and there is no risk for STI transmission), only abstinence from penile/vaginal intercourse is needed. Abstaining from all types of sexual activity requires a high level of commitment from both partners, and honest communication about other ways to show affection. It avoids the physical and emotional impact of sexual activity and is often chosen for religious or spiritual reasons. While it is 100% effective when it is practiced, those using abstinence as a method of contraception rarely have a backup method available if a different decision is made in a heated moment. Also, few people choose lifetime celibacy, so it is worthwhile to learn about other contraceptive methods.

Fertility Awareness Based Methods

Another behavioral method of contraception is fertility awareness. This method, also referred to as the rhythm method or natural family planning, requires the female to track her menstrual cycle in a variety of ways. The couple avoids penile/vaginal intercourse in the days just prior to and following ovulation to help prevent the sperm from reaching a viable egg. The menstrual cycle can be charted simply with a calendar (if the woman's cycle is very regular or predictable) or by using body measurements like the basal body temperature or cervical mucus tracking. The surge of estrogen just before ovulation makes the cervical mucus thin and watery, giving sperm an easy path to reach the egg. Basal body temperature (temperature at rest) rises a little bit at ovulation.

Barrier Methods

A physical barrier like a male condom, female condom, cervical cap, or diaphragm prevents the partners' genitalia from coming in full contact with each other. The male and female condoms offer some STI protection as well as pregnancy prevention if used consistently and correctly. Because the diaphragm and cervical cap only cover the woman's cervix, they do not protect against STIs. All barrier methods can be used in combination with spermicide, which inactivates sperm and increases the protection against pregnancy. Barrier methods do not interfere with a woman's hormones, but do require planning for use before beginning sexual activity.

Hormonal Methods

Currently, hormonal methods of contraception, also known as birth control, are only available for females. Hormonal methods of contraception do not offer any protection against STIs. These methods contain estrogen and progestin (synthetic form of progesterone) and primarily work to prevent pregnancy by stopping ovulation. By having a consistent level of estrogen and progestin, the woman's body does not get the surge of these hormones that usually precedes ovulation. Hormonal contraceptive methods also thicken the cervical mucus, making it difficult for the sperm to reach the egg, and prevent the lining of the uterus from thickening, making it less likely for a fertilized egg to implant (American College of Obstetricians and Gynecologists, 2014). Combined hormones can be delivered through a pill, injections, a skin patch, or a vaginal ring. Each method offers advantages and disadvantages related to effectiveness, ease of use, and potential side effects.

Another group of hormonal methods are called long-acting reversible contraceptives. These include the intrauterine device (IUD) and birth control implants. Both of these methods release hormones, primarily progestin, to prevent fertilization of the egg by sperm. They work in a similar way to short-term hormonal contraceptive methods by also thickening cervical mucus and thinning the uterine lining. Long-acting reversible contraceptive methods have a higher effectiveness rate than other methods and can help prevent pregnancy for 3–5 years (American College of Obstetricians and Gynecologists, 2016). Again, these methods do not offer any protection against STIs. Couples using hormonal methods of contraception who might be at risk for STI transmission also need to use a barrier method to decrease STI risk.

Emergency Contraception

Emergency contraception (EC) helps prevent pregnancy in the case of unanticipated sexual intercourse, contraceptive failure, or sexual assault (Bounds, Brekken Shea, Agnor, Darnell, 2012). These methods, like hormonal contraceptive methods, help prevent the sperm from fertilizing the egg and do not offer any protection against STIs. They are not a medical abortion and do not terminate an existing pregnancy. Two options exist for emergency contraception: a copper IUD inserted up to 5 days after unprotected intercourse, or emergency contraceptive pills (ECPs) taken up to 72 hours after unprotected intercourse. According to researchers at the Office of Population Research at Princeton University, progestin-only ECPs are the most effective type of pill at inhibiting or delaying ovulation. One pill of this type, Plan-B, became available over-the-counter in 2006. Women are still encouraged to visit a healthcare provider and not rely on EC as a regular method of contraception (Trussell, Raymond, & Cleland, 2016).

Sterilization

Male and female sterilization are surgical, permanent methods of contraception. The female procedure, called tubal ligation, permanently blocks the fallopian tubes, which is where sperm usually fertilize the egg. Vasectomy, the male procedure, permanently blocks the vas deferens, which transports sperm.

These methods are almost 100% effective in preventing pregnancy, but do not offer any STI protection (Bounds, Brekken Shea, Agnor, Darnell, 2012).

Sexually Transmitted Infections

Other than unintended pregnancy, sexually transmitted infections (STIs) are another possible consequence of unprotected sexual activity. STIs

© Annette Shaff/Shutterstock.com

can be passed from person to person through sexual contact with the penis, vagina, rectum, or mouth. The 2015 Sexually Transmitted Disease Surveillance Report showed that levels of chlamydia, gonorrhea, and syphilis all increased in the past year, despite declines in years prior to 2014. Young people aged 15–24 (regardless of sexual orientation) have the highest rates of chlamydia and gonorrhea, and syphilis rates are highest in gay and bisexual men of all ages. One in four sexually active adolescent females has an STI such as chlamydia or human papillomavirus (HPV) (CDC, 2015). Untreated STIs are a leading cause of preventable infertility by possibly causing an increased risk of ectopic pregnancy (pregnancy outside the uterus) and permanent damage to reproductive organs (NIH, accessed 2017) and can also lead to chronic health conditions such as cervical cancer.

Sexually transmitted infections, also known as sexually transmitted diseases, are divided into 3 categories: bacterial, viral, and parasitic. As discussed in the Wellness and Disease Prevention chapter of this textbook, infections caused by bacteria can be treated with antibiotics. Antiviral treatments can decrease the symptoms of infections caused by viruses, but almost all viral STIs are lifelong conditions. Prescription medications are also used to treat parasitic STIs such as pubic lice, scabies, and trichomoniasis.

Table 13.1 lists the transmission, symptoms, complications, treatment, and prevention methods for bacterial and viral STIs. While symptoms are listed for each type of infection, individuals must know that many diseases are asymptomatic, meaning that no outward signs are visible or may go unnoticed.

Prevention and testing are crucial steps in decreasing STI risk and infection rates. The best way to prevent contraction of an STI is to practice sexual abstinence or have a mutually monogamous relationship with an uninfected partner. If an individual chooses to be sexually active, he or she should limit the number of sexual partners and use condoms consistently and correctly. If an individual suspects infection, he or she should avoid any sexual contact until getting tested for STIs (Bounds, Brekken Shea, Agnor, and Darnell, 2012).

No single test can be administered for all types of sexually transmitted infections. Table 13.2 below describes the testing techniques for various STIs.

TABLE 13.2

STI	Test
Chlamydia	Swab of genital area or urine sample
Gonorrhea	Swab of genital area or urine sample
Syphillis	Blood test or sample from sore
HIV	Blood test or swab from inside of mouth
Genital Herpes	Swab of affected area and/or blood test
HPV	Visual diagnosis of genital warts; HPV DNA test and biopsy after abnormal Pap test if cervical cancer
Hepatitis B	Blood test
Pubic lice and scabies	Visual diagnosis
Trichomoniasis	Visual diagnosis or swab of infected area

(American Sexual Health Association, 2017 and Bounds, Brekken Shea, Agnor, and Darnell, 2012)

Organizations such as student health centers, county health departments, hospitals, and other clinics offer free and low-cost STI testing. Programs such as Get Your Test (CDC) and World AIDS day promote regular STI testing and support for those with STIs like HIV/AIDS.

TABLE 13.1 ♦ What Are the Common Sexually Transmitted Infections (STIs)?

STI	Transmission (Body Fluids and/or Direct Contact)	Symptoms
Chlamydia	**Fluids**—contact of mucous membranes (cervix, urethra) with infected person's fluids (semen and mucus). Most common with exposure through vaginal or anal sex. Casual contact considered to be safe.	Most patients have no symptoms. If present, they may be: *Women*—pain or dull aching in lower abdomen, heavy feeling in pelvic area, pain with urination or intercourse, heavier menstrual flow, breakthrough bleeding, heavy cervical discharge. *Men*—urethral discharge, pain with urination, pain in scrotum (epididymitis).
Human Papillomavirus (HPV)/Genital Warts/Precancerous Tissue Change (Intraepithelial Neoplasia)	**Contact**—touching (hands/genital, genital/genital, or ano-genital) an infected person's lesions can transmit cells containing the virus. Can be transmitted through non-penetrative sexual contact.	Usually no symptoms, but external lesions may itch. Lesions on the skin can be either raised or flat. Most lesions on the cervix can be seen only with the use of acetic acid and magnification.
Herpes Simplex (HSV) both types I and II	**Contact**—touching (hand/genital, genital/genital, oral/genital, or ano-genital) an infected person's lesions. Can be transmitted through non-penetrative sexual contact. Transmission commonly occurs in the absence of lesions.	Single or multiple fluid-filled blisters appear typically in the ano-genital area and mouth. They rupture, sometimes leaving extremely painful shallow ulcers, which heal in about twelve days.
Pelvic Inflammatory Disease (PID)	**Fluids**—contact of mucous membranes with infected person's body fluids (mucus, semen). Transmission most common with exposure through anal and vaginal sex, or rarely, oral sex. Casual contact considered to be safe.	There may be no symptoms, but PID is usually characterized by moderate to severe lower abdominal pain, fever, chills, and possibly bowel symptoms. May mimic appendicitis, ureteral stones, twisted or ruptured ovarian cyst, and other acute lower abdominal conditions.

From *Sexually Transmitted Infections: What Everyone Should Know,* by American College Health Association. Copyright © 2011 by American College Health Association. Reprinted by permission.

Potential Complications/ Course of Infection	Treatment	Prevention—For all STIs, abstinence is the best protection
In women, serious complications can occur if spread to fallopian tubes. May result in tubal scarring, infertility, and risk of tubal pregnancy.	A number of commonly used antibiotics are effective. Partners **must** be treated at the same time.	Condoms (latex or polyurethane) reduce but do not eliminate risk.
Cervix—Most cervical infections are invisible to the naked eye. Occasionally, visible cervical warts may be present. Cervical cancer can be prevented by detection and treatment of pre-cancerous changes. *External skin and anus of men and women, and the vagina*—warty lesions, flat or raised. Some may be pre-cancers, but natural history of lesions is not to become cancers until advanced age. Long-term complications are not yet known.	Many treatments are available. The most expensive does not necessarily mean the best. *Cervix*—cryo (freezing), laser, and LEEP. *External*—Aldara, cryo, laser, liquid N, TCA/BCA, podophyllin, and interferon. In some individuals, the virus is cleared from the body. In others, viral particles remain latent after treatment. Lesions can be eliminated. It is unlikely that the presence of latent viral particles without lesions can result in transmission.	Barrier methods reduce but do not eliminate risk. With condoms, for example, lesions may be present in uncovered areas. Only total absence of any touching of infected tissue will avoid transmission. When both partners are infected, they probably do not continue to transmit to each other.
Recurrent painful attacks. Infants infected at or before delivery may sustain severe neurological damage or death.	Antiviral drugs are effective if taken early in the infection or continuously in a preventive regimen. Topical anesthetics may be helpful in reducing discomfort.	Barrier methods reduce but do not eliminate risk. With condoms, for example, lesions may be present in uncovered areas.
May progress to abscesses and injury resulting in infertility, ectopic pregnancy, chronic pain, and even death.	Therapy with one or more antibiotics with broad coverage. Individuals must always be treated for chlamydia and gonorrhea; management sometimes requires hospitalization. Partners **must** be treated at the same time.	Condoms (latex or polyurethane) reduce but do not eliminate risk.

(continued)

TABLE 13.1 ♦ What Are the Common Sexually Transmitted Infections (STIs)? *(continued)*

STI	Transmission (Body Fluids and/or Direct Contact)	Symptoms
Human Immunodeficiency Virus (HIV)/AIDS	**Fluids**—contact of open skin or mucous membranes with infected person's body fluids (blood, mucus, semen). Most common with exposure through anal or vaginal sex, and, though uncommon, oral sex. Casual contact considered to be safe. Health care workers at risk through scalpel cuts and needle sticks.	Divided into four stages: *Infection and Seroconversion*—flu-like illness for approximately two weeks. *Symptom-Free*—few months to many years. *Early Symptoms*—fevers, shingles, yeast infections—few months to several years. *AIDS*—opportunistic infections, neoplasia (Kaposi's sarcoma, lymphoma, cervical cancer), dementia, and other neurological symptoms—few months to several years.
Gonorrhea	**Fluids**—contact of mucous membranes (cervix, urethra) with infected person's fluids (semen, mucus). Most common with exposure through vaginal or anal sex. Casual contact considered to be safe.	Very similar to chlamydia for both women and men.
Hepatitis B (HBV)	**Fluids**—contact with mucous membranes (cervix, urethra, anal area) with infected person's fluids (semen, saliva, blood, mucus). Most common with exposure through vaginal or anal sex. Casual contact considered to be safe. Health care workers at risk through scalpel cuts and needle sticks.	At first, usually no symptoms. If disease progresses, symptoms may occur—fatigue, nausea, and jaundice (yellowing of the skin and eyes) with dark urine.
Syphilis	**Fluids** and **Contact**—Also, 50% risk of transmission from mother to infant in utero.	Occurs in three stages: *Primary*—painless ulcer. *Secondary*—rash, condylomata lata, lymph node enlargement, spotty baldness. *Late/Latent*—vascular and neurological damage may be occurring.

References

American Pregnancy Association. (2017). Retrieved from http://americanpregnancy.org/getting- pregnant/fertility-window/

Ariely, D. & Loewenstein, G. (2006). The heat of the moment: The effect of sexual arousal on sexual decision making. *Journal of Behavioral Decision Making.* 19: 87-98. doi: 10.1002/bdm.501

Bounds, L., Brekken Shea, K., Agnor, D., & Darnell, G. (2012). *Health and fitness: A guide to a healthy lifestyle.* (5th ed.). Dubuque, IA: Kendall Hunt

Centers for Disease Control and Prevention. *Sexually Transmitted Disease Surveillance 2015.* Atlanta: U.S. Department of Health and Human Services; 2016.

Combined Hormonal Birth Control: Pill, Patch, and Ring: American College of Obstetricians and Gynecologists. July 2014. Retrieved from http://www.acog.org/Patients/FAQs/Combined-Hormonal- Birth-Control-Pill-Patch-and-Ring

Potential Complications/ Course of Infection	Treatment	Prevention—For all STIs, abstinence is the best protection
Signs and symptoms of AIDS, death (current medications lengthening survival). Treatment of pregnant women with HIV greatly reduces the risk of maternal-fetal transmission.	Antivirals and specific medications for complications.	Condoms (latex or polyurethane) reduce but do not eliminate risk. Avoid contact with needles, particularly IV drug use.
In women, serious complications can occur if spread to fallopian tubes. May result in tubal scarring, infertility, and risk of tubal pregnancy.	A number of commonly used antibiotics are very effective. Partners **must** be treated at the same time.	Condoms (latex or polyurethane) reduce but do not eliminate risk.
Cirrhosis, liver cancer, liver failure, death.	Antiviral medications are indicated in certain circumstances.	Vaccination of infants and non-immunized adolescents and adults is highly recommended. Avoid contact with blood, needles, etc.
Late complications include: severe neurologic dysfunction, aortic aneurysm.	Penicillin or doxycycline—based on darkfield or blood test. Very important that pregnant women with positive blood tests be treated to prevent congenital syphilis. **Must** treat all contacts.	Condoms, spermicides.

Crivello, J. (2013). *Anatomy and physiology.* (2nd ed.). Dubuque, IA: Kendall Hunt.

Derbyshire, E. (2012). Correct timing of folic acid supplementation during pregnancy. *British Journal of Midwifery.* 20(11): 774-778.

Get Tested: American Sexual Health Association. (2017). Retrieved from http://www.iwannaknow.org/teens/sti/testing.html

Hamilton BE, Martin JA, Osterman MJK, et al. Births: Final data for 2014. National vital statistics reports; vol 64 no 12. Hyattsville, MD: National Center for Health Statistics. 2015.

Long-Acting Reversible Contraception: American College of Obstetricians and Gynecologists. (May 2016). Retrieved from http://www.acog.org/Patients/FAQs/Long-Acting-Reversible-Contraception-LARC-IUD- and-Implant

Mihaila C, Schramm J, Strathmann FG, Lee DL, Gelein RM, et al. (2011). Identifying a window of vulnerability during fetal development in a maternal iron restriction model. *PLoS ONE* 6(3): e17483. doi:10.1371/journal.pone.0017483

Paulson, J. (2012). Prenatal exposures: A continuum of vulnerability to environmental toxins. *Environmental Health Policy Institute.* Retrieved from http://www.psr.org/environment-and- health/environmental-health-policy-institute/responses/prenatal-exposures.html

SEER Training Modules, *Male Reproductive System.* U. S. National Institutes of Health, National Cancer Institute. Accessed 5 February 2017. https://training.seer.cancer.gov/.

Trussell, J., Raymond, E., & Cleland, K. (2016). Emergency contraception: A last chance to prevent unintended pregnancy. Princeton University Office of Population Research. Retrieved from http://ec.princeton.edu/questions/EC-Review.pdf

What is the link between sexually transmitted diseases or sexually transmitted infections (STDs/STIs) and infertility?: National Institutes of Health. (Accessed 8 February 2017). Retrieved from https://www.nichd.nih.gov/health/topics/stds/conditioninfo/Pages/infertility.aspx

Your Developing Baby: Office on Women's Health, U.S. Department of Health and Human Services (1 February 2017). Retrieved from https://www.womenshealth.gov/pregnancy/youre-pregnant-now- what/stages-pregnancy

Index

CPSIA information can be obtained
at www.ICGtesting.com
Printed in the USA
LVOW02s1350230717

542079LV00001B/1/P